DVANCE PRAISE FOR *THE BUSINESS*
OF TRANSITION

mportant book, as the emergence of Myanmar from decades of relative isolation
another round of debates about the relationship between law and development.
utors share their wealth of experience with law and business reform projects in
and enable readers to understand the difficulties and prospects of success.'

   – Christoph Antons, Professor, Newcastle University Faculty of Law

of Transition offers a new and searching critique of the decades-long enterprise
velopment. Myanmar cross-disciplinary specialists in law and markets superbly
conventionalities, boldly encounter intricate complexities, and refuse to be
ormulaic answers. Through intensive case studies the authors skillfully explore
fraught and sometimes paradoxical interplay between international donors and
domestic actors, whether political elites, businesses, non-profits, civil society
munities. Every specialist in globalization, law and markets will benefit greatly
ful engagement with this excellent volume as it reveals again the intricacy and
f every country's encounter with the transnational and global.'

– Terence Halliday, Professor, Center on Law and Globalization, American Bar
                    Foundation

ors to this volume, diverse in origin, expertise and experience, blend to give an
mentary on and exposition of the present realities and future possibilities of
nsitional economy. It places contemporary empirical data in a broader context.
economic, legal, social, political, moral and humanitarian issues as well as the
f the interaction between domestic, regional and international regimes make
t should be on the shelves of scholarly and business readers alike.'

   – Mary E. Hiscock, Emeritus Professor of Law, Bond University, Australia

lsory reading for policy analysts and/or academics interested in the process
d commercial legal reform. Through the prism of Myanmar – a country at
of geoeconomics, political and economic transition – the contributors to
ng to bear theoretical sophistication alongside deep empirical knowledge to
iness of transition. The book eschews technocratic analysis of legal reform,
lyses how social forces such as business, labour, the legal profession as well
s and multilateral organisations are engaged in contestations that shape the
sition. It is essential reading material for anyone wishing to understand the
ics of legal change, not just in Myanmar but in an array of transitional econ-
es.'

     – Kanishka Jayasuriya, Professor, Murdoch University, Australia

des a particularly instructive context for exploring the relationship between
ment as it undergoes two dramatic and simultaneous transitions: from mili-
i-democracy, and from socialism to a market economy. The essays in this
ompelling case that "best practices" transplanted from foreign jurisdictions
purchase on the unique challenges that such transitions entail and imply
an has often been the case on the part of external agencies in promoting
of an appropriate law reform agenda.'

      – Michael Trebilcock, Professor, University of Toronto

THE BUSINESS OF

This interdisciplinary volume offers a tim[...] and economics through empirical and [...] temporary Myanmar. The book explor[...] times of major political change throug[...] and foreign investment. The expert co[...] the ways in which law reform creates n[...] social transformation, while also being [...] gain. This book is an invitation to thir[...] intersection between law, developmer[...] ical transition. The chapters speak to [...] rights, access to finance, economic d[...] ing its potential and its limits, and th[...] globalised ideas and the internationa[...] book is for students, scholars and pr[...] Asian Studies, political science and ir[...]

MELISSA CROUCH is Senior Lecturer [...] of New South Wales. She has publisl[...] of Myanmar and Indonesia.

A[...]

'This is an i[...] triggers yet [...] The contrib[...] the country[...]

'The Busines[...] of law and d[...] question gli[...] locked into f[...] the complex,[...] advisors and [...] or local comr[...] from though[...] particularity [...]

'The contribu[...] insightful cor[...] this unique tr[...] Its coverage of[...] examination c[...] this a book tha[...]

'This is compu[...] of business an[...] the confluence[...] this volume br[...] explore the bu[...] and instead an[...] as political elit[...] business of trar[...] complex dynar[...] omies and polit[...]

'Myanmar prov[...] law and develop[...] tary rule to sen[...] volume make a [...] provide limited [...] more modesty t[...] their conception[...]

THE BUSINESS OF TRANSITION

Law Reform, Development and Economics in Myanmar

Edited by

MELISSA CROUCH

CAMBRIDGE
UNIVERSITY PRESS

CAMBRIDGE
UNIVERSITY PRESS

University Printing House, Cambridge CB2 8BS, United Kingdom

One Liberty Plaza, 20th Floor, New York, NY 10006, USA

477 Williamstown Road, Port Melbourne, VIC 3207, Australia

314–321, 3rd Floor, Plot 3, Splendor Forum, Jasola District Centre, New Delhi – 110025, India

79 Anson Road, #06-04/06, Singapore 079906

Cambridge University Press is part of the University of Cambridge.

It furthers the University's mission by disseminating knowledge in the pursuit of
education, learning, and research at the highest international levels of excellence.

www.cambridge.org
Information on this title: www.cambridge.org/9781108416832
DOI: 10.1017/9781108236737

First published 2017

Printed in the United Kingdom by Clays, St Ives plc

A catalogue record for this publication is available from the British Library.

Library of Congress Cataloging-in-Publication Data
Names: Crouch, Melissa, editor.
Title: The business of transition: law reform, development and economics
in Myanmar / edited by Melissa Crouch.
Description: New York: Cambridge University Press, 2017. |
Includes bibliographical references and index.
Identifiers: LCCN 2017034629 | ISBN 9781108416832 (hardback)
Subjects: LCSH: Burma – Economic conditions – 1988– | Economic development – Burma.
Classification: LCC HC422.B925 2017 | DDC 330.9591–dc23
LC record available at https://lccn.loc.gov/2017034629

ISBN 978-1-108-41683-2 Hardback

CONTENTS

v

FIGURE AND TABLES

Figure

Tables

Figure

Tables

CONTRIBUTORS

MATTHEW ARNOLD is an academic and aid worker specialising in conflict resolution and governance issues and has extensive field experience in assorted parts of Asia and Africa. Currently he works as Program Director for The Asia Foundation in Myanmar. Matthew received his doctorate from the London School of Economics and has written extensively about post-conflict transitions in Sudan, South Sudan and Timor-Leste, as well as conflicts in Iraq, Afghanistan and Thailand. His research has appeared in leading academic journals, and he has co-authored two books: *Militias and the Challenges of Post-Conflict Peace* (2011) and *South Sudan: From Revolution to Independence* (2013). He is the author and organiser of a highly influential policy paper series in Myanmar funded by The Asia Foundation.

MELISSA CROUCH is Senior Lecturer at the Law Faculty of the University of New South Wales (UNSW), Sydney, Australia. She is the co-editor of *Law, Society and Transition in Myanmar* (2014) and the author of *Law and Religion in Indonesia: Conflict and the Courts in West Java* (2014). She is the editor of a volume on *Islam and the State in Myanmar: Muslim-Buddhist Relations and the Politics of Belonging* (2016). She teaches in the areas of constitutional law, administrative law, Islamic law and the legal traditions of Southeast Asia.

JOHN DALE is Associate Professor of Sociology at George Mason University. He has conducted fieldwork on the politics and creative collective action of civil society in Burma/Myanmar since 1997, served as an Open Society Foundation international liaison to University of Yangon in 2014, and is a frequent commentator on the country's contentious politics for major news organizations around the world. He is author of *Free Burma: Transnational Legal Action and Corporate Accountability* (2011), and co-author (with Anthony Orum) of *Political Sociology: Power and Participation in Modern World* (2009).

MICHELE FORD is Professor of Southeast Asian Studies and Director of the Sydney Southeast Asia Centre at the University of Sydney, Australia. She holds an ARC Future Fellowship. Michele's research interests focus on Southeast Asian labour movements, trade union aid and trade union responses to labour migration in East and Southeast Asia. She is the author of *Workers and Intellectuals: NGOs, Unions and the Indonesian Labour Movement* (2009), editor of *Social Activism in Southeast Asia* (2013) and co-editor of several volumes including *Labour Migration and Human Trafficking in Southeast Asia: Critical Perspectives* (2012) and *Beyond Oligarchy: Wealth, Power, and Contemporary Indonesian Politics* (2014).

TIM FREWER is a PhD candidate at the University of Sydney in the Department of Geosciences (human geography). He has worked in various research roles in Southeast Asia over the past ten years and has published numerous articles on development issues in the region. His current research looks at the politics of climate change aid, with a particular focus on Myanmar.

MICHAEL GILLAN is Senior Lecturer at the University of Western Australia where he teaches globalisation and work and international employment relations. He has published in a wide range of international journals including *Economic Geography, Journal of Contemporary Asia, Asian Studies Review, South Asia, Australian Journal of Labour Law* and the *Journal of Industrial Relations*. His current research interests include the role of global union federations in employment relations in India and Indonesia; employment relations in global production networks; labour movements and politics in India; and employment relations in Myanmar (Burma). He is President of the South Asian Studies Association of Australia.

MARTIN KRYGIER is Gordon Samuels Professor of Law and Social Theory, UNSW; Honorary Professor at RegNet, ANU; and a Fellow of the Australian Academy of Social Sciences. He has edited and contributed to *Spreading Democracy and the Rule of Law?* (2006); *Rethinking the Rule of Law after Communism* (2005); *Community and Legality* (2002); *The Rule of Law after Communism* (1999); *Marxism and Communism: Posthumous Reflections on Politics, Society, and Law* (1994); *Bureaucracy: The Career of a Concept* (1980). His most recent book is *Philip Selznick: Ideals in the World* (2012). He has written extensively on the nature of the rule of law, and on attempts to promote it worldwide. He has a particular interest in the place of law in countries recovering from dictatorship and conflict, prominent among them post-communist countries of central and eastern Europe. In 2016, he was awarded the prestigious Dennis Leslie Mahoney Prize in Legal Theory.

DAVID KYLE is Associate Professor of Sociology at the University of California, Davis. He has a Ph.D. in sociology from Johns Hopkins University. He is the author of two books, *Transnational Peasants: Migrations, Networks, and Ethnicity in Andean Ecuador* (2000), and *Global Human Smuggling: Comparative Perspectives* (2nd Ed., 2011) with Rey Koslowski. Recent research in Mexico and Myanmar (with John Dale) seeks to understand the changing social relations, digital and communication technologies, and institutional dynamics of knowledge production and the politics of democratic transition and development (see 'Smart Transitions? Foreign Investment, Disruptive Technology, and Democratic Reform in Myanmar', *Social Research: An International Quarterly*, Summer 2015). Prof. Kyle was the Director of the Gifford Center for Population Studies at UC Davis from 2009 to 2012. He has given numerous national and international talks and media interviews on the topic of human smuggling.

LAUREN NISHIMURA is a doctoral candidate in the Law Faculty, the University of Oxford and a Grotius Research Scholar at the University of Michigan Law School. Prior to beginning her DPhil, Lauren spent two years in Myanmar and Thailand, where she worked as an attorney with EarthRights International (full time) and as a consultant with the International Commission of Jurists. From 2006 to 2012, she was a litigator in the United States, with a focus on environmental law and renewable energy. She holds an MSt in International Human Rights Law from University of Oxford and a JD from Georgetown University Law Center. Lauren has published on climate change, displacement and migration, and human rights.

CATHERINE RENSHAW is an associate professor in the School of Law at the Australian Catholic University. Her research focuses on human rights and democracy in Southeast Asia. With Professor Ben Saul, she is editor of *Human Rights in Asia and the Pacific* (2014). She is an editor of the *Journal of South Asian Law*, the author of numerous journal articles and book chapters, and between 2008 and 2010 was Director of an Australian Research Council project based at the Australian Human Rights Centre at the University of New South Wales, Australia. She has been a Visiting Scholar at the Regulatory Institutions Network, Centre for International

Governance and Justice, Australian National University. Catherine acts as an advisor to several human rights non-governmental organisations in the Asia Pacific region.

ADAM SIMPSON is Director of the Centre for Peace and Security within the Hawke Research Institute and Senior Lecturer in the International Relations program within the School of Communication, International Studies and Languages, University of South Australia. He is Adjunct Research Fellow at the Centre for Governance and Public Policy, Griffith University. He prepared Chapter 3 of this volume during his time as a Visiting Research Scholar at the Centre for Southeast Asian Studies, Kyoto University. He previously taught at the University of Adelaide where he remains an Associate in the Indo-Pacific Governance Research Centre. His research adopts a critical perspective and is focused on the politics of the environment and development in Southeast Asia. He has published in journals such as *Pacific Review, Third World Quarterly* and *Environmental Politics*. He is the author of *Energy, Governance and Security in Thailand and Myanmar (Burma): A Critical Approach to Environmental Politics in the South* (2014; updated paperback edition, 2017) and is lead editor of the *Routledge Handbook of Contemporary Myanmar*.

HTWE HTWE THEIN is Senior Lecturer in International Business at the School of Management, Curtin University, Australia. Her research applies institutional theory within the field of international business through her work on 'home' and 'host' institutions and the impact of supra-national institutions on firm strategy, primarily in Myanmar, since the early 1990s. Htwe Htwe has published in leading journals including *Journal of World Business, International Journal of Cross-Cultural Management* and *Feminist Economics*. She has also co-authored numerous research reports for business and government.

SEAN TURNELL is Associate Professor in Economics at Macquarie University, Sydney, Australia. He is the author of numerous academic papers on Myanmar, and has been a regular commentator on the country in the international press. His book on Burma's financial history, *Fiery Dragons: Banks, Moneylenders and Microfinance in Burma*, was published in 2009. He has been a Visiting Fellow at the University of Cambridge, the Southeast Asia Program, Cornell University, and the Paul H. Nitze School of Advanced International Studies, Johns Hopkins University.

JOSH WOOD is a research officer at the East Asian Bureau of Economic Research and a PhD student in Economics at the Crawford School of Public Policy, the Australian National University. In 2014, he was a visiting research fellow at the Myanmar Development Resource Institute's Centre for Economic and Social Development in Yangon where he completed a report on the country's three special economic zones. He has conducted extensive field research on the special economic zones in Myanmar.

FOREWORD

MARTIN KRYGIER

This book is the third of a trilogy (so far) that Dr Melissa Crouch has recently edited on many of the distinctive characteristics of Myanmar's social and political fabric, and some of the major challenges and opportunities that country faces today and for some considerable time to come. The first was *Law, Society and Transition in Myanmar* (co-edited with Tim Lindsey, 2014); the second *Islam and the State in Myanmar* (2016); and now *The Business of Transition*. So her work has quickly come to be associated with penetrating analyses of the central issues and challenges facing Myanmar – legal, social, religious and now economic. Given the extent to which all these domains are interwoven, it would be best to buy all three books and read them together, with the awareness that their subjects constantly act and interact with each other in many, various and changeable ways. Short of that, any one of them is an edifying treat, and this one particularly so.

For this is the first academic treatment of 'the business of transition' in Myanmar, taken in the round. As such, and given the huge novelty, range, complexity, volatility and unpredictability of developments included in and related to this subject, it is appropriate that rather than a monograph by one person with one point of view, one thesis about one subject, it brings together a selection of diverse, though related, essays by different authors on different elements and aspects of this difficult 'business'. The essays in this book identify a range of major domains and issues of significance, situate them in Myanmar's historical and social context, survey current problems, develop educated conjectures about future developments and introduce a variety of viewpoints – about a range of different elements that make up the hugely complex and layered course of events we try to gesture at with optimistic umbrella words such as 'development' or 'transition'.

The challenge for the analyst is to penetrate the crowded realities sheltering under such capacious umbrellas. The challenge for 'change agents' is to recognise the complexity and volatility of 'development' or 'transition'

without succumbing helplessly before them. This work rises to those challenges by presenting characterisations, diagnoses and prognoses from a
number of leading specialists on many of the central constituents of these
processes. Encouraging its authors to speak in their individual voices and
deliver individual assessments of a variety of problems has been the successful strategy of this work.

The title of the work is usefully ambivalent. Taken in a broad sense,
'the business of transition' suggests – what is the truth – that 'transition'
is no foreordained linear passage from a rejected dysfunctional past to a
wished-for and promised future, for example, military dictatorship to liberal democracy. Rather, like so many other countries 'in transition' (Krygier
and Czarnota 2006), whatever course it takes, Myanmar's passage will be
a difficult, tricky, even perilous business, with surprising trajectories; wins
for some and losses for others; wins for some that *depend upon* losses for
others; moves forward and back; full – as Tim Frewer's chapter in this volume emphasises – of unintended consequences, some fortunate, others not.
Frequently espoused as a self-evident good for all, transition rarely turns
out that way. And however it turns out, there will be surprises en route.

Even a successful transition is rarely a simple 'break with the past', for
we never 'break' with the past, however much things change. That is one
thing that all 'transitional' orders have in common, and that paradoxically
makes them all different: they all have particular histories and traditions
which leave lasting particular legacies, with which present and future generations will have to deal, indeed *within which* present and future generations think and act. No slates are clean; all is bricolage, picking from
existing shards and fragments, adding to them novel bits and pieces, coming up with something both old and new. If for Tolstoy, 'happy families
are all alike; every unhappy family is unhappy in its own way,' countries
in transition are more like unhappy families. For precisely the fact that
the presence of particular pasts is a universal phenomenon means that no
transition is the same as another.

The presence of the past is exacerbated in Myanmar, since we are not
talking merely of relics or legacies. The polity, the economy, indeed the
whole society remains in considerable part under the control of the military, which controlled it without competition for more than fifty years,
and retains control of central domains today. As Matthew Arnold points
out in Chapter 6 of this book,

> Full military rule in Myanmar ended in April 2011. However, overcoming
> the legacies of decades of such authoritarianism will take a long time. This

is primarily because the military penetrate deeply into the bureaucracy starting in the early 1960s ... The influence of military authoritarianism on the bureaucracy had significant effects on economic governance as well. Namely, economic governance was not focused benignly on the full empowerment of the private sector, but rather part of a wider bureaucratic intent of surveillance and control of the population. Current economic realities in Myanmar are also compounded by the socialist tendencies of the junta.

There is thus a real risk, in 'transitional' societies in general, and in Myanmar in particular as it moves, in Frewer's terms, from aid orphan to aid hub, not merely that aid will serve *donor* interests more than is publicly averred, but that it will serve, as he also stresses, overlapping interests of donors and existing elites, rather than and possibly at the expense of those of its ostensible and announced target populations. This is yet another reason, and a theme of many of the chapters of this book, why it is as important as it is rare that people involved in this business know as much about what and where the country which they are keen to transform *is* as they do about where they want it to get to. It is also a reason, as the chapters by Arnold, Nishimura, Renshaw and Frewer stress, why it is misguided to treat development as a purely, or even primarily, technical matter. It has many technical aspects, as Turnell emphasises, which cannot be wished away, but framing the whole process is *politics*, and in Myanmar politics of a distinctly and pervasively militaristic cast.

And so, particularly in the case of Myanmar, where the past and present are so complex, close knowledge of the particular country and domain involved is crucial for anyone involved in this business. On the other hand, insiders – particularly in countries such as Myanmar that have been cut off from much of the rest of the world for several generations – need exposure to experiences beyond their own. It is a key achievement of this work that it brings together general reflections on 'development' with particular, nuanced understandings of Myanmar, without subordinating either to the other.

While in the broad sense, the business of transition encompasses all the domains of life with which Dr Crouch's three collections have been concerned, there is of course a narrower sense at the forefront of many people's minds when they think of transition and development, and when they hear the phrase '*economic* development'. That is the focus of this work, and it is crucial in a country such as Myanmar, which has managed to combine rich natural resources with dramatic poverty. Like every other domain of development, it has multiple elements and impacts, many of which are illuminated by the various essays in this collection. As for elements, one soon learns at least two, apparently but not really contradictory, lessons. One is that economic development has its own imperatives and constraints. Ignoring them can be costly, even in pursuit of virtuous ends, and not merely in economic terms. Thus, Sean Turnell stresses in relation to microfinance, 'The lesson for microfinance in Myanmar from the long and sorry history (and recent past) of its financial cooperatives is a simple one. The provision of financial services, even in their micro form, are best left unburdened by aims and objectives that have little to do with such services, but much more to do with utopian visions of societal transformation.' This is not a caution that should stop with financial services.

On the other hand, to adapt Kipling on English parochialism, 'what do they know of economics who only economics know?' To understand, still more effectively to promote economic development, one needs to think about law, administration, political structures and incentives, in Myanmar's case especially *military* structures and incentives, social organisation, culture, religion and many other things. One is put in mind of Amartya Sen's mordant observation, in his influential speech to the World Bank,

> Even when we consider development in a particular sphere, such as economic development or legal development, the instruments that are needed to enhance development in that circumscribed sphere may not be confined only to institutions and policies in that sphere ... If this sounds a little complex, I must point out that the complication relates, ultimately, to the interdependences of the world in which we live. I did not create that world, and any blame for it has to be addressed elsewhere. (Sen 2000, and see Tamanaha 2011)

Not only will the *instruments* of development overlap any particular designated sphere, so too will their effects. For example, even were special economic zones to be economically warranted (which, in the case of two of the three in Myanmar, Wood questions), there remain the issues that Nishimura raises about the effects on local communities. More generally, economic development can encourage both social inclusion and exclusion, and it matters a great deal which, as Chapter 2 on labour standards, Chapter 4 on social enterprise, Chapter 8 on local effects of special economic zones and Chapter 10 on the differential effects of international aid illustrate. Even where such effects are unintended, they are not all unpredictable, and those interested in development that is at once effective *and* equitable need to take them into account. The essays in this volume are useful guides to several.

This book is a rich resource in all these ways and more. It is not the task of a book's foreword, however, to anticipate all the riches to come. So, aside from recommending this work with enthusiasm, I will stop here.

References

Krygier, Martin and Adam Czarnota. 2006. 'After Postcommunism. The Next Phase'. 2 *Annual Review of Law and Social Science* 299.

Sen, Amartya. 2000. 'What is the role of legal and judicial reform in the development process?' Washington, DC: World Bank Legal Conference, 5 June, p. 10, http://siteresources.worldbank.org/INTLAWJUSTINST/Resources/legalandjudicial.pdf.

Tamanaha, Brian. 2011. 'The Primacy of Society and the Failures of Law and Development: Decades of Refusal to Learn'. 44 *Cornell Journal of International Law* 209.

ACKNOWLEDGEMENTS

I would like to thank the law faculty for its generous support of the workshop held on 27 November 2017, through the Faculty Workshop Scheme at the University of New South Wales, Sydney. I would also like to thank the Law and Economics Initiative of Professor Rosalind Dixon and Professor Richard Holden for also funding the workshop. Sincere thanks also go to the anonymous reviewers and their extremely useful comments and feedback.

ACRONYMS

AGRAM	Action Group for Resource Accountability in Myanmar
ASEAN	Association of Southeast Asian Nations
CSOs	civil society organisations
DAO	Development Affairs Organisations; municipal offices
DDA	Dawei Development Association
DfID	UK Department for International Development
DICA	Directorate of Investment and Company Administration
ECL	Environmental Conservation Law
EIA	environmental impact assessment
EITI	Extractive Industries Transparency Initiative
FDI	foreign direct investment
FER	Foundation for Ecological Recovery
FESR	Framework for Economic and Social Reforms
FLA	Fair Labor Association
FLEGT	Forest Law Enforcement, Governance and Trade
GAD	General Administration Department
GSP	Generalised System of Preferences
IATI	International Aid Transparency Initiative
ILO	International Labour Organisation
ITD	Italian-Thai Development PLC
JICA	Japan International Cooperation Agency
KNU	Karen National Union
MaBaTha	Committee for the Protection of Nationality and Religion
MATA	Myanmar Alliance for Transparency and Accountability
MCDC	Mandalay City Development Committee
MDRI	Myanmar Development Resource Institute
MEITI	Myanmar Extractive Industries Transparency Initiative
MGMA	Myanmar Garment Manufacturing Association
MIC	Myanmar Investment Commission
MJTD	Myanmar Japan Thilawa Development

MoC	memorandum of cooperation
MOGE	Myanmar Oil and Gas Enterprise
MoHA	Ministry of Home Affairs
MOLES	Ministry of Labour Employment and Social Security
MSG	multi-stakeholder group
MSMEs	micro- and small- and medium-sized enterprises
MTUG	Myanmar Trade Union Federation
NCA	National Ceasefire Agreement
NHRCT	National Human Rights Commission of Thailand
NLD	National League for Democracy
NRGI	Natural Resources Governance Institute
OECD	Organisation for Economic Co-Operation and Development
OFAC	Office of Foreign Assets Control
OGM	Operational Grievance Mechanism
PDCs	peace and development committees
PHR	Physicians for Human Rights
SDN	Special Designated Nationals
SEA	strategic environmental assessment
SEZs	special economic zones
SGM	Shwe Gas Movement
SLORC	State Law and Order Restoration Council
SPDC	State Peace and Development Council
SPV	special purpose vehicle
SSN	Southern Society Development Network
TDAC	Township Development Affairs Committee
TERRA	Towards Ecological Recovery and Regional Alliance
TNI	Transnational Institute
TSDG	Thilawa Social Development Group
UMEHL	Union of Myanmar Economic Holdings Ltd
UMFCCI	Union of Myanmar Federation of Chambers of Commerce and Industry
YCDC	Yangon City Development Committee

Understanding the Business of Transition in Myanmar

MELISSA CROUCH

A joke was going around about the impact of development in the country since Myanmar began its controlled transition to a quasi-civilian government in 2011. The word for 'to develop', 'to progress' or 'to improve' in Burmese is 'တိုးတက်'. This is made up of two words, which mean, respectively, 'to push, to advance or to go forward' and 'to climb up, to advance or to get on'. The joke would begin with one person commenting, 'The country is really *developing*.' To which another person would reply, 'Yes, now you have to *push* to get on the bus.' The play on the double-meaning of the word 'to develop' and 'to push' here is a telling sign of the illusive promise of development. The joke is a reference to the fact that the only thing that has changed for many people in Yangon is that the public buses are more crowded. This is not to mention that the traffic on the roads is often at a standstill because of the dramatic increase in car imports.

This book is oriented around the theme of the 'business of transition'. It is concerned with how to understand the 'business' that takes place in times of major political change. There has been growing recognition of the commercial stakes and business activities of the rule-of-law industry (Marshall 2014: xiv). This book identifies the way in which law creates new markets, law embodies hopes of social engineering and law reform is motivated by the goal of economic gain. This book is an invitation to think carefully and critically about the intersection between law, development and economics in times of political transition. This theme is one that has caused considerable angst and soul-searching in academia and public policy and amongst legal practitioners. It is hoped that by focusing on one specific context – Myanmar – as the latest site for law and development and rule-of-law reforms fresh insights can be gained. The importance of Myanmar cannot be underestimated, given its strategic location between China and India and the perception that it is the newest frontier in Southeast Asia for foreign investment and law and governance initiatives. Building on recent work (Crouch and Lindsey 2014), the case of Myanmar can be used as a gauge of the current trends in the law and development movement.

This chapter introduces the Myanmar context by sketching out the contours of the business of transition, with a focus on local engagement and responses to law reform and rule-of-law promotion. Given that Myanmar finds itself as the latest site for law reform, the chapter situates developments in Myanmar within the broader trends in law and development. It argues that we must continue to grapple with the legacy of past law and development efforts, and remind ourselves of lessons learnt from past failures, because many of the concerns around court reform, legal education and model laws remain directly relevant to contexts such as Myanmar today.

The chapter first turns 'Back to Business', which is a reference to the failed attempt in Myanmar to shift from a socialist to market-based economy after 1988. The chapter argues that the past history of law and economic reform is shaping future efforts at reform. Many of the economic and business reforms since 2011 have built on these earlier foundations in some way. I emphasise the importance of understanding current reforms in light of past political, legal and economic practices. In short, law and development initiatives need to take into consideration the path dependency of a country's legal culture to support efforts that can build on or disrupt this trajectory.

The chapter then questions 'Whose Business?' is involved in the post-2011 reform frenzy of new rule-of-law and economic development initiatives. While so often attention is drawn to laws or institutions, it is of course people who are the actors and agents engaged in the business of law reform. This focus on agents is an intentional reminder that despite the persistence of legal technical assistance, these efforts all rely on and are determined by the people who inhabit and animate these institutions.

The chapter concludes with attention to 'Business Matters', that is, distinctive features or characteristics of debates on law reform and economic development as it is playing out in Myanmar. At a time when aid, diplomacy and business interests are closer than ever, there is an emphasis on greater transparency, participation and distribution of resources; the reform of legal texts and institutions; and the awareness of foreign involvement in the process of aid delivery, development assistance and foreign investment. These concerns are addressed in more detail in other chapters throughout the book.

Myanmar in the History of Law and Development

This chapter repositions Myanmar in light of what is often referred to as the 'law and development' movement, a broad and contested term that is used to describe the use of law reform to pursue goals of political, economic and social development. In more recent decades, the field has been described by the less contested term 'law and governance', or through the prominence of overarching themes such as the globalisation of the rule of law (Morgan 2010). The literature on the history of law and development is largely dominated by a focus on Western actors and institutions, particularly the United States and institutions such as the World Bank and the Ford Foundation (Kleinfeld 2012; Carothers 1999; Carothers and De Gramont 2013). I acknowledge that, with more time and space, a broader perspective could also include law reform under Myanmar's period of British colonial rule (1885–1947). Nevertheless, I begin in the 1960s and seek to demonstrate modern Myanmar's paradoxical position within the law and development movement. I do so to highlight Myanmar's current curious status as the latest site for rule-of-law initiatives and foreign investment.

In the 1960s, Myanmar was in a paradoxical situation in terms of its connections to the law and development movement. On one hand, Myanmar was thrust onto the world stage of diplomatic peace-building and development in a very unlikely way. The unexpected death of the then–UN Secretary-General Dag Hammarskjöld created an opportunity for U Thant, a Burmese diplomat, to be appointed in his place (U Thant 1978). U Thant's term (1961–1971) was historic for many reasons, not least because this was the first time a non-European was elected to the position, and it was during a period when many former colonies had gained independence and were entering into membership of the UN. In December 1961, under the leadership of U Thant as the new secretary-general, the General Assembly declared the First Decade of Development. While this declaration did not place an emphasis on law, it did pave the way for international technical assistance in a range of areas and became the platform on which subsequent international development efforts were based. Just several months later in 1962, Ne Win executed a coup in Burma. In the ensuing years, General Ne Win shut off the country from the outside world, driving out most foreign embassies and international organisations.

It was also in the 1960s when the law and development movement took off, driven by US lawyers and professors in Latin America and the United States Agency for International Development (USAID) (Scott 2008). The focus of these modernisation initiatives was on civic education, courts, the legal profession and legal education (Carothers 1999: 20–29). In short, the emphasis was on legal technical assistance (Arndt 1987). This first decade of practice was driven by a small pool of lawyers (Paul 2003). Some academic practitioners amongst these ranks were soon overcome with a sense of crisis and disillusionment due to the paternalistic and top-down approach taken, as articulated in a famous article by Trubek and Galanter (1974).

Trubek and Galanter suggest that legal reform efforts had been based on many wrong assumptions. They identify that many efforts had started from the assumption of an individualised view of society. Reform efforts had presumed that the state has control over individuals, that individuals would conform to legal rules and that the state was central to law reform. Practitioners had acted upon the belief that the design of laws can achieve social goals and that law can be used to justify injustice by the state. Yet of course law reform is not able to change behaviour in predictable ways. Efforts to train and support the legal profession ignored the fact that the growth in the legal profession is not in itself neutral, and may actually increase social inequality because the legal profession does not necessarily uphold the public interest. Further, while many technical assistance programmes focused on the courts as central to the legal order, it was often the case that courts were inaccessible and biased, while informal dispute resolution forums were overlooked. In response to these criticisms, Trubek and Galanter suggested that there was a need to enhance empirical understanding of local cultures and institutions, and the assumption that US law serves as an appropriate model needs to be questioned. Many of the assumptions about the role of the courts, legal education and the legal profession are still evident in contemporary rule-of-law programmes, and so Trubek and Galanter's critique remains an important reminder.

The year of publication of Trubek and Galanter's article, 1974, also marked the death of U Thant, the former Secretary-General of the UN (1961–1971). When his body was returned from New York to Yangon, a stand-off ensued between the military and students over whether he should be given a proper state burial. The conflict resulted in the military blowing up the student union building, causing an untold number of deaths. Over the coming decades, the memory of U Thant and his service to the global community was suppressed in Myanmar.

The 1980s are often seen as the second moment in the Western liberal narrative of law and development. This time has been depicted as a period of law and the neo-liberal market, in which law took centre-stage in development (Trubek and Santos 2006). Globally, the belief that law enables economic growth comes with a standard set of requirements – protection of property rights, enforcement of contracts, banking regulations and intellectual property regimes, amongst others (see, for example, Ginsburg 2000; Pistor and Wellons 1999; Jayasuriya 1999). This period was also marked by an absence of accountability of donors and providers of law and development initiatives, such as the World Bank. This vacuum of accountability has been labelled the 'lawlessness of development' (Paul 2003: xiii). It was a growing industry, but one that was yet to enter Myanmar. The 1980s in Myanmar were a period of public dissatisfaction with the dysfunctionalities of socialist rule under Ne Win, such as the imposition of harsh demonetisation policies. In 1988, the democratic uprising in Myanmar began, only to be suppressed by another two decades of military rule.

The 1990s were marked by the ascendance of the rule of law as the dominant mantra of law and development. Law became both central to social and economic development and was seen as a remedy for market failures. This era ushered in a renewed emphasis on institutional reform, including courts, due to the impact of new institutionalist economics (North 1990). The number of international agencies that have rule-of-law programmes has grown significantly, and globally there are at least forty UN agencies alone that offer some form of rule-of-law assistance (O'Connor 2015). In Myanmar, the 1990s marked an attempt by the military to shift the economy from a socialist to a market-based system. Various legislative reforms on economic and commercial affairs were passed as the regime made a desperate effort to revamp the economy by attracting significant foreign investment and tourism. This failed, and Western sanctions remained a significant deterrent.

In the 2000s and beyond, at the international level there was a renewed focus on development through the Millennium Development Goals, and, more recently, the Sustainable Development Goals. However, it was only the latter goals that explicitly put law and justice on the global development agenda. These efforts were complemented by the 2005 Paris Declaration on Aid Effectiveness, which affirmed principles of local ownership and the need for greater accountability of the aid industry itself. While legal technical assistance often remained a core part of rule-of-law programmes, ideas of legal empowerment and access to justice gained traction (Golub 2006). Further, a new industry of measuring the rule of law has emerged, although measuring the impact of rule-of-law programmes remains a complex and fraught endeavour (Engel Merry, Davis and Kingsbury 2015). At present Myanmar remains close to the bottom of most indexes, such as Transparency International's Corruption Perception Index (see Simpson, Chapter 3) or the World Bank's Doing Business report, although of course such rankings have been criticised.

The range of professionals now driving rule-of-law programmes is diverse, and this has drawn attention to the emergence of the global 'rule of law profession' (Simion and Taylor 2015). This profession has had to rethink the assumption that law can and does play a role in social and economic change, an assertion that is far more challenging than we have previously assumed. The results from socio-legal studies on whether law can engender social and behavioural change are mixed at best (Gillespie and Nicholson 2012: 2). In many ways, while the current phase in law and development may bear renewed emphasis on the rule of law as a good in and of itself, it still carries the remnants of old approaches such as the belief in the utility of legal transfers and assumptions about the desirability of recourse to best practice (Tamanaha 1995). There has also been a renewed turn to the political economy of rule-of-law reforms (Carothers and De Gramont 2013), and a re-emphasis of the role of law in development more generally (WDR 2017).

In Asia, much of this Western or internationally driven law reform frenzy primarily took place in the wake of the financial crisis of 1997. At times, loan agreements came with heavy conditionality clauses (Antons 2003; Antons and Gessner 2007). The law and development industry continued to pursue a standard core of activities – judicial reform, police and security sector reform, legal education, professional regulation, corporate and trade law reforms (Trebilcock and Daniels 2008) – although often infused with a new emphasis on access to justice, gender sensitivity and legal empowerment (Golub 2006).

Throughout the 1990s and 2000s, Myanmar remained under tight military control. The points of interaction on law and development with the outside world were minimal, such as the in-country work of the UN Office of Drugs and Crime to address the opium trade and the International Labour Organisation's work on the cronic problem of child labour. By the late 2000s, the British Council's Pyoe Pin programme was one of few to explicitly include a rule-of-law component. In 2012 the grandson of U

Thant (former Secretary General of the UN) gained permission from the government, and financial backing from donors, to renovate U Thant's former house as a museum in honour of his service to the global community through the United Nations. In the same year, many international organisations, businesses and foreign embassies once again began to set up shop in Myanmar.

By 2013–2014 Myanmar was the highest recipient of development assistance from the Organisation for Economic Co-Operation and Development (OECD). One does not need to go far on the OECD website to see the connection that is increasingly being drawn between aid and foreign investment, referenced in slogans such as 'aid for trade' or 'financing for sustainable development'. The largest donor by far to Myanmar is Japan, yet the efforts of Japan or other countries such as China in terms of their development impact in the region and around the globe are often overlooked. The role of law reform and economic development in times of political transition therefore requires particular attention.

In some respects, a conventional history of law and development would position Myanmar as largely absent from the picture. However, I have tried to demonstrate that in fact the legacy of U Thant as former secretary-general of the UN at a time when the First Decade of Development was launched is in fact a significant event in itself. Although the socialist regime of Burma ultimately denied his global contribution by refusing an official state burial, fast-forward to 2012 shows U Thant's legacy slowly coming to light. Further, it is essential to bear in mind the turbulent history of the law and development movement itself, as well as the recent avalanche since 2012 in Myanmar in order to understand the trends in law reform today.

I turn now to consider the two decades prior to Myanmar's official semi-democratic turn, to examine the local context and legal culture in which the contemporary business of transition is taking place.

Back to Business

All efforts at law reform take place against the backdrop of a particular historical trajectory. In Myanmar, efforts to kick-start a market economy and undertake law reform are not new. After the fall of the socialist regime in 1988, measures were taken to reorient away from a socialist economy towards a market-based economy. The abrupt change from socialism to a market economy was accompanied by a push to open up opportunities for foreign investment in Myanmar, as well as to establish private banks (Turnell 2009: 256–260). In the 1990s, the abolition of the socialist economic system and the introduction of new laws on foreign investment followed. Yet the business sector remained under the control and surveillance of the regime, and there was little emphasis on innovation (Tin Maung Maung Than 2007). The post-1988 efforts to shift to a market economy were largely stillborn. This was made more difficult by heavy Western sanctions in the 1990s–2000s. As Renshaw points out (Chapter 9 in this volume), the example of US sanctions under military rule is one demonstration that targeted sanctions may simply exacerbate the situation due to a lack of legitimacy.

Many of the reforms introduced since 2011 – from the Central Bank Law to the Foreign Investment Law – began with the legal framework from the 1990s as a background template. These laws have created new tensions and new forms of conflict (Crouch 2016b). In this sense, 'Back to Business' in Myanmar is more about returning to the legislative foundations and regulatory practice laid in the 1990s on business and economic reforms, and expanding on and liberalising these measures. In many ways this is not surprising. While there are many international experts offering advice, the reality is that local legal drafters often stick with familiar strategies and procedures rather than introduce the radically unknown.

While the business of transition may involve an intensive effort at law reform, efforts at law reform are not new in Myanmar. In fact, every regime has placed some emphasis on the idea of law reform. For example, in the 1880s as Burma was being annexed to British India in several stages, authorities in the British Indian empire were appointed to various law commissions to draft the Penal Code, the Code of Civil Procedure and Criminal Procedure Code, and a range of staple laws that remain in existence today, including the Contract Act, Specific Relief Act, Evidence Act, Transfer of Property Act, Succession Act and Negotiable Instruments Act. After independence in 1947, the parliamentary government established a Laws Revision Committee in 1954 to compile and publish the thirteen-volume Burma Code. Many of the laws from the Burma Code still remain in force with few amendments today. After the coup of 1962 and the takeover by General Ne Win, a Laws Revision Committee chaired by the attorney general was established in October 1963 with the task of reviewing legislation. A similar pattern was established by the State Law and Order Restoration Council (1988–2010), which set up a committee in 1995 to review all laws and consider amending or repealing existing laws. The post-2011 governments have followed this pattern by establishing law reform committees with the task of considering laws that require amendment, replacement or cancellation. This obsession with reform of legal texts shows no sign of abating, with the creation of Thura Shwe Mann's Commission for the Assessment of Legal Affairs and Special Issues and its primary mandate of legislative review.

The key distinction since 1988 is that the economic and legal system has been oriented away from socialism and towards a market economy. The current basis for economic reform is the 2008 Constitution. The emphasis on the market economy is in fact embedded in the Constitution. The Constitution specifies that Myanmar is based on a 'market economy', and this is explicitly attributed to the former State Peace and Development Council in the Preamble to the Constitution. While it may seem unusual to recognise the market economy in the Constitution, Myanmar in fact joins a growing number of countries that explicitly enshrine the market economy in the constitution. This list includes the Constitution of Afghanistan (2004), Albania (1998), Andora (1993), Angola, Bosnia and Herzegovnia (1995), Cambodia (1993), Guatemala (1985), Kosovo (2008), Laos (1991), Malawi (1994), Moldova (1994), Romania (1991), Serbia (2006), Slovakia (1992) and Spain (1978).[1] This long list of constitutions from Asia to Eastern and Central Europe to the Middle East is just one indication of the way in which the idea of the 'market economy' has embedded itself in constitutional law. This is particularly the case in countries that have made a shift from a socialist economy to a market economy. The inclusion of a 'market economy' provision in a constitution is an overt effort to distinguish economic reforms from the past and to enshrine the concept of the market economy in the Constitution, as a form of 'higher' law. Perhaps more distinctive to Myanmar is the constitutional promise not to nationalise or demonetise the currency, as the previous military regime had done with devastating consequences.

In terms of the intersection between the legal system and the economy in Myanmar, many new laws address economic reforms geared towards greater foreign investment and the market economy, including in the banking sector, establishment of special economic zones and potential reform of the Company Law. This churn in legal policies and regulations has created significant challenges for commercial lawyers, where responding to a client's request often requires investigative journalism as much as

---

[1] See the Comparative Constitution-Making Project: http://comparativeconstitutionsproject .org/. This is not including constitutions that recognise a qualified market economy, such as the 'socialist market economy' of the China Constitution 1982 and the 'socialist-oriented market economy' of the Vietnam Constitution 1992 (art 51).

it does legal research, given the challenges of finding and matching legal text with administrative practice.

In sum, law reform in Myanmar, as in any other developing context, is not new. The genesis of the market economy can be traced to post-1988 trends, and yet the post-2011 period with its relative freedoms is clearly marked by a greater effort to enshrine a market-based system, or to get 'Back to Business'. At the heart of this controlled reform process are local actors. I turn now to consider whose business is at the heart of the law and development agenda.

Whose Business?

Times of political change involve intensive efforts at economic and legal reform, and often raise concerns about who should be able to participate in and benefit from the business of transition. The chapters in this book pay particular attention to local actors in contemporary Myanmar. Amongst the most prominent are civil society organisations (CSOs) working in a range of sectors that advocate for and with local communities and interest groups. This includes advocacy on matters as important and diverse as land rights for farmers, labour rights for factory workers, protection from domestic violence for women and the right to education for children. There has certainly been an increase in scope and influence of CSOs in Myanmar in recent years, and many have traced this to the post–Cyclone Nargis recovery activities in 2008.

The renewed agency of CSOs in Myanmar is evident throughout this book, from Simpson's concern with the CSOs that form part of the Multi-Stakeholder Group for the Extractive Industries Transparency Initiative (Chapter 3), to Dale and Kyle's concern with social enterprise (Chapter 4), to Turnell's focus on microfinance initiatives (Chapter 5) and Nishimura's attention to CSOs that advocate for the rights of communities affected by special economic zones such as Dawei Watch (Chapter 8). CSOs face ongoing challenges in their efforts to participate in the law reform process, and some have had more meaningful opportunities than others in being able to engage in consultation with government agencies. While these chapters recognise the new space that has opened up for CSOs since 2011, they are also alert to the ongoing challenges and struggles that remain in the quest for genuine consultation, transparency and advocacy for social justice and equality.

A shift from authoritarian rule inevitably leads to renewed focus on the state as a key actor in law reform. In Myanmar, state actors include various government departments that may be responsible for drafting laws, including the Union Attorney General's Office (as the de facto ministry of law), various ministries, parliamentary committees and members of parliament. Yet the focus on the state and its institutions is in tension with more recent scholarship that recognises that legal transfers and efforts at law reform must be decentred to include the role of non-state or hybrid actors. In Myanmar there is no shortage of non-state actors that seek to have an influence on the process of reform: from armed ethnic groups to the private sector to religious or ethnic-based social and political organisations. On many issues and in many sectors, the interests run across state and non-state lines. Ford, Gillan and Thein's chapter on labour standards (Chapter 2) is one demonstration of a sector where reform affects not only the government's Ministry of Labour Employment and Social Security, but involves the International Labour Organisation, unions and private companies local, regional and transnational.

The national parliament has been one of the most interesting and surprising developments in the post-2011 era. After the 2015 elections, the state and region parliaments will also potentially become more active in law-making. State and region parliaments have already raised questions with the Constitutional Tribunal regarding its capacity to raise taxes under the Constitution. The government administration plays a significant role in implementing many of the new laws and government policies. In particular, new research has demonstrated the significant, but at times subversive, role played by the General Administration Department, as the core of the administrative structure, and the Development Affairs Organisation (Arnold et al. 2013; Arnold and Kyi Pyar Chit Saw 2015). It is at the sub-national level that a range of administrative procedures take place in relation to business permits and licences for use of land and taxation, and it is imperative that these local governance institutions are recognised as key actors in development. The importance of regional regulations to enable local business is aptly illustrated by Arnold (Chapter 6, this volume).

In contrast to the legislative and executive branch, the courts have played less of a role in the business of reform in Myanmar. This is because many of the new national laws on business reforms do not allow disputes to be heard by the courts (Crouch 2017). Instead, disputes under a range of new laws are to be resolved by commissions established by statute. There are some exceptions to this tendency of preventing disputes from going to court, such as the Minimum Wage Law that specifically refers to the writs as an avenue to challenge unlawful decisions (Ford, Gillan and Thein, Chapter 2 this volume). Supreme Court judges have, however, played an extra-judicial role because at times they have been asked to assist in drafting legislation according to the court's responsibilities under the Constitution. This includes the draft Insolvency Law, the Legal Aid Law and the Monogamy Law. The courts will begin to see more cases related to business disputes due to new legislation on aspects of commercial and corporate law being considered by parliament. While the courts have also been amongst the most resistant institutions to reform, they have begun to engage more with international donors. For example, the Union Supreme Court holds an annual Strategic Action Plan meeting to co-ordinate engagement with the donor community. There will potentially be significant changes to the court system, and the potential introduction of specialised courts as has occurred in other parts of Asia, in coming years.

The legal profession has been reinvigorated in its new-found role as a mediator of the business of law reform. Traditionally, in Myanmar the basic structure of legal practice includes a senior lawyer, who bears the title of 'advocate' and chamber master, and his chamber students, who are usually recent law graduates known as 'higher grade pleaders' (junior lawyers). Most lawyers in Myanmar are litigation lawyers, undertaking mostly criminal and to a lesser extent civil cases. The pool of local commercial lawyers is small but growing. In the 1990s a handful of commercial law firms were established during the military turn to a market economy. However, it was not until 2012, after the political shift under President Thein Sein, that foreign commercial law firms began to establish offices in Yangon in large numbers. The market is now, in the words of one lawyer, the most crowded legal market in Southeast Asia, and includes Korean, Japanese, American, UK, Thai, regional and global law firms. At present there are no regulations concerning foreign lawyers.[2] This area of practice is likely to undergo significant change in the future, because tensions between local litigators and commercial lawyers may lead to some form of regulation of foreign lawyers. In fact, many of the activities of foreign commercial law firms (such as offering pro bono training to the Attorney General's Office or the courts) at present are precisely an effort to win the favour of the government and therefore prevent a situation where foreign lawyers are regulated out of the local market.

---

[2] While there are many parallels between Vietnam's period of renovation after 1996 and Myanmar, one difference is that Vietnam set out clear restrictions on how foreign lawyers could operate in country (Rose 1998).

Law professors are another crucial actor in the business of transition. All universities at present are under the control of the government, and so all law professors are civil servants. Many law professors (all of whom are women) from the eighteen law departments across the country are regularly called upon by the government to assist in the drafting of legislation, the translation of laws, teaching in the judicial and military institutes, and marking judicial entrance exams, depending on their area of expertise. This has been the case in areas as diverse as intellectual property, children's rights and the national higher education law. Their position remains precarious, however, as professors must navigate their obligations to the institution and the government amidst calls for greater institutional and academic autonomy. Further, the issue of student activism remains a major concern, and, in the past, academics have been co-opted by the state to help contain and control student demonstrations. While students are still unable to form unions, in 2015 the arrest, assault and arbitrary detention of students were a reminder that many actors are still not free to participate in the process of transition.

The list of actors in law and economic development also includes the private sector. The business community is a diverse mix, including military businesses, state-owned economic enterprises and business cronies (Ford, Gillan and Thein 2015). It also includes newer actors such as social enterprises, as explained by Dale and Kyle (Chapter 4). The challenges of understanding the extent and scale of state-owned enterprises in Myanmar, and ways in which future policy should respond to them, are extremely complex (Rieffel 2015; Heller and Delesgues 2015). The sheer size and scale of some of the industries in which they are involved – such as the jade industry (Global Witness 2015) – suggest that even if these actors are not involved in official law reform, they clearly remain a major determinant of economic success.

As opportunities for foreign investment open up, foreign companies also vie for influence in this process. Other foreign organisations such as multilateral and bilateral agencies are also present in large numbers. A visit to the hotel zones in the capital city of Naypyidaw reveals the diverse international actors engaged in development – the alphabet soup of acronyms includes the United Nations Development Programme (UNDP) and United Nations High Commission for Refugees (UNHCR), to national aid agencies such as the United States Agency for International Development (USAID), the Japanese International Cooperation Agency (JICA) and the Korea International Cooperation Agency (KOICA), to supra-regional bodies such as the European Union, to international non-governmental organisations (INGOs) such as the International Development Law Organisation (IDLO), and development banks such as the World Bank and Asian Development Bank (ADB). This is not to mention bilateral donors, foundations such as the Open Society Institute, other INGOs, quasi-INGOs or global network organisations such as the International Bar Association. Many of these organisations have now been involved in rule-of-law projects for decades in a range of other contexts around the globe. There have been some high level government efforts towards co-operation and co-ordination amongst donors. In 2013, the Thein Sein government established the Myanmar Development Cooperation Forum and issued the Naypyidaw Accord for Effective Development Cooperation. Under the NLD government from 2016, a Development Assistance Coordination Unit was established (known as 'DACU'). Yet the extent to which these agencies co-ordinate and share information, or fail to do so, in Myanmar is in part conditioned on their past interactions and institutional histories in other contexts.

This survey of the range of actors involved can be taken as a neutral and open-ended response to the question of 'Whose Business?' Alternatively, the question of 'Whose Business?' may provoke a more hostile response, suggesting that for some it is 'none of their business'. This more suspicious response has surfaced as part of the debates on economic law reforms in terms of nationalist and protectionist sentiment. Further, many local actors play multiple roles and therefore have overlapping ties of allegiance, and yet these ties will no doubt continue to shift with the political landscape under the National League for Democracy (NLD) government. Attention needs to focus on who can or should participate in, and benefit from, rule-of-law reform. While the rule-of-law industry is now a standard fixture in developing contexts, the necessity for locally driven initiatives remains paramount. In fact, on one reading, Cheesman's study of the rule of law may lead us to conclude that the rule of law can only effectively be promoted by local actors in Myanmar (Cheesman 2015). At the very least, his work points to the necessity of reform driven by those with an intimate knowledge and appreciation of local context.

Business Matters

This chapter now turns to consider the core contemporary issues at stake in the business of transition. The reform process reflects broader trends in the current phase of law and economic development, while also attesting to the persistent weaknesses and bias in law reform. Our attention needs to focus on how local actors respond to and participate in law reform (Gillespie and Nicholson 2012), not simply focus on how legal texts have changed. I identify three trends that are evident in the business of transition in Myanmar. The first is the heightened demands for genuine participation, transparency in governance and equitable distribution of resources, and the benefits of democracy generally. The second is the technical reform of legal texts and institutions and the borrowing of legal models. The third is foreign aid, investment and expertise, with Myanmar now home to a large proportion of the law and development sector. These overlapping trends and concerns demonstrate some of the central issues in contemporary efforts of law and development. I explore these issues with reference to the chapters that follow in this volume.

Demands for Participation, Transparency and Equitable Distribution

One characteristic of the business of transition is the heightened expectations of public participation in business and economic reforms and demands for transparency in the reform process. Of course, all INGOs today, as well as most business activities, would claim to include some consultation as part of their process. Yet the challenge is often about how to ensure effective participation and consultation, and the inclusion of vulnerable groups such as women and youth in particular. Nishimura (Chapter 8) grapples with the issue of managing expectations and ensuring meaningful and genuine consultation on projects such as the special economic zones. In Myanmar, this has taken place as media restrictions have been lifted and limitations on civil-society organisations relaxed. The increase in public participation in law reform has taken several forms. There has been greater participation in the national law-making process for some draft laws, although more often the consultation process is too little, too late.

Another form of participation has been demands for local community consultation regarding business plans and foreign investment, particularly in areas such as the special economic zones. Special economic zones have been marked out for Dawei, Thilawa, Kyaukphyu and Kokang, and these are in varying stages of progress (see Nishimura, Chapter 8; Wood, Chapter 9).[3] The idea of special economic zones is one that has spread across Asia (World Bank 2008; Harding and Carter 2010), and the concept

---

[3] Myanmar Special Economic Zones Law No 1/2014; Kokang Economic Zone, Myanmar Investment Commission Notification 59/2014.

itself is not new in Myanmar (Turnell 2014: 194). While the original legislation was modelled on that of Vietnam and China, further detail was
added to the expanded 2014 law in relation to income tax exemptions,
land use and labour requirements. Wood demonstrates, however, that the
difference between the regulations on the special economic zones and on
foreign investment more generally is negligible, and that this may negatively impact the possibility for success of the zones (Chapter 7). The chapters in this volume seek to capture local perspectives and responses to
legal change. All chapters show some concern with the role of civil society,
with what people think the law is capable of, or what they expect it can or
should do.

Access to dispute resolution mechanisms and the resolution of past
grievances has been another area of demand. Restrictions on freedom of
association have been lifted, although not completely removed, and it is
now legal to form a union (with the exception of student unions, which
remain illegal). Demands for dispute resolution have often revolved
around the issue of land and natural resources. There has been renewed
focus on labour standards (Kyaw Soe Lwin 2014) and the recent introduction of a minimum wage. As Ford, Gillan and Thein (Chapter 2) demonstrate, the minimum wage introduced by law in Myanmar in 2015 came
close to meeting the expectations of CSOs, and claims by the private sector that this would negatively affect their business viability appear to be
largely unfounded.

In addition, the demands for more meaningful and genuine public participation and consultation are often combined with demands for transparency. Such calls for transparency may be made by both local actors as
well as foreign actors. For example, many have called for greater reporting
and accountability in Myanmar's state economic enterprise sector (Rieffel
2015). The calls for transparency have also been made of the rule-of-law
and aid industry itself, in part due to recognition that this is now 'big business' (Zurn, Nolkaemper and Peerenboom 2012). In 2014, Burma signed
up to the International Aid Transparency Initiative (IATI), a voluntary
code, and a website has been launched to manage aid data (mohinga.
info). The site documents that at least US$5.31 billion in aid has been
committed to Burma between 2011 and 2015 (*The Irrawaddy* 2015). The
information the site contains on the amount and purpose of aid of course
depends on the willingness of agencies to submit to the voluntary reporting requirements. This also raises the concern that the combination of
aid and investment may swamp the demand-side of change, and distort
priorities.

Further, there is an understandable and pressing concern that natural resources should not be subject to exploitation by outsiders or by local cronies, but rather be of benefit to local communities. The 'resource curse' is a well-known phrase in Myanmar, as a reference to the challenges facing the state in the management of natural resources (Humphreys, Sachs and Stiglitz 2007). Many are keen to use their new freedoms to avoid the resource curse. The post-2011 environment and the greater freedoms of speech and association have led to countless complaints about land grabs and resource allocation and distribution, past and present. This has been typified in local protests against the Letpadaung copper mine, a joint venture between a Chinese company and the military-owned Union of Myanmar Economic Holdings Ltd, as discussed by Simpson (Chapter 3).

Yet the law reform process has shown little signs of genuine improvement in how land is allocated, how disputes over land are resolved or how natural resources can be used in a more sustainable way. While parliament has passed several laws on the use of land, regulating farm land specifically and mandating environmental protection, many argue these laws do not go far enough in addressing the protracted issue of land confiscation.[4] While the vast majority of people in Myanmar depend on agriculture for their livelihood, little has changed in terms of their prospects for meaningful property rights.

In addition to land, Myanmar has an abundance of natural resources from oil and gas to gems and precious stones. Concerns over natural resource use and the exploitation of the environment and of workers in industries such as oil and gas have implicated foreign firms in the past and have had a negative effect on human capital. A major court case during the military era was filed in the United States against Unocal. In this case Burmese peasants brought claims against Unocal alleging violations of rights in the course of the natural gas pipeline project.[5] This case was possible because of the efforts of transnational legal actors and the social movements that energised this case (Dale 2011). After eight long years of winding its way through the courts, Unocal announced that a settlement had been reached with the plaintiffs. While this case was less about the environmental impact and more about the high human cost involved, the potential for foreign firms to face responsibility at home remains. This has led to a range of new regulatory initiatives in the resource sector, such

---

[4] Environmental Conservation Law No 9/2012; Administration of Vacant, Fallow and Virgin Lands Law No 10/2012; Farmland Act No 11/2012.
[5] See *Doe v. Unocal*, 395 F.3d 932 (9th Cir. 2002).

as the Extractive Industries Transparency Initiative (EITI), although as Simpson identifies this comes with a new set of challenges and problems (Chapter 3). These challenges are urgent given that industries such as the jade sector are worth an estimated US$31 billion per year on the black market (Global Witness 2015).

The concern over natural resources in Myanmar has often been generated at the local level, yet there remains disconnect between the powers of the state/region governments and the ability of these governments to use the resources for the public benefit. Natural resource governance has been a key theme of discussion and debate at the 21st Century Panglong Union Peace Conference, which began in 2016.

Reform of Legal Texts and Institutions

Law and development initiatives have fixated on the borrowing of ideas, and the reform of legal texts and institutions through legal technical assistance (Arndt 1987). This is certainly the case in Myanmar, as not only have a whole host of laws been passed, but a wider range of efforts are taking place to enhance legal education, establish an independent bar association, create rule-of-law training centres and open legal aid clinics.

In the same way that many development professionals have packed up their bags in Cambodia, Vietnam, Pakistan and Iraq and moved to Myanmar, so too have foreigners brought in their ready-made programmes and legal models from outside, often with little time to consider the local context and culture. Model legislation is increasingly promoted by specialised interest groups. Yet this preoccupation with legal models that embody 'international best practice' is more nebulous than it seems, as the idea of international best practice is never a neutral variable (Gillespie and Nicholson 2012: 6). Rule-of-law projects do not have inherent meaning, but rather the process of interpretation and contextualisation takes place on the ground by local actors (Gillespie 2014). This should lead to renewed attention to local context and meaning-making by local actors. This is particularly so because it is often local actors within government agencies who feel the pressure to have a new law for their sector.

One feature of legal reform is the tendency to look to common law models given the insistence by the government that Myanmar is a common law legal system. For example, the Company Act 1914 is still on the books in Myanmar and largely remains unamended up until now. There are efforts to revise and update both the Company Act and the Insolvency Act in co-operation with the Directorate of Investment and Company

Administration (DICA), the Union Supreme Court and the ADB (Tun 2014). In many ways Myanmar is a latecomer in the region in terms of corporate and commercial law reform, with organisations such as the ADB assisting in the reform of insolvency laws in at least eleven countries in Asia since 1998. Even once these draft laws are approved, it will take significant efforts to implement new systems and shift the mentality of government agencies from surveillance and restrictions on companies to one of facilitating business formation, innovation and growth. The preference to look to common law best practice must not overlook the reality that in many respects the legal system in Myanmar functions according to latent socialist principles and favours vested military interests.

Model legislation has been considered in relation to a range of areas of law. One example is the new Central Bank law that has been introduced.[6] In theory, this law grants independence to the Central Bank from the Ministry of Finance, reforms the position of the governor of the Central Bank and its board, and restricts the printing of money (Turnell 2013). Myanmar therefore joins a range of countries around the world that have taken steps to increase the independence of the central bank through legal reform (Polillo and Guillen 2005). However, in reality the Central Bank of Myanmar does not yet function independently. The future operation of banks, including foreign banks, will depend on the implementation and regulations under the new Financial Institutions of Myanmar Law 2016.

As Myanmar continues to open up and engage with the international community, this raises questions about the role and impact of international standards, upon which model legislation is sometimes based. Several chapters in this volume consider the relevance of international law in Myanmar. Myanmar is a dualist system, that is, any international treaty or convention must also be passed as a national law before it is recognised as law in the domestic context. One example is the Child Law No 9/1993, although this does not fully meet Myanmar's obligations under the UN Convention on the Rights of the Child. While Myanmar has signed the International Covenant on Economic, Social and Cultural Rights, it has not yet introduced legislation in this regard. Some select aspects of international law, such as the law of the sea, have been the focus of study in Myanmar as a 'safe' issue in light of Myanmar's success in its dispute over the maritime border with Bangladesh.

---

[6] The Central Bank of Myanmar Law No 16/2013.

In terms of rule-of-law programmes, some aid has gone to fund the involvement of foreign experts in law reform, although this does not necessarily equate to actual foreign influence in the draft law. This is not new, and some laws in the State Law and Order Restoration Council (SLORC)/State Peace and Development Council (SPDC) era were also drafted with degrees of assistance by foreign experts and institutions. The Anti-Trafficking in Persons Law No 5/2005 was drafted in consultation with international actors and with reference to international standards. More recently, several international organisations were involved in the consultation and drafting of the Small and Medium Enterprise Law. While engagement with foreign expertise creates more opportunities to consider best practice, it has also led to local concerns, perceptions and rumours of unwarranted foreign influence in the drafting process. This necessitates greater awareness of power disparities and greater transparency in the drafting and consultation process.

Many actors are pointing out the gaps between the situation in Myanmar and international standards and norms (regardless of whether Myanmar has actually signed on to these conventions), such as the standards expected of consultation on special economic zones (Nishimura, Chapter 8). Yet there is a need to go beyond this line of analysis to consider what meanings international law has in Myanmar, the areas in which it does or does not have traction, and to what extent it is useful to measure Myanmar against international standards.

Finally, regionalism is likely to have an influence on Myanmar's law reform process in the future. Myanmar became a member of the Association of Southeast Asian Nations (ASEAN) in 1997, although it was not until 2014 that it was finally permitted to take its turn as chair. Given the turn to ASEAN economic integration, this may influence future law reform efforts. More likely, in an informal sense, local actors in Myanmar often refer to or inquire about examples from ASEAN countries, regardless of whether legal models in the ASEAN region are of any use or relevance to Myanmar. This demonstrates a close affiliation with and desire to learn from successful legal reforms in the region.

Foreign Aid, Investment and Expertise

Law and economic development efforts are marked by an increase in foreign involvement. This may take the form of foreign aid, the involvement of foreign experts in law reform projects, foreign volunteers and foreign investment. While foreign involvement cannot necessarily be equated with foreign influence, there has clearly been a major increase in efforts at foreign engagement. Structurally, some government aid agencies in the West have been collapsed into departments for foreign affairs, including in Canada, New Zealand and Australia. There has been a corresponding rise in the language of 'economic diplomacy' as a substitute for traditional aid programmes. Foreign aid is increasingly tied explicitly to foreign affairs, and while this aid may still also be in the interests of the recipient country, at other times it may have a neutral or negative effect (Carothers and De Gramont 2013).

Law and development initiatives also now involve a host of bilateral and multilateral actors. Foreigners involved in these endeavours are likely to export legal ideas and development concepts that they are most familiar with (Schimmelfennig 2012: 115). Some have questioned whether the sheer avalanche of foreign aid in Myanmar since 2011 is 'too much too soon' (Rieffel and Fox 2013). The politics surrounding the provision of humanitarian aid reached a new low in 2013 when aid organisations were forced out of Rakhine State due to tensions over aid delivered to the displaced Rohingya population (see Cook 2016). This highlights the precarious and highly contested nature of humanitarian aid delivery in Myanmar.

The programmes and agendas of these agencies are inevitably shaped by their political and economic interests (Schimmelfennig 2012). After Myanmar's historic 2015 elections, these forms of engagement are increasing. There was talk of Myanmar becoming a 'One UN' community in the future. The UN's slogan of 'Delivering as One' includes four aspects: one leader, programme, budget and office. In essence, it is a bureaucratic merger of all UN aid agencies on the ground, which requires the consent of the host country. The intention is to make it easier for the host country to deal with one centralised agency. While this bureaucratic merger has taken place in other countries at the invitation of the government, there is no available evidence yet of the merits of such an approach.

Discussions on trends in aid and technical assistance often focus on the West, and yet this fails to recognise different approaches taken by other foreign actors. For example, the Japanese have a long history of engagement with Myanmar, including the provision of various forms of financial assistance through JICA (Steinberg 2001: 253–258; Seekins 1992). The Japanese operate outside the Western law and development paradigm (Nicholson and Hinderling 2013; Taylor 2005). As the primary shareholder in the ADB, and the second largest shareholder in the World Bank after the United States, Japan has a significant influence through the programmes of these multilateral banks. Japan has had an impact in the region through legal technical assistance in countries such as Vietnam, Cambodia and Mongolia. However, in Myanmar, the Japanese are less likely to directly influence the Myanmar model of law reform, due to the perceived gap between the civil law and common law heritage. This is not to discount the considerable informal influence that the Japanese have due to their long-standing ties and financial commitments to Myanmar.

The Japanese have a history of providing aid to Burma. In 1987, aid from Japan made up 20 per cent of Burma's national budget. After the coup of 1988, Japan was the first country to recognise the military government and continue aid relations (Oishi and Furuoka 2003: 898). Japan was the only government to continue providing scholarships to civil servants to study in Japan during the military regime. It has even been said that in 1998 SLORC released Daw Aung San Suu Kyi in part to please the Japanese, who had promised a significant amount of aid and financial assistance (Fink 2009: 78). Japan was amongst the first to establish ties with the University of Yangon Law Department, and to set up a Myanmar-Japan Legal Resource Centre on campus, with a particular focus on business law reforms. JICA has negotiated physical desk space in a range of government ministries, from the Union Attorney General's Office to the Ministry of Mining. In 2014, there were reports of a backlash in Myanmar against development plans in co-operation with JICA (DVB 2014). While the involvement of Japan in development is less well-known, it is clearly one of the major foreign actors in the business of transition in Myanmar because of the long-term relationships it has fostered amongst the civil service and the long-term commitment it has already demonstrated.

A final issue that many chapters in this volume touch on is the perceived need to attract foreign investment and the challenges of regulating it for the benefit of the people. Between 1989 and 2010, China, Hong Kong, South Korea and Thailand were the major investors in Myanmar (Bissinger 2012). Few Western countries invested at this time due to the imposition of Western sanctions (Pederson 2008). In 2016, curiosity about potential foreign investment opportunities has slowed, with many Western firms adopting a wait-and-see approach given potential changes under the NLD government. The Union Parliament has spent a significant amount of time over the past few years debating and then reconsidering the provisions of the Foreign Investment Law 2012, followed by a separate law relating to investment by Myanmar citizens.[7] In 2016, these

---

[7] Foreign Investment Law No 21/2012; Myanmar Citizens Investment Law No 18/2013.

two laws were combined and revised, passed by the new NLD-led government. This has potential implications for land use, labour and taxation, although given the broad terms of the legislation it often comes down to subsequent regulations to clarify the details.

The influence of foreign involvement through aid and humanitarian programmes, technical assistance and private sector investment is rarely black and white. But the grey shadow it does cast means that foreign involvement is ripe for manipulation or complaints from nationalists who wish to protect an aspect of the market or of the perceived national culture. This places greater weight on the need for transparency and accountability across these areas of foreign investment, and for sustained attentiveness and priority accorded to understanding local context.

Outline of the Book

The chapters that follow share a concern that Myanmar offers an opportunity for the international community to learn from past mistakes in terms of its involvement in the business of transition. The chapters in this volume speak to a range of common issues – land rights, access to finance, economic development, the role of law including its potential and its limits, and the intersection between local actors, globalised ideas and the international community. All chapters are based on new empirical evidence and insights from living, working and conducting field research in Myanmar.

In Chapter 2, 'Labour Standards and International Investment in Myanmar', Michele Ford, Michael Gillan and Htwe Htwe Thein focus on the critical issue of labour standards and the implications for international investment in Myanmar. They profile a case study of the garment industry, which is largely populated by Asian businesses, and the response of the introduction of a minimum wage. The fact that the garment sector was not exempt from the minimum wage law is significant. The authors note that international firms are keen to affiliate with international labour standards as a strategy to manage any possible reputational risk. In contrast, Asian firms are only now facing pressure from trade unions and civil society networks to comply with this labour regime due to their relative disconnect from global networks. The authors point to the future necessity of social mobilisation by unions and civil society to make real the minimum wage for all workers.

Similar themes are explored in Chapter 3, 'The Extractive Industries Transparency Initiative: New Openings for Civil Society in Myanmar', where Adam Simpson focuses on the impact of the EITI international regulatory scheme and its operation in Myanmar. He intentionally considers the EITI as one of the most public, high-profile and globalised natural resource governance tools. Yet his chapter identifies a paradox inherent in this project. On one hand, the EITI process has a fairly narrow and carefully defined scope as a mechanism to check that government revenue lines up with company payments. On the other hand, civil society activists hold high expectations that the EITI must also act as a means of fair distribution of natural resources. Yet this is a task the EITI was not designed to address. Simpson's chapter suggests that the perceived success or failure of a particular development initiative is in part conditioned by the gap between what the project is designed to do and what local actors expect the project to be able to achieve. This points to the importance of understanding local expectations of development and accountability projects. His chapter also struggles with the important question of representation, such as in areas where a particular minority group is affected (for more, see Crouch 2016a), and the challenges of ensuring representation in a divided society.

Two chapters in this volume look at particular areas of innovation where law reform often lags behind. In Chapter 4, 'The Risky Business of Transformation: Social Enterprise in Myanmar's Emerging Democracy', John Dale and David Kyle consider the emergence of social enterprises, as both a global and a regional phenomenon, and one that has potential to empower entrepreneurs in the Myanmar context. As in many of the chapters, Dale and Kyle emphasise the broader trend in social enterprise and the regulatory responses that it has entailed in Malaysia, Vietnam and Thailand, as well as in established democracies such as the United Kingdom and United States. The value of emerging social enterprise in Myanmar at present might in part lie in its ability to avoid regulation to date. Dale and Kyle focus on the example of employment opportunities for former political prisoners in Myanmar and the way in which social enterprise initiatives have emerged to fill a gap in addressing this important social need. They focus on the need for development reforms to foster individual creativity and initiative, and for any future regulation of social enterprise by the state to be for the protection of workers and to foster rather than stifle innovation.

In Chapter 5, 'Microfinance in Myanmar: Unleashing the Potential', Sean Turnell assesses the state of the microfinance sector in Myanmar, which is of critical importance given the state of the banking sector. The leading scholar of Myanmar's economy, Turnell first highlights both the promise and the potential of microfinance, although he cautions us that we should not overemphasise either its successes or its failures in other contexts. Turnell identifies two major benefits of microfinance: the way it can meet a critical need for poor people to be able to access financial services, and the way it can offer a tangible sense of institutional reliability that is otherwise out of reach of the poor. Turnell familiarises the reader with the history of microfinance in Myanmar and the recent efforts by the government to regulate the sector. He argues that the present environment for microfinance remains hampered by past 'myopic policy-making' practices. While he remains optimistic about the possibilities microfinance represents, he concedes that it remains no solution to a fully functioning financial sector. There are no short cuts to financial reform.

Critical for local business is the need to focus on local economic governance, rather than just foreign investment alone. In Chapter 6, 'The Governance of Local Businesses in Myanmar: Confronting the Legacies of Military Rule', Matthew Arnold considers the role and function of the General Administration Department (GAD) and the Development Affairs Organisations (DAOs), the two major administrative institutions in Myanmar that regulate the business and economic sector at the local level. Arnold notes that the law and development literature has in recent decades affirmed the importance of local governance and administration. In this chapter he identifies how local governance matters to development in Myanmar. By offering new empirical analysis of administrative realities in Myanmar, Arnold identifies the major shifts that are taking place in the role and function of the GAD and DAOs. He acknowledges the need to overcome the legacy of the military as a constraining factor on the potential contribution to economic development.

Two chapters in this volume consider the importance and implications of reforms to establish special economic zones (SEZs) in Myanmar. In Chapter 7, 'Special Economic Zones: Gateway or Roadblock to Reform?', Josh Wood focuses on the economic viability and the importance of the SEZs as forms of collaboration with China, Thailand and Japan, respectively. He situates developments in Myanmar within the broader trend in the Asia-Pacific to stimulate economic growth through the creation of SEZs, though he notes the difficulties with comparative exercises. Debunking the myth that these SEZs are 'new', Wood shows how the plans for these sites evolved over the past two decades. In addressing the question of whether SEZs can contribute to economic reform in Myanmar, Wood argues that each of the sites – Dawei, Kyaukphu and Thilawa – needs to be considered on their merits. His sobering final analysis suggests that poor economic plans may mean that the SEZs in fact place the reform agenda in jeopardy, rather than bringing in economic benefits for the country as espoused. His chapter is a reminder that economic initiatives cannot be evaluated in isolation and that the relative success of an SEZ will depend on how it compares to the broader economic reform environment within which it is created.

In a separate chapter on SEZs, Chapter 8, 'Facing the Concentrated Burden of Development: Local Responses to Myanmar's Special Economic Zones', Lauren Nishimura takes a different angle by focusing on how local communities have responded to the development of SEZs and the way these plans have imposed a concentrated burden on these communities. This relates back to the core themes of the volume, including the demands for heightened and meaningful public participation, concerns over the distribution of land and the uncertainty created by the involvement of foreign investors. Nishimura examines law as one means that communities and civil society organisations use to influence the development of projects such as SEZs. Like other authors, Nishimura is concerned with the intersection between international standards, government policies and the concerns of local communities. She argues for the need to evaluate law from the perspective of its impact on local communities and the extent to which it facilitates, or impedes, participation and accountability. She also recognises that it is often non-legal strategies adopted by local communities that may have just as much, or even greater, impact than following legally mandated grievance procedures. Nishimura highlights the potentially devastating impact of SEZs on both individuals and the environment. She charts the way that local communities navigate national, regional and global advocacy strategies, enabled by the fact that SEZs involve the interests of foreign governments and donors, as much as national ones. This is a timely reminder of the challenges of ensuring that development works for local people.

In the final two chapters, there is a focus on the interaction between the international community and the Myanmar context. In Chapter 9, 'Top-Down Transitions and the Politics of US Sanctions', Catherine Renshaw looks at the impact of sanctions in Myanmar past and present. Focusing primarily on US sanctions, Renshaw draws on the overwhelming body of scholarship that suggests that sanctions did not engender political reform in Myanmar. Renshaw examines the legacy of US sanctions (1990–2010) in light of the contemporary transition to draw broader conclusions about the business of transition. She argues for the importance of timing in the success of political and economic reform, and stresses the moral imperatives bound up in the business of transition that go beyond a mere cost-benefit analysis. Renshaw suggests that US sanctions may be more of a response to internal domestic sentiments than they are a rational and effective means of diplomacy. In doing so she undermines the belief of foreign countries that still hold to the view that they can influence the course of political change in Myanmar. As the volume went to press in 2016, the US had just made the decision to lift the remaining sanctions.

In the final chapter, 'The Politics of Aid in Myanmar', Tim Frewer identifies both the potential and the perils of aid, combined with the dramatic increase in CSOs, in Myanmar. Frewer charts how Myanmar has shifted from an aid orphan, largely denied access to aid under the military regime, to an 'aid hub' that may rival Cambodia as an aid recipient. This also means that Myanmar may run the risk of aid dependency, although it has access to far greater natural resources than a country such as Cambodia. Frewer identifies Cyclone Nargis in 2008 as a critical juncture that led to the expansion of aid and the activities of CSOs in Myanmar. Frewer remains cautious about the impact of aid in the contemporary period, given that the regime remains authoritarian at heart, despite the reforms that have taken place. Frewer identifies how bilateral and multilateral donors and their programmes are intimately entangled with geopolitical and economic concerns. He suggests that our focus should turn to the unintended effects of aid in terms of the relationship between elite interests and aid programmes, and the way aid is used to legitimise the pursuit of political and economic interests of the donors.

All of the chapters in this volume share a common orientation: a deep intellectual understanding and concern for the local Myanmar context, while acknowledging the pressing need to analyse the influence of regional and international engagement on the business of transition in Myanmar. At its core, the business of transition is concerned with the interaction between economic, business and legal developments in times of major political transition. Such efforts at reform often seek similar outcomes (such as access to the law and legal certainty) even if by different means. This volume offers critical insights about Myanmar as the latest site for development, and in doing so this timely contribution will stand as a reminder of the ongoing challenges posed by the intersection between business, law, economics and development in a globalised world.

References

Antons, Christoph (ed.). 2003. *Law and Development in East and Southeast Asia.* London: Routledge.

Antons, Christoph and Volkmar Gessner. 2007. *Globalisation and Resistance: Law Reform in Asia Since the Crisis.* Oxford: Hart Publishing.

Arndt, H. W. 1987. *Economic Development: The History of an Idea*. Chicago: University of Chicago Press.

Arnold, Matthew and Kyi Pyar Chit Saw. 2015. *Municipal Governance in Myanmar*. Paper No 7. www.theasiafoundation.org.

Arnold, Matthew et al. 2013. *State and Region Governments in Myanmar*. www.theasiafoundation.org.

Bissinger, Jared. 2012. 'Foreign Investment in Myanmar?' 34 *Contemporary Southeast Asia* 23.

Carothers, Thomas. 1999. *Aiding Democracy Abroad: The Learning Curve*. Washington DC: Carnegie Endowment for International Peace.

Carothers, Thomas and Diane De Gramont. 2013. *Development Aid Confronts Politics: The Almost Revolution*. Washington DC: Carnegie Endowment for International Peace.

Cheesman, Nick. 2015. *Opposing the Rule of Law: How Myanmar's Courts Make Law and Order*. Cambridge: Cambridge University Press.

Cook, Alistair D. B. 2016. 'The Global and Regional Dynamics of Humanitarian Aid in Rakhine State' in M. Crouch (ed.), *Islam and the State in Myanmar: Muslim-Buddhist Relations and the Politics of Belonging*. Oxford: Oxford University Press, pp. 258–278.

Crouch, Melissa. 2017. 'Myanmar's Courts in an Era of Quasi-Military Rule' in H. P. Lee (ed.), *Asia-Pacific Judiciaries: Independence, Impartiality and Integrity*. Cambridge: Cambridge University Press.

2016a. *Islam and the State in Myanmar: Muslim-Buddhist Relations and the Politics of Belonging*. Oxford: Oxford University Press.

2016b. 'Legislating Reform? Law and Conflict in Myanmar' in Nick Cheesman and Nich Farrelly (eds), *Conflict in Myanmar: War, Politics, Religion*. Singapore: Institute for Southeast Asia Studies, pp. 219–239.

Crouch, Melissa and Tim Lindsey. 2014. *Law, Society and Transition in Myanmar*. Oxford: Hart Publishing.

Dale, John. 2011. *Free Burma: Transnational Legal Action and Corporate Accountability*. Minneapolis: University of Minnesota Press.

Democratic Voice of Burma (DVB). 2014. 'Karen CSOs reject JICA plans'. 10 September.

East Asian Bureau of Economic Research. 2015. *Myanmar Trade and Investment Strategy*. Canberra: MDRI and East Asian Bureau of Economic Research, Australian National University. Available at http://www.eastasiaforum.org.

Engel Merry, S., K. Davis and B. Kingsbury (eds). 2015. *The Quiet Power of Indicators: Measuring Governance, Corruption & the Rule of Law*. Cambridge: Cambridge University Press.

Fink, Christina. 2009. *Living Silence in Burma: Surviving under Military Rule*. Chiang Mai: Silkworm Books.

Ford, Michele, Michael Gillan and Htwe Htwe Thein. 2015. 'From Cronyism to Oligarchy? Privatisation and Business Elites in Myanmar'. *Journal of Contemporary Asia* 1.

Gillespie, John. 2014. 'Development of a Theoretical Framework for Evaluating Rule of Law Promotion in Developing Countries' in M. Zurn, A. Nollkaemper and R. Peerenboom (eds), *Rule of Law Dynamics in an Era of International and Transnational Governance*. Cambridge: Cambridge University Press.

Gillespie, John and Pip Nicholson. 2012. 'Taking the Interpretation of Legal Transfers Seriously' in J. Gillespie and P. Nicholson (eds), *Law and Development and the Global Discourses of Legal Transfers*. Cambridge: Cambridge University Press, pp. 1–26.

Ginsburg, Tom. 2000. 'Does Law Matter for Economic Development? Evidence from East Asia'. 34(3) *Law & Society Review* 829.

Global Witness. 2015. *Jade: Myanmar's Biggest Secret.* https://www.globalwitness.org/reports/myanmarjade/

Golub, Stephen. 2006. 'The Legal Empowerment Alternative' in Thomas Carothers (ed.), *Promoting the Rule of Law Abroad: In Search of Knowledge*. Washington DC: Carnegie Endowment for International Peace.

Harding, Andrew and Connie Carter (eds). 2010. *Special Economic Zones in Asian Market Economies*. London: Routledge.

Heller, Patrick R. P. and Lorenzo Delesgues. 2015. *Gilded Gatekeepers: Myanmar's State-Owned Oil, Gas and Mining Enterprises*. New York: National Resource Governance Institute.

Hiscock, Mary. 1995. 'Changing Patterns of Regional Lawmaking in Southeast Asia'. 5(3) *Australian Journal of Corporate Law* 364.

Humphreys, M., J. Sachs and J. Stiglitz. 2007. 'What Is the Problem with Natural Resource Wealth?' in M. Humphreys, J. Sachs and J. Stiglitz (eds), *Escaping the Resource Curse*. New York: Columbia University Press.

Jayasuriya, K. 1999. *Law, Capitalism and Power in Asia: The Rule of Law and Legal Institutions*. London: Routledge.

Kleinfeld, Rachel. 2012. *Advancing the Rule of Law Abroad: Next Generation Reforms*. Washington DC: Carnegie Endowment for International Peace.

Kyaw Soe Lwin. 2014. 'Legal Perspectives on Industrial Disputes in Myanmar' in M. Crouch and T. Lindsey (eds), *Law, Society and Transition in Myanmar*. Oxford: Hart Publishing.

Marshall, David (ed.). 2014. *The International Rule of Law Movement: A Crisis of Legitimacy and the Way Forward*. London: HUP.

Morgan, Bronwyn. 2010. 'Forward' in A. Perry-Kessaris (ed.), *Law in the Pursuit of Development: Principles into Practise?* New York: Routledge.

Newton, Scott. 2008. 'Law and development, law and economics and the fate of legal technical assistance, in Arnscheidt, J, B van Ruiji, and J M Otto (eds)

Law-making for Development: Explorations into the Theory and Practise of International Legislative Drafting. Leiden: Leiden University Press.

Nicholson, Pip and S. Hinderling. 2013. 'Japanese Aid in Comparative Perspective'. 5 *Hague Journal on the Rule of Law* 274–309.

North, Douglas. 1990. *Institutions, Institutional Change and Economic Performance.* Cambridge: Cambridge University Press.

O'Connor, Vivienne. 2015. *Understanding the International Rule of Law Community, its History and its Practise.* International Network to Promote the Rule of Law, Washington DC: US Institute of Peace.

Oishi, M. and Fumitaka Furuoka. 2003. 'Can Japanese Aid be an Effective Tool of Influence? Case Studies of Cambodia and Burma'. 43(6) *Asian Survey* 890.

Paul, James C. N. 2003. 'Law and Development' in John Hatchard and Amanda Perry-Kessaris (eds), *Law and Development: Facing Complexity in the 21st Century: Essays in Honour of Peter Slinn.* London: Cavendish Publishing.

Pederson, Morten. 2008. *Promoting Human Rights in Burma: A Critique of Western Sanctions Policy.* New York: Rowman & Littlefield.

Pistor, K. and Wellons, P. A. 1999. *The Role of Law and Legal Institutions in Asian Economic Development 1960–1995.* Oxford: Oxford University Press.

Polillo, S. and M. Guillen. 2005. 'Globalisation Pressures and the State: The Worldwide Spread of Central Bank Independence'. 110(6) *American Journal of Sociology* 1,764.

Rieffel, Lex. 2015. *Policy Options for Improving the Performance of the State Economic Enterprise Sector in Myanmar.* Singapore: ISEAS Working Paper, No 1.

Rieffel, Lex and James W. Fox. 2013. *Too Much Too Soon? The Dilemma of Foreign Aid in Myanmar/Burma.* Virginia: Nathan Associates Inc.

Rose, Carol. 1998. 'The New Law and Development Movement in the Post-Cold War Era: A Vietnam Case Study'. 32 *Law & Society Review* 93.

Schimmelfennig, Frank. 2012. 'A Comparison of the Rule of Law Promotion Policies of Major Western Powers' in M. Zurn, A. Nolkaemper and R. Peerenboom (eds), *Rule of Law Dynamics in an Era of International and Transnational Governance.* Cambridge: Cambridge University Press.

Seekins, Donald M. 1992. 'Japan's Aid Relations with Military Regimes in Burma, 1962–1991: The Kokunaika Process'. 32(3) *Asian Survey* 246–262.

Simion, Kristina and Veronica Taylor. 2015. *Professionalising the Rule of Law: Issues and Directions.* Sweden: Folke Bernadotte Academy.

Steinberg, David I. 2001. *Burma: The State of Myanmar.* Washington DC: Georgetown University Press.

Tamanaha, Brian. 1995. 'The Lessons of Law and Development Studies'. 89 *American Journal of International Law* 470.

Taylor, Veronica. 2005. 'New Markets, New Commodity: Japanese Legal Technical Assistance'. 23 *Wisconsin International Law Journal* 251–281.

The Irrawaddy. 2015. 'Aid transparency improving but not enough'. 2 July. http://www.irrawaddy.org/burma/aid-transparency-improving-but-not-enough-report.html.

Tin Maung Maung Than. 2007. *State Dominance in Myanmar: Political Economy of Industrialisation*. Singapore: ISEAS.

Trebilcock, Michael J. and Ronald J. Daniels. 2008. *Rule of Law Reform and Development: Charting the Fragile Path of Progress*. Cheltenham, UK: Edward Elgar.

Trubek, David and Mark Galanter. 1974. 'Scholars in Self-Estrangement'. *Wisconsin Law Review* 1,062.

Trubek, David M. and Alvaro Santos. 2006. 'The Third Moment in Law and Development Theory and the Emergence of a New Critical Practise' in D. M. Trubek and A. Santos (eds), *The New Law and Economic Development*. Cambridge: Cambridge University Press, pp. 1–19.

Tun, Melinda. 2014. 'Company Law Reform in Myanmar' in M. Crouch and T. Lindsey (eds), *Law, Society and Transition in Myanmar*. Oxford: Hart Publishing, pp. 225–245.

Turnell, Sean. 2014. 'Legislative Foundations of Myanmar's Economic Reforms' in M. Crouch and T. Lindsey (eds), *Law, Society and Transition in Myanmar*. Oxford: Hart Publishing, pp. 183–201.

2013. 'Banking and Financial Regulation and Reform in Myanmar'. 31(2) *Journal of Southeast Asian Economies* 225–240.

2009. *Fiery Dragons: Banks, Moneylenders and Microfinance in Burma*. Copenhagen, Denmark: NIAS Press.

U Thant. 1978. *View from the UN: The Memoirs of U Thant*. New York: Doubleday.

UNDP. 2015. *Local Governance Mapping* (reports for all fourteen states and regions). www.undp.org.

World Bank. 2008. *Special Economic Zones: Performance, Lessons Learned and Implications for Zone Development*. Washington DC: World Bank Group.

World Development Report (WDR. 2017. *Governance and the Law*. Washington: World Bank Group.

Zurn, M., Andre Nolkaemper and Randall Peerenboom. 2012. 'Introduction' in Zurn et al. (ed.), *Rule of Law Dynamics in an Era of International and Transnational Governance*. Cambridge: Cambridge University Press.

2

Labour Standards and International Investment in Myanmar

MICHELE FORD, MICHAEL GILLAN AND
HTWE HTWE THEIN

In Myanmar, the improvement of labour standards and human rights has been closely linked not only to the government's reform programme but also to efforts to attract increased foreign investment. Labour standards are of particular concern for multinational corporations from the United States and the European Union because of post-sanctions reporting requirements and the reputational risks associated with criticism from activists. This focus on labour standards by business and government has been complemented by the emphasis of the International Labour Organisation (ILO) on promoting 'core' labour standards as a component of a business-enabling environment, which is also in alignment with the agendas of the International Monetary Fund and the World Bank.

Exploring the interaction between normative and regulatory institutions, this chapter provides a critical analysis of the effectiveness of labour law and regulatory reforms in meeting international expectations in regard to labour standards. It does so through a case study of the different responses of high-profile international brands sourcing garments from Myanmar and local garment manufacturing enterprises, many owned by Asian investors, to the implementation of a new minimum wage law. The responses of the former demonstrate a desire to be seen to conform with international labour standards to manage reputational risk. The responses of the latter reflect their disconnection from global buyer and sourcing networks under trade sanctions and the fact that they are only now beginning to confront pressure from buyer firms, international bodies and national organisations to comply with a labour standards regime.

Labour Standards and the Enabling Environment for Business

The study of international investment and the strategies and determinants that shape the behaviour of multinational corporations spans several disciplines, each of which employs a different analytical lens. In recent years, international business – the discipline most closely focused on these questions – has become increasingly engaged in attempts to understand the influence of institutional variation on these core concerns. As this emerging literature has recognised, local and international institutions constitute a key element of the enabling environment in terms of attracting or deterring foreign direct investment. This 'institutional turn' has opened space for considering how supra-national regulation, civil society organisations and different social and political institutional variables can be factored into analysis of investment patterns and multinational corporations.

As a discipline, international business initially described the behaviour of multinational corporations headquartered in developed markets. As a consequence, research focused primarily on firm behaviour, paying little attention to environmental factors (Meyer and Peng 2005). With the emergence of Central and Eastern Europe as investment destinations in the 1990s, scholars began to question the adequacy of this approach, pointing to the importance of host-country institutional settings, as well as factors such as entry timing, investment locations and level of commitment, in shaping firms' investment strategies in those contexts (McCarthy and Puffer 1997; Meyer 2002). Research on corporate governance has also demonstrated the need to broaden the framework of analysis to include government and non-government stakeholders (Buck, Filatotchev and Wright 1998; Mygind 2001; McCarthy and Puffer 2003). These insights are relevant throughout the developing world, but perhaps particularly so in Myanmar, which shares many of the characteristics found in the emerging economies of Central and Eastern Europe – most notably political and economic transition from an authoritarian political system and a centrally planned economy towards a market economy and a more democratic polity.

International and home-country institutions also shape the investment choices and practices of multinational corporations in foreign countries, including their practices in relation to labour (Sirait 2014). Drawing on Scott (2001) in their analysis of firm strategies in Myanmar during the embargoed period (1996–2011), Meyer and Thein (2014) identify three groups of institutions: regulative (regulatory), normative and cognitive. 'Normative institutions' establish expectations of how businesses will act, for example, not investing in countries with poor human rights records or by ensuring that subcontractors do not employ child labour. By contrast, 'regulative institutions' consist of substantive legal and other requirements imposed on multinational corporations by their home governments, for example, a tariff regime or reporting requirements. In some cases, these are supported by 'cognitive institutions', such as the perceptions of consumers and corporate decision-makers of particular foreign business contexts, and how those contexts intersect with business practices.

Garment and footwear brands such as Nike and Gap are influenced by anti-sweatshop campaigns, which expose both labour violations perpetrated directly by multinationals and a lack of due diligence regarding the employment conditions of the workers in their supply chains. The presence of a punitive authoritarian regime may also shape consumer perceptions of products made in a particular source country. Media and non-governmental organisation (NGO) reports provide fertile ground for labour, human rights and democracy advocates seeking to exert pressure on these brands. Decision-makers in high-profile multinational corporations are sensitive to criticism, particularly where those criticisms tap in to broader normative institutions regarding business and human rights. One recent study has gone so far as to argue that, 'as public pressure has become a major influence on MNCs, consumers rather than governments have become the critical third party influencing the dynamics of labor governance' (Donaghey et al. 2014: 234).

High-profile multinational corporations have responded to this risk by establishing codes of conduct, a form of private normative institution designed to mediate reputational risk with consumers.[1] The branded garment and footwear industries, and in particular prominent leisurewear brands, have been a major focus for the development of this tool since the 1990s. Such has been their popularity that up to one-quarter of apparel companies have implemented a code of conduct to which subcontractors are (at least nominally) required to adhere (Wetterberg 2010, cited in Esbenshade 2012). Some codes of conduct are simply window-dressing. Others have a degree of regulatory influence through monitoring and remediation implemented by the lead firm itself, or externally by

---

[1] As Ross (2004) has observed, these private regulatory approaches lie at the opposite end to mobilisational pressure from unions and government enforcement, with international law and trade sanctions falling somewhere in between.

a consultancy firm, an NGO, or a government or a trade union, in some cases as part of a multi-stakeholder initiative (Esbenshade 2012).

Codes of conduct are just one of a number of normative instruments that have emerged around the labour practices of multinational corporations. Other normative instruments include the ILO's system of conventions and, more recently, its identification of 'core' labour standards, namely freedom of association and the right to collective bargaining; the elimination of all forms of forced or compulsory labour; the effective abolition of child labour; and the elimination of discrimination in respect of employment and occupation. With the identification of these core standards in the Declaration on Fundamental Principles and Rights at Work in 1998, the ILO shifted its focus from regulation – where member nations signed and ratified individual conventions by which they were then nominally bound – to a primarily normative approach, which emphasised the promotion of these shared principles (Alston 2004). Although the core standards are associated with eight 'fundamental' conventions, ratification of those conventions is no longer considered necessary for the standards to apply.

The core labour standards have been reproduced in a range of other normative instruments, including the United Nations Guiding Principles on Business and Human Rights, also known as the Ruggie Principles (UNHCR 2011: 13). The Ruggie Principles are explicitly normative in nature, as recognised in their formulation, which emphasises 'the responsibility of business enterprises to respect human rights' as 'distinct from issues of legal liability and enforcement' (UNHCR 2011: 14). At the same time, they insist that states not only have a duty to monitor and manage the human rights practices of businesses operating in their territory, but also to set a clear expectation that 'businesses respect human rights abroad'. Examples cited in the document include 'requirements on "parent" companies to report on the global operations of the entire enterprise; multilateral soft-law instruments such as the Guidelines for Multinational Enterprises of the Organisation for Economic Co-operation and Development [OECD Guidelines]; and performance standards required by institutions that support overseas investments', but also 'direct extraterritorial legislation and enforcement' (UNHCR 2011: 4). Interpretations of the significance of the introduction of the core labour standards differ greatly, as do assessments of their impact on business practice through normative institutions such as the Ruggie Principles. What is clear, however, is that they have fed into a discourse in which attempts to protect basic labour rights and trade have become increasingly connected. As

Alston (2004: 471) observes, 'The [ILO's] 1998 Declaration was, in many respects, a product of the almost universal lip service which is paid to the view that the liberalization of international trade and improved labour standards at the national level are, in some way, linked.'

The broad acceptance of this view is reflected in the willingness of multilateral institutions such as the International Monetary Fund and the World Bank – institutions traditionally hostile to the interests of labour – to engage with the ILO and the international labour movement on labour standards. Although the International Monetary Fund refused the ILO's request that it impose the newly formulated core labour standards as an object of loan conditionality, it agreed to encourage the observation of those core labour standards (Fischer 1999). The World Bank had already adopted a firm position on the necessity of equal opportunity and the prohibition of forced and child labour in the mid-1990s. At the end of that decade, it indicated that it was prepared to promote the core labour standards but not to impose freedom of association and the right to collective bargaining as a condition on lending (Holzmann 1999). Four years later, the head of the International Finance Corporation signalled that he had come to accept that borrowers should be required to comply with all core labour standards. This position became policy in 2006, when compliance was imposed as an element of conditionality on World Bank loans (Bakvis and McCoy 2008).

Normative institutions do not always translate into regulatory institutions, but these categories are in many cases mutually reinforcing. As early as the mid-1980s, the United States incorporated its normative position on labour rights and trade in the Generalised System of Preferences Renewal Act, which explicitly linked eligibility for investment, trade and development assistance to labour rights through its labour clause (Alston 2004). Countries can lose their most favoured nation status under the Generalised System of Preferences (GSP) if they are found to be failing to act on labour rights violations. The petition mechanism designed for the scheme allowed American unions and non-governmental organisations to file complaints on behalf of their foreign counterparts – a tactic that, while not always successful, proved useful in a number of contexts (Compa and Vogt 2001). Since 1994, the European Union has also tied labour standards to trade through a GSP mechanism through which states and individuals can request that labour rights violations be investigated, possibly leading to suspension of a country's most favoured nation status (Portela and Orbie 2014). Countries may also request to have tariff rates reduced for complying with core labour standards (European Commission 2004).

As Tsogas (2000) has noted, the significance of GSP mechanisms has declined as tariffs have been cut. To some extent they have been superseded by free trade agreements, fifty-eight of which included labour provisions as of June 2013, up from only four in 1995 (ILO 2015). This number includes most North American and European Union free trade agreements, some of which also incorporate measures to encourage the implementation of core labour standards through national labour law (Bakvis and McCoy 2008). The first of this kind was the US–Cambodia Bilateral Textile Trade Agreement, signed in January 1999, which not only required the Cambodian state to improve employment relations regulations but also encouraged the garment industry to comply with international labour standards in order to access trade-related incentives. Under the agreement, it was the United States government that would determine whether those standards had been met (Kolben 2004).[2]

Perhaps the strongest regulatory response has taken the form of trade sanctions. In the case of Myanmar, the European Union imposed diplomatic restrictions and an arms embargo in 1996, extending restrictions a decade later to trade in timber, metal and precious stones. However, the most influential sanctions regime was that imposed by the United States between 1996 and 2011. The United States government initially banned new investment by United States citizens or companies in 1997, a provision that was later extended to ban effectively all imports from Myanmar. A number of other countries followed suit, although their sanctions were generally weaker than those imposed by the United States (Thein and Pick 2009). Although sanctions are primarily regulatory in that they suspend or limit trade and/or impose regulatory oversight on the investment activities of a 'home' origin business in the target nation, they may also act as a normative institution. In the case of US-based multinational corporations operating in Myanmar, Meyer and Thein (2014) found that a significant proportion responded in ways that exceeded their legal obligations under the sanctions regime, reflecting the influence of normative pressure on firm strategy. While not subject to a regulatory requirement to withdraw,

---

[2] ILO analysis suggests that North American free trade agreements tend to have economic consequences for non-compliance while those originating from the European Union tend to take a 'promotional' approach, for example, providing a framework for dialogue or monitoring (ILO 2015). Several free trade agreements involving the United States include provisions for the establishment of co-operative activities to strengthen labour inspection or improve the implementation of the labour law, as indeed has been the case in Cambodia (Kolben 2004; Ward and Mouyly 2016).

many Western businesses chose to do so to avoid the reputational risk of being associated with the regime.

Labour Standards in Myanmar's Reforming Institutional Environment

The government of President Thein Sein (2011–2016) introduced a series of reforms in various policy areas, which led to the establishment or reshaping of state agencies and institutions. While these reforms have been remarkable in many respects – resulting most notably in a significant expansion of freedom of expression and political representation – the intent and capacity of the state to implement legislative reform have been inconsistent, not least because of the enduring influence of the military and associated businesses (Ford, Gillan and Thein 2016). Reforms designed to attract foreign investment and to establish a regulatory framework for labour based on internationally accepted labour standards have occurred simultaneously. While at first glance these reform processes might appear to be unrelated or even contradictory, they have in fact been explicitly linked together not only by the ILO and foreign governments but by the government of Myanmar and multinational corporations seeking to invest in Myanmar.

In 2012, the government set out a reform agenda in anticipation of establishing a national comprehensive development plan. The Framework for Economic and Social Reforms (FESR) was premised on the need to open the economy and significantly increase foreign investment and trade, although it also acknowledged that there were substantial barriers to achieving this aim. As noted in a diagnostic study conducted by the Asian Development Bank, while 'natural resources, geographic advantage, low-cost labor, and potential market access are driving FDI', the low labour cost base in manufacturing is undercut by higher than average distribution, procurement, rental and property costs and low productivity (Asian Development Bank 2014: 157–158).[3] As this suggests, the key obstacle Myanmar must overcome to expand its industrial development through foreign investment is not merely easier access to hitherto untapped pools of low-cost labour but rather the need for massive and sustained investment in economic and social infrastructure.

---

[3] For a discussion of the role of the Asian Development Bank in regulating risk in Myanmar, see Simpson and Park (2013).

The FESR and a subsequent OECD Investment Policy Review (2014) conducted in partnership with the government of Myanmar and the secretariat of the Association of Southeast Asian Nations (ASEAN) identified a series of legal and institutional reforms necessary to improve the investment climate. Some of these reforms had preceded the publication of these reports. In 2012, the official exchange rate was brought into alignment with the real market exchange rate, and foreign investors were permitted to establish joint ventures with private sector firms. The government introduced a revised law on foreign direct investment (FDI) in 2012 – repealing a law that had been in place since 1988 – and released detailed procedural rules for FDI in early 2013. In the following year, the Special Economic Zone Law was promulgated, and the rules for special economic zones (SEZs) were released in mid-2015.[4] There was a considerable increase in FDI approvals after these reforms were initiated, with annual government targets for FDI exceeded every year. The bulk of this investment came from Southeast Asia and East Asia.[5] There was also a deliberate strategy by the government, with the assistance of international agencies, to try to link export-oriented industries into global supply chains.

In addition to examining matters such as the policy and institutional reforms required to promote and protect investment, the OECD policy review focused on the need for investors to 'act responsibly and contribute to inclusive and sustainable development' (OECD 2014: 3). The normative dimension of international labour governance was invoked in references to the need for foreign investors to conform to 'international standards of behaviour beyond what is required by the host government'; to exercise 'vigilance' to 'ensure that their investments do not cause harm'; and to 'fully respect both the laws of Myanmar – whether or not they are actually implemented – and international expectations about responsible business conduct in weak governance zones' (OECD

---

[4] See Turnell (2015) for analysis of the limits and effect of exchange and investment reforms and Wood (this volume) on SEZs. The government of Myanmar has accepted the OECD Investment Policy Review recommendation that there should not be separate laws for foreign and domestic investors to promote fair competition and enhanced investment, and a new investment law is pending (presentation by Aung Naing Oo, director-general of the Myanmar Directorate of Investment and Company Administration and secretary of the Myanmar Investment Commission, Perth, 16 October 2015).

[5] Presentation by Aung Naing Oo, director-general of the Myanmar Directorate of Investment and Company Administration and secretary of the Myanmar Investment Commission, Perth, 16 October 2015.

2014: 63). While such statements could be dismissed as empty rhetoric, both the OECD review and the FESR report provide concrete examples of how international normative institutions have been translated into institutional reform in Myanmar. The OECD review noted the links between preferential market access in the European Union, the ratification of ILO Conventions and the general status of labour and human rights: the European Union had removed Myanmar's most preferred nation status under its GSP system in 1997, restoring it only in mid-2013 on the advice of the ILO (OECD 2014: 69, 278). The FESR, meanwhile, pointed to the initiation of legal and regulatory reforms to eliminate forced labour and to enable freedom of association; the formation of employer associations and trade unions; and the introduction of minimum wage legislation – alongside close co-operation between the government and the ILO – as components of the economic development plan (Republic of the Union of Myanmar 2012: 38–39).

The ILO has been an influential intermediary in the process of embedding these international regulatory and normative institutions in Myanmar's legal and policy frameworks.[6] Its role has been especially important given the acknowledged weaknesses of the state bureaucracy in designing and implementing labour policy and regulation. It has worked closely with the Ministry of Labour, Employment and Social Security (MOLES) and other government agencies in technical areas including occupational health and safety regulation and procedures; labour inspection; and the formation and functioning of dispute resolution bodies such the Dispute Settlement Arbitration Council.[7] It also provided significant technical assistance in the drafting of the Labour Organisation Law 2011 and the Settlement of Labour Disputes Law 2012, and has sought to build bridges between the government of Myanmar, international and domestic business, emerging civil society groups and trade unions.[8]

---

[6] The discussion of the ILO presented here draws on Ford, Gillan and Thein (in press). For a discussion of labour law and dispute resolution procedures during the Ne Win and State Law and Order Restoration Council (SLORC)/State Peace and Development Council (SPDC) military regimes see Lwin (2014a).

[7] The creation of this national dispute settlement body, along with corresponding dispute resolution bodies at workplace, township and regional levels, were required by the Settlement of Labour Disputes Law 2012.

[8] These laws comprise an industrial relations architecture that is at least minimally acceptable by international standards, and in recognition of this and progress made by the government in addressing forced labour, the ILO ended its restrictions on Myanmar's membership status in June 2012. Nonetheless, there has also been ongoing criticism about the design and

The link between labour relations and foreign investment is explicitly recognised through the ILO's Labour Law Reform and Institutional Capacity Building program, funded and supported by Denmark, Japan and the United States. In a joint statement, donors, the ILO and the Myanmar government described the 'labour regime' as an 'important component of its investment environment' which, in conjunction with other measures, can assist in repositioning Myanmar as an 'attractive sourcing and investment destination' and thus advance 'overall sustainable growth and development' (ILO 2014b). The ILO has also taken on a direct intermediary role in Myanmar's reintegration with global production networks. Well-known international consumer goods brands have consulted with the Liaison Office prior to investing to mitigate or lessen the potential reputational risk of expanding production or distribution within the country.[9]

It is within this context that the ILO has sought to facilitate foreign investment in Myanmar with the stated goal of supporting employment generation and development goals while also seeking to assist it to comply with international standards. In recognition of the low level of capacity in the country's formal economy – in terms of skills, industry development and management competence – to respond to an upsurge of interest from potential investors, the ambit of the ILO's 'responsible business' programme has been particularly broad, including many multinational corporations in the consumer goods sector. In an attempt to enhance the capacity of industries to work more closely with global trade and supplier networks, the ILO has – in conjunction with government and business – initiated value chain assessments and development plans for industries with a current or potential export profile. The ILO has also begun groundwork for the development of factory-level training and measurement programmes in addition to implementing a suite of activities designed to promote 'social dialogue' and 'awareness raising' around corporate social responsibility and labour standard issues in value chains (ILO 2014a).

Engaging with the ILO has been especially important to investors based in the United States, as the possible restoration of Myanmar's GSP status is clearly linked to international labour standards. Myanmar was suspended from inclusion in the system in 1989 due to its failure to comply with criteria on workers' rights (Trautwein 2015). At a 2013 public hearing by the United States government to review Myanmar's GSP status, the

---

effect of the legal and institutional framework from the international labour movement and from within the ILO.

[9] Interview with the ILO Chief Liaison Officer, January 2014, Yangon, Myanmar.

delegation from Myanmar was confronted with a series of questions pertaining to freedom of association, union registration and the dismissal of trade union activists (Executive Office of the President 2013). Inclusion in the GSP was not granted. In late 2015, the United States announced a further review, which would again focus on the progress of labour reforms (Trautwein 2015). As a consequence, the observance of labour standards by United States investors in Myanmar is likely to be watched closely by local and international policy-makers as well as trade union and civil society networks.

Responsible investment reporting requirements for firms originating in the United States also mean that these firms must provide regular reports to the State Department on environmental and social impacts if their aggregate investment in Myanmar exceeds US$500,000. Most of the information in the reports is publicly accessible.[10] The scope of public reporting encompasses information on 'due diligence' and 'policies and procedures' that pertain to the impact of direct business operations or the supply chain on workers' rights. These reporting requirements do not give rise to any additional legal liability; rather, they are intended as useful information for the United States government to assess the 'impact and effects' of new investments after the suspension of the sanctions regime. In this respect, while the regulatory effect of reporting is weak, it could be seen as making a contribution in the normative domain.

In the context of these normative influences, it is not surprising that the apparel firm Gap – the first major retail brand based in the United States to begin sourcing from Myanmar-based suppliers since 2011 – has participated in ILO 'stakeholder forums' on labour law and standards as well as publicly stating its commitment to the labour law reform process (Gap Inc. 2015). As a sourcing company, rather than a direct producer or investor, Gap considers itself to be technically exempt from the United States government's responsible investment reporting requirements (Gap Inc. 2015), but has nonetheless volunteered to provide publicly accessible

---

[10] The reporting requirements allow for the confidential reporting to the United States government of the persons involved in preparing the document; any communications with military personnel; and risk prevention and mitigation policies and measures; otherwise all reporting items are publicly accessible. Nonetheless, most businesses have included all of the reporting items in their public reports. There is also another separate stream of required reporting on the exercise of rights or new investment by United citizens involving an agreement with Myanma Oil and Gas Enterprise (MOGE). For more information see http://www.humanrights.gov/wp-content/uploads/2013/05/responsible-investment-reporting-requirements-final.pdf.

reports to the State Department. In its 2015 report, Gap noted that while it has 'significantly increased' the quantum of products sourced from two Korean-owned firms based in Myanmar its policies and codes of conduct for itself and its suppliers are 'grounded in internationally recognized standards' such as ILO core labour conventions and the OECD Guidelines (Gap Inc. 2015). It also described its collaboration with the ILO to establish 'workplace coordinating committees' to facilitate worker-management dialogue and its engagement of auditors to assess health, safety and labour conditions in the factories of those suppliers.

The case of Gap – as a prominent American firm in an industry sector characterised by regulatory weakness, labour standards violations and international civil society and labour movement advocacy networks – illustrates the relevance of normative institutions for high-profile investors. Many studies have suggested that worker – management consultative committees and corporate-directed reporting, audits and professed commitment to international labour standards belie limited real gains in labour rights and working conditions, and can under some circumstances even be a substitute rather than a complement to independent worker representation.[11] In Myanmar, Gap has engaged with local industry associations, labour NGOs and the ILO-directed multi-stakeholder initiatives on the observance of core labour standards and the implementation of local labour law. Its willingness to do so is clearly driven more by normative than regulatory pressures. It is also reflective of how Gap is positioned relative to other garment producing and sourcing firms, a point that we will explore in the next section with reference to the implementation of a minimum wage.

Regulatory and Normative Pressures in the Application of Labour Standards

The interaction between normative and regulatory institutions in labour standards can be understood by examining the drivers of actual change. An important example in Myanmar has been garment industry responses to the introduction of a new minimum wage determination process. International buyers seek to form links with contracting suppliers from Myanmar because of the relatively low cost of labour there and to diversify their sourcing networks. At the same time, the high-profile brands

---

[11] For a useful summary of this literature, see Esbenshade (2012).

they represent are responsive to normative pressures at play internationally, which have led them to support the application of (minimum) labour standards in supplier factories, as well as making their own investments in auditing and reporting systems and working with preferred suppliers to mitigate reputational risk. Established 'local' garment manufacturing enterprises (many of which are in fact Korean- or Chinese-owned) are articulated with local or regional – rather than global – buyer networks and have less lucrative supply contracts, and thus both rely more on an extremely low-cost labour process for realising profit and face lower normative pressures in regard to labour standards. As a consequence, they are much more resistant to improvements in wages, conditions and management practices, and this resistance has led to a series of strikes and labour protests from 2011 in the industry.[12]

The Myanmar Minimum Wage Law, which repealed the Minimum Wages Act of 1949 and the Agricultural Labourers Minimum Wages Act of 1948, came into effect in June 2013.[13] In conjunction with the more detailed implementation rules (Notification No. 64/2013) that followed, the Law required the formation of a national minimum wages committee composed of 'representatives of the relevant government departments, government organizations, labour organizations or representatives of workers, employer organizations or representatives of employers and other persons who are experienced, expert and fair in matters related to wage prescription'.[14] While the Law requires equal numbers of employer and worker representatives, they were to be appointed by the government. The national committee is complemented by regional and state committees, all of which are required to consider research, submissions and relevant information on, amongst other things, current salaries, social security, living costs and standards, employment opportunities, commodity prices, inflation and productivity.

---

[12] A 2013 study produced by local labour NGOs reported the very poor employment conditions and wages for workers in the industrial zones in which most garment factories are located (Labour Rights Clinic et al. 2013). In the context of expanded capacity after 2011 for workers to associate and represent their interests, the reluctance of managers and owners to improve basic wages and conditions has fuelled labour protests and strikes (Lwin 2014b; Gillan and Thein 2016).

[13] The Law (in Burmese, along with the Draft Act and an unofficial translation in English) and the implementation rules are available from http://www.ilo.org/dyn/natlex/natlex4 .detail?p_lang=en&p_isn=90652&p_classification=12.02.

[14] In chapter VI of the Act there is also an obligation for the management committees of SEZs to submit proposed minimum wages for workers in the zones to the national committee for consideration and determination.

The national committee was formed in late 2013, and the state and regional committees in early 2014. The formation of these bodies involved considerable effort given the multiple stakeholders and the general lack of experience of all parties in participating in such a wage determination process.[15] There were seven national meetings and thirty at the other levels over a period of eighteen months to assess data, including a cost-of-living survey of more than 22,000 households and submissions relevant to determining the minimum wage. This series of meetings to consider relevant data was followed by a two-day consultative workshop in mid-2015 immediately prior to the announcement of the minimum wage that involved, amongst others, employers, labour organisations, committee members and ILO staff (Republic of the Union of Myanmar 2015). Set at 3,600 kyat (approximately US$3) for a standard eight-hour working day, the minimum wage was established at a level that was reasonably close to the 4,000 kyat per day claim by labour organisations. Importantly, it was to apply across the nation without variation for the relevant industry or location of work – although it did exclude enterprises with fifteen or fewer workers, small family businesses and trainee probationary workers. The penalty for employer non-compliance was set at a prison term of up to one year and/or a fine of up to 500,000 kyat (approximately US$413), although the capacity to enforce these provisions remains limited.

After the announcement of the minimum wage there were vociferous objections from labour-intensive manufacturing enterprises based in industrial zones in Yangon and Mandalay – by no coincidence the same areas and industries that have seen a growth in strikes centred around wage demands as well as union and labour NGO activity in the period from 2012 (Gillan and Thein 2016). The Myanmar Garment Manufacturing Association (MGMA) complained of the possible impact on investment, suggesting that the minimum wage would lead to a 'more-than doubling of the industry average introductory wage for unskilled workers' and pointing to high rates of overtime pay that would apply on top of the minimum wage after forty-four hours were worked per week (MGMA 2015a). It also convened a meeting of 150 member enterprises, including locally owned businesses and South Korean- and Chinese-owned firms, to demand that the wage be rescinded and to reiterate their preferred outcome of 2,500 kyat (Snaing 2015).

---

[15] Interview with the director-general of the Department of Labour, Ministry of Labour Employment and Social Security, January 2014, Yangon, Myanmar.

The MGMA subsequently made a formal request to the national minimum wage committee that garment workers be excluded from the wage award on the basis of the need to maintain industry competiveness and incapacity to pay. The Korean Garment Manufacturers Association and the Chinese Investors Association (representing investors from Taiwan, Hong Kong and mainland China) warned of widespread closures and job losses, with the latter depicting the wage decision as 'shocking' and as undermining the basis of their investment in Myanmar (*Eleven Myanmar* 2015) – a claim that was clearly absurd given the significant depreciation in the value of the kyat. These threats also proved to be greatly exaggerated: when the minimum wage came into effect in September 2015, there were reports that just 1,000 garment workers had been retrenched. It was unclear, moreover, whether these retrenchments were a consequence of the introduction of the minimum wage. According to local trade unions, the difficulties of many garment factories are caused not by labour costs but by poor market planning and a general 'overcrowding' of the industry (Aung and Phyu 2015).

The strong response from the industry association also reflected deep differences in terms of enterprise scale, access to capital and management competence between these old players in the Myanmar garment industry and a new group of firms that have proven better able to embed themselves in the more profitable buyer-driven supply networks of leading global brands. Lacking incentives or access to capital to upgrade factories, many long-established garment enterprises have operated labour-intensive and low-productivity production regimes at a relatively small scale. During the trade sanctions period (1997–2012), these established local garment manufacturing firms were linked to Japanese and Korean intermediate buyer networks rather than larger global sourcing firms, and thus had little knowledge and experience in managing the reporting and auditing requirements of global buyers.[16] As a consequence, they have been largely unable to tap into the surge of European firms sourcing garments after Myanmar's access to the European Union GSP scheme was restored, generating an estimated US$256 million of garment imports in 2014 (Mullins 2015). Indeed, the lion's shares of large supply contracts have been captured by a select group of foreign-owned firms with operations in Myanmar. This is certainly evident for high-profile brands such as Gap and H&M, which prefer to source from a small number of Korean

---

[16] Interview with MGMA secretary-general, January 2013, Yangon, Myanmar.

(Gap) or Chinese (H&M) owned supplier firms that have established manufacturing units in Myanmar and with whom they have worked in the past in other garment-producing nations.[17]

In the context of these obvious limitations, there have been some efforts to improve local firms' capacity to comply with international labour standards. Against a backdrop of rolling strikes by garment workers for better wages in late 2014, the MGMA issued a joint statement of intent for consultation with the Myanmar Trade Union Federation (MTUF),[18] which called for 'collective dialogue and factory productivity' and trying to achieve where possible 'bipartite settlements of disputes and constructive dialogue before disputes arise' (MGMA 2014). In the following year, the MGMA introduced a code of conduct for its members with the stated intention of enhancing management standards and practices across a range of areas, including labour relations, and inclusive of a commitment for members to 'uphold the eight core labour standards of the International Labour Organization' and to 'commit to create a safe and humane working environment' (MGMA 2015b). The accompanying press release explicitly recognised the connection between prospects for success and compliance with international norms, noting that 'garment exports from Myanmar to the EU doubled in 2014, but nearly all of these orders went to producers able to pass international social compliance audits' (MGMA 2015c). After introducing the code of conduct the MGMA also consulted with twelve leading European buyer brands, and then made a public commitment to request that the government 'establish and enforce a consistent policy framework on labour-related laws' (MGMA 2015d).

While these initiatives indicate a degree of formal recognition of the need to improve working conditions and stabilise labour relations in the industry, there was nevertheless a striking contrast between the reaction of MGMA members and global garment brands to the announced minimum wage. The latter responded positively, and advocated publicly for its

---

[17] Interview with ILO project officer, December 2014, Yangon, Myanmar.

[18] The MTUF was formed in 2014. It aims to be a national union federation but is currently a cluster of basic (enterprise) and township trade unions in and around Yangon and Mandalay. Unlike the Confederation of Trade Unions of Myanmar (CTUM) and the Agriculture and Farmers Federation of Myanmar (AFFM) (affiliated with the International Union of Food, Agricultural, Hotel, Restaurant, Catering, Tobacco and Allied Workers' Associations (IUF)) the MTUF is yet to be officially registered and recognised as a national union federation. For more detail on trade unions in Myanmar see Gillan and Thein (2016).

implementation. The Fair Labor Association (FLA)[19] wrote a letter to the minister of labour in Myanmar – co-signed by seventeen of its members, including the well-known brands New Balance, Adidas and Patagonia – to raise concerns about the exemption request for garment workers. The letter stated that the 'suggestion made by trade associations that a higher minimum wage will discourage international investment is based on a false premise' and that a 'minimum wage set through consultation with relevant stakeholders will attract rather than deter international companies buying garments from Myanmar' (FLA 2015). A similar stance was taken by the Myanmar Responsible Sourcing Working Group and the Ethical Trade Initiative, both corporate social responsibility organisations involving leading garment retail brands. In a formal submission to the government in support of the implementation of the minimum wage, the Ethical Trade Initiative, for example, stated that its members wished to 'counter the claims of Myanmar's garment manufacturers and employers' associations'. It went on to acknowledge that the requested exemption 'would mean garment workers being unfairly denied a wage that meets their basic needs' which, it argued, 'could lead to work stoppages and industrial unrest – conditions that are far more likely to see international brands reconsider their investment in Myanmar than payment of a national minimum wage' (ETI 2015). Several brands also issued individual statements, which were reported widely in English-language media outlets (Zaw 2015; Global New Light of Myanmar 2015; Barron 2015).

Conclusion

The final decision of the government of Myanmar to implement the minimum wage with no exemption in the garment sector could be interpreted as a sign of how normative pressures were brought to bear on local industry by powerful European and North American buyers. It is important to remember, however, that the low-cost base of labour supply, even with a minimum wage, remains a key attraction for foreign investors. Inevitably, as noted in our discussion of voluntaristic and market-guided self-regulation, there are real tensions between the corporate imperative to squeeze suppliers on cost and their professed commitment to labour

---

[19] The Fair Labor Association is based in the United States and describes itself as a 'collaborative effort of socially responsible companies, colleges and universities, and civil society organizations' that engages in advocacy and audit activities around workers' rights and labour standards. See http://www.fairlabor.org/about-us.

standards and levelling up workers' wages. It is also necessary to recognise that pressures for the introduction and implementation of labour regulation and improved standards do not emanate only from a top-down process of market direction through multinational corporations and trade preference arrangements: the normative pressures that now apply to multinational corporations in the garment sector are a consequence of decades of sustained campaigning by civil society organisations and trade unions around the globe. In Myanmar itself, too, trade unions and labour NGOs mobilised around the introduction of the minimum wage, with the MTUF even conducting its own cost-of-living survey as a means of spurring the official state-directed process into action (Nyein 2014). The agency of workers themselves is also significant, as the many strikes in the industry over insufficient wages have also shaped the process and the outcome.

These caveats notwithstanding, it is clear that the social responsibility sourcing and auditing requirements of high-profile international brands and corporations are shaping state and business discourses and practices in Myanmar. Formally, this has led to an acceptance that minimum labour standards are necessary for national economic development and the integration of local industry with global production networks. As the experience of other nations in Southeast Asia shows, however, an enormous gulf exists between formal standards and their realisation – with the latter almost always requiring social mobilisation by unions and civil society to secure major advances in workers' having a voice, welfare and ability to exercise rights. This point highlights the significance of the future development and industry-specific effects of employment regulation and industrial relations organisations and institutions in post-authoritarian Myanmar.

References

Alston, P. 2004. '"Core Labour Standards" and the Transformation of the International Labour Rights Regime'. 15(3)*European Journal of International Law* 457–521.

Asian Development Bank. 2014. *Myanmar: Unlocking the Potential. Country Diagnostic Study*. Mandaluyong City, Philippines: Economics and Research Department.

Aung, N. L. and K.W.P. Phyu. 2015. 'Thousands out of Work as Minimum Wage Kicks Off'. *Myanmar Times*. 4 September. Available at http://www.mmtimes.com/index.php/national-news/yangon/16332-thousands-out-of-work-as-minimum-wage-kicks-off.html.

Bakvis, P. and M. McCoy. 2008. 'Core Labour Standards and International Organizations: What Inroads has Labour Made?' Briefing Paper No. 6. Berlin: Friedrich Ebert Stiftung.

Barron, L. 2015. 'High-profile Foreign Brands Back Minimum Wage for All'. *Myanmar Times*. 23 July. Available at http://www.mmtimes.com/index.php/national-news/15629-high-profile-foreign-brands-back-minimum-wage-for-all.html.

Buck, T., I. Filatotchev and M. Wright. 1998. 'Agents, Stakeholders, and Corporate Governance in Russian firms'. 35 *Journal of Management Studies* 81–104.

Compa, L. and J. Vogt. 2001. 'Labour Rights in the Generalised System of Preferences: A 20-Year Review'. 22 *Comparative Labour Law and Policy Journal* 199–238.

Donaghey, J., J. Reinecke, C. Niforou and B. Lawson. 2014. 'From Employment Relations to Consumption Relations: Balancing Labor Governance in Global Supply Chains'. 53(2) *Human Resource Management* 229–252.

Eleven Myanmar. 2015. 'Garment Manufacturers Threaten to Close Factories if Minimum Wage Implemented'. 3 July. Available at http://www.elevenmyanmar.com/local/garmentmanufacturersthreatenclosefactoriesifminimumwageimplemented.

Esbenshade, J. 2012. 'A Review of Private Regulation: Codes and Monitoring in the Apparel Industry'. 6/7 *Sociology Compass* 541–556.

Ethical Trading Initiative (ETI). 2015. 'ETI Supports Calls for New Myanmar Minimum Wage to Apply to Garment Sector'. 15 July. Available at http://www.ethicaltrade.org/news-and-events/news/ETI-supports-calls-for-Myanmar-minimum-wage-to-apply-to-garment-sector.

European Commission. 2004. 'The European Union's Generalised System of Preferences'. Brussels: The European Commission Directorate-General for Trade. Available at http://trade.ec.europa.eu/doclib/docs/2004/march/tradoc_116448.pdf (accessed 15 November 2015).

Executive Office of the President. 2013. Public Hearing for US Generalized System of Preferences (GSP), Review of GSP Eligibility. 4 June. Washington DC: Office of the US Trade Representative. Available at http://business-humanrights.org/sites/default/files/media/us-gsp-myanmar-hearing-jun-2013.pdf (accessed 16 November 2015).

Fair Labor Association (FLA). 2015. '17 FLA Affiliates Oppose Unfair Minimum Wage Exemption For Myanmar Garment Workers'. 15 July. Available at http://www.fairlabor.org/report/17-fla-affiliates-oppose-unfair-minimum-wage-exemption-myanmar-garment-workers.

Fischer, S. 1999. Statement by IMF First Deputy Managing Director Stanley Fischer at the Seminar and Panel Discussion, 'A Role for Labor Standards in the New International Economy?' 29 September. Washington DC: Omni-Shoreham Hotel. Available at https://www.imf.org/external/np/tr/1999/tr990929.htm (accessed 16 November 2015).

Ford, M., M. Gillan and H. Thein. In press. 'The International Labour Organization as a Development Actor' in A. McGregor, L. Law and F. Miller (eds), *Routledge Handbook of Southeast Asian Development*. Abingdon and New York: Routledge.

Ford, M., M. Gillan and H. Thein. 2016. 'From Cronyism to Oligarchy? Privatisation and Business Elites in Myanmar'. 46(1) *Journal of Contemporary Asia* 18–41.

Gap Inc. 2015. 'Responsible Sourcing in Myanmar Gap Inc., Update Report for the Period August 26, 2014–May 31, 2015'. Submitted 1 July. Available at http://photos.state.gov/libraries/burma/895/pdf/20150701GapIncMyanmar PublicReport.pdf (accessed 15 November 2015).

Gillan, M. and H. Thein. 2016. 'Employment Relations, the State and Transitions in Governance in Myanmar'. 58(2) *Journal of Industrial Relations* 273–288.

Global New Light of Myanmar. 2015. 'Global Brands Voice Support for Minimum Wage Proposal'. 15 July. Available at http://globalnewlightofmyanmar.com/ global-brands-voice-support-for-minimum-wage-proposal/.

Holzmann, R. 1999. Statement by World Bank Social Protection Director Robert Holzmann at the Seminar and Panel Discussion, 'A Role for Labor Standards in the New International Economy?' 29 September. Washington DC: Omni-Shoreham Hotel. Available at https://www.imf.org/external/np/tr/1999/ tr990929.htm (accessed 16 November 2015).

ILO. 2014a. 'National Tripartite Dialogue: Presentation on ILO's Programme of Work in Myanmar'. 4 December. Nay Pyi Taw: ILO Liaison Office in Myanmar. Available at http://www.ilo.org/yangon/whatwedo/events/WCMS_329889/ lang–en/index.htm (accessed 18 August 2015).

2014b. 'New Initiative to Improve Labour Rights in Myanmar: Joint Statement of the Republic of the Union of Myanmar, the United States of America, Japan, Denmark and the International Labour Organization (ILO)'. 14 November. Yangon, Myanmar. Available at http://www.ilo.org/yangon/info/public/ speeches/WCMS_319811/lang–en/index.htm (accessed 18 August 2015).

2015. 'Studies on Growth with Equity: Social Dimensions of Free Trade Agreements'. Geneva: International Labour Organization. Available at http://www.ilo.org/wcmsp5/groups/public/–dgreports/–inst/documents/ publication/wcms_228965.pdf (accessed 16 November 2015).

Kolben, K. 2004. 'Trade Union Monitoring, and the ILO: Working to Improve Conditions in Cambodia's Garment Factories'. 7 *Yale Human Rights and Development Law Journal* 79–107.

Labour Rights Clinic et al. 2013. *Modern Slavery: A Study of Labour Conditions in Yangon's Industrial Zones 2012-2013*. Yangon: Labour Rights Clinic, Cooperation Program of Independent Labourers, Construction-based Labour Union and Workers Support Group.

Lwin, K. 2014a. 'Legal Perspectives on Industrial Disputes in Myanmar' in M. Crouch and T. Lindsey (eds) *Law, Society and Transition in Myanmar*. Oxford: Hart Publishing.

2014b. 'Understanding Recent Labour Protests in Myanmar' in N. Cheesman, N. Farrelly and T. Wilson (eds) *Debating Democratization in Myanmar*. Singapore: Institute of Southeast Asian Studies.

McCarthy, D. and S. Puffer. 1997. 'Strategic Investment Flexibility for MNE Success in Russia: Evolving beyond Entry Modes'. 32 *Journal of World Business* 293–319.

2003. 'Corporate Governance in Russia: A Framework for Analysis'. 38 *Journal of World Business* 397–415.

Meyer, K. 2002. 'Management Challenges in Privatization Acquisitions in Transition Economies'. 37 *Journal of World Business* 266–276.

Meyer, K. and M. Peng. 2005. 'Probing Theoretically into Central and Eastern Europe: Transactions, Resources, and Institutions'. 36 *Journal of International Business Studies* 600–621.

Meyer, K. and H. Thein. 2014. 'Business under Adverse Home Country Institutions: The Case of International Sanctions against Myanmar'. 49(1) *Journal of World Business* 156–171.

Mullins, J. 2015. 'Big Western Brands Sew Way Forward'. *Myanmar Times*. 29 May. Available at http://www.mmtimes.com/index.php/business/14755-big-western-brands-sew-way-forward.html.

Myanmar Garment Manufacturing Association (MGMA). 2014. 'Joint Statement of MGMA & MTUF (English Version)'. 24 November. Available at http://www.myanmargarments.org/wp-content/uploads/2014/12/Joint-Statement-of-MGMA-MTUF-English-Version-24.11.2014.pdf.

Myanmar Garment Manufacturing Association (MGMA). 2015a. 'Ministry of Labour Proposes Minimum Wage Amount'. 30 June. Available at http://www.myanmargarments.org/2015/06/ministry-of-labour-proposes-minimum-wage-amount/.

Myanmar Garment Manufacturing Association (MGMA). 2015b. 'Code of Conduct for the Member Companies of the Myanmar Garment Manufacturers Association'. January. Available at http://www.myanmargarments.org/about/mgmas-code-of-conduct/.

Myanmar Garment Manufacturing Association (MGMA). 2015c. 'Myanmar Garment Manufacturers Association Publishes First-ever Code of Conduct for Myanmar's Apparel Industry'. 1 February. Available at http://www.myanmargarments.org/wp-content/uploads/2015/02/MGMA-Code-of-Conduct-Press-Release.pdf.

Myanmar Garment Manufacturing Association (MGMA). 2015d. 'Statement: Conclusions on Code of Conduct Implementation Reached after Discussion between MGMA Factories and Visiting EU Brands'. 24 March. Available at http://www.myanmargarments.org/wp-content/uploads/2015/03/MGMA-Statement-about-CoC-Discussion.pdf.

Mygind, N. 2001. 'Enterprise Governance in Transition: A Stakeholder Perspective'. 51 *Acta Oeconomica* 315–342.

Nyein, N. 2014. 'As Lawmakers Raise Pay, Minimum Wage Law Languishes'. *The Irrawaddy*. 19 November. Available at http://www.irrawaddy.com/burma/lawmakers-raise-pay-minimum-wage-law-languishes.html.

OECD. 2014. *OECD Investment Policy Reviews: Myanmar 2014*. Paris: OECD Publishing. Available at http://dx.doi.org/10.1787/9789264206441-en.

Portela, C. and J. Orbie. 2014. 'Sanctions Under the EU Generalised System of Preferences and Foreign Policy: Coherence by Accident?' 20(1) *Contemporary Politics* 63–76.

Republic of the Union of Myanmar. 2012. *Framework for Economic and Social Reforms: Policy Priorities for 2012–15 towards the Long-Term Goals of the National Comprehensive Development Plan*. Yangon: Republic of the Union of Myanmar.

Republic of the Union of Myanmar. 2015. Announcement on Proposed Minimum Wage No. 1/2015. 29 June. Myanmar National Minimum Wage Committee. Available at http://www.myanmargarments.org/factory-information/laws-regulations/.

Ross, R. 2004. *Slaves to Fashion: Poverty and Abuse in the New Sweatshops*. Ann Arbor: University of Michigan Press.

Scott, W. 2001. *Institutions and Organization: Ideas and Interests*. Thousand Oaks: Sage.

Simpson, A. and S. Park. 2013. 'The Asian Development Bank as a Global Risk Regulator in Myanmar'. 34(10) *Third World Quarterly* 1,858–1,871.

Sirait, G. 2014. *Employment Relations in Indonesia's Retail Sector: Institutions, Power Relations and Outcomes*. Doctoral Thesis. The University of Sydney.

Snaing, Yen. 2015. 'Garment Industry Rejects Minimum Wage Proposal'. *The Irrawaddy*. 3 July. Available at http://www.irrawaddy.com/business/garment-industry-rejects-minimum-wage-proposal.html.

Thein, H. and D. Pick. 2009. 'International Trade and Business Investment in Myanmar: Scope, Strategic Development, and Social Implications' in M. Gillan and B. Pokrant (eds), *Trade, Labour and Transformation of Community in Asia*. London: Palgrave Macmillan, pp. 36–68.

Trautwein, C. 2015. 'US Reconsiders Myanmar for Special Trade Preferences'. *Myanmar Times*. 8 December. Available at http://www.mmtimes.com/index.php/business/18018-the-united-states-reconsiders-myanmar-for-special-trade-preferences.html.

Tsogas, G. 2000. 'Labour Standards in the Generalized Systems of Preferences of the European Union and the United States'. 6(3) *European Journal of Industrial Relations* 349–370.

Turnell, S. 2015. 'Burma's Economic Transition: Hopes and Hurdles'. 82(2) *Social Research: An International Quarterly* 481–506.

UNHCR. 2011. 'Guiding Principles on Business and Human Rights: Implementing the United Nations "Protect, Respect and Remedy"'. *Framework*. Geneva: UNHCR.

Ward, K. and V. Mouyly. 2016. 'Employment Relations and Political Transition in Cambodia'. 58(2) *Journal of Industrial Relations* 258–272.

Zaw, N. 2015. 'Minimum Wage Gathers Support From Abroad'. *The Irrawaddy*. 17 July. Available at http://www.irrawaddy.com/business/minimum-wage-gathers-support-from-abroad.html.

3

The Extractive Industries Transparency Initiative

New Openings for Civil Society in Myanmar

ADAM SIMPSON

Myanmar's broader economy and society are dominated by agriculture, but primitive accumulation through natural resource extraction has become a fundamental driver of national economic growth. It has cemented

> Myanmar's structural position as a producer and exporter of raw commodities. This has given rise to a highly rapacious, uneven and often violent mode of development, and a configuration of socio-political forces that is less amenable to genuine democratisation than to violent unrest. (Jones 2018)

The key challenges for the National League for Democracy (NLD) government are to both manage a long-term political transition from military to civilian rule and initiate a durable economic transformation towards a more broad-based economic growth model with the benefits of development spread more evenly amongst the population. In the short-to-medium term, however, natural resource extraction will remain a key source of national income and foreign exchange. A successful political and economic transition to entrenched democratic rule therefore requires a far more comprehensive and inclusive approach to natural resource governance than has previously been attempted (Bauer, Shortell and Delesgues 2016).

To ensure more equitable development the issue of resource distribution must be addressed geographically and ethnically amongst the country's various states and regions, but also within society's social and economic hierarchies. For society-wide acceptance of resource distribution policies, the decision-making processes require greater public and civil society involvement. The legal frameworks for implementing policies of resource extraction and use must not only be seen to be fair and equitable, they must be applied fairly and rigorously to improve confidence in the legal system, which has traditionally been considered ad hoc and largely existing to serve the goals of the military and its associated business interests. Indeed, while the political and economic reform process under the Thein Sein government (2011–2016) transformed many areas of government administration, the judiciary, considered representative of 'a larger political order' (Cheesman 2015: 10), is widely seen as unreformed (Crouch 2018).

While a wholesale overhaul of the court system is required, other processes of environmental and natural resource governance may act as conduits towards more inclusive policy-making and assist in overcoming historical distrust and enmity between ethnic groups, government and civil society organisations (CSOs). Within the Environmental Conservation Law 2012 and its associated rules and procedures, which took several years to develop, there are requirements for project proponents to consult with civil society, community-based organisations and project-affected people (Simpson 2015). The Environmental Impact Assessment (EIA) Procedures and National Environmental Quality (Emission) Guidelines were finally launched in January 2016 in the last days of the Thein Sein government (ADB 2016).

These requirements are, however, somewhat novel in Myanmar – although EIAs have been required for foreign investments since 2012 – and their efficacy will take some time to determine. The role of EIAs in promoting sustainable development will become more important over time, as skills in environmental assessment increase and the regulation expertise improves. The Ministry of Natural Resources and Environmental Conservation (MONREC), formed by the NLD government in 2016 from the former Ministry of Environmental Conservation and Forestry (MOECAF) and Ministry of Mines, chairs the National Environmental Conservation Committee (NECC), which issues EIA approvals for projects if environmental protection measures have been met. MONREC should have more influence enforcing environmental protection for mining projects now that they are within its remit (Cornish and Vivoda 2016).

Another natural resource governance tool, which I argue played a crucial role in legitimising civil society's role within natural resource governance in Myanmar, is the Extractive Industries Transparency Initiative (EITI). Legislation formalising the EITI is scheduled for early 2017 (MEITI 2016), but the first of Myanmar's EITI Reports, which determine Myanmar's progress on EITI implementation, was published in January 2016 (Moore Stephens 2015b). The second EITI Report was due by March

2017, although an extension was granted to March 2018, with Validation against the EITI Standard now due to commence in July 2018.

The progress of EITI implementation in Myanmar has closely shadowed the economic and political reform process since 2012 – initially under President Thein Sein and now under the NLD government – and has come to symbolise a new deliberative form of governance. While the EITI is certainly more participatory than previous state-led environmental governance policies, the scope of the original EITI was quite narrow, although it has expanded over time. At its core it is simply a tool for matching government revenues with company payments to minimise the corrupt leakage of funds. This limited remit is completely at odds with the expectations of many activists and communities in Myanmar: that the EITI is a key tool for the equitable distribution of resources.

As with many other governance ventures in Myanmar, implementation of the EITI has been stymied by the shortcomings or interests of the individuals involved and a lack of capacity or resources dedicated to it. Nevertheless, in the multi-stakeholder group (MSG), which is the in-country decision-making and implementing body that drives the EITI process, the government, business interests and civil society each have equal decision-making power. In a country such as Myanmar, emerging from five decades of authoritarian rule, this body has the potential to transform the traditionally antagonistic relations between government and civil society (Doyle and Simpson 2006). If it were merely a body set up and overseen by the Myanmar government it would be subject solely to the whims of individual ministers, potentially undermining its rationale and effectiveness. This would have severely restricted its activities during the military-backed Thein Sein government. Under the EITI, however, the MSG and the entire process are supervised by the international EITI Board, which was chaired through most of Myanmar's accession period under Thein Sein by former UK Development Secretary Clare Short.

For the Thein Sein government, the EITI came to epitomise Myanmar's successful return to the international community, but it also came with the cost of potential meddling by the EITI Board, which has not baulked from downgrading a wayward country; due to concerns over a government crackdown on civil society, Azerbaijan became the first country to be downgraded by the Board, from Compliant to Candidate status, in April 2015.[1] Increased international oversight entailed potential risks for

---

[1] Prior to the EITI Standard 2016 a country was defined as an EITI Candidate country when it was implementing the EITI but not yet Compliant. A country was defined as

the Myanmar government, but successful engagement with this process has brought international praise and exposure to international norms, which is essential for the equitable development of the country.

The NLD government, with its history of street activism and opposition to the military, has further dismantled some aspects of the authoritarian state, although it has also demonstrated its own illiberal tendencies (Simpson 2017: 201–204). It should prove more open to engagement with civil society actors – for example, Maung Tin Thit, a civil society representative on the MSG, won a seat for the NLD in the 2015 elections – but it has been somewhat aloof towards civil society since forming the government, implying that, having won a landslide election victory, the NLD is the only valid actor in the governance of the country (Fink and Simpson 2018). In addition, active support for the EITI was limited during the government's first year in office. Nonetheless, as the senior technical and policy analyst at MEITI notes, no one is criticising the government for inactivity on the EITI just yet, because the people of Myanmar feel that, for the first time, 'this is our government'.[2]

This chapter therefore examines the role of the EITI, particularly in facilitating and legitimising civil society activism, in the ongoing political and economic transition in Myanmar. It examines how political and economic reforms mediated through an internationally supervised governance process can assist in the establishment of civil society engagement and international democratic norms at a local level. Nevertheless, it also contemplates the limitations of such a process, particularly when transparency norms are faced with structural local impediments that are driven by the benefits that accrue to the current owners and controllers of the natural resources sector.

The EITI and Myanmar

The EITI is a 'global standard to promote open and accountable management of natural resources' (EITI International Secretariat 2017). It

---

EITI Compliant when the EITI Board considered that it met all the EITI requirements. The new Standard changed the assessment nomenclature for implementing countries to a more nuanced four-level assessment based on a country's progress towards each requirement, including civil society participation, and their overall implementation of the EITI Standard: Satisfactory, Meaningful, Inadequate or No Progress. Implementing countries must undergo Validation at least once every three years.

[2] Interview with Min Zar Ni Lin, EITI senior technical and policy analyst, MEITI, Yangon, 5 September 2016.

emerged in the early 2000s as part of a shift in global governance towards revenue transparency, particularly in the extractive sector (Haufler 2010; Van Alstine 2014). Countries implementing the EITI disclose information on tax payments, licences, contracts and production from natural resource extraction in an annual EITI Report, which is compiled by an independent administrator, allowing civil society and community groups to track the revenue from natural resources from production to the government accounts.

The income received by the government is reconciled against the payments made by companies to the government. If the figure that the government reports is less than that of the companies, there are likely to be corrupt payments to government officials. This reconciliation therefore deals with only reported payments, so it is still possible for informal 'brown paper bag' corruption to occur, but Western companies, in particular, face increasing scrutiny and pressure by shareholders and governments over transparency and potential corrupt practices. Legislation in the United States initially from 2010 (Securities and Exchange Commission 2016) and the European Union in 2013 (European Parliament and Council of the European Union 2013) has ensured that large American and European extractive companies investing in Myanmar will be required to report their payments to the government; with Myanmar in the EITI, companies from Australia, Asia and elsewhere will be required to follow suit.

The EITI is, however, extremely limited as a governance tool. Indeed, it is this limitation that can make it attractive to corporations and governments. It makes no direct contribution to debates over the distribution or ownership of resources, the levels or type of environmental protection or the use of government funds resulting from resource extraction. These governance concerns are largely beyond the remit of the EITI, which can be considered as having a depoliticised focus on transparency that is not unproblematic (MacLean 2014). Throughout Myanmar, however, there exist inflated expectations, regarding the determination of resource distribution and ownership, in relation to what the EITI can achieve. This misunderstanding is echoed in other areas of political reform including parliamentary politics where the limitations on Aung San Suu Kyi's ability to institute reform when in opposition were not well understood.

Expectations may have been raised by the extensive media coverage the EITI received, which occurred concurrently with the emergence of a free press in the country from 2013. While in some countries the EITI has not been widely publicised (Aaronson 2011), in Myanmar, as in Liberia (Rich and Warner 2012), it received widespread coverage, resulting in some parts of society viewing it as a panacea for corrupt or incompetent natural resource governance. The scope of the EITI is far narrower. Numerous studies on the EITI suggest that implementation in its earlier form had a limited effect on natural resource governance (Aaronson 2011; Kolstad and Wiig 2009; Mouan 2010; Sovacool and Andrews 2015; Sturesson and Zobel 2015; Van Alstine 2014), although there is some evidence that joining the EITI reduces corruption (David-Barrett and Okamura 2013).

While the focus remains on 'transparency', the EITI Standard was launched at the EITI Global Conference in April 2013 to improve governance aspects such as civil society participation; EITI Requirement 6 within this Standard instructed applicant governments 'to ensure that civil society is fully, independently, actively and effectively engaged' in the process (EITI International Secretariat 2013: 40). This civil society participation was further refined in the EITI Standard 2016, launched at the EITI Global Conference in Lima, Peru, in February 2016 (EITI International Secretariat 2016: 14). A protocol on 'Participation of civil society', which provides an assessment framework for the provisions related to civil society, was also included in the 2016 Standard. The main vehicle for civil society engagement is the MSG; its horizontal distribution of authority is unique in Myanmar. The EITI is therefore a compelling case study of the implementation of internationally mandated norms for civil society participation in natural resource governance in the South.

Why Implement the EITI?

The rationale behind the EITI is to ensure that government revenues from natural resource extraction are measurable and transparent, thereby reducing corruption and providing citizens with a tool to apply pressure on governments regarding budget expenditures. The need for greater transparency and better governance in Myanmar is evident in Myanmar's performance in related indicators. In Transparency International's Corruptions Perception Index 2016 Myanmar was perceived as one of the most corrupt countries in the world, ranked 136 out of 176 countries (Transparency International 2017). This result was a significant improvement on its 2010 result, the last year of direct military rule, when it was ranked second-to-last, equal with Afghanistan out of 178 countries, with only Somalia perceived as more corrupt.

Corruption in the natural resources sector – a sector that is particularly susceptible to corruption (Simpson 2018) – was even worse. The Resource Governance Index was launched by the Revenue Watch Institute, now the

Natural Resources Governance Institute (NRGI) (2013), at the 2013 EITI and Mining for Development Conferences in Sydney. As the Myanmar minister for Mines looked on the Index was unveiled, revealing that Myanmar ranked last out of fifty-eight resource-rich countries in terms of the quality of governance in the extractive sector. Its composite score of 4 out of 100 was also particularly low; Equatorial Guinea, which ranked fifty-sixth, still managed a score that was more than three times higher. This assessment was undertaken before many recent reforms had come into play; with, for instance, improved transparency in the auctions for oil and gas blocks in 2014,[3] Myanmar's score and ranking will no doubt improve in the next Index. Nevertheless, as the baseline report of the extractives industry prepared by Adam Smith International noted,

> Previously, many grievances with the extractive industries sector were resolved by fiat or use of force, rather than through policy-making, mediation or dialogue. We must therefore begin by acknowledging the reality that misinformation and historically derived distrust still exists. (Adam Smith International 2015: 9)

Myanmar's ethnic diversity and history of conflict and authoritarianism have resulted in incredibly complex political and economic systems with overlapping and contested de jure and de facto authority structures (Joliffe 2015). Many of Myanmar's natural resources are situated in ethnic minority areas, which has resulted in civil society opposition (Simpson 2007; 2013) and exacerbated long-term civil conflicts (see Simpson, Farrelly and Holliday 2018; South 2009); in their statistical study on forest resources and conflict Rustad et al. (2008) found that forest resources generally have a negligible influence on both conflict onset and conflict duration, but they cited Myanmar as the clearest case where it did exist. The EITI is generally supported across Myanmar's society, but there is some concern in ethnic areas that it will reinforce centralised control of natural resources in ethnic areas, as the EU's Forest Law Enforcement, Governance and Trade (FLEGT) Facility may do with forests.[4]

Due to conflict and corruption there is a significant black economy that is not captured when measuring the official economy. In addition, all levels of government and bureaucracy in Myanmar have extremely limited capacity and resources; although there is a concerted effort underway to digitalise the information, much of the government data remains

---

[3] Interview with Asia Pacific/Myanmar manager, NRGI, 3 February 2015, Yangon.
[4] Interview with Wong Aung, former co-ordinator, Shwe Gas Movement, 21 January 2015, Yangon.

on paper.[5] These factors have resulted in the resources sector being particularly opaque with related economic flows difficult to quantify and the
resultant data unreliable. Analysis of the gemstones industry, which is
dominated by jade mining and trade, has indicated just how unreliable
government data can be (Irwin 2016).

Officially, all gemstones and jade produced in Myanmar must be sold
at the government's annual Myanmar Gems Emporium, and the government insisted that this be the figure that was used for the EITI. In the 2015
Emporium, gemstone sales were US$1.26 billion, down from a record
US$3.4 billion the previous year, with jade accounting for about 90 per cent
of the total sales (Reuters 2015). According to Myanmar's Central Statistical
Organization jade *exports* were approximately US$1 billion, or 10 per cent
of the total, in the financial year April 2013–March 2014, with around the
same amount in 2014–2015 (Central Statistical Organization 2016a; 2016b;
Moore Stephens 2015a: 15). However, according to Chinese customs
data provided to the UN's Comtrade database, China imported US$12.3
billion of gemstones from Myanmar in 2014, with most of the trade being
jade (NCRA 2015). While almost all of Myanmar's jade is ultimately
exported to China,[6] the discrepancy between these figures indicates that
there may be far more jade being mined and exported than the government
admits. The Chinese figures also include only official exports; there may be
significant flows of gemstones in the black economy not being accounted
for in these figures.

Furthermore, an extensive report by Global Witness (2015) employed
two separate estimates of the jade sector: a primary methodology based on
a complex analysis of jade grades and volumes and a secondary approach
employing the aforementioned Chinese data. Both methods concluded
that the value of the jade mined in 2014 was worth more than US$30
billion, which was almost half Myanmar's total estimated 2014 GDP of
US$64 billion (World Bank 2015a). Both estimates were based on official
production data that took no account of the jade production kept entirely
off the books, which was likely to be significant.

There is great uncertainty and unreliability in the gemstone sector
data, however, with recent UN Comtrade figures from China suggesting

[5] As an incredulous economic specialist with the Korea International Cooperation Agency
(KOICA) who was assisting with Myanmar's calculation of GDP noted: 'in the office
there were large bundles of papers everywhere – these are the sources to calculate GDP'.
Interview, 30 January 2014, Naypyidaw.
[6] Email correspondence with researcher at Global Witness, 2 March 2016.

that the US$12.3 billion in official gemstone imports from Myanmar in 2014 was almost an order of magnitude greater than any other year. In 2013, only US$1.2 billion was registered. In 2015 imports fell from the high in 2014 to US$2.3 billion and in 2016 they collapsed even further to US$179 million (United Nations 2017). As a senior researcher at Global Witness suggested, these fluctuations could have been due to the anti-corruption drive in China.[7] Some of the highest profile cases involved jade, which could have resulted in more trade being declared in the short term with demand dissipating in the longer term. Without greater transparency in government data it remains extremely difficult to understand the nature and dynamics of the industry as a whole. Nonetheless, all the available analysis suggests that the figures used in the EITI for gemstones are likely to be a small fraction of what the industry actually produces, which highlights a severe limitation of the EITI process.

Even before the EITI Standard was adopted, however, the EITI Board and Secretariat made clear that transparency was only a starting point for the EITI. From the earliest moments of implementation in Myanmar, Zaw Oo, the national co-ordinator of Myanmar EITI (MEITI), which was based in the Centre for Economic and Social Development (CESD) within the Myanmar Development Resource Institute (MDRI), saw the EITI and MSG primarily as a vehicle for getting tripartite co-operation between government, business and civil society, rather than as a 'standalone process' or 'an end in itself'.[8] As trust-building activities these processes could provide opportunities to not only improve environmental governance across the country but also to facilitate the evolving peace process, which is intimately tied to the equitable sharing of natural resources.[9] Nevertheless, decades of authoritarian rule and disinvestment in education and institution-building in the country left government administration and trust between actors in a parlous state resulting in a challenging environment for negotiations.

Joining the EITI Club

The political and economic transformation that is currently taking place in Myanmar has brought Myanmar in from the cold in relation to the West

---

[7] Email correspondence with senior researcher at Global Witness, 16 May 2017.

[8] Interview with Zaw Oo, director of research and program leader, MEITI, 23 May 2013, Sydney, Australia.

[9] Interview with Aung Naing Oo, associate program director, Myanmar Peace Centre, 13 June 2013, Yangon.

with foreign governments, international financial institutions and many international organisations working with the Myanmar government for the first time since the late 1980s (Simpson and Park 2013). Since 2011 aid agencies, such as Australian Aid and the UK Department for International Development (DfID), have rapidly expanded their aid programmes in Myanmar and, having bypassed the state for much of the previous two decades, now work directly with the state to provide international expertise in environmental and natural resource governance, as well as health and education. As the Western sanctions regime fell away under the Thein Sein government, the EITI became one of the key indicators of this increased engagement between Myanmar and the international community, which saw the EITI as a vehicle for both increasing civil society engagement and promoting international governance norms. In July 2012 Jonas Moberg, the head of the EITI Secretariat, visited Myanmar for the first time at the invitation of the government, which had indicated it wanted to join the EITI. Myanmar's intentions were confirmed in December of that year by Thein Sein in a Presidential Decree, and Soe Thein, minister of the President's Office, was appointed to chair the EITI Leading Authority, the executive-level body (EITI International Secretariat 2017).

Consequently, in May 2013 Australian Aid sponsored a Myanmar delegation to Australia to attend the Global EITI and Mining for Development Conferences in Sydney and conduct field trips to Australian mines. Anticipating the membership of the EITI MSG, the delegation included civil society activists, civil servants and the ministers of Mines and Energy. Although the minister for Finance attended only briefly, the minister for Mines, Myint Aung, spent most of the trip with the group, giving activists and government officials an unprecedented opportunity for interaction and laying the groundwork for much of the collaboration to come. Most activists involved with the EITI agree that the Ministry of Mines was the most helpful of the bureaucracies with the Ministry of Finance also relatively open; the Ministry of Energy was, however, 'tougher' to engage with.[10] The openness of the minister for Mines to outside influences was evident by his interest in the views of foreign academics on contract renegotiation and civil society, particularly in relation to the Shwe Gas Project.[11] Although significant renegotiation of the Shwe Gas contract was unlikely, given its intense importance to China's energy

---

[10] Interview with Asia Pacific/Myanmar manager, NRGI, 3 February 2015, Yangon; interview with Ko Ko Lwin, Myanmar associate, NRGI, 21 January 2015, Yangon.

[11] Interview with Myint Aung, Union minister, Ministry of Mines, Union of Myanmar, 23 May 2013, Sydney, Australia.

security, the minister announced to parliament two months later that the contract for the Letpadaung (Letpadan/Monywa) Copper Mine had been renegotiated to provide more favourable terms for the government and local communities at the expense of China's Wanbao Mining Ltd.

Despite this hitherto unknown willingness by some parts of government to work closely with non-government actors, the attitude of much of government remained antagonistic and aloof when negotiating with civil society. It gradually became clear that although the Thein Sein government had signed up to the EITI and the civil society commitments that it entailed, they were largely unprepared to actually undertake it. The residual militarism and authoritarianism of the government resulted in a limited acceptance of the role of civil society as designated equal partners within the MSG.

Civil society within Myanmar mostly comprises activists who opposed military rule, either within the country or in the border areas, although some activists such as Win Myo Thu of ECODEV had previous experience of working with the government. Negotiations between civil society and the government, and to some extent the MEITI team within MDRI, were therefore often fractious, with a lack of negotiating expertise on both sides, leading to regular threats to walk away from the process.[12] Nevertheless, throughout 2013 civil society undertook a significant national consultation programme to determine the CSO membership of the MSG. In October 2013, 150 representatives of CSOs from all over the country met in Yangon to discuss the EITI and elect the civil society representatives for the MSG.[13] This civil society movement eventually formalised into the Myanmar Alliance for Transparency and Accountability (MATA), which became the main umbrella CSO negotiating the EITI.[14]

The Multi-Stakeholder Group

The MSG is the driving force of the EITI in each country. In Myanmar under President Thein Sein, it was chaired by Maung Maung Thein, the deputy finance minister. MEITI eventually settled on nine CSO representatives, eight government representatives and six business representatives for the MSG, although each group had an equal vote in decision-making.

---

[12] Interview with international adviser to MEITI, 27 July 2015, Yangon.
[13] Interview with Ko Ko Lwin, activist with Spectrum (now Myanmar associate, NRGI), 3 February 2014, Yangon.
[14] Interview with Ma Taryar, national co-ordinator, MATA, 30 January 2015, Yangon.

Civil society had successfully argued to the international EITI Secretariat that their historical political marginalisation, together with the complexity of ethnic areas, required nine members to adequately represent the sector. To manage the MSG workload, three technical subcommittees were established: Governance, Technical, and Communication and Outreach.[15]

Limitations on Myanmar's governance capacity, and potentially the government's interest in the EITI, were evident throughout the MSG selection and operation period. Although the first MSG meeting was finally held in Naypyidaw on Saturday 8 February 2014 there was a sense of chaos in the MEITI office in the lead-up to the meeting as the designated dates shifted to and fro with MEITI receiving instructions from the Ministry of Finance.[16] The date was finalised only on the afternoon of Tuesday 4 February. The MEITI international consultant therefore notified business representatives on Wednesday 5 February, leaving them only two business days to organise their teams, with no flights back to Yangon on Saturday afternoon. The consultant argued that setting the meeting in Naypyidaw on the weekend with such short notice and limited travel options would result in business not being seriously engaged: 'they won't send MDs [managing directors] they'll send a minion'.[17]

Although a diverse range of ethnic minority members were elected to the MSG, Bamar (Burman) CSO representatives still dominated; the Shwe Gas Movement representative from Rakhine State joined the group only due to pressure from international EITI advisers rather than through the Yangon-dominated civil society.[18] Some observers argued that two leading Bamar representatives dictated the October 2013 meeting, and tended to 'bully' other representatives.[19] Although personal traits can also play a role, the 'blindness' (Walton 2013) of Bamar society to their privileged position under military rule can result in the replication

---

[15] Interview with Min Zar Ni Lin, EITI senior technical and policy analyst, MEITI, Yangon, 5 September 2016.
[16] Interview with Min Zar Ni Lin, research associate and deputy leader, MEITI, 3 February 2014, Yangon.
[17] Interview with international adviser to MEITI, 4 February 2014, Yangon.
[18] Interview with Wong Aung, former co-ordinator, Shwe Gas Movement, 25 March 2014, Yangon.
[19] Interview with head of an international organisation in Myanmar, 25 March 2014, Yangon. As Brooten and Metro note, while undertaking research in Myanmar anonymity of local subjects 'cannot always be guaranteed if the organization, the setting, or the individual may be identified even if anonymised' (2014: 12). This applies equally to Western subjects or 'internationals' based in the country who require their identity to be withheld to continue their work (Simpson 2017: 158).

of this dominance within civil society. Some of this dominance was also reflected in technical expertise, however; in a meeting with Clare Short in Naypyidaw in December 2013, civil society proved themselves much more organised and impressive than the government and MDRI.[20] The issue of ethnic representation in the MSG was raised again by some foreign governments and international organisations who tried to include Muslim representation or voices in the process. This was particularly pertinent for the Rohingya and other Muslims who make up one-third of Rakhine State, given that the rationale of the MSG was to give voice to marginalised sectors of society. In response to such suggestions the second Rakhine representative announced: 'if you include *Kala* [a derogatory term for Rohingya], I'll walk out'.[21]

Myanmar's EITI candidature application was eventually submitted on 7 May 2014 (MEITI 2014), and at the EITI Board Meeting in Mexico City on 2 July 2014 Myanmar was formally accepted as a Candidate country. MEITI then had eighteen months to produce the first EITI Report, due on 2 January 2016, which fell during the Thein Sein government's caretaker period after the NLD's election win. The Ministry of Finance, now the Ministry of Finance and Planning, created a secretariat to assume MEITI responsibilities after publication of the first report, but six months before the handover it still had no staff working on the EITI full time.[22]

Despite the limited remit of the EITI, CSOs endeavoured to broaden the role of the MSG to deal with any related natural resource governance issues. This became evident in January 2015 when CSOs called an emergency MSG meeting in January 2015 over the shooting of a protester at the Letpadaung Copper Mine in December 2014 (Fortify Rights and International Human Rights Clinic 2015).[23] Following the aforementioned contract renegotiation in mid-2013, Wanbao Mining became a minority stakeholder in the mine, holding 30 per cent, with its business partner, the military-backed Union of Myanmar Economic Holdings Ltd (UMEHL), holding 19 per cent; the Myanmar government (No.1 Myanmar Enterprise) took a 51 per cent share. Due to disagreements over the shooting and its relevance to the EITI MSG both the government and civil society threatened to withdraw from the entire EITI process,

[20] Interview with International Adviser to MEITI, 21 January 2015, Yangon.
[21] Interview with Min Zar Ni Lin, Research Associate and Deputy Leader, MEITI, 3 February 2015, Yangon; Interview with International Adviser to MEITI, 21 January 2015, Yangon.
[22] Interview with international adviser to MEITI, 27 July 2015, Yangon.
[23] Interview with Ko Ko Lwin, Myanmar associate, NRGI, 21 January 2015, Yangon.

although the CSOs were split with 'personalities' causing ruptures in the decision-making processes.[24] The head of the EITI Secretariat, Jonas Moberg, flew in to try and placate both sides.[25]

CSOs were attempting to deploy the EITI as a human rights grievance mechanism, which the MEITI international consultant argued reflected a 'lack of understanding' of what the EITI was for.[26] An alternative interpretation of the action is that the EITI was one of the few channels where government was forced to sit down with CSOs and listen to their grievances. It is therefore unsurprising that CSOs would leverage their internationally mandated influence by attempting to expand the issues to be dealt with by the EITI and MSG. As a consequence of the dispute, the international consultant offered to meet with Wanbao to discuss issues related to the EITI and the mine. The response was an email in which Wanbao argued that they were only a minority shareholder and they would be bound by the EITI, so there was no need to meet; they added 'we wish you well with your little project'.[27]

To decentralise management of the EITI the MSG agreed in October 2014 to establish four pilot 'MEITI subnational coordination units', in Mandalay Region, Magway Region, Shan State and Rakhine State. The aim of these units was to provide a 'local-level platform for dialogue on local issues of concern relating to the extractive industries' (MEITI 2015: 5). There was no local-level reporting process, but each unit was to develop their own work plans with activities that focused on public consultation. By late 2016, however, only Magway had established an MSG, although some progress had also been made in Mandalay.[28]

Nevertheless, the inclusion of Rakhine State as a sub-national unit caused some consternation amongst the international advisers, given the communal conflict in the state and the general Rakhine aversion to the inclusion of Muslim or Rohingya voices in the process. The World Bank was pushing to include Rohingya in the process through MATA, but its national co-ordinator, Ma Taryar, argued that the CSO did not work that way: 'if they have a natural resource governance CSO then that is fine but so far

---

[24] Interview with Wong Aung, former co-ordinator, Shwe Gas Movement, 21 January 2015, Yangon.

[25] Interview with Min Zar Ni Lin, research associate and deputy leader, MEITI, 3 February 2015, Yangon.

[26] Interview with international adviser to MEITI, 21 January 2015, Yangon.

[27] Interview with international adviser to MEITI, 27 July 2015, Yangon.

[28] Interview with Min Zar Ni Lin, EITI senior technical and policy analyst, MEITI, Yangon, 5 September 2016.

we haven't seen one.'[29] Given the restrictions placed on the movement and activities of the Rohingya community, with more than 100,000 still in internment camps, it could be argued that greater civil society outreach could be undertaken for this community in Rakhine State.

Improving Resource Governance through the EITI Report

The annual EITI Report contains the reconciliation data and determines a country's progress on EITI implementation. It is therefore the main document available to civil society to pursue improved resource governance goals. The sectors assessed in Myanmar's first EITI Report, released in January 2016 (Moore Stephens 2015b), were set out in the Scoping Report prepared by the consultancy Moore Stephens, which was finalised 12 November 2015 (Moore Stephens 2015a). Their first contract was to prepare a Scoping Report and prepare a five-year reporting roadmap. Prior to their arrival in Myanmar in mid-2015 they sent numerous requests to MEITI to set up meetings. When they arrived, however, no meetings had been organised, significantly delaying the report.[30] The second contract was to produce the final EITI Report on the reconciliation between the company and government figures for the financial year April 2013–March 2014 (Moore Stephens 2015b).[31]

The only sectors to be included in the reconciliation were oil and gas (including transportation), which was relatively simple due to the involvement of international business and large contracts, and mining (including gems and jade), which, with its diverse scales, multitude of stakeholders and deep integration with the economies of the ethnic minority–controlled areas, presented a more complex array of challenges. The government initially argued that gems and jade should be excluded from the EITI process,[32] but the benefits of an internationally supervised process meant that the international consultant, backed by the EITI Secretariat and Board, ensured that these core sectors were included.

Although some CSOs wanted to include hydroelectricity, it was agreed that it would be left out of the reconciliation in the first report but that a schedule would be incorporated into the report to include it at a later date.

---

[29] Interview with Ma Taryar, national co-ordinator, MATA, 30 January 2015, Yangon.
[30] Interview with international adviser to MEITI, 27 July 2015, Yangon.
[31] Email correspondence with international adviser to MEITI, 19 November 2015.
[32] Interview with international adviser to MEITI, 21 January 2015, Yangon.

The EITI has not traditionally encompassed hydroelectricity, but it has begun to be included by some countries, such as Albania. In Myanmar, the prospect of numerous large dams in ethnic areas on the Thanlwin (Salween) and Ayeyarwady (Irrawaddy) Rivers made this a priority for some ethnic CSOs (Kirchherr, Charles and Walton 2016; Simpson 2013). Other CSOs wanted either forestry or fisheries included; forestry was excluded because the FLEGT process has set up a parallel internationally mediated governance regime, and fisheries was considered non-core for the initial EITI Report. Moore Stephens's Scoping Report recommended hydropower and fisheries be included in future EITI Reports (Moore Stephens 2015a: 7).

The reconciliation was difficult because not only are most of the government records kept on paper, there are also no records of disaggregated tax revenue by company. The reconciliation was therefore based on non-tax data such as royalties, customs and production. As difficult as this task was, government intransigence, particularly from the Ministry of Energy, made the task even more difficult. Some of the limitations to the Scoping Report were set out by Moore Stephens:

(i)   The conclusions of our work have been based partially on data and information provided by government entities which have not been previously audited or reconciled ...

(ii) We did not obtain the statement of revenues collected from the extractive sector from the IRD and Custom Department.

(iii) We did not obtain the desegregated data (by licensee) on revenue streams collected from small operators from the MoM [Ministry of Mines], except for emporium data for Jade and Gemstone.

(iv) We did not obtain the comprehensive list of Military Holding companies and their related subsidiaries.

(v)   We did not obtain the list of operators in the Gems and Jade sectors from the MoM (Moore Stephens 2015a: 6).

Each of these limitations is a key issue, but it is clearly difficult to undertake a thorough reconciliation of the extractive sector without taking into account tax data from the Internal Revenue Department. Similarly, like many other sectors of the economy, the mining industry in Myanmar is dominated by opaque military-owned corporations – including the enormous holding companies UMEHL and Myanmar Economic Corporation (MEC) – and their associated 'cronies' who have created oligopolistic wealth (Ford, Gillan and Thein 2016; Irwin 2016; Moore Stephens 2015b: 48–49). As Moore Stephens note, they did not even receive a list of these holding companies, nor of their subsidiaries, so their assets and activities are clearly shielded from view. Until these corporations are forced to reveal their activities the EITI Reports will be necessarily lacking. In addition, military cronies have bankrolled peace negotiations in the past between the military and ethnic armed groups, such as the KNU and Kachin Independence Organisation, illustrating the importance to corporate interests of access to ethnic states for natural resource extraction (Jones 2014).

The lack of disaggregated company data, and other associated data limitations, also means that it has been difficult to assess the government revenue from a particular company or mine. To take one example, civil society activists want to investigate government receipts and other governance issues related to the Letpadaung Mine.[33] The Scoping Report was woefully out of date on this issue; it failed to mention Wanbao and instead listed the Myanmar Ivanhoe Copper Company Ltd, owned by Canada's Ivanhoe, as the major foreign company with a 50:50 joint venture with No.1 Mining Enterprise. Ivanhoe's interest in the mine was taken over by Wanbao in 2011. In addition, the contract was renegotiated in July 2013, early in the year of reconciliation, but the 19 per cent interest of the military-backed UMEHL is not mentioned (Moore Stephens 2015a: 28). Letpadaung is the most high-profile mine in the country, so the erroneous information in the Scoping Report was not encouraging, although it was corrected in the final report (Moore Stephens 2015b).

When the final report on fiscal year 2013–2014 was released in January 2016 much of the material had been flagged in the draft and Scoping Reports; the reconciliation covered three sub-sectors – oil and gas, gems and jade, and other minerals – and total Union government revenue collected from the extractive sector amounted to MMK3,011 billion (Myanmar *kyat*) (approximately US$3.1 billion). The oil and gas sector generated the most revenue with the government collecting MMK2,569 billion (US$2.7 billion) representing 85 per cent of total revenues. In the minerals sector the government collected MMK388 billion from gems and jade and MMK54 billion from other minerals in 2013–2014: a total of MMK442 billion (US$460 million) which represented 15 per cent of revenues (Moore Stephens 2015b: 8–9). While not insubstantial, the gems and jade revenues represent a very small fraction of the value of the jade sector, which is more than US$30 billion, as estimated by Global

---

[33] Interview with Ma Taryar, national co-ordinator, MATA, 30 January 2015, Yangon.

Witness (Global Witness 2015). The report indicates that the extractives sector comprised 6 per cent of Myanmar's GDP, 23.6 per cent of state revenues and 38.5 per cent of total exports (Moore Stephens 2015b: 10), but these statistics employ the government's figures relating to the size of Myanmar's GDP, which likely significantly undervalue the size of the jade industry.

Most of the state revenues were collected by state-owned enterprises (SOEs),[34] which raised MMK2,554 billion (US$2.7 billion) representing 85 per cent of the total. During reporting for the EITI, information on the operations and accounts of SOEs was made publicly available in Myanmar for the first time. A governance shortcoming that was highlighted in the report was the use of 'other accounts' by SOEs. From 2012–2013 government reforms allowed 55 per cent of revenues to be withheld by SOEs in these accounts, which are not counted in the state budget and can be used for their own purposes with only limited government oversight (Heller and Delesgues 2016: 28–31). In 2013–2014 SOE transfers amounted to MMK2,676 billion of which MMK1,543 billion, representing 58 per cent, was held in the 'other accounts', while the other 42 per cent was transferred to the state's budget. For instance, Myanmar Oil and Gas Enterprise (MOGE), the SOE that foreign companies must partner with in oil and gas investments, moved approximately MMK1,320 billion (US$1.4 billion) into these off-budget accounts in 2013–2014 (Moore Stephens 2015b: 8–10), more than Myanmar spent on either health (MMK528 billion) or education (MMK909 billion) in the same period (Open Myanmar Initiative 2016; see also World Bank 2015b).

A key point Moore Stephens also highlighted in the final report was the lack of legal support for the EITI. They noted that 'the EITI reporting obligations are not covered by any other Law organising the process of collection in the current Legislation', and they recommended developing a legal framework including an EITI law that could be harmonised with existing legislation with provisions relating to:

> reporting obligations for extractive companies and government entities alike, while specifying the level of disaggregation of the data to be submitted; and a time schedule for updating and publishing forms and instructions and selection of the reporting entities and submission of declarations and completion of all reconciliation work. (Moore Stephens 2015b: 79–80)

---

[34] SOEs are sometimes referred to as state-owned economic enterprises (SEEs) in Myanmar (see Heller and Delesgues 2016), but here I have used the standard international acronym.

These requirements, which were supported by NGOs such as Global Witness,[35] would improve the legal standing of the EITI in Myanmar and underpin its integration into the country's broader natural resource governance framework. MATA also supported an overarching EITI law,[36] while the manager of the Extractives Programme in the Myanmar Centre for Responsible Business indicated that Union-level legislation would provide more support for both CSO and MEITI representatives at township level.[37] He indicated that many of the CSO representatives from the MSG were not from NGOs registered with the government; they therefore receive curt treatment from township-level authorities, most of which have lived their entire lives within an authoritarian military structure that precluded civil society engagement. In contrast, the Myanmar manager of NRGI, an organisation with extensive multi-country experience on the EITI, argued that an EITI law was not necessary for successful implementation of the EITI.[38] Regardless of the law's necessity, however, MEITI planned to develop legislation to support the EITI with lawmakers in early 2017 (MEITI 2016).

Conclusion

Myanmar's journey in joining the EITI has shone a spotlight on the limitations of existing natural resource governance in the country. Many of these constraints were to be expected in a country with such an authoritarian history, but significant progress has been made in improving its complex political and economic systems. Effective reform of the extractive industries' legal and governance frameworks is an enormous challenge, but one that reflects the broader difficulty of encouraging equitable and sustainable development in a highly unequal and poverty-stricken country.

For the foreseeable future, it will be NLD-led governments that are tasked with navigating Myanmar through its ongoing EITI commitments and other natural resource governance reforms. The government took its first tentative step in reforming the gemstone sector in July 2016 when it announced it would not renew mining permits for gems and jade when they expired and

---

[35] Email correspondence with researcher at Global Witness, 2 March 2016.
[36] Interview with co-ordinator, MATA, Yangon, 30 January 2015.
[37] Interview with manager, Extractives Programme, Myanmar Centre for Responsible Business, Yangon, 7 September 2016.
[38] Interview with Asia Pacific/Myanmar manager, NRGI, 6 September 2016, Yangon.

would not issue new permits until the by-laws associated with the amended Myanmar Gemstones Law had been passed (Ye Mon and Kyi Kyi Sway 2017). In an echo of the EITI MSG, a new trilateral committee, comprising government, industry and civil society representatives, is being established to advise on the development of a new jade policy, although some of the proposed legislative changes are superficial and would do little more than maintain the status quo (Paul Shortell 2017).[39]

Progress on the EITI itself was limited during the government's first year in power. The MSG associated with the Thein Sein government was disbanded, as was the EITI Leading Authority and all other government committees as the NLD sought to break with the past and stamp its authority on the new government. Unfortunately, the centralised decision-making processes of the NLD and the new government, with all significant decisions flowing through the office of Aung San Suu Kyi, meant that reconstituting these committees was a slow process. In addition, in her first year Suu Kyi appeared to focus almost exclusively on the peace process, assuming that once a comprehensive agreement was reached, other areas such as the economy could be prioritised. In reality, economic concerns, and natural resource governance in particular, are intimately interwoven with issues of ethnic and civil conflict in Myanmar. Improved natural resource governance, through greater transparency, effective environmental assessment and resource redistribution (Bauer et al. 2016), is likely to facilitate the peace process rather than flow from it.With the MSG in abeyance throughout 2016, the three technical subcommittees continued meeting to maintain some momentum,[40] but funding difficulties and a lack of commitment or apparent interest from the new government meant that there were difficulties in finalising the second EITI Report, then due in March 2017.[41] The NLD government eventually appointed a new EITI Leading Committee in December 2016 and applied for an extension to the EITI International Board on 31 January 2017, the last possible day. In April 2017 the Board acquiesced to their request and they were granted twelve month extensions: the second EITI Report became due on 31 March 2018 with Validation commencing 1 July 2018 (EITI International Secretariat 2017). Despite the extension, progress on the issues highlighted in the first report is likely to be limited;

---

[39] Email correspondence with senior campaigner, Global Witness, 16 May 2017.
[40] Email correspondence with regional director, EITI International Secretariat, 22 December 2016.
[41] Interview with Min Zar Ni Lin, EITI senior technical and policy analyst, MEITI, Yangon, 5 September 2016.

priorities for the government to address included establishing greater parliamentary oversight of SOEs, applying transparency requirements to military-owned companies and, as a result, improving documentation of beneficial ownership.

These issues all point to an underlying difficulty for the NLD government: the structural power of the military within Myanmar's political economy and its formal authority under the military-written 2008 Constitution. The military control of the ministries associated with defence, interior and border affairs, in addition to other constitutional powers, meant that the NLD was extremely limited in its ability to manage the ethnic minority border areas, where most conflict occurs and natural resources are found.

Nevertheless, strong leadership from the government on the EITI, whether legislative or administrative, would promote the values of transparency and accountability in government that it espoused in opposition, providing it with moral authority to pursue recalcitrant businesses or sectors. Continuing with the EITI, which is widely considered to be a Thein Sein initiative, and giving credit to his government for what it achieved in this area, would earn it plaudits, and possibly greater co-operation, from the military and its associated businesses. Support for the EITI would create a culture of disclosure that spreads to other parts of the natural resources sector, and eventually to other parts of government and society as well.

A potential danger for civil society actors participating in the EITI is that its administrative requirements and focus on transparency consume scarce resources, preventing them from addressing other governance issues, such as human rights or environmental degradation. From the evidence of the process so far, however, CSOs have managed to both participate in the EITI and continue with work in other areas; their attempts, which were often successful, to broaden the agenda of the MSG demonstrated their power, with international support, in pursuing broader goals within the EITI process itself.

In a sense the EITI is an iterative process. Myanmar's first EITI Report was full of omissions and inaccuracies, but by documenting and highlighting these errors subsequent reports should improve the accuracy of reporting. As these reports are published it is the role of civil society and other stakeholders to analyse the information and use it to advocate for more broad-based and equitable development strategies than the ones that have hitherto been adopted. Given Myanmar governments' historical lack of consultation with civil society, the EITI and its international oversight played a crucial role in establishing civil society as a legitimate actor within natural resource governance in the country. As EIAs and public consultation become the norm within Myanmar's environmental governance system it should not be forgotten how paradigm-shattering the initial negotiations associated with the EITI were.

References

Aaronson, S. A. 2011. 'Limited Partnership: Business, Government, Civil Society, And The Public in the Extractive Industries Transparency Initiative (EITI)'. 31(1) *Public Administration and Development* 50–63.

Adam Smith International. 2015. *Institutional and Regulatory Assessment of the Extractive Industries in Myanmar*. London: Adam Smith International and MDRI-CESD. Available at http://documents.worldbank.org/curated/en/docsearch/report/96445 (accessed 1 September 2015).

Asian Development Bank (ADB). 2016. *Launch Ceremony: EIA Procedures and Environmental Quality Guidelines*. Bangkok: Asian Development Bank, Greater Mekong Subregion, Core Environment Program. Available at http://www.gms-eoc.org/events/launch-ceremony-eia-procedure-and-environmental-quality-guidelines (accessed 10 October 2016).

Bauer, A., P. Shortell and L. Delesgues. 2016. *Sharing the Wealth: A Roadmap for Distributing Myanmar's Natural Resource Revenues*. New York: Natural Resource Governance Institute (NRGI). Available at http://www.resourcegovernance.org/sites/default/files/nrgi_sharing_Myanmar_Revenue-Sharing.pdf (accessed 18 February 2016).

Brooten, L. and R. Metro. 2014. 'Thinking about Ethics in Burma Research'. 18(1) *Journal of Burma Studies* 1–22.

Central Statistical Organization. 2016a. *Central Statistical Organization*. Naypyitaw: Ministry of Planning and Finance. Available at http://www.csostat.gov.mm/ (accessed 21 June 2016).

2016b. *Myanmar Statistical Information Service (MMSIS)*. Available at http://www.mmsis.gov.mm/ (accessed 22 December 2016).

Cheesman, N. 2015. *Opposing the Rule of Law: How Myanmar's Courts Make Law and Order*. Cambridge: Cambridge University Press.

Cornish, G. and V. Vivoda. 2016. 'Myanmar's Extractive Industries: An Institutional and Regulatory Assessment'. 3(4) *Extractive Industries and Society* 1,075–1,083.

Crouch, M. 2018. 'Judiciary' in A. Simpson, N. Farrelly and I. Holliday (eds), *Routledge Handbook of Contemporary Myanmar*. London and New York: Routledge.

David-Barrett, L. and K. Okamura. 2013. *The Transparency Paradox: Why do Corrupt Countries Join EITI?* Berlin: European Research Centre for Anti-Corruption and State-Building. Available at http://www.againstcorruption.eu/ (accessed 20 November 2015).

Doyle, T. and A. Simpson. 2006. 'Traversing More than Speed Bumps: Green Politics under Authoritarian Regimes in Burma and Iran'. 15(5) *Environmental Politics*. November 750–767.

EITI International Secretariat. 2013. *The EITI Standard*. Oslo: Extractive Industries Transparency Initiative (EITI) International Secretariat. Available at http://eiti.org/files/English_EITI STANDARD_11July_0.pdf (accessed 10 November 2015).

———. 2016. *The EITI Standard 2016*. Oslo: Extractive Industries Transparency Initiative (EITI) International Secretariat. Available at https://eiti.org/files/english_eiti_standard_0.pdf (accessed 15 March 2016).

———. 2017. *Extractive Industries Transparency Initiative*. Oslo: Extractive Industries Transparency Initiative (EITI). Available at http://eiti.org (accessed 1 June 2017).

European Parliament and Council of the European Union. 2013. EU Accounting (and Transparency) Directives (Country by Country Reporting): New Disclosure Requirements for the Extractive Industry and Loggers of Primary Forests (Directive 2013/34/EU). Strasbourg: European Union. Available at http://eur-lex.europa.eu/legal-content/EN/TXT/PDF/?uri= CELEX:32013L0034&from=EN (accessed 1 December 2016).

Fink, C. and A. Simpson. 2018. 'Civil Society' in A. Simpson, N. Farrelly and I. Holliday (eds), *Routledge Handbook of Contemporary Myanmar*. London and New York: Routledge.

Ford, M., M. Gillan and H. H. Thein. 2016. 'From Cronyism to Oligarchy? Privatisation and Business Elites in Myanmar'. 46(1) *Journal of Contemporary Asia* 18–41.

Fortify Rights and International Human Rights Clinic. 2015. *Crackdown at Letpadan: Excessive Use of Force and Violations of the Rights to Freedom of Peaceful Assembly and Expression in Letpadan, Bago Region, Myanmar*. Bangkok: Fortify Rights and Harvard Law School International Human Rights Clinic. Available at http://www.fortifyrights.org/ downloads/FR_Crackdown_At_Letpadan_October_2015.pdf (accessed 11 October 2015).

Global Witness. 2015. *Jade: Myanmar's 'Big State Secret'*. London: Global Witness. Available at https://www.globalwitness.org/reports/myanmarjade/ (accessed 23 October 2015).

Haufler, V. 2010. 'Disclosure as Governance: The Extractive Industries Transparency Initiative and Resource Management in the Developing World'. August, 10(3) *Global Environmental Politics* 53–73.

Heller, P. R. P. and L. Delesgues. 2016. *Gilded Gatekeepers: Myanmar's State-Owned Oil, Gas and Mining Enterprises*. New York: Natural Resource Governance

Institute (NRGI). Available at http://www.resourcegovernance.org/sites/default/files/nrgi_Myanmar-State-Owned-Enterprises_Full-Report.pdf (accessed 18 February 2016).

Irwin, E. 2016. *Gemstone Sector Review (Summary Version): In support of Myanmar EITI*. Yangon: Myanmar Extractive Industries Transparency Initiative (MEITI).

Joliffe, K. 2015. *Ethnic Armed Conflict and Territorial Administration in Myanmar*. Yangon: Asia Foundation. Available at http://asiafoundation.org/resources/pdfs/ConflictTerritorialAdministrationfullreportENG.pdf (accessed 15 November 2015).

Jones, L. 2014. 'The Political Economy of Myanmar's Transition'. 44(1) *Journal of Contemporary Asia* 144–170.

——— 2018. 'Political Economy' in A. Simpson, N. Farrelly and I. Holliday (eds), *Routledge Handbook of Contemporary Myanmar*. London and New York: Routledge.

Kirchherr, J., K. J. Charles and M. J. Walton. 2016. 'The Interplay of Activists and Dam Developers: The Case of Myanmar's Mega-Dams'. 33(1) *International Journal of Water Resources Development* 111–131.

Kolstad, I. and A. Wiig. 2009. 'Is Transparency the Key to Reducing Corruption in Resource-Rich Countries?' 37(3) *World Development* 521–532.

MacLean, K. 2014. 'Counter-Accounting with Invisible Data: The Struggle for Transparency in Myanmar's Energy Sector'. 37(1) *PoLAR: Political and Legal Anthropology Review* 10–28.

MEITI. 2014. *MEITI Candidacy Application Form*. Naypyitaw: Myanmar Extractive Industries Transparency Initiative (MEITI). Available at http://eiti.org/files/MEITI-application.pdf (accessed 9 June 2014).

——— 2015. *Myanmar EITI Annual Activity Report: July 2014-June 2015*. Yangon: Myanmar Extractive Industries Transparency Initiative.

——— 2016. *Myanmar EITI Annual Activity Report: July 2015-June 2016*. Yangon: Myanmar Extractive Industries Transparency Initiative.

Moore Stephens. 2015a. *Myanmar Extractive Industries Transparency Initiative: Scoping Study for the First EITI Report – For the Period April 2013-March 2014*. London: Moore Stephens.

——— 2015b. *Myanmar Extractive Industries Transparency Initiative: EITI Report for the Period April 2013-March 2014 – Oil Gas and Mining Sectors*. London: Moore Stephens.

Mouan, L. C. 2010. 'Exploring the Potential Benefits of Asian Participation in the Extractive Industries Transparency Initiative: The Case of China'. 19(6) *Business Strategy and the Environment* 367–376.

Natural Resource Governance Institute. 2013. *The 2013 Resource Governance Index: A Measure of Transparency and Accountability in the Oil, Gas and Mining Sector*. New York: Natural Resource Governance Institute (formerly

Revenue Watch Institute). Available at https://resourcegovernance.org/sites/
default/files/rgi_2013_Eng.pdf (accessed 1 June 2017).

NCRA. 2015. *A $12bn Jade and Gem Industry Rides to the Kyat's Rescue*. Yangon:
New Crossroads Asia. Available at http://www.newcrossroadsasia.com/
(accessed 10 November 2015).

Open Myanmar Initiative. 2016. *OMI Budget Explorer*. Available at http://budget
.omimyanmar.org/ (accessed 24 December 2016).

Reuters. 2015. 'Myanmar Gems Sales Slump as Conflict Stems Jade Supply'. 9 July.
Available at http://www.reuters.com/article/2015/07/09/myanmar-jade-idU
SL3N0ZP2DH20150709 (accessed10 November 2015).

Rich, E. and T. N. Warner. 2012. 'Addressing the Roots of Liberia's Conflict
through the Extractive Industries Transparency Initiative' in P. Lujala and S.
A. Rustad (eds), *High-Value Natural Resources and Peacebuilding*. London:
Earthscan.

Rustad, S. C. A., J. K. Rød, W. Larsen and N. P. Gleditsch. 2008. 'Foliage and
Fighting: Forest Resources and the Onset, Duration, and Location of Civil
War'. 27 *Political Geography* 761–782.

Securities and Exchange Commission. 2016. *Disclosure of Payments by Resource
Extraction Issuers, Final Rule*, 17 CFR Parts 240 and 249b, Release No. 34–
78167; File No. S7-25-15, RIN 3235-AL53. Washington DC: US Securities and
Exchange Commission.

Shortell, P. 2017 'Does Myanmar Need a Gemstone Law?'. *Myanmar Times*. 25
January. Available at http://www.mmtimes.com/index.php/opinion/24686-
does-myanmar-need-a-gemstone-law.html (accessed 2 June 2017).

Simpson, A. 2007. 'The Environment-Energy Security Nexus: Critical Analysis of
an Energy 'Love Triangle' in Southeast Asia'. April, 28(3) *Third World Quarterly*
539–554.

2013. 'Challenging Hydropower Development in Myanmar (Burma): Cross-
Border Activism under a Regime in Transition'. 26(2) *The Pacific Review*
129–152.

2015. 'Starting from Year Zero: Environmental Governance in Myanmar'
in S. Mukherjee and D. Chakraborty (eds), *Environmental Challenges
and Governance: Diverse Perspectives from Asia*. London and New York:
Routledge.

2017. *Energy, Governance and Security in Thailand and Myanmar (Burma):
A Critical Approach to Environmental Politics in the South*. Updated edition.
Copenhagen: NIAS Press.

2018. 'Corruption, Investment and Natural Resources' in S. Alam, J. Bhuiyan
and J. Razzaque (eds), *International Natural Resources Law, Investment and
Sustainability*. London and New York: Routledge.

Simpson, A., N. Farrelly and I. Holliday (eds). 2018. *Routledge Handbook of
Contemporary Myanmar*. London and New York: Routledge.

Simpson, A. and S. Park. 2013. 'The Asian Development Bank as a Global Risk Regulator in Myanmar'. 34(10) *Third World Quarterly* 1858–1871.

South, A. 2009. *Ethnic Politics in Burma: States of Conflict*. London and New York: Routledge.

Sovacool, B. and N. Andrews. 2015. 'Does transparency Matter? Evaluating the Governance Impacts of the Extractive Industries Transparency Initiative (EITI) in Azerbaijan and Liberia'. September, 45 *Resources Policy* 183–192.

Sturesson, A. and T. Zobel. 2015. 'The Extractive Industries Transparency Initiative (EITI) in Uganda: Who Will Take the Lead When the Government Falters?'. January, 2(1) *The Extractive Industries and Society* 33–45.

Transparency International. 2017. *Corruption Perceptions Index 2016*. Berlin: Transparency International. Available at https://www.transparency.org/news/feature/corruption_perceptions_index_2016 (accessed 1 June 2017).

Van Alstine, J. 2014. 'Transparency in Resource Governance: The Pitfalls and Potential of "New Oil" in Sub-Saharan Africa'. 14(1) *Global Environmental Politics* 20–39.

United Nations (2017) *UN Comtrade Database*. Available at https://comtrade.un.org/data/. (accessed 2 June 2017).

Walton, M. J. 2013. 'The "Wages of Burmanness": Ethnicity and Burman Privilege in Contemporary Myanmar'. 43(1) *Journal of Contemporary Asia* 1–27.

World Bank. 2015a. *Myanmar*. Washington DC: World Bank. Available at http://www.worldbank.org/en/country/myanmar (accessed 10 January 2016).

2015b. *Myanmar: Public Expenditure Review*. Washington DC: The World Bank. Available at http://documents.worldbank.org/curated/en/5041214 67987907393/pdf/103993-WP-P132668-PUBLIC-Myanmar-PER-Dec-2015.pdf (accessed 1 December 2016).

Ye Mon and Kyi Kyi Sway. 2016. 'Jade Mining Permit Extensions Suspended'. *Myanmar Times*. 27 July. Available at http://www.mmtimes.com/index.php/business/21593-jade-mining-permit-extensions-suspended.html (accessed 2 February 2017).

4

The Risky Business of Transformation

Social Enterprise in Myanmar's Emerging Democracy

JOHN DALE AND DAVID KYLE

Democratic Transformation Is Risky Business

Social enterprises – businesses that trade for a social or environmental purpose – have been gaining currency in the United Kingdom, the United States and many countries of Southeast Asia as well. This chapter examines the emerging social enterprise sector in Myanmar (see Table 4.1), which is poised to expand in the wake of the country's democratic political transition. Increasingly, international development institutions and investors embrace the notion that social enterprises can play an important role in promoting social inclusion and reducing inequality. The collective consensus is that a thriving social enterprise sector might serve as a democratising force in Myanmar. However, the relationship between social enterprise and democracy remains unclear, even where it thrives outside Myanmar. Can social enterprise thrive in societies with weak democratic institutions? And if not, what kinds of basic democratic safeguards are necessary for a sustainable social enterprise sector that might, in turn, strengthen existing democratic institutions and contribute to the creation of new ones?

We suggest that the value of social enterprises in Myanmar lies in its capacity to transform structures of social inequality in ways that deepen democracy in the polity, economy and society. Such a transformation requires democratic experimentation and risk-taking that invites political opposition. A sustainable social enterprise sector will require social entrepreneurs who have sufficient democratic rights, backed by the law *and practice* of the state, to engage in the ongoing risky business of deepening democracy. It also will require conditions in which *all* citizens are free to engage in social entrepreneurship.

Myanmar's general elections in November 2015 culminated in a landmark victory for the country's pro-democracy movement. But the democratic transition is far from over. The new government will face resistance from many camps in its own continuing efforts to advance democracy. The country's transition is not only a struggle for political democracy, but also for economic democracy. And that struggle to achieve both is taking place within a fragmented nation, but also within a rapidly changing global society.

The new government seeks to address the many social inequalities that the Myanmar state has institutionalised in law, policy, rules and regulations over the past decades under the military's leadership. It also will have to do so under rapidly changing economic conditions that threaten to introduce new sources of social inequality. The past legacy of military rule still hampers the ideas and initiatives of individuals, particularly of those who engage in the work of democratic social change. Later in this chapter, we devote special attention to Myanmar's former political prisoners – activists, artists, journalists, students, monks, politicians and others – who remain stigmatised with criminal records for their past efforts to institutionalise democracy in Myanmar. We explain how recent legal reform intended to improve the operational environment for Myanmar's business and civil society organisations (CSOs), combined with existing law, has failed to address the basic conditions necessary for the participation of former political prisoners in the creation of democratically transformative social enterprises.

What Is a Social Enterprise?

Appreciation for the activity comprising social enterprise in Myanmar begins with understanding the practice, scale and transnational ecosystem of support for social enterprise beyond Myanmar. Business with a social conscience is not new. There have been philanthropists as long as there have been exploitative industrialists. What is becoming a rising force are the networks of regional and interregional entrepreneurs – often distinguished as 'social entrepreneurs' – who have the same goal of benefitting society through more profit-conscious and efficient means. Social Enterprise UK, the United Kingdom's national body for the social enterprise sector, defines social enterprise as

> a business that trades for a social and/or environmental purpose. It will have a clear sense of its 'social mission', which means that it will know what difference it is trying to make, who it aims to help, and how it plans to do it.

> It will bring in most or all of its income from selling goods or services, and it will also have clear rules about what it does with its profits, reinvesting these to further the 'social mission'.[1]

Social enterprise has been gaining currency in North America and Europe for a generation. The United Kingdom has more than 60,000 social enterprises, according to a 2009 government study, which contribute more than US$34 billion to the economy (Bland 2010: 14). But this movement has experienced a particular rise from a new generation of college-educated graduates unable to find employment in the wake of the global financial crisis. These self-employed social entrepreneurs are creating a new vocabulary to describe their practices. Many of them work together through a transnational network of 'social impact hubs' in more than seventy cities spanning five continents that encourage 'creative collaboration', 'knowledge sharing' and 'social networking'. These social entrepreneurs have emerged as a new category of brokers between 'social impact investors' and the social beneficiaries whose lives they primarily seek to transform or the social problems they seek to solve. They work with (and often as) social enterprise 'incubators' and connect their members to businesses, governments and non-governmental institutional investors who serve as 'accelerators', helping them to 'scale-up' their operations in an effort to achieve greater financial sustainability and social impact.

Social enterprises are distinguishable from non-governmental organisations (NGOs). The main difference between them is the revenue model. NGOs rely primarily on foundation grants, public funding and charitable donations to support their programmes and cover their administrative overhead. Social enterprises rely less heavily on donor funds because they create social programmes that are meant to be self-sustaining. Social entrepreneurs invest in social ventures and generate their own revenues to sustain themselves.

A social enterprise is thus, first and foremost, a business, although like an NGO, it constitutes part of the social sector. It has a steady stream of income, and just like any other company, it takes loans, invites capital investments and forms partnerships to expand its business activities. The main goal of an NGO is to create social value, without much regard for the business bottom line, while the social enterprise aims, within a business model, to achieve sustainability in the financial and social (and often even the environmental) sense.

---

[1] http://www.socialenterprise.org.uk/about/about-social-enterprise/FAQs.

The creators of these social enterprises, particularly those in or from the United States, United Kingdom or Western Europe, but increasingly in parts of Southeast Asia as well, say that they inhabit a social frontier, sometimes referred to as the 'emerging fourth sector'. This is a projected space of entrepreneurial action where outmoded laws and inappropriate, old-style legal entities hamstring their socially transformative plans. Increasingly, they are pressuring governments to legislate new laws, particularly new types of hybrid business entities, to provide a more variegated legal structure to this emerging fourth sector.

There are a variety of ways social enterprises may be legally structured. In the United States, social enterprises may be legally structured as non-profit organisations, for-profit companies, co-operatives, microenterprises, benefit (or B) corporations, low-profit limited liability corporations (L3Cs) or flexible-purpose corporations, amongst others. In the United Kingdom, social enterprises are classified under the legal form 'community interest company'. Not to be confused with just any 'social business' that may endorse or sponsor a charitable cause or campaign for social change (for example, Body Shop) while selling shares on the stock exchanges of New York or London, the primary objective of a social enterprise's action is social in nature. It is not primarily profit-driven. Again, this does not mean that social enterprises do not generate profits or revenues, but rather that they primarily reinvest any profit to expand or enhance the achievement of the venture's social objectives. The profits do not accrue to owners or shareholders. A social enterprise does not exist to remunerate capital. And social enterprises are audited accordingly. In principle, they are regulated within the terms and boundaries of the legal organisational form through which they are constituted.

More recently, with the encouragement of the Asian Development Bank (ADB) and the Asia-Europe Foundation, emerging economies in Asia have embraced the development of social enterprises. Perhaps the strongest example is Thailand, which has created an infrastructure for social enterprises that is seen as a model in Southeast Asia. The sector has its own representative body, the Thai Social Enterprise Office (TSEO). The sector also has the support of political and business leaders, attracts consistent mainstream media coverage and has established organisational ties to social enterprise sectors in the United Kingdom and other countries.

There is also a rapidly developing social enterprise scene in Malaysia, and Vietnam's Enterprise Law was revised in 2014 to provide a legal definition of social enterprise. According to the legislation, social entrepreneurs will be 'considered for special treatment' in the granting of licences and certificates. They will also be able to obtain funding, sponsorship and investment from Vietnamese and foreign individuals, enterprises and NGOs to cover their operational and administration costs. Recognising the importance of social enterprises to national growth, the Vietnamese government promised to 'encourage, support and promote the development of social enterprises' (Jenkins 2015).

Social Enterprise in Myanmar

Reflecting the global trend in the rise of social enterprise, Myanmar is now home to many such initiatives. In Yangon, the organisation FXB Myanmar provides vocational training and business opportunities to HIV-positive workers and women rescued from the Thai sex industry and transnational human-smuggling operations (with links to Myanmar) that supply it. Proximity Designs, a manufacturer of locally affordable foot-powered irrigation pumps, has a network of distribution channels to up-country farmers that surpasses those of NGOs and governmental organisations. BusinessKind-Myanmar sells low-cost mosquito netting in malarial and dengue fever regions, and half of its workforce is also HIV-positive. Myanmar Business Executives provides low-interest micro-credit and networking outlets to needy individuals and organisations. What these initiatives have in common is that they use business models to achieve social benefits. These companies produce multiple products and services, have sales strategies and target markets, and even make a profit, though much of that is redirected to social causes. Some receive grants from international NGOs or aid agencies, but the products are generally low-cost necessities accompanied by community-based education instructing how to maximise their effectiveness and/or maintain the technologies. They generally avoid donations and charity, and strive to achieve financial sustainability. There are many examples of these kinds of ventures operating in Myanmar – most of which have emerged in the wake of the 2008 Cyclone Nargis disaster that occurred at the height of the global financial crisis. All of these ventures may be considered social enterprises (see the Appendix).

Yet, in Myanmar, the vast majority of ventures operating in ways that might fit the definition of a social enterprise do not refer to themselves as such. There are many small for-profit businesses that give priority to their social mission, and many NGOs that, under newly drafted Association Laws in Myanmar, are now able and eager to generate revenues or 'transform' themselves into microfinance institutions (Duflos et al. 2013) that provide investment and training to the many individuals, groups and communities with whom they have been working for decades (when they were funded largely by grants and philanthropic donations).

Unlike its counterparts in the United States, United Kingdom, Western Europe and parts of Southeast Asia, the social enterprise sector in Myanmar is emerging in the absence of legal recognition for such entities – no such legal recognition for social enterprises exists. In a legal sense, all social enterprises in Myanmar operate in the informal economy. Nevertheless, many ventures operating in Myanmar are already self-identifying as 'social enterprises'. Some, especially those with experience in social enterprise sectors in the United States, United Kingdom and parts of Southeast Asia outside Myanmar, are operating in the hope that, as their practices gain social recognition, acceptance and appeal, they one day will also gain what they perceive to be the benefits of legal recognition.

These benefits extend beyond consideration for special treatment in granting licences and certificates, and the ability to cover operational and administrative costs through local and foreign funding, sponsorship and investment. They help to reinforce the kind of legal entity that distinguishes a social enterprise from existing for-profit and non-profit enterprises. For example, for-profits emphasise shareholder value, yet social enterprises pay more attention to their impact on all stakeholders. For-profit and non-profit legal and tax models are not designed for the simultaneous pursuit of social and financial bottom lines. When founders choose a for-profit form, they have no reliable way of ensuring commitment to the social mission. And board members, mindful of their fiduciary duty, may find it hard to prioritise social and environmental concerns over the interests of shareholders. But legally recognised social enterprises, after identifying the groups that are essential to their organisation's success and clarifying the value proposition for each, have been able to negotiate unconventional roles, responsibilities and incentives that increase stakeholders' engagement with the mission – and to have this reflected in shareholder agreements, loan contracts and other financial instruments.

Furthermore, one of the most difficult challenges that social enterprises face is preserving their social mission after an ownership transfer. It is often assumed that owners drive governance, but ownership is a collection of legal rights that can be unbundled and repackaged in creative ways. Thoughtful ownership and governance design can protect the mission over the long term and deepen stakeholder engagement. But this can be difficult in the absence of legal recognition (and accompanying rights), as well as in the absence of a supportive institutional ecosystem that recognises and values the legitimate differences between for-profit, non-profit and social enterprises.

It is becoming clear that, since 2014, Myanmar is beginning to gain transnational access to a supportive institutional ecosystem that is largely operating outside the country. Social enterprises, or 'for-benefit' enterprises, increasingly are finding access to such a supportive institutional ecosystem (Sabeti 2011). These institutions provide services beyond those of traditionally business-minded legal and accounting firms or consultancies. They represent an emerging inter-organisational field (Warren 1967; Wooten and Hoffman 2013) in which institutional entrepreneurs (Dimaggio 1988; Fligstein 1997; Zucker 1988; Lawrence 1999; Beckertt 1999; Maguire, Hardy and Lawrence 2004; Rao, Monin and Durand 2003) are attempting to create a new space, language and identity for the meaningful action of social enterprises.

But the socially transformative power of social enterprises does not lie in its ability to financially 'do better' than traditional non-profit or donor-dependent 'do-gooders'. Such a strategy could amount only to privatising the 'third sector', and possibly marginalising important areas of development that require great courage and risk to address – often over extensive periods of time. Rarely are such endeavours financially rewarding in terms imagined at the outset of most business proposals. Nevertheless, such endeavours can have invaluable unforeseen social gains. Rather, the critical difference lies in the quality of *social innovation* that such a sector might bring to bear on the institutions that generate social inequality.

The promise of social enterprises in Myanmar lies in its capacity to address social inequality in ways that deepen democracy. It is too soon to say whether social enterprises can deliver on this promise. We do not argue for or against the legal recognition of social enterprises in Myanmar. Instead, we raise as a question what foreign advocates of social enterprise and many transplanting social entrepreneurs in Myanmar have taken for granted: can you have transformative social enterprises if you do not have democracy? Or, more pointedly, in the absence of democratic safeguards for all social entrepreneurs, not just some or many, does the promotion of a social enterprise sector simply amount to a new strategy for introducing market discipline to the work that NGOs and other CSOs have been doing for decades? How much risk can social entrepreneurs afford to take in attempting to solve the most durable or pressing problems of inequality under conditions in which their own equality remains legally, politically or culturally unprotected? Despite rhetoric to the contrary, can Myanmar harness and legitimate the potential power of its emerging social enterprise sector in ways that prevent it from becoming just another means of social and political marginalisation?

What makes Myanmar an interesting case study in the development of the social enterprise movement is that it offers an opportunity to study how not only a social enterprise sector emerges, but also the dynamics of the broader institutional context that shape and are shaped by its emergence. From the perspective of international investors, Myanmar now represents a 'frontier market', ripe for risky, potentially high-yielding investment returns – particularly in the area of Internet and communications technology (ICT) (see Dale and Kyle 2015). Many social enterprises in Myanmar are already incorporating such technology into business plans and their quest to solve social problems.

From the perspective of international development institutions such as the ADB, Myanmar represents a developing economy in Southeast Asia that will have to incorporate frontier technologies and develop public policies encouraging social entrepreneurship and social impact investing as the region shifts its primary strategy for economic growth from export-led, cheap-labour manufacturing to an integrated network of innovation-based knowledge economies. In doing so, it argues that its strongest emerging economies will be able to escape the 'middle-income trap' and revitalise economic growth through qualitative innovation that will make up for the economic drag of these countries' rising wages (and consumption) and concomitantly falling rates of productivity.

At the same time, the ADB envisions the region's emerging (and frontier) economies as being able to bring innovative codified and tacit knowledge – technologies and communities of practice – to bear on its fundamentally agricultural economy. The ADB plans to do so while also laying the infrastructural groundwork in other sectors (for example, cultural heritage and tourism, public health, the environment and especially education and ICT) to leap-frog the development problems that it anticipates (based on past experience) the region soon will face as its cities rapidly become new Asian 'megacities'.

Yangon, Mandalay and even Naypyidaw are on course to become megacities within the next one to two decades (Dale and Kyle 2015). As a result, Myanmar now finds itself awash in financial capital and celebrated as one of Asia's most alluring 'frontier markets'[2] and potentially lucrative

---

[2] The term 'frontier market' was coined by International Finance Corporation's Farida Khambata in 1992, and is commonly used to describe the equity markets of the smaller and

destinations for foreign direct investment, including venture capital investment. Myanmar's government too is garnering substantial credit, loans and investment from regional and global financial institutions.

The social enterprise context in Myanmar is complicated by high levels of investment due to the promise and opportunity of a democratic transition. To fulfil its promise to lead the country towards a more meaningful democratic transformation, Myanmar's newly elected government will have to make tough decisions about how to manage these new economic flows in ways that do not create greater social inequality amongst its citizens. Simply opening the floodgates to flows of global capital will not ensure inclusive or sustainable growth. Indeed, as has been the case for many countries in Asia (and in other regions of the world), such an economic strategy may serve only to exacerbate or deepen existing social inequality within Myanmar.

The New Development Discourse on Inequality

The rise of social enterprise in Myanmar comes at a time of a global shift in development discourse on inequality. In its 2012 Annual Report, the ADB declared that social inequality posed the greatest threat to stability and future economic growth in the Asian region (ADB 2012a: 2, 8). The report begins by highlighting the strength and success of Asia's economies. Over the past twenty-five years, driven mostly by cheap labour, economies in Asia have yielded unprecedented growth rates and contributions to the global economy. Asia is now the growth engine of the global economy. This report also emphasises that, in the past two decades, the drivers of Asia's economic success, such as new technology, globalisation and market-oriented reforms, have served to create disparities not only between but also within Asian countries. In some Asian countries, for example, the richest 1 per cent of households account for close to 10 per cent of total consumption. The ADB notes that 'the widening gap is not only in income, but rather inequality of opportunity and access to public services is also prevalent, and a crucial factor in widening income inequality' (ADB 2012a: 2, 8). This emphasis on inequality reflects a

---

less accessible, but still 'investable', countries of the developing world. It is understood to be less developed than an 'emerging market', yet more developed than the economies of 'least developing countries'. The frontier, or pre-emerging, equity markets are typically pursued by investors seeking high, long-run return potential as well as low correlations with other markets.

general and significant shift in discourse deployed by international development institutions.

In 2000, when the United Nations announced its Millennium Development Goals for 2030, the focus was clearly on eradicating poverty. Inequality, however, was not on the agenda. The World Bank as well was focused squarely on poverty, as evident in its 1999 report (World Bank 1999). Fifteen years later, and in the wake of a long global financial crisis, international governmental development institutions are putting economic and social inequality on their agendas.

Although slow to acknowledge it, the United Nations, the World Bank, the International Monetary Fund (IMF), the Organisation for Economic and Co-Operative Development (OECD), the British Council and the World Economic Forum have also produced reports over the past two years that highlight the threats that not only poverty, but social inequality, pose to sustainable global economic growth (United Nations 2014; Gill and Kharas 2015; Lagarde 2015; OECD 2015; British Council 2015; World Economic Forum 2015). Recent reports capture this shift in discourse on economic development (British Council 2015: 6–7).

Neoliberal economists have long suggested that global economic growth since the 1970s has overall benefitted both the rich and poor. The rich and poor alike have experienced improved standards of living – even if the rich have experienced greater improvement in their standard of living. The painful exception to this, they acknowledge, by the end of the 1990s was Africa – where the poor have become poorer. Neoliberal economists' concern with *poverty* is that it contributes to conflict and global economic stability. The same economists, however, saw inequality as unproblematic. The fact that inequality was growing substantially during this same period was explained away as a moral trade-off – the necessary incentives required to attract the most productive economic leaders driving the benefits of a larger global economic pie that met a greater proportion of the world's basic needs were understood to trump moral concerns about inequality. Overall, democracy would find more fertile soil globally in a world characterised by greater global economic growth.

Today, however, there is increasing concern that inequality, not just poverty, may also be contributing to conflict and global economic instability. While the British Council has framed this concern in what may sound like moral terms, alluding to an economic democratic deficit, most international development institutions describe the problem in more pragmatic terms. Regardless, the Council's new emphasis on social inequality as a problem for economic growth represents a window of opportunity for longtime proponents of efforts to address global inequality and more democratic global development.

Driving these international organisations' new development discourse on inequality is a broader vision of the role that innovation can play in revitalising economic growth. The development agencies of the United States, United Kingdom, European Union and, now, Asia are trying to focus not simply on models of 'efficiency innovation' (such as Wal-Mart's strategy of doing more with less – a strategy that does not create jobs but instead replaces them, as in the unfortunate case of Mexico). Instead, they are focusing on models that embed 'efficiency innovation' within models of 'market-creating innovation'. This latter type of model hitches the former to existing growth sectors of the global economy – such as ICT. This strategy of growth has resulted in net job gains for countries such as Taiwan.

Alongside growth, however, this new emphasis on inequality (particularly in developing and emerging economies) is focused on the role that business can play in supporting inclusive economic and social development, and shaping the institutional ecosystems, cultures and mindsets of people in developing countries in ways that contribute to financially sustainable social problem-solving. The idea is to channel 'social impact' investment capital to cultivate 'social entrepreneurship' in the hope of producing new forms of 'social innovation' that can address problems of inequality through the development of financially sustainable 'social enterprises'. As with the focus on poverty in the past, these development institutions still see markets as the source of solutions to social problems, including accessibility to healthcare, education, food – and even inequality.

Yet, there is little discussion at this point of how the social and legal organisation of markets, and relations of production and provision, may *introduce their own sources of social inequality* – even as they work, guided by 'missions with a social purpose', to attenuate social inequalities that stem from other relations. This is not to suggest that only profit-seeking enterprises introduce their own sources of social inequality (through, for example, capitalist/labour relations) that countervail their efforts to attenuate social problems of inequality. Large international non-governmental organisation (INGOs) and even small non-profit organisations are also susceptible to generating new sources of inequality through the ways in which they organise the (unevenly empowered) social relations through which they produce forms of transnational solidarity that span the global North and South (see Dale 2010a; 2010b; 2011; 2013; Bob 2002; Kurasawa 2007).

The point, rather, is that social innovation will require democratic experimentation in the ways that we socially organise (financially, socially and environmentally sustainable) social enterprises to solve the deep-rooted problems of inequality that global economic growth has both produced and amplified.[3] Short of such a transformative vision of social innovation, a development agenda that focuses on commodifying social problems in the name of social entrepreneurship and social innovation could be seen simply as a move to hijack the more (but still insufficient) transformative work that social activists have been doing for many decades, or to circumscribe the kind of activism that has focused on corporate accountability in cases where corporations have engaged in abusive human rights practices or extreme environmental degradation.

In Myanmar, international development institutions are promoting social enterprises that are forming primarily in the areas of ICT development, agricultural innovation and tourism-related services. To better understand this new emphasis on developing a social enterprise sector in Myanmar, and to appreciate the promises and perils facing the contested vision of social innovation shaping its currently emerging landscape, we must first understand its relationship to a broader growth and development strategy focused on innovation-based knowledge economies.

Creative Equality? Asian Innovation-Based Knowledge Economies

Myanmar's new government will also have to navigate a rapidly changing context of regional development in South and Southeast Asia. Development financial institutions such as the ADB have begun to frame a regional strategy that seeks to address what it characterises as the looming threat of slowing economic growth rates and social inequality. While countries such as China, Japan, the Republic of Korea and the city-state of Singapore all have been successfully developing innovation-based knowledge economies, most others in the region have hitched their economic growth more singularly to a manufacturing export-led strategy based on a strong supply of cheap labour and natural resources. Although there is no consensus on the definition of a 'knowledge economy'[4] there

---

[3] For a particularly robust vision of democratic experimentation and the potential benefits of the social innovation movement, see Roberto Unger (2015).

[4] Indeed, some question whether such a phenomenon is new, or whether it exists at all. The term 'knowledge economy' emerged in the 1960s (see Machlup 1962; Bell 1974; Porat and Rubin 1977). Smith (2002: 6) argues that it is a ubiquitous metaphor, not a useful scientific concept. Roberts and Armitage (2008) challenge the concept's validity by arguing that

have been various efforts to define the concept (see, for example, OECD 1996; Department for Trade and Industry 1998; Smith 2002; Powell and Snellman 2004; Brinkley 2006; Roberts and Armitage 2008). In line with these definitions, the United Kingdom's Economic and Social Research Council (ESRC) argues that the term 'knowledge economy' is used to describe the economic structure emerging in the global information society in which economic success increasingly depends on the effective use of intangible assets such as knowledge, skills and innovative potential (Economic and Social Research Council 2007; on the global information society, see for example Castells 1996). Now, with most low-income countries in the region expected to reach middle-income status by 2020, the ADB is urging these countries to catch up and create knowledge-based economies of their own. Failing to do so, they warn, most of these countries may find themselves stuck in the 'middle-income trap'.

Gill and Kharas (2015) coined the term 'middle-income trap' to describe economies like Asia's that were being 'squeezed between the low-wage poor-country competitors that dominate mature industries and the rich-country innovators that dominate in industries undergoing rapid technological change'. It is a condition in which rising wages and declining productivity (patterns associated with a growing middle class, as in the cases of Thailand, Indonesia, Malaysia and the Philippines) gradually contribute to slower overall economic growth (ADB 2014: 10). This diminishes the economic success that a country has achieved through its prior comparative labour advantage and once-plentiful natural resources.

The ADB is promoting a shift from a manufacturing export-led strategy based on a strong supply of cheap labour and natural resources to a strategy that fosters entrepreneurship within these countries, harnesses and institutionalises their creativity, and regionally integrates these countries' development of innovation-based knowledge economies. The idea behind this economic strategy is that creativity – the formulation of 'functional creations, scientific inventions and technological innovations' (UNCTAD 2008) – plays a critical role in shaping societies and economies. As the ADB succinctly puts it, '[f]ostering innovation, entrepreneurship, and creativity translates into direct and tangible economic

the contemporary economy is characterised as much by ignorance as it is by knowledge. Roberts (2009) extends the case more forcefully in challenging the notion of a 'global knowledge economy', which is characterised by highly uneven development with 'core' and 'periphery' economies to the extent that its meaningful integration is questionable and its utility for developing countries is suspect and likely more hegemonically beneficial to the core economies that promote its development in the peripheral ones.

outcomes' (ADB 2014a: 9). This understanding derives from an accumulating body of research and theoretical models associated with what economists refer to as 'new growth theory' (see for example Romer 1990; Lucas 1988; Burger-Helmchen 2013).

New growth theory, which began to emerge in the 1980s, changed the way that international development financial institutions such as the World Bank, IMF and OECD (amongst others) think about how capital and labour are combined to produce economic output. It suggests that something additional in the economic recipe has the effect of making already-productive economies even more productive. This additional element is technology, or human capital, or innovation. This theory was new in the sense that it tried to *explain* the role of technology within the model rather than *assuming* it, as had the 1987 Nobel Prize–winning research of economist Robert Solow. It is for this reason that this literature is also called '*endogenous* growth theory'. New growth theorists Paul Romer and Robert Lucas each suggested, in different ways, that knowledge, in the form of technology embodied in physical capital (Romer 1990; 1994) or in the form of technology as a part of the human capital stock (Lucas 1988), enables economies that have reached a high level of development to sustain or revitalise their growth momentum by increasing the *quality* of their productivity, rather than suffer a kind of inevitable decline in growth.

In 2014, in the wake of its 2012 annual report's emphasis on the threat posed to Asia by inequality, the ADB published two additional reports that elaborate on, and attempt to provide an empirical basis for measuring, the future progress towards the new strategy for Asia's economic growth and development – *Innovative Asia: Advancing the Knowledge Economy* (ADB 2014b) and, with the Economist Intelligence Unit, *Creative Productivity Index: Analyzing Creativity and Innovation in Asia* (ADB 2014c). The first report draws heavily on the World Bank's Knowledge Economy Index,[5] described in more detail later in this chapter, to measure and compare overall levels of knowledge production within Asian economies. The Knowledge Economy Index takes into account whether the environment is conducive for knowledge to be used effectively for economic development. It is an aggregate index that represents the overall level of development of a country or region towards the knowledge economy. The Knowledge Economy Index is calculated based on the average of the

---

[5] The World Bank's Knowledge Economy Index data is available at http://data.worldbank .org/data-catalog/KEI.

normalised performance scores of a country or region on four 'pillars' related to the knowledge economy: economic incentive and institutional regime; education and human resources; the innovation system; and ICT.

The second report proposes a new Creative Productivity Index to measure 'progress in fostering creativity and innovation' in twenty-two Asian economies (along with the United States and Finland). Other innovation-related indexes exist, such as the Global Innovation Index published by the World Intellectual Property Organization and INSEAD (one of the world's largest graduate business schools[6]) and the Global Creativity Index published by the Martin Prosperity Institute. But unlike these indexes, the Creative Productivity Index focuses on *efficiency*. The Creative Productivity Index comprises thirty-six input indicators and eight output indicators to measure how efficiently countries turn their creative inputs into innovation outputs, rather than just the overall level of creative inputs. This index measures creative inputs along three dimensions: capacity to innovate; incentives to innovate; and environment conducive to innovation (which also includes corruption and bureaucracy). It measures creative productivity (that is, creative outputs) by considering conventional indicators, such as the number of patents filed or scientific output, as well as a number of broader measures of knowledge creation. This, the report suggests, allows countries to seek the most effective – and affordable – innovation investments, and also captures elements of creativity that are more relevant in less developed countries, for example, agricultural innovation.

Taken together, these reports suggest a strategy in which the ADB already has started investing heavily. The ADB's strategy is to address the region's social inequality relative to other regions of the globe. Furthermore, they seek to address social inequality *between* countries in the region in ways that have implications for social inequality *within* these countries – including Myanmar.

The Measured Creativity of an Imagined Innovative Myanmar

Based on the Knowledge Economy Index and the Creative Productivity Index, we might conclude that Myanmar is a place where knowledge and creativity are scarce commodities. Myanmar ranks near or at the bottom of every dimension measured in both indexes. According to the Knowledge Economy Index, Myanmar does not have an environment

---

[6] See www.about.insead.edu/who_we_are/.

conducive to knowledge being used effectively for economic development. The Creative Productivity Index tells us that Myanmar lacks creative productivity. Myanmar's workers and enterprises have little capacity
or incentive to innovate. Nor does Myanmar appear to be efficient with
what little it has. Myanmar ranks 'low', twenty-second out of the twenty-
four countries measured – just below Bangladesh and Fiji, and just above
Pakistan and Cambodia. By contrast, Lao People's Democratic Republic
ranks 'high' (ninth), just above Singapore, People's Republic of China,
Indonesia and Malaysia. In short, it hardly seems likely that Myanmar
would be able to compete with other economies in the region by pursuing
the development of an innovation-based knowledge economy.

The construction of indexes such as the Knowledge Economy Index
and the Creative Productivity Index measures all economies in terms of
features associated with a knowledge economy, whether those countries
are actually attempting to develop one or not. It then uses these indexes
to compare their performance and ranks them in relation to each other
as though they are competing to develop knowledge economies. This
then lends the impression that there exists a regional or global knowledge
economy. The ADB claims, for instance, that Asia is poised to become a
leader in the 'global knowledge economy'. Yet, there is significant evidence
to suggest that the existence of a global knowledge economy is more a
value-laden projection than an empirical reality (see for example Roberts
2009; Graham 2014).

Indexes and ratings like these play a critical, and often problematic,
disciplinary role in global governance. The ranking and comparison of
states in indexes and ratings like these do not always help hold governments accountable in practice as they may simplify highly complex issues
and fail to contribute to genuine reform (Cooley and Snyder 2015: 102).
Particularly when these rankings are tied to sources of institutional investment or support, states are more likely to make changes that boost their
scores on particular indicators that, while improving their rankings, do
not reflect a commitment to the ideal being measured.

Today, the World Bank's vision of 'Knowledge for Development' is
about more than filling knowledge gaps in the unevenly developed global
economy. It is about putting creativity to work. It is a measured creativity (Kyle and Dale, forthcoming) that disciplines individual economies
to more efficiently produce not only knowledge as a commodity, but all
commodities – and with the aim of achieving more qualitative economic
growth or, better, innovative new directions that can be scaled up to
achieve new growing markets.

It is in the context of these reports that the ADB articulates its strategy for escaping the middle-income trap for Asia, which, it asserts, is likely to hold 50 per cent of the global middle class and 40 per cent of the global consumer market by 2020: 'It is time for Asia to consolidate and accelerate its path of growth.... And many developing economies are well placed to assimilate frontier technologies into their manufacturing environments' (ADB 2014a: 1).

It is also becoming increasingly apparent that this new government will have to confront the ongoing threat that both old and new sources of social inequality pose to the democratic transformation of its institutions – not only to the state, but also the economy and civil society. In this regard, it will have to carefully negotiate a growing international development paradigm that promotes social entrepreneurship and social enterprise as the prescriptive remedy for treating the local symptoms of social inequality caused by under- or mis-regulated global economic growth.

Social Entrepreneurship: Business as Usual or Transformative Agency?

Pursuing democratic institutional change in a climate of international development that is promoting social entrepreneurship raises a host of questions concerning what role the emerging social enterprise sector might play beyond merely attenuating social inequality through the creation of 'inclusive business' or 'business with a social purpose'. In particular, can a social enterprise sector stem the institutional production of inequality? Is it capable of fostering the kind of local democratic experimentation that could generate or unleash innovative social knowledge and practices that enhance the agency of social entrepreneurs – as both workers and citizens? Can such a sector create new, more democratically organised social enterprises and complementary institutions to expand the individual freedom and social wellbeing of those who work for and with them? What are the barriers (and limits) to its capacity to contribute to democratic institutional development? What are its proponents' priorities in fostering this nascent sector's growth? What international experience can be usefully applied in Myanmar, a frontier market in the midst of a critical period of democratic transition within an emerging regional knowledge economy?

It is useful at this point to consider what we might mean by 'social entrepreneurship'. In general, the organisational ventures themselves often are referred to as 'social enterprises'. But academic and business communities (mostly from the United States and Europe) have devised and distinguished several different conceptions of, and approaches to, social entrepreneurship. In the United States, the emphasis tends to focus on individual entrepreneurs and their creative business talent and leadership skills. In Europe, approaches to social entrepreneurship focus more on the organisation and the broader network in which it operates. In other words, there is a tendency in the United States to focus the agency of social entrepreneurship as the product or trait of atomistic individuals, while in Europe the tendency is to focus on the ways that the agency of social entrepreneurship is socially embedded in organisational and networked structures that enable, constrain or transform it. Nevertheless, Anja Cheriakova (2013) usefully identifies four concepts of social entrepreneurship, or schools of thought, spanning both sides of the Atlantic, each of which focuses on a different aspect of social entrepreneurship.

The first school of thought associates social entrepreneurship primarily with generating earned revenue. It reflects a socially justified commercial vision. This approach considers financial sustainability to be as important as a social mission. In the United States, the Social Enterprise Alliance, which began in 1998 as the National Gathering of Social Entrepreneurs, promotes this concept. According to its website, Social Enterprise Alliance is the largest network of social entrepreneurs and social enterprise practitioners in the United States.[7] Social enterprises seek to make a profit, or at least not to make a loss (Austin, Stevenson and Wei-Skillern 2006). As non-dividend companies designed to address a social objective (Yunus 2010), they can enhance their effectiveness by competing with commercial businesses in the market.

In Myanmar, where many basic needs have been unmet for so long, many commercial entrepreneurs claim that starting any financially sustainable business yields social benefits and might therefore well be considered a social enterprise. Building Markets is an organisation headquartered in New York that has projects in Afghanistan, Haiti, Mozambique and, as of 2013, Myanmar. Its Sustainable Marketplace Initiative in Myanmar (SMI-Myanmar) leverages the increasing scope and volume of international investment and assistance into opportunities for local small and medium-sized enterprises (SMEs) to grow their businesses and create jobs, 'thereby reducing poverty and guiding the economy on a path to sustainable

[7] See https://socialenterprise.us/about/what-we-do/.

development'.[8] They provide services and work with buyers to break down barriers to local procurement and build the capacity of local small and medium-sized enterprises, brokering their linkages to domestic and international opportunities. In its first three years, SMI-Myanmar helped local businesses win 200 contracts worth more than US$16 million, trained more than 500 businesses to navigate complicated international contractual standards and procurement requirements, and organised workshops for local CSOs to improve and formalise their local procurement strategies as well.

Complementing this vision of social entrepreneurship, the Myanmar Business Forum provides platforms for public-private dialogue – channels of exchange between the Myanmar government and the private sector, both domestic and foreign – to promote business reform, and to help companies grow and create jobs in a variety of sectors that sorely need them. The Forum consists of seven working groups in the sectors: natural resources; infrastructure; manufacturing/trade and investment; hotels and tourism; services; banking and finance; and agriculture, fisheries and forestry. Each working group identifies a limited number of common and significant issues that are critical to the effective development of the sector, and that require changes in law, regulation, policy or practice.

Impact hubs in Yangon, such as Project Hub and Ideabox, provide co-working space for young entrepreneurs and help them to incubate sustainable business and social enterprise plans. These hubs generate sustainable revenues through monthly membership fees. From the perspective of this first school of thought, all such activity might be seen as social entrepreneurship.

The second school of thought associates social entrepreneurship with social inclusion – typically, but not necessarily, in the formal market – through job creation. The main objective is to create employment for people such as the low-qualified unemployed or the disabled, who are normally excluded from the labour market. The social mission of work integration social enterprises (WISE) is to integrate excluded members into work and society through a productive activity. One example, to which we alluded earlier in this chapter, is BusinessKind-Myanmar, a non-profit organisation that establishes social businesses in poor and neglected Myanmar communities. Their businesses provide valued products and services at affordable prices and create employment opportunities for

[8] See http://buildingmarkets.org/our-impact/myanmar

vulnerable Myanmar women. For example, one of its social businesses, Good Sleep, sells low-cost mosquito netting in malarial and dengue fever regions, and through this venture has created jobs for many HIV-positive Myanmar women. Indeed, these women constitute half of its workforce.[9]

In Myanmar, WISEs like these are not uncommon. Another notable example is FXB Myanmar,[10] which rehabilitates victims of the sex-trafficking industry. It equips them with the tools and training to weave and make furniture, and enables them to work outside the sex industry. FXB has also developed a tailor-made 'mobile' professional training course to reach young girls living in the most remote regions of Myanmar, who do not have access to any of these kinds of services. When the budget allows, they provide these girls with their own sewing machines. Social enterprises like these, while emphasising their social mission to create employment for the low-qualified unemployed or disabled, are still subject to the pressures of competition from for-profit businesses, and internal politics within their own governing structure and associated with their own sources of finance. For instance, Pomelo, a WISE in Myanmar that produced handicrafts made by street children and persons with disabilities, was recently the subject of a 'hostile takeover',[11] and claims that its original team of designers is working to create a new social enterprise.

There are also many new WISEs emerging in the hospitality and tourism sectors. For example, Shwe Sa Ba, a hotel and restaurant training centre, and Linkage Restaurant and Art Gallery provide training to financially disadvantaged Myanmar youth who hope to pursue a career in the country's hospitality industry. And the Yangon Bakehouse Training Café trains disadvantaged women in baking and hospitality, and also teaches them 'livelihood' classes.

The third school of thought associates social entrepreneurship with social value and social impact more than revenue generation. That a social enterprise also engages in commerce is beside the point. The idea of doing so in ways that transcend the financial approach of traditional philanthropy is still important (Trexler 2008). But what matters most for this school of thought is the social impact that the organisation has on

---

[9] See http://www.businesskind.org/goodsleep/.

[10] See https://fxb.org/programs/myanmar/.

[11] See 'Get in Touch' at the bottom of Pomelo's website: http://www.pomelomyanmar.org/about-us#our-model. See also R. J. Vogt, 'Pomelo Founders Squeezed Out', *Myanmar Times* (Wednesday 2 March 2016), at http://www.mmtimes.com/index.php/lifestyle/19273-pomelo-founders-squeezed-out.html.

the local community. For example, Green Waves[12] is a social enterprise that has been evolving through a pilot project in Bogalay Township in the Ayeyarwaddy Delta, which was hit hard by Cyclone Nargis in 2008. For this project, Green Waves acquired 100 acres of damaged and abandoned land to be restored to productivity. They employed landless farm labourers from nearby communities, and provided them with training from volunteer visiting experts. They shared the profits from the harvests equitably between the labourers and the Green Waves social enterprise. The farmers they employed used their earnings to secure land as tenant farmers, and Green Waves used its share both to reinvest in the land and to distribute community-level grants to three local villages. They used these grants to start rural social enterprises (mostly livestock breeding), and then reinvested the profits from these enterprises into community education and infrastructure projects. Within three years, this project became financially self-sufficient.

The idea of using social innovation to solve everyday problems with new services and products fits into this school of thought. 'Social innovation' refers to the development of concepts and ideas that meet the social needs of people and that extend and strengthen civil society. Indeed, promoters of this idea of social entrepreneurship understand the concept itself to be a social innovation. More specifically, however, the term has commonly been used to describe how services and products can be made that can solve real problems in society, looking not only to technology as a solution, but also seeking new forms of organisation.

Proximity Designs, for example, winner of both the Skoll Foundation's and Schwab Foundation's Award for Social Entrepreneurship,[13] began in 2004 as a small social enterprise in Myanmar providing innovative irrigation foot-pumps to rural farmers in 600 villages. Today, Proximity Designs are accessible to 80 per cent of the rural population of Myanmar, a country in which 70 per cent of the population lives in rural areas. They have improved the incomes of roughly half a million farmers. Under their product brand name Yetagon, they now offer 'game-changing, smart designs that are having a major impact'.[14] They have diversified their design and product line of water pumps, and have developed drip irrigation systems, water storage tanks and, more recently, solar lighting products. The co-founders (and co-spouses) Jim Taylor and

---

[12] See http://www.greenwavessocialenterprise.org/index.html.
[13] See http://skoll.org/about/skoll-awards/.
[14] See http://proximitydesigns.org/products-services/irrigation-products.

Deddie Aung Din have created innovative short-term financing solutions for rural smallholders in need of crop loans, and have begun spinning these off into Proximity Finance, which provides growers with ongoing access to credit.[15]

This concept of social innovation has been related to social entrepreneurship, but not exclusively. All kinds of organisations can be involved, since social innovators strive to build (and socially broker) relationships between previously separated individuals and groups. Like social entrepreneurship, social innovation has been diversely conceptualised. The narrow definition of solving a local problem is more akin to the school of thought that focuses on social impact within social entrepreneurship.

This is related as well to the traditional definition of social innovation that gives priority to the internal organisation of firms to increase productivity. This is also the kind of social innovation that the ADB is focusing on when it uses the Creative Productivity Index to rank countries' progress towards knowledge innovation and development. It is related to the concept of 'disruptive innovation', a term of art coined in 1995 by Clayton Christensen to describe a process by which a product or service takes root initially in simple applications at the bottom of a market and then relentlessly moves up market, eventually displacing established competitors (Christiansen, Rayner and McDonald 2015). More recently, the international development community, including NGO practitioners, philanthropists and research experts, as well as social entrepreneurs, social enterprises and social impact investors, has been deploying the kindred concept of 'disruptive development', to refer to solutions that have a transformational impact on society and that improve lives.[16]

Increasingly, the scope and scale of such social impact entrepreneurship have turned to ICT solutions. For example, it has served as a critical dimension of one mode of social entrepreneurship that we have called 'smart humanitarianism' (Dale and Kyle 2015), which promotes a new kind of empathy required for social problem-solving and humanitarian action – one less sentimental, much more technocratic and managerial. Smart humanitarianism emphasises the human-machine partnership via online technologies, apps and expert systems management strategies, and redistributes the cognitive responsibilities of determining and delivering goods for greatest measurable impact with a quid pro quo of reframing inequality.

---

[15] See http://www.proximitydesigns.org/products-services/financial-services.
[16] See http://www.seattleglobalist.com/event/global-washington-7th-annual-conference-disruptive-development.

However, social innovation that focuses on the actual process of innovation – how innovation and change take shape – is more akin to a fourth school of thought that defines social entrepreneurship as socially transformative change agents. The focus is on the process of innovation through new forms of co-operation to find sustainable solutions to social problems (Unger 2015). J. Gregory Dees (1998), for example, defines social entrepreneurs as

> playing the role of agents in the social sector by adopting a mission to create and sustain social value, recognizing and relentlessly pursuing new opportunities to serve that mission, engaging in a process of continuous innovation, adaptation, and learning, acting boldly without being limited by resources currently in hand, and finally exhibiting a heightened sense of accountability to the constituencies served and for the outcomes created.

The objective is not simply to solve a single social problem, but rather to find sustainable solutions to the causes of a problem within a broader context and embedded in a process of continued learning and community participation. Social entrepreneurship in this sense means creating viable socioeconomic structures and relations that yield and sustain social benefits. As we alluded to earlier in the chapter, this concept of social entrepreneurship is also related to a particular, yet broadly conceived, understanding of social innovation that focuses on the actual process of innovation – how innovation and change take shape. This is a focus on the process of innovation with new forms of co-operation – particularly in a spirit of democratic experimentation (Unger 2015) – to find sustainable solutions to social problems.

Ashoka, now the largest worldwide network of social entrepreneurs, initially defined a social enterprise as 'disruptive innovation' in resolving social problems in an entrepreneurial way. It began with a concept of social entrepreneurship more akin to social impact entrepreneurship. More recently, however, it has come to emphasise a new conception of social entrepreneurship as change agents, working to achieve large-scale social innovation, and even what they call a 'social revolution'. As they describe it Ashoka's mission has evolved beyond catalysing individual entrepreneurs to enabling an 'everyone a changemaker' world.[17] Although self-descriptions like these may represent rhetorical flourish, we emphasise that in practice social enterprises are often guided by more than one of these concepts of social entrepreneurship, not only over time, but concurrently.

---

[17] See https://www.ashoka.org/about.

Some argue that because social entrepreneurship is a hybrid concept – combining as it does the already vague terms 'social' and 'entrepreneurship' – it will remain a contested concept. Of course, the same can be said of 'sustainability' or 'democracy' or 'human rights', yet this should not prevent us from struggling to give these concepts richer meaning. The implication of this criticism, however, is that social entrepreneurship can never be a category in itself that is separate from non-profit charities and for-profit businesses. Yet, as we have discussed, there are already new legal forms in the United States and the United Kingdom, and South Korea passed in 2006 the Social Enterprise Promotion Act. According to Bidet and Eum (2011), it was inspired by both the British policy and the Italian social co-operative law of 1991, which distinguishes between social enterprises providing social services and WISEs.

There do seem to be limits to how far we can reasonably stretch the concept. We can distinguish the well-established concept of corporate social responsibility from social entrepreneurship. The latter, unlike the former, entails embedding social goals in the organisation's core objectives. In the corporate social responsibility approach, these goals are added to the overall corporate objectives at different levels. An enterprise that is unwilling to accept a significant reduction in profits in the pursuit of its social goals should not be considered a social enterprise. A for-profit business with a corporate social responsibility strategy does not qualify since it might abandon its social aims if it believed its profits were at stake. The social goal is incidental to (or only instrumentally pursued in relation to) the business model.

The main challenge for social enterprises in Myanmar is to strike a balance between its social and financial mission, and to create new forms and practices that perhaps later – through public dialogue, policy debate, activist lawyering, legislative initiatives, social movement campaigns, transnational advocacy or other forms of influence – can serve as the grounds for deepening democracy, not only in the polity, but in the economy and civil society as well. Myanmar's social enterprise sector is ripe for such experimentation.

Marginalising a Critical Source of Grass-Roots Social Entrepreneurship

In an effort to govern and regulate what constitutes a social enterprise, some non-profit organisations such as the Global Impact Investing Network (GIIN), as well as brokerage firms such as Acumen, have developed various impact measurement tools to help entrepreneurs to understand and improve their impact on society. Universities – mostly business schools – are developing courses in social entrepreneurship to show how using a business model can improve the way entrepreneurs generate a social mission to become part of the overall focus of a social enterprise. Typically, these tools emphasise financial sustainability, leaving the 'social' problem-framing, research and social impact assessment to the entrepreneur (who is understood to be an entrepreneur in a largely 'commercial' sense). Again, these initiatives to govern what constitutes a social enterprise are largely shaped by understandings of social entrepreneurship that are common in the United States – understandings which focus on individual business leadership skills. This raises a question that is vigorously debated in US business schools: Can you really teach people to be entrepreneurs – socially or commercially? And it raises further questions that business schools in the United States are not asking: is it really 'problem-solving'? Can you just give people the right tools and assume that they will do the right thing? Who is excluded despite the rhetoric of 'inclusion'? This reduces or oversimplifies what is a social problem or moral problem – or even social inequality itself.

Some organisations go further in attempting to distinguish legitimate from illegitimate social enterprises and social entrepreneurs. For example, Social Enterprise Mark,[18] a UK initiative, is working to set up a certification system for social enterprises (similar to the Kimberly Process that was established to certify non-conflict, or 'blood', diamonds). A certification system offers the advantage of encouraging the development of social enterprises. It also persuades mainstream businesses to include social enterprises in their supply chains. In general, a certification system offers a procedure for strengthening a social enterprise's brand values, positioning and credibility. It creates an improved degree of transparency for customers or clients, as well as for partners, investors and beneficiaries. However, a certification system can also marginalise some social entrepreneurs and their social enterprises. As Cheriakova (2013: 14) has observed, '... those who work on promoting social innovation might fall outside the qualification, resulting in them pushing social change further without their efforts being recognized'. This is an important point, and one that we think has serious implications for social entrepreneurs in Myanmar – in particular, those who have been working as change agents on the political front lines to institutionalise democracy and human rights.

[18] See http://socialenterprisemark.org.uk.

Becoming Change Agents: The (Political) Prisoners' Dilemma

Although there are no laws in Myanmar distinguishing social enter-prises as a special form of business, the legality of certain kinds of social entrepreneurship – shaped by the remnants of a legal culture that has been forged by decades of repressive authoritarian rule – still plays a criti-cal role in shaping the emergence and vitality of social enterprises. An important way in which it does so is by retaining legal meanings asso-ciated with democratic practice that the former military government in Myanmar institutionalised as 'criminal'. Developing a capacity for criti-cally engaging the state and holding it accountable for addressing not only market failure but also the pursuit of profits at the expense of social and environmental injustice is a fundamental function of a democratic civil society – and it is a pattern not uncommon in even the highest-ranking knowledge economies. But for decades, the military government's addi-tional practices of socio-cultural (as distinguished from legal) regulation and community intimidation fostered de facto as well as de jure discrimi-nation against Myanmar's pro-democracy activists. This pattern contin-ued even under the new civilian government after former President Thein Sein released those designated as 'political prisoners'. In the months prior to the 2015 elections, both former political prisoners and NGO human rights defenders were being arrested, contributing to a new generation of political prisoners (many of whom were students protesting education reform).

Current efforts to foster and institutionalise social entrepreneurship in the form of social enterprises in Myanmar currently overlook and threaten to marginalise a key social group that represents a significant source of entrepreneurial leadership: former political prisoners jailed for peacefully challenging social and economic injustice in the name of democracy and human rights. As we are writing this, the Myanmar gov-ernment, including local agents of the state, still discriminates against for-mer political prisoners, refusing to expunge their stigmatising criminal records. Local agents of the state discourage others from associating with them and their families, rendering them social pariahs. The practice of intimidating even the family members of these former political prisoners has been commonly reported to us. This contributes to a culture of de facto discrimination in which former political prisoners and their family members suffer. They are blocked from access to travel and hospital care. It is very difficult for them to find employment. The children of former political prisoners suffer discrimination by association – finding themselves unable to gain acceptance to university despite having passed the national standard exams with high scores.

The strategy of investing in social enterprises in the absence of basic democratic safeguards has already created obstacles for these former leaders of Myanmar's pro-democracy movement, thus robbing the investment strategy of much of its potential for true social transformation. Starting businesses, much less social enterprises, is disproportionately difficult and risky for the very civil society leaders the West seeks to engage. This is in part due to both de jure and de facto forms of discrimination against former political prisoners. The interaction of existing regulations (for requesting a business incorporation certificate to register a company) and newly revised laws (the Companies Act[19] and the Association Registration Law No. 31/2014), in combination with prevailing laws (the Electronic Transactions Law No. 5/2004, the 2011 Peaceful Assembly and Peaceful Procession Act No. 15/2011, the Myanmar Microfinance Law No. 13/ 2011, the Telecommunications Law No. 31/2013), has thus far contributed to the marginalisation of former political prisoners, and thus undermines potential efforts to incorporate their social entrepreneurship into the formal economy.

In 2015, the Directorate of Investment and Companies Administration (DICA) began the process of revising the century-old Companies Act. If approved 'as is' by Parliament in 2016, it would mandate that all companies still in operation must be formally registered.[20] Private companies and (I)NGOs each initially register under separate laws – both of which have been recently revised. In the absence of any law distinguishing a social enterprise as a unique legal entity, social entrepreneurs seeking to establish a social enterprise must choose between these existing laws when registering their organisations.

Former political prisoners who have criminal records face immediate obstacles when requesting a business incorporation certificate from DICA. Two prior steps are required to do so. First, applicants must obtain a reference letter from the ward chief.[21] For example, Yangon is divided into four districts and thirty-three townships. Each township is then

---

[19] The Companies Act is still subject to further revision as of March 2016.
[20] See http://www.luther-lawfirm.com/en/news/directorate-of-investment-and-company-administration-dica.html.
[21] World Bank Group, 'Starting a business in Myanmar' (June 2015), at http://www.doingbusiness.org/data/exploreeconomies/myanmar/starting-a-business/.

divided into a certain number of wards. A ward is the smallest and most local administrative unit, comprising several households. The ward chief (a local agent of the state who is typically familiar with the residents of the ward) provides a letter confirming the address of the new business. The second step is to obtain a signed letter verifying the applicant's criminal history from the township police station.[22] Under such local conditions in which de facto discrimination is routinely practised by authorities against former political prisoners, formally registering a company can be very difficult. Faced with the choice of formally registering an enterprise versus operating in the informal economy, many former political prisoners choose the latter, hoping that they do not get caught.

(I)NGOs, unlike private companies, must register under the new Association Registration Law No. 31/2014. The Association Registration Law envisions a decentralised registration system implemented by the Ministry of Home Affairs (MoHA), with six registration committees, including at the Union (national) level, region or state level, Naypyidaw Council level, self-administered region or state level, divisional level and township level. Domestic associations may apply at any level, based on their anticipated territorial sphere of activities. INGOs must apply for registration with the Union registration committee. Yet, according to the International Center for Not-for-Profit Law (ICNL), amongst the most significant changes introduced by the Association Registration Law is the replacement of the mandatory registration system with a voluntary registration system.[23] As the ICNL points out, however, whether and how the new law will be implemented remains uncertain.[24]

This ambiguity has implications for the freedom of expression and advocacy of social enterprises that might choose to register (or not) as NGOs. One of the most significant changes of the political transition period in Myanmar relates to the freedom of expression. When the Censorship Board was abolished in 2012, individuals began criticising the government and CSOs (including community-based organisations, as well as local and international NGOs) began advocating for politically contentious causes. CSOs suddenly found increased opportunity to contribute to law and policy-making.

However, Myanmar's civilian government established subsequent law upon which it relied to hinder the freedom of expression. The

---

[22] Ibid.
[23] See http://www.icnl.org/research/monitor/Myanmar.html.
[24] See 'Barriers to Entry', at http://www.icnl.org/research/monitor/Myanmar.html.

Telecommunications Law (Telecom Law), enacted under Myanmar's civilian government in 2013, established the regulatory framework for foreign investment into Burma's telecommunications infrastructure. Section 66(d) of this law prohibits using a telecommunications network to extort, coerce, defame, disturb, cause undue influence or threaten any person.[25] Similarly, Burma's Electronic Transactions Law, section 33, criminalises using electronic transactions technology to commit any 'act detrimental to the security of the State or prevalence of law and order or community peace and tranquility or national solidarity or national economy or national culture'.[26] Myanmar's military government has used these articles in the past to jail dissidents, activists, CSO leaders and others for merely expressing opinions.

In addition, the Telecom Law, section 77, authorises the Ministry of Communications and Information Technology to order the suspension of telecom services in emergency situations. However, there are no criteria as to what can trigger such a suspension. This allows the government to shut down Internet and mobile communications arbitrarily, which often immediately precedes crackdowns on peaceful demonstrators or other human rights violations (as we witnessed in 2007, for example, during Myanmar's so-called Saffron revolution).[27]

Freedom of assembly also remains legally ambiguous for social enterprises that might attempt to address issues concerning democratic reform that the Myanmar government (or its influential foreign political or economic advisors) deems too contentious. In 2011, the Peaceful Assembly and Peaceful Procession Act came into force, providing partial protection for the freedom of assembly. The Act proved problematic, however, as it required prior authorisation from the respective police station. Where assemblies proceeded without authorisation, the military government used the notorious section 18 to arrest and imprison organisers and protestors. Some CSOs, including the prominent 88 Generation Students, initiated broad-based public consultation and advocacy processes against the 2011 Act. In June 2014, the Parliament adopted amendments to the Act. Most significantly, the Act now provides that while prior approval is required, the request for authorisation shall be rejected only if the authorities provide 'valid reasons'. In addition, the amendments have reduced

---

[25] See 'Barriers to Speech/Advocacy', at http://www.icnl.org/research/monitor/Myanmar.html.
[26] Ibid.
[27] Ibid.

the available punishments in case of violation (for example, reducing the imprisonment period from one year to six months).[28] The problem is that the term 'valid reasons' is undefined and can be arbitrary.

Finally, the Association Registration Law affirms that 'Any registered domestic organization may accept support in accordance with the prevailing law, provided by a foreign government or international NGO or domestic organization, or any individual.' Under prevailing law, an officially registered domestic NGO can open an account in the organisation's name at the Myanmar Foreign Trade Bank, with approval from the Ministry of Finance and Revenue, and with a recommendation letter from the MoHA. And with a registration number and copy of its registration certificate, a registered domestic NGO may also open an organisational bank account in a private bank. Before the Microfinance Law 2011 was adopted to provide a framework for the licencing and operation of microfinance institutions in Myanmar, there was no clear law or regulation affirming the right of NGOs to conduct income-generating activity. This law has been important to providing the poor and marginalised with financial services. But the Association Registration Law 2014 does not make clear whether *unregistered* domestic NGOs can open a bank account in the organisation's name, or generate revenues.[29] The uncertainty of the implications of this law for social enterprises that might choose to operate informally is therefore significant.

This raises an important question for proponents of social enterprises pursuing social inclusion in formal markets as a strategy for reducing inequality. Under what social conditions do informal actors move into the formal economy? Human capital, money and a regulatory environment – are these enough? Informal economies are often filled with actors who have developed strategies of social caretaking that provide certain dimensions of wellbeing – for example, childcare provision – that formal employment may not allow them to sustain. Not all social enterprises operating in the informal sector necessarily want to become part of the formal sector (Williams and Nadin 2011), yet most of the recommendations recently proposed to Myanmar by international development institutions, and even organisations like the British Council, which has conducted considerable research on social enterprises (British Council 2013; 2014; 2015), assume that they do, or that they should. It would seem that the current trend in reforming laws pertaining to the registration of companies are

---

[28] See 'Barriers to Assembly', at http://www.icnl.org/research/monitor/Myanmar.html.
[29] See 'Barriers to Resources', at http://www.icnl.org/research/monitor/Myanmar.html.

institutionalising conditions that would make it difficult for viable social enterprises driven by politically contentious transformative democratic visions to continue operating in Myanmar's informal economy.

NGOs in Myanmar that are registering their organisations, and receiving investments to operate essentially as social enterprises, are likewise dissuaded from working with foreign political prisoners. NGOs in Myanmar have long worked informally with political prisoners, drawing extensively on their combination of language skills and social capital (for example, their extensive networks of contacts and influence). But in a changing business climate of increased accountability within newly organised public-private bureaucratic structures (such as INGO Forum Myanmar),[30] fewer NGOs are willing to risk the government harassment and threat to the formally registered organisation that could come from getting caught. Increasingly, therefore, NGOs that venture into the world of social enterprise in Myanmar, required by law to add a certain percentage of local Myanmar employees to their workforce, are turning to less risky, but also less democratically risk-taking, citizens of Myanmar.

Some former political prisoners, despite these obstacles, have demonstrated their interest in creating social enterprises. One example of a social enterprise in Myanmar that was started by former political prisoners is Golden Harp Taxi service.[31] The drivers are all former political prisoners, and they serve mostly former political prisoners. Their business has started to attract foreign clients (including diplomats) who sympathise with their political efforts to democratise Myanmar. Their profits go back into the company to maintain and expand the fleet of taxis – employing more former political prisoners – and to meet the needs of the broader community of former political prisoners and their families. Some of the informal businesses like Golden Harp Taxi, which represent worker integration social enterprises, may be nurturing the conditions for creatively engaging social and economic injustice in the future. These informal social enterprises may also provide a social space for democratic experimentation, and a means for creating new, more socially sustainable relations, practices and identities that cannot be formalised (cf. Yockey 2015).

---

[30] See http://ingoforummyanmar.org/en/about-us.
[31] Interview with Golden Harp Taxi's founders, October 2014, in Yangon. See also http://www.aljazeera.com/indepth/features/2012/11/201211289210776231.html.

Towards a Sustainable Democratic Transition

While attending the ATHGO International/World Bank Social Innovation Conference in May 2013 in Washington DC, we listened to the cellphone tycoon Denis O'Brien address that year's competitors, billed as the world's top one hundred prospective social entrepreneurs between the ages of eighteen and thirty. O'Brien is the chairman of Digicel Group, one of the fastest-growing cellphone companies in the world. Born and educated in Ireland, and officially residing in Malta for tax-sheltering purposes, he is one of the world's wealthiest people (wealthier than Oprah Winfrey and Richard Branson). In 2001, he donated US$3 million to help found Front Line Defenders, or the International Foundation for the Protection of Human Rights Defenders, a human rights organisation based in Dublin, to protect human rights defenders at risk. The organisation has Special Consultative Status with the Social and Economic Council of the United Nations. When one young social entrepreneur in the audience asked O'Brien what he thought about corporate accountability, O'Brien responded, 'Corporate accountability is dead; everyone's a social entrepreneur now.' At the conclusion of the talk, he was rushing to catch a flight to Myanmar – where his private company was competing with more than ninety others for one of the Myanmar government's newly de-monopolised telecom licences. Digicel's bid was ultimately unsuccessful, but O'Brien's comment on corporate accountability raises an important question for social entrepreneurs who seek to address the kinds of social inequality that stem from the operations and interests of large and powerful corporations. The social enterprise sector may find that it is easier to attract start-up capital and social impact investment financing when they are targeting the aspects of an 'economic democratic deficit' that stems from the purposive action of undemocratic states than from the purposive action of undemocratic corporations or global financial institutions, or of the international governmental and non-governmental development organisations they influence.

Social entrepreneurship is diverse in its origins and motives, responding to what is seen as government failure or corporate exploitation, or even a civil society that is insufficiently democratic in its modes of practice. Creating a framework of the various aspects that social entrepreneurship should ideally include could help improve understanding of whether and how it could be supported and accelerated by policies and educational systems. Social entrepreneurship should be ambitious, socially innovative and democratically experimental. It must not only generate social impact, but also must be embedded in a process of continuous learning and participation, by the community, with the aim of becoming a change agent. Revenues and profits should be largely reinvested to fulfil the social mission. Establishing a framework built on such principles could serve to bring substance and order to the social enterprise bubble, a necessity if the concept is to be a serious alternative for commercial businesses and traditional NGOs.

In the absence of particular legal reforms, the focus on social entrepreneurship could undermine rather than bolster Myanmar's efforts to secure a sustainable democratic transition. Former political prisoners, whose only crime was peacefully pursuing democratic change, require basic democratic safeguards that would enable them to participate, without facing threat of de jure or de facto legal discrimination and harassment in the creative production of social enterprises. Moreover, social enterprises pursuing emancipatory, not just ameliorative, projects targeting institutional sources of social inequality in Myanmar would require similar protections.

If inclusive business development becomes only a project to advance an equal right to work, but not also a right to protection from the inequalities that the organisation of work often creates, then it risks becoming mainly a (false) advertising slogan for business as usual. Myanmar's government should strive for more than social inclusion in its continuing quest for a democratic transformation of its institutions.

The first meaningful legal changes that the Myanmar government can make to improve its prospects of enhancing its socially creative productivity (although this might not be well-measured by the ADB's index) are to release its currently detained and imprisoned persons whose only 'crime' has been to protest against social and economic injustice in the defence or advancement of democratic reforms, and to expunge such crimes from their records. The government could rely on the meticulously managed database of political prisoners kept by the Assistance Association for Political Prisoners (AAPP), a social enterprise legally organised as an NGO founded and operated by former political prisoners.[32] These diverse citizens from across Myanmar have already passed the 'social entrepreneurship' test. They have proven their entrepreneurial leadership through their creative action and willingness to take personal risks for a social purpose – to transform political and economic conditions of inequality to achieve a more sustainable democratic society.

[32] See http://aappb.org/.

APPENDIX

Table 4.1. *A sample of social enterprises in Myanmar*

Organisation name	Description	Type of social enterprise	Legal form	Social enterprise code
Shwe Sa Bwe	Restaurant that also acts as a training centre for disadvantaged youth	Local inclusive business	Private company	1, 2
Golden Harp Taxi	Taxi company in Yangon that helps political prisoners to find work	Political prisoners	Private company	2
Peak Point Travel	Ecotourism company	Repatriates	Private company	1
Yangon Bakehouse Training Café	Trains disadvantaged women in baking and hospitality and provides livelihood classes	Local inclusive business	Private company	3
Linkage Restaurant and Gallery	Restaurant that provides street children with vocational training	Local inclusive business	Private company	3
Sunflowers Art, Organic Dye Textile and Crafts Store	Gallery, art studio, handicraft store that is produced and designed by rural women	Local inclusive business	Private company	2, 3
Proximity Designs	Provides rural farmers access to affordable services that can help increase their income.	Rural development, agriculture	NGO	1, 2, 3, 4

Myanmar Business Forum	Public-private dialogue platform to help companies grow and create jobs	Tech start-up	NGO	1
Building Markets	E-learning system that modernises business culture	Tech start-up	NGO	1
Yangon Institute of Economics	Entrepreneurship centre that helps cultivate small businesses and support future business leaders	Tech start-up	Other	1
DuPont Myanmar	Uses science and technology to modify seeds	Agriculture	Private company	1, 2
Pomelo and Helping Hands	Handicraft business that has products made by people with HIV, street children and people with disabilities	Local inclusive business	Private company	2, 3
HarmonEat Cooking Classes	Community programme to teach people how to cook locally sourced food.	Local inclusive business	Private company	3
FXB Myanmar Handicrafts	Provides weaving and furniture-making training to victims of trafficking	Local inclusive business	Private company	2
DevLab	Open office space to support entrepreneurs	Tech start-up	Other	1
Project Hub	Co-working space for young entrepreneurs	Tech start-up	Other	1

(continued)

Table 4.1 (*continued*)

Organisation name	Description	Type of social enterprise	Legal form	Social enterprise code
Ideabox	Incubator/accelerator network in Myanmar	Tech start-up	Other	1
Opportunities Now	Business skill training and microfinancing company	Tech start-up	Other	1
Shan Maw Myae	Operates an organic farm and produces/distributes fertiliser	Rural development, agriculture	Private company	2, 3
Samrong Yea Mean Chay	Co-operative that benefits farmers	Rural development, agriculture	Co-op	3
Evergreen Group	Invests money to develop local processer enterprises	Rural development, agriculture	Co-op	1
Green Waves	Restores damaged land to productivity	Rural development, agriculture	Foundation	3
Snowball Soy	High-end soy milk business sourcing soybeans from minority producers	Rural development, agriculture	Private company	1, 2.3

Key: 1. Income generation
2. Job creation/WISEs
3. Social value/impact
4. Change agents

Note: We thank Samantha Samuel-Nakka for her research assistance in preparing this Appendix.

References

Asian Development Bank (ADB). 2012a. *2012 Annual Report: Advancing Regional Cooperating and Integration in Asia and the Pacific.* Mandaluyong City, Philippines: Asian Development Bank.

Asian Development Bank (ADB). 2012b. *Myanmar in Transition: Opportunities and Challenges.* Mandaluyong City, Philippines: Asian Development Bank.

Asian Development Bank (ADB). 2014a. *Innovative Asia: Advancing the Knowledge-Based Economy- Highlights of the Forthcoming ADB Study Report.* Mandaluyong City, Philippines: Asian Development Bank.

Asian Development Bank (ADB). 2014b. *Innovative Asia: Advancing the knowledge-based economy: the next policy agenda.* Mandaluyong City, Philippines: Asian Development Bank.

Asian Development Bank (ADB). 2014c. *Creative Productivity Index: Analysing Creativity and Innovation in Asia.* Report by the Economist Intelligence Unit for the Asian Development Bank. Mandaluyong City, Philippines: Asian Development Bank.

Austin, J., H. Stevenson and J. Wei-Skillern. 2006. 'Social and Commercial Entrepreneurship: Same, Different, or Both?' 30(1) *Entrepreneurship Theory and Practice* 1–22.

Beckertt, J. *Economic Action and Embeddedness: The Problem of the Structure of Action.* Unpublished ms. October 1999. Paper presented at the Stockholm Conference on Economic Sociology, 2–3 June 2000.

Bell, D. 1974. *The Coming of the Post-Industrial Society.* London: Heinemann.

Bidet, E. and H. S. Eum. 2011. 'Social Enterprise in South Korea: History and Diversity'. 7(1) *Social Enterprise Journal* 68–85.

Bland, J. 2010. *Social Enterprise Solutions for 21st Century Challenges: The UK Model of Social Enterprise and Experience.* Publications of the Ministry of Employment and the Economy, Strategic Projects 25/2010. London: Social Business International Ltd.

Bob, C. 2002. 'Merchants of Morality'. March/April, 129 *Foreign Policy* 36–45.

Brinkley, I. 2006. *Defining the Knowledge Economy: Knowledge Economy Programme report.* London: The Work Foundation. Available at http://www.theworkfoundation.com/Reports/65/Defining-the-knowledge-economy-knowledge-economy-programme-report.

British Council. 2013. *Social Enterprise Landscape in Myanmar.* Rangoon: British Council.

Allman, S. and B. Brown. 2014. *Exporting Social Enterprise: A Survey of Overseas Trade by UK Social Enterprises – and how to Foster its Growth.* British Council, Social Enterprise UK.

Gregory, D., P. Holbrook, P. Woodman and D.F. Angel-Urdnala. 2015. *Think Global Trade Social: How Business with a Social Purpose can Deliver more Sustainable Development.* British Council, Social Enterprise UK.

Burger-Helmchen, T. (ed.). 2013. *The Economics of Creativity: Ideas, Firms, and Markets.* New York: Routledge.

Castells, M. 1996. *The Information Age: Economy, Society, and Culture Volume I: The Rise of the Network Society.* Oxford: Blackwell.

Cheriakova, A. 2013. 'The Emerging Social Enterprise: Framing the Concept of Social Entrepreneurship'. 28 October. *The Broker.* Available at http://www .thebrokeronline.eu/Articles/The-emerging-social-enterprise.

Christiansen, C., M. E. Rayner and R. McDonald. 2015. 'What is Disruptive Innovation? December. *Harvard Business Review.* Available at https://hbr.org/ 2015/12/what-is-disruptive-innovation.

Cooley, A. and J. Snyder. 2015. 'Rank Has Its Privileges: How International Ratings Dumb Down Global Governance'. November/December. *Foreign Affairs.* Available at https://www.foreignaffairs.com/articles/2015-10-20/ rank-has-its-privileges.

Dale, J. 2010a. 'Democratizing the Production of Human Rights in Burma'. Fall, 6(3) *Global Studies Review.* Available at http://www.globality-gmu.net/archives/ 2303.

    2010b. 'Poverty & Power: The Problem of Structural Inequality'. January, 39 *Contemporary Sociology: A Journal of Reviews* 82–83.

    2011. *Free Burma: Transnational Legal Action and Corporate Accountability.* Minneapolis, MN: University of Minnesota.

    2013. 'Internal Affairs: How the Structure of NGOs Transforms Human Rights.' November, 119(3) *American Journal of Sociology.*

Dale, J. and D. Kyle. 2015. 'Smart Transitions? Foreign Investment, Disruptive Technology, and Democratic Reform in Myanmar'. 82(2) *Social Research: An International Quarterly,* 'Special Issue: From Burma to Myanmar: Critical Transitions' 291–326.

    2016. 'Smart Humanitarianism: Re-imagining Human Rights in the Age of Enterprise'. September, 42(6) *Critical Sociology,* 783–797.

Dees, J. G. 1998. 'The meaning of social entrepreneurship'. Available at https:// entrepreneurship.duke.edu/news-item/the-meaning-of-social-entrepreneurship/.

Department for Trade and Industry. 1998. *Our Competitive Future: Building the Knowledge-driven Economy.* White paper. London: Department for Trade and Industry. Available at http://webarchive.nationalarchives.gov.uk/ 20070603164510/http://www.dti.gov.uk/comp/competitive/wh_int1.htm.

DiMaggio, P. 1988. 'Interest and Agency in Institutional Theory' in Lynne Zucker (ed.) *Institutional Patterns and Organizations.* Cambridge: Ballinger, pp. 3–21.

Duflos, E., P. Luchtenberg, L. Ren and L. Y. Chen. 2013. *Microfinance in Myanmar Sector Assessment.* Washington DC and Yangon: CGAP and International Finance Corporation, World Bank Group.

Economic and Social Research Council. 2007. 'ESRC Society Today – Knowledge Economy Fact Sheet.' Available at http://webarchive.nationalarchives.gov.uk/20071204130131/http://esrc.ac.uk/ESRCInfoCentre/facts/UK/index4.aspx?ComponentId=6978&SourcePageId=18132.

Fligstein, N. 1997. 'Social Skill and Institutional Theory'. 40 *American Behavioral Scientist* 397–405.

Gill, I. and H. Kharas. 2015. *The Middle-Income Trap Turns Ten*. Policy Research Working Paper 7403. World Bank.

Global Impact Investing Network. 2015. *The Landscape for Impact Investing in South Asia: Understanding the Current Status, Trends, Opportunities and Challenges in Bangladesh, India, Myanmar, Nepal, Pakistan and Sri Lanka*. GIIN.

Graham, M. 2014. 'The Knowledge Based Economy and Digital Division of Labour' in V. Desai and R. Potter (eds) *Companion to Development Studies, 3rd edition*. London: Hodder, pp. 189–195. Available at http://papers.ssrn.com/sol3/papers.cfm?abstract_id=2363880.

Jenkins, M. 2015. 'It's not Charity: The Rise of Social Enterprise in Vietnam'. 31 March. *The Guardian*. Available at http://www.theguardian.com/sustainable-business/2015/mar/31/its-not-charity-the-rise-of-social-enterprise-in-vietnam.

Kurasawa, F. 2007. *The Work of Global Justice: Human Rights as Practices*. New York: Cambridge University Press.

Kyle, D. and J. Dale. 2016. *Inventing Scientific Creativity: A Forgotten Space Age Project to Mine 'Psychological Uranium' for War and Profit*. Unpublished ms. Under contract with Stanford University Press.

Lagarde, C. 2015. *Lifting the Small Boats*. 17 June. International Monetary Fund. Available at https://www.imf.org/external/np/speeches/2015/061715.htm.

Lauer, K. 2008. *Transforming NGO MFIs: Critical Ownership Issues to Consider*. Washington DC: CGAP.

Lawrence, T. B. 1999. 'Institutional Strategy'. 25(2) *Journal of Management* 161–168.

LEAP. 2014. *Bridges to Impact: A New Paradigm for Agri-Social Enterprises in Cambodia and Myanmar*. Singapore: LEAP.

Lucas, R. Jr. 1988. 'On the Mechanics of Economic Development'. 22 *Journal of Monetary Economics* 3–42.

Lwin, K. 2015. 'Entrepreneur Taps into the Travel Market'. 7 April. *The Myanmar Times*. Available at http://www.mmtimes.com/index.php/business/property-news/13953-entrepreneur-taps-into-the-travel-market.html.

Machlup, F. 1962. *The Production and Distribution of Knowledge in the United States*. Princeton, NJ: Princeton University Press.

Maguire, S., C. Hardy and T. B. Lawrence. 2004. 'Institutional Entrepreneurship in Emerging Fields: HIV/AIDS Treatment Advocacy in Canada'. 47 *Academy of Management Journal* 657–679.

Martin, R. L. and S. R. Osberg. 2015. *Getting Beyond Better: How Social Entrepreneurship Works*. Boston: Harvard Business Review Press.

Min, K. 2014. 'Yangon Institute of Economics Launches Entrepreneurship Program'. 5 March. *Myanmar Business Today*.

Oo, M. 2015. 'Local Enterprise Designs Affordable Solar Irrigation Pump'. 25 October. *Myanmar Business Today*.

Organisation for Economic Co-Operation and Development. 1996. *The Knowledge-based Economy*. OCDE/GD(96)102. Paris: OECD.

Porat, M. U. and M. Rubin. 1977. *The Information Economy: Development and Measurement*. Washington DC: Office of Telecommunications/US Government Printing Office.

Powell, W. W. and K. Snellman. 2004. 'The Knowledge Economy'. 30 *Annual Review of Sociology* 199–220.

Pwint, Z. 2015. 'Helping Hand: Three Social Enterprise Restaurants in Yangon'. 4 September. *The Myanmar Times*. Available at http://www.mmtimes.com/index.php/lifestyle/dining/16312-helping-hand-three-social-enterprise-restaurants-in-yangon.html.

Rao, H., P. Monin and R. Durand. 2003. 'Institutional Change in Tocqueville: Nouvelle Cuisines in French Gastronomy'. 108 *American Journal of Sociology* 795–843.

Roberts, J. 2009. 'The Global Knowledge Economy in Question'. 5(4) *Critical Perspectives on International Business* 285–303.

Roberts, J. and J. Armitage. 2008. 'The Ignorance Economy'. 26(4) *Prometheus: The Journal of Issues in Technological Change, Innovation, Information Economics, Communications, and Science Policy* 335–354.

Romer, P. 1990. 'Endogenous Technical Change'. 98(5) *Journal of Political Economy* 71–102.

    1994. 'Origins of Endogenous Growth'. 8(1) *Journal of Economic Perspectives* 3–22.

Roughneen, S. and S. Aung. 2014. 'In Burma, Some Ex-Political Prisoners Heed Capitalism's Calling'. 8 February. *The Irrawaddy*. Available at http://www.irrawaddy.com/feature/burma-ex-political-prisoners-heed-capitalisms-calling.html.

Sabeti, H. 2011. 'The For-Business Enterprise'. November. *Harvard Business Review*. Available at https://hbr.org/2011/11/the-for-benefit-enterprise.

Slow, O. 2013. 'Myanmar Ready for Social Enterprises'. January, 24 *Myanmar Business Today*.

Smith, K. 2002. 'What is the knowledge economy? Knowledge intensity and distributed knowledge bases'. Discussion paper. Tokyo: United Nations University/Institute for New Technologies.

Trexler, J. 2008. 'Social Entrepreneurship as an Algorithm: Is Social Enterprise Sustainable?' 10(3) *E:CO* 65–85.

UNCTAD. 2008. 'Summary: Creative Economy Report 2008'. UNCTAD/DITC/ 2008/2. Geneva and New York: UNCTAD. Available at http://unctad.org/en/ Docs/ditc20082ceroverview_en.pdf.

Unger, Roberto Mangabeira. 2015. 'Conclusion: The Task of the Social Innovation Movement' in Alex Nicholls, Julie Simon and Madeleine Gabriel (eds) *New Frontiers in Social Innovation Research*. New York: Palgrave Macmillan, Kindle Edition, Location 5319–7037.

United Nations. 2014. *Millenium Development Goals Report*. New York: United Nations.

Wai, Z. 2015. Building Markets Open Training Center for Entrepreneurs in Mandalay. 9 July. *Myanmar Business Today*.

Warren, R. L. 1967. 'The Inter-organizational Field as a Focus for Investigation'. 12 *Administrative Science Quarterly* 396–419.

Williams, C. and S. Nadin. 2011. 'Entrepreneurship in the Informal Economy: Commercial or Social Entrepreneurs?' 8(3) *International Entrepreneurship and Management Journal* 309–324.

Win, S. 2015. 'US Agricultural Giant Ramps up in Myanmar'. 27 October. *The Myanmar Times*.

Wooten, M. and A. J. Hoffman. 2013. 'Organizational Fields: Past, Present and Future' in R. Greenwood, C. Oliver, R. Suddaby and K. Sahlin (eds) *The Sage Handbook of Organizational Institutionalism*. Los Angeles: Sage, pp. 130–148.

World Bank. 1999. *Knowledge for Development: World Development Report*. New York: Oxford University Press.

2012. *International Development Association and International Finance Corporation Interim Strategy Note For the Republic of the Union of Myanmar For the Period FY13–14*. Southeast Asia Country Management Unit.

2015. *Myanmar Investment Climate Assessment: Sustaining Reforms in a Time of Transition*. Washington DC: World Bank.

World Economic Forum. 2015. *Outlook on the Global Agenda 2015*. Geneva: WEF.

Yockey, J. W. 2015. 'Does Social Enterprise Law Matter?' 66 *Alabama Law Review* 767.

Yunus, M. 2010. *Building Social Business: The Kind of Capitalism That Serves Humanity's Most Pressing Needs*. New York: PublicAffairs.

Zucker, L. 1988. *Institutional Patterns and Organizations*. Cambridge: Ballinger.

5

Microfinance in Myanmar

Unleashing the Potential

SEAN TURNELL

Microfinance will play an outsized role in any plausible financial sector reform programme in Myanmar. Already well-entrenched, but unnecessarily restricted by a range of inhibiting regulations and a lack of supporting legal and other infrastructure, microfinance has yet to make the impact it could in expanding financial inclusion.

One of the factors that differentiates microfinance institutions (MFIs) in Myanmar's financial ecosystem is that, uniquely, they are free to lend without demanding collateral. They are, however, at present much held back by restrictions on their ability to raise funds – from owners and principals, and even from their own members in the form of deposits. The latter restriction is an especially damaging one that flies in the face of what we now understand is amongst the most important roles that MFIs play in financial inclusion, and in allowing poor households and small businesses to accumulate capital and to protect themselves against some of the vicissitudes of life.

This chapter explores the current state of microfinance in Myanmar, looks at the legal framework that has allowed its expansion and shaped its form, and critiques the factors that continue to hold it back. Along the way recommendations are offered to advance microfinance in ways that will expand financial inclusion in Myanmar and, as a consequence, contribute to achieving sustainable and inclusive economic development more broadly.

Microfinance: Promise and Potential

While the over-inflated claims of the benefits that have sometimes been made for microfinance have receded in recent years, the idea that microfinance institutions offer an answer to the problem of financial exclusion – the iniquity of people being unable to access conventional banking and financial services – retains great weight.[1] Unencumbered by the legacies that continue to undermine Myanmar's formal banks, MFIs are regarded by their backers and proponents as just the sort of nimble, low-cost institutions Myanmar needs to extend financial outreach. The intellectual arguments behind this advocacy, which enjoy a broad consensus amongst the multilateral financial institutions and other development partners active in Myanmar (World Bank, IMF, Asian Development Bank and so on), comprise the conventional arsenal of ideas that have backed microfinance more or less from the moment it burst into global prominence. This includes several common claims.

First, through the use of innovative methods and techniques, not least 'peer group lending', MFIs are said to be able to deliver credit at lower cost, and at lower risk. Peer group lending establishes essentially a group liability contract that transfers agency costs from an MFI to its borrowers, surmounting the information asymmetries that face the lender through the co-option of peer knowledge (that borrowers have of each other). Just about all of Myanmar's MFIs employ peer group lending, and all claim loan repayment rates in excess of 95 per cent.

Further, MFIs' low-cost/low-risk lending allows them to lend to borrowers who are unable to access formal finance, either because of the absence of banks in their proximity, or because they were not regarded as conventionally creditworthy. This directly enhances financial inclusion – and in so doing delivers some of the virtues of access to finance otherwise denied. This is achieved by generating greater incomes and employment by financing poor, unbanked entrepreneurs. It is also attained by allowing poor households to smooth consumption against fluctuating incomes (through saving as well as borrowing), and to insure themselves against (predictable and unpredictable) financial 'events'.

In addition, by lending primarily to women, microfinance empowers the marginalised and enhances gender equality. Female-focused lending is also held to be another factor promoting MFI sustainability. Conventionally regarded as less selfish and socially destructive, more risk averse, less mobile and more vulnerable to social sanction – women are

---

[1] For the purposes here, the definition of microfinance employed is that used by the Consultative Group to Assist the Poorest (CGAP, the World Bank-originated body that is the global industry's pre-eminent research and information exchange), as 'the provision of formal financial services to poor and low-income people, as well as others systematically excluded from the financial system' (CGAP 2012: 4).

more likely to repay their debts. Nearly all of Myanmar's MFIs have a bias (for most, an exclusivity) to lending to women. In a related virtue (predicated on alleged gender spending proclivities), microfinance is meant to promote schooling and improved health for children. Microfinance has also proved that the poor are 'bankable', and that financial institutions created for the poor can be profitable and self-sustaining.[2]

As hinted at already, the delivery of these virtues by microfinance, accepted without much scrutiny during the first flush of the movement's global momentum (which reached its apogee with the award of the Nobel Peace Prize to the most globally well-known MFI, Grameen Bank, and its charismatic founder, Muhammad Yunus, in 2006), has come under a cloud in recent years. Some high-profile MFI customer suicides in India (which fairly or unfairly were blamed on microfinance debt burdens); the simple loss of novelty of the idea; and, perhaps above all, some important findings from the growing use of randomised trials to test the claims of microfinance have dulled the movement's brand. The broad consensus of these trials and other empirical work is that, on the whole, microfinance does not *itself* empower women or lead to better education outcomes for children, and 'does not lead to the miraculous social transformation some proponents have claimed' (Banerjee et al. 2014: 5).[3]

And yet, critics of microfinance, not least politicians looking for easy scapegoats, have been guilty of over-emphasising its failures. This has particularly been the case in the context of what might reasonably be regarded as the core business of MFIs – the simple provision of affordable financial services. This has been addressed in a seminal book by Roodman, *Due Diligence: An Impertinent Inquiry into Microfinance*. In considering the genuine success of microfinance, Roodman identifies that 'Its strength lies not in lifting people out of poverty ... [but] rather, in leveraging modest subsidies to build financial institutions and industries that give millions of poor families more control over their finances' (Roodman 2012: 6).

Why is such control important? Roodman explains this by noting that the necessity of financial services for the poor is an even greater need than

---

[2] For a taste of such claims, see the speech of the chairman of the Norwegian Nobel Prize Committee, Ole Danbolt Mjos, awarding the Nobel Peace Prize to Grameen Bank and its founder, Muhammad Yunus, on 10 December 2006, http://www.nobelprize.org/nobel_prizes/peace/laureates/2006/presentation-speech.html (accessed 16 March 2016).

[3] Banerjee et al.'s findings are supported by near identical ones from other randomised evaluations, including those of Angelucci, Karlan and Zinman (2013), Attanasio et al. (2013), Augsberg et al. (2012), Crepon et al. (2014) and Tarozzi, Desai and Johnson (2013) – amidst a fast-growing literature.

that for the rich. This is because 'For people navigating the unpredictable and unforgiving terrain of poverty, any additional room for manoeuvre, any additional control, can be extremely valuable' (Roodman 2012: 34).

Another related aspect of microfinance is the creation of a sense of institutional reliability. This is a point made well in Collins et al.'s seminal work on *Portfolios of the Poor: How the World's Poor Live on $2 a Day*, which explores the *economic theory* underlying microfinance. They depict the value of reliability, in terms of the timely delivery of goods and services in the amount ordered and paid for, as 'the single biggest improvement that microfinance can bring to the financial lives of the poor ... ' (Collins et al. 2009: 180–181). They attribute the significance of reliability for the poor to the fact that in most other aspects of their lives, the poor face significant uncertainty. This includes uncertainty in terms of inconsistent income, the unpredictable nature of work and therefore the difficulty of planning ahead for the future. The contribution that the availability of microfinance makes to stability and reliability of income for the poor is therefore profound.

Microfinance in Myanmar: The State of Play

MFIs in Myanmar exist to service individuals and communities otherwise excluded from accessing formal finance. Myanmar's nascent (if growing) banking sector has a relatively small geographic footprint, is still widely distrusted beyond fairly limited demographic groups and is not structurally built to cater to small, isolated and poor borrowers (Turnell 2014). The Myanmar Agricultural Development Bank (MADB), a state-owned monolith that was for a long time the monopoly supplier of rural finance and a 'should be' provider to such borrowers, is underfunded, slowly de-capitalising and in need of fundamental restructuring (World Bank 2014). A not-surprising consequence of all of this are the metrics of financial access in Myanmar. In 2015 only around 10 per cent of people in Myanmar had a bank account in their own name, while only 3 per cent had access to formal insurance. Private sector credit to GDP (a crucial measure of the contribution of the financial sector to economic growth and development) stood at 15 per cent the same year, compared to 39 per cent for Laos, 45 per cent for Cambodia and 97 per cent for Vietnam (Almekinders et al. 2015). Observing the sector overall, the German development agency, GIZ, concluded in 2015 that the 'financial sector in Myanmar is the least developed of all countries in Southeast Asia' (Foerch et al. 2015: 15).

Of course, an obvious consequence of all of this is that Myanmar is a country for which microfinance *should* have a lot to offer. It is to the background of microfinance in Myanmar, and the current state of play of its leading MFIs, that we now turn.

Myanmar's Leading MFIs

Microfinance has a long and difficult history in Myanmar, the latter not least due to the fact that through much of its history the sector has existed (in various forms since 1997) at the fringes of legality. Dependent on specific 'understandings' of foreign non-governmental organisations (NGOs), and often simply on regulators looking the other way, for the longest time microfinance in Myanmar teetered between achieving genuine success and coming to an abrupt and inglorious halt.[4]

In 2016 microfinance in Myanmar exists on sound (if only partially exercised) legal foundations, and has achieved growth and outreach. Altogether around 250 MFIs are now present in the country, serving more than 1.2 million clients and with a total loan portfolio of just more than US$200 million (LIFT 2013: 1).

Most of Myanmar's MFIs were established in the life of the Thein Sein administration, during which time Myanmar became (and, to some extent, remains) something of a hot spot for footloose international investors, NGOs and global charities, multilateral lending institutions, as well as the development agencies of a number of governments. A great proportion of all of these, in turn, promote microfinance as a sector into which they will allocate funds. For such actors, microfinance ticks all sorts of boxes for their donors and constituencies back home – an obvious and good place to start programmes of broader assistance and engagement.[5]

---

[4] For more on the establishment and history of microfinance in Myanmar, see Turnell (2009: 319–352).

[5] Of course, the influx of funds and new players into microfinance, especially into countries that lack supporting infrastructure, can be destructive of prudence and good practice. The collection of savings can be discouraged, and excessive lending can create bubbles that (as recent global experiences attest) are difficult to detect and deflate in time. As Roodman (2012: 275–279) notes, the disasters created by excessive flows of donors' funds into microfinance lending entail a 'long list' that includes recent crises in Bangladesh, Bosnia, India, Mexico, Nigeria and Pakistan. So far in Myanmar the problem of excessive funding is not yet in evidence. However, a proliferation of the number of MFIs themselves is already a cause of concern, and in early 2015 the regulator of microfinance in Myanmar began to issue new MFI licences of just one-year duration. Clearly there is more to come on this front.

Table 5.1. *The leading MFIs in Myanmar*

Institution	Number of depositors	Deposits US$000s	Number of borrowers	Loans outstanding US$000s
ACLEDA Myanmar*	46,202	302.6	32,863	8,572.3
DAWN Microfinance	44,703	582.4	43,437	9,960.0
PACT Global Microfinance Fund	623,828	35,689.2	623,864	112,151.6
Proximity Finance	n.a.	n.a.	35,808	5,982.3
Vision Fund Myanmar	n.a.	n.a.	63,363	8,847.0

* As of late June 2015.
Source: Microfinance Information Exchange (MIX Market).[6]

Table 5.1 provides some data on the largest and most promising of Myanmar's MFIs.

As can be seen from Table 5.1, microfinance in Myanmar is greatly dominated (more than 50 per cent of all microfinance lending) by the very large PACT Global Microfinance Fund. An institution with a long history in Myanmar, the PACT scheme began as a United Nations Development Programme (UNDP) 'project' in 1997 with a bespoke ministerial 'memoranda of understanding' against what was, otherwise, a singular lack of legal authorisation to conduct microfinance. After fifteen years of operating under such a precarious existence (during which time, nevertheless, the PACT MFI grew and expanded), in February 2012 it was transformed (and legally established under the new microfinance law) into the PACT Global Microfinance Fund (PGMF). It mixes Grameen bank-lending methodologies, at the core of which are the peer group–lending model, the lending-only-to-women stipulation and the provision of business training of various forms. PGMF is both an MFI and a development-minded NGO. The latest data on PGMF lending are included in Table 5.1, but collectively since its creation the scheme claims around one million borrowers.[7]

Joining PGMF in the first tier of professional MFIs are a number of other prominent institutions, but all (with the exception of Proximity)

[6] Mix Market microfinance data for Myanmar can be found at www.mixmarket.org/mfi/country/Myanmar/ (accessed 15 March 2016).
[7] Much of the following is gleaned from PGMF's website, www.pactworld.org/country/pact-global-microfinance-fund (accessed 6 November 2015). Background on the MFI's early years in Myanmar can be found in Turnell (2009).

are ultimately entities created by foreign NGOs and banks. These include ACLEDA Myanmar, a subsidiary of the Cambodian bank of the same name, but which has the backing of World Bank Group's International Finance Corporation.[8] ACLEDA runs a reasonably substantial microfinance business in Myanmar. It currently has around a dozen branches, but is licensed to eventually operate in nearly eighty townships in Yangon and Bago regions. In its March 2015 Annual Report, ACLEDA noted that it was examining 'the possibility of becoming a full commercial bank.'[9]

Vision Fund Myanmar was founded in 1997 by the global World Vision charity.[10] It does not seek to be a financial institution in the narrow sense, but uses its MFI to further the organisation's broader humanitarian and development goals. Dawn Microfinance was created with a similar motivation, in 2002, by Save the Children.[11] In 2015, however, this MFI was effectively 'taken over' by a tripartite consortium that included the prominent MFI incubator Accion International (which now owns 40 per cent of Dawn), the Netherlands government development bank, FMO (30 per cent), and the Dutch emerging-markets investment fund Triodos Investment Management (30 per cent).[12] Injecting nearly US$7 million into the venture, the declared intent of the consortium is to 'establish Dawn as a prime example for the underdeveloped microfinance industry in Myanmar'. In creating this 'demonstration effect', professional Accion staff have been seconded to key positions within Dawn.[13]

---

[8] The IFC has a 15 per cent stake. COFIBRED (a co-operative bank from France which had been a bidder for one of Myanmar's foreign bank licences) and the German government–owned development bank, KfW, hold another 15 per cent each, while ACLEDA Bank (Cambodia) itself owns the remaining 55 per cent. The existence of IFC as a shareholder in ACLEDA has proved valuable for the MFI in raising offshore funds, including (granted as a one-off authorisation) the ability to pay a higher interest rate (13 per cent) on such funds than those permitted to other foreign MFIs. See ACLEDA Myanmar's website, www .acledamfi.com.mm/mm/eng/ (accessed 6 March 2016).

[9] Report available at the ACLEDA website, www.acledamfi.com.mm (accessed 17 March 2016).

[10] For more on the background of Vision Fund's early history in Myanmar, see Turnell (2009). See also Vision Fund's website, www.visionfund.org/1966/about/ (accessed 6 November 2015).

[11] For a broad overview of Dawn, see www.accion.org/our-impact/dawn-microfinance (accessed 15 March 2016).

[12] For details of this transformation, see 'Accion, FMO and Triodos Investment Management Form Consortium to Strengthen Financial Inclusion in Myanmar', Press Release, Accion International, 28 April 2015, www.accion.org/content/accion-fmo-and-triodos-investment-management-form-consortium-strengthen-financial-inclusion (accessed 15 March 2016).

[13] Ibid.

Proximity Finance is the MFI unit of the venerable Proximity Designs firm of Myanmar.[14] A social business (established in 2004) with an array of products and services designed to match the needs of rural dwellers in Myanmar, Proximity's initial contact with finance was stimulated by its need to fund its customers (Proximity is discussed in broader detail in the chapter by Dale and Kyle in this volume).

Beyond the major MFIs in Myanmar are a myriad of others of varying forms, size and quality. They include around twenty local NGO-run operations, nearly eighty financial co-operatives, a dozen or so foreign microfinance companies and nearly one hundred local microfinance companies. Many of the latter are former (and current) commercial moneylender firms. Many of these smaller MFIs are effective, efficient and built upon experience and expertise from which much might be expected. Some are moribund institutions established merely to 'sit' on a licence in the hope of speculative gain, while others raise prudential and consumer protection concerns. The latter cohort includes aforementioned money-lending outfits masquerading as MFIs, the former many of the 'rebranded' financial co-operatives (more on which later in the chapter).

The long informality (even suppression) of microfinance in Myanmar deferred the establishment of collective representation of MFIs. The growth of the sector since the promulgation of the Microfinance Law in 2011, however, has stimulated both interest and activity on this front. After a number of false starts (and certain tensions between the different cohorts of MFIs), in 2016 the Myanmar Microfinance Association (MMFA) emerged as a reasonably effective voice for the sector. As shall be examined later in the chapter, this includes efforts at sector improvement and expansion through lobbying for a more liberal approach to MFI regulation.

The Microfinance Law

The most important development affecting microfinance in Myanmar under the Thein Sein administration has been its formalisation and legalisation – in November 2011, via the Myanmar Microfinance Law (MFL). Consistent with the broad and ambitious mandates associated with the halcyon days of microfinance, the objectives of the MFL encompass job creation and poverty reduction, the lifting of health, education and social

---

[14] See the Proximity Finance website, www.proximitydesigns.org/products-services/financial-services (accessed 6 November 2015).

conditions of poor households,[15] the nurturing of thrift, the creation of small businesses, the expansion of opportunities beyond agriculture and the dissemination of higher technologies.

Meanwhile, to deliver this, the MFL authorises the establishment of MFIs to carry out a liberal array of activities, including to:

a. extend microcredit;
b. accept deposits;
c. receive and accept remittances;
d. carry out insurance business;
e. borrow locally and from abroad; and
f. carry out 'other' financial activities.

In fact, two categories of MFIs are authorised (s 19) under the MFL – deposit-taking MFIs that (theoretically) can do all of the above and non-deposit-taking institutions whose funding cannot be secured by accepting voluntary deposits from members. As defined in the MFL, however, MFIs can take a number of organisational forms (foreign or domestic), including partnership firms, private corporations, co-operative societies and other financial institutions, but all authorised to carry out microfinance business (s 2b).

Minimum capital standards are specified under the MFL, appropriately at differential levels depending on whether an MFI takes in voluntary deposits or not. For deposit-taking MFIs the minimum amount of paid-up capital is set at MMK30 million (slightly less than US$30,000), and for non-deposit-taking MFIs capital must be a minimum of MMK15 million.[16] Such an initial capital requirement is common throughout the microfinance industry (but the capital minimums in Myanmar are *very* low), as are the different amounts for deposit- and non-deposit-taking institutions. Effectively doubling (over time) the capital requirements of the MFL, however, is another provision (s 33b) that compels MFIs to 'deposit 25% of net profit to a general reserve account ... until it is equivalent to 100% of deposited paid-up capital'.

Meanwhile, under the MFL the taking of collateral by MFIs is effectively prohibited by the MFL's very definition of microlending as that 'without requiring to submit surety' (s 2b).

---

[15] The direct translation of the cohort targeted for assistance under the MFL is rendered as 'basic class people'. Such people would roughly correspond to the 'working poor' classification typically in focus for MFIs around the world.
[16] Myanmar's currency is the *kyat*, denoted throughout as 'MMK'.

The initial set of implementing regulations for MFIs specifies a number of other allowances and requirements.[17] These include very prescriptive lending procedures (amongst which is a maximum allowable loan size of MMK50 million, or around US$5,000) and the use of standardised forms (reasonably common in the sector internationally). The information MFIs must collect from borrowers seeking a loan includes their intent on the use of funds, the minutes of meetings of peer-group members and a pledge that they intend to repay. Group members must sign loan applications for all other group members, likewise against a pledge that they will make good on any defaults. If a borrower is illiterate, borrowers and group members are permitted to use a thumb-print.

Other regulations on MFI access to wholesale funding, regulations on allowable interest rates and other constraints are taken up in more detail later in the chapter.

Overseeing the evolving regulation and supervision of microfinance in Myanmar is the Financial Regulatory Department (FRD) of the Ministry of Finance.[18] This body was formed out of the Myanmar Microfinance Supervisory Enterprise, which was itself spun out of the long-standing state-owned pawn shop in Myanmar, the Myanmar Small Loans Enterprise. The chair and vice chair of the FRD are the minister and deputy minister of the Department of Finance, respectively, while other ex-officio members of the FRD include the governor of the CBM, the managing directors of each of Myanmar's major state-owned banks and the director-general of Myanmar's Directorate of Investment and Company Administration (DICA).

Fetters, Failures and Ways Forward

As can be seen from the previous discussion, and in keeping with the sector's broad mandate, the MFL *in principle* authorises a range of MFI activities to fully exploit the opportunities ostensibly allowed. In practice, however, the absence of enabling regulation in many areas, and somewhat myopic and excessively conservative regulators, continue to deny

---

[17] Financial Regulatory Department, Ministry of Finance and Revenue, *Microfinance Procedures, Instructions and Accounting and Reporting Formats for the Microfinance Organization*, Notification 277/2011, 23 December 2011.

[18] The website of the FRD is included in the pages belonging to the Ministry of Finance, but they are shared with the Myanmar Small Loans Enterprise – underlining the point that MFI regulation in Myanmar is yet to be placed within an appropriate framework. See www .mof.gov.mm/en/content/myanma-small-loans-enterprise (accessed 18 March 2016).

the sector the necessary permissions to engage in activities that can (and should) make significant contributions, especially for financial inclusion. These include deposit and other funding restrictions, product and service restrictions, regulatory agency problems, interest rate restrictions and an array of miscellaneous technical barriers. Naturally this has created frustration for Myanmar's MFIs, and along with it a lobbying platform for the aforementioned industry association, the MMFA (whose efforts on this front also enjoy the support of the leading sectoral donors).

In the following section, we outline the most important of these barriers to the success of microfinance in Myanmar, some related contextual problems and, after each item so outlined, some suggested solutions.

Limitations on Funding: The Need to Make the MFL Operational

Mobilising deposits is a raison d'être of the MFL which, as noted, specifies higher capital and other prudential standards for institutions that seek to do so. This being the case, it comes as something of a shock to find that the taking of deposits by MFIs *in practice* is currently greatly restricted in Myanmar. For reasons that are not entirely clear (but which centre upon a certain innate conservatism within the FRD, on top of 'capacity constraints' in the same), deposits in all MFIs (including those capitalised and licensed as voluntary deposit-takers) are limited to 5 per cent of a member's approved loans. The taking of deposits from non-borrowers is prohibited completely.[19]

In a similar vein, the FRD has also banned the provision of term deposits and other (what it calls) 'bank like' products. Another device through which MFIs might legitimately fund themselves, such deposit types also greatly assist MFIs in their ability to properly deal with the liquidity 'mismatch' that naturally arises from financial intermediation.[20]

These limitations on deposits, ostensibly made out of a concern for the safety of depositors' savings against the backdrop of Myanmar's long history of financial crises – and the great number of small, (possibly) poorly managed and relatively obscure MFIs that have been allowed to spring

---

[19] For this ruling, see Ministry of Finance, Financial Regulatory Department, 'Receiving Voluntary Saving and Compulsory Saving by MFIs', 13 January 2015, Regulation 39/2015.

[20] Adding salt in to this wound is the fact that the injunction was almost certainly enacted under pressure from the formal banks – leaning on the regulator at a time when they feared losing market share to rivals who could not only offer a higher interest rate than they could but, because of the international backing of many of the MFIs, offered a certain extra dose of perceived safety and security along the way.

into existence – are greatly damaging. In the first instance, it undermines the ability of MFIs to properly fund themselves via the contributions of their own members, and to recycle savings through the economy and so expand the country's stock of financial capital. Restricting all forms of deposits to just 5 per cent of an MFI's (by definition, *micro*) loans unnecessarily endangers institutional and systemic stability.

But the restriction also flies in the face of all that the evidence tells us about the importance of savings, especially when compared to what the same evidence suggests with the somewhat compromised benefits that sometimes accrues from an exclusive focus on credit. Adroitly summarising the literature on this, Roodman (2012: 282) asserts:

> Savings is a conceptually simpler service, with much going for it … Experience and common sense say that the poorest are more willing to save than to shoulder the risk of credit. Meanwhile … savings can do almost anything credit can. People can save to start a business, pay tuition, finance a funeral. And, like insurance, it can buffer families against financial shocks.

The importance placed on saving by everyday people in Myanmar themselves is reflected in the fact that it is done – by all but the poorest of households, albeit in 'informal' ways. Remote from, excluded from or untrusting of banks and other formal institutions, savings for many in Myanmar primarily take the form of items of intrinsic value, the exact type depending upon wealth and occupation. Thus savings take the form of gold, jewellery (often worn, especially for women, as bangles), stored paddy, other durable foodstuffs and cash (with US dollars, in mint condition, greatly preferred). Storage of all of these items is overwhelmingly in the home and its surrounds, in boxes, trunks, tins, pots and sometimes even safes. Few of the richest residents of Myanmar will be without gold or the ubiquitous wad of pristine US$100 notes.[21] Where such savings are not manifest, alas, are in a monetary shape in Myanmar's MFIs – which otherwise *could* convert inert capital into a more dynamic form, benefitting the MFIs and potential borrowers alike.

But Myanmar's MFIs are not just constrained in raising funds via deposits. MFIs' equity capital and wholesale borrowing are also restricted. For local MFIs these restrictions are due both to regulatory constraints and to practical barriers related to the lack of a functioning financial system more broadly. For instance, under enabling regulations issued by the FRD in 2014, domestic MFIs are supposed to be able to borrow from

---

[21] For more on savings patterns in Myanmar, see Turnell (2016).

the Myanmar Economic Bank (MEB, the principal state-owned commercial bank in Myanmar).[22] In practice, however, this is not possible. The MEB continues to insist (in keeping with the broad habit of banks in Myanmar) on collateral for its loans which, almost universally (given the uncollateralised loans that MFIs themselves must make), MFIs do not have.

Meanwhile, MFIs face a maximum debt-to-equity ratio of 5:1. The latter greatly adds to the effective capital requirements imposed on MFIs as they expand and, in so doing, limits their ability to do so. Adding an unhelpful level of confusion on this front is the fact that it is currently unclear whether the 5:1 debt ratio includes deposits in its measure of 'debt'. Should it do so the constraints on MFI growth are severe indeed.

Foreign MFIs are not permitted to borrow from the MEB, or any other local bank, but they are authorised to borrow up to US$3 million overseas, provided this receives the approval of their home regulators *and* the Central Bank of Myanmar (CBM). This wholesale funding arrangement is, however, likewise problematic. First up, the US$3 million limit is a low and confining one, especially when combined with the 5:1 debt/equity rule. Second, the injection of the CBM into the process is an unnecessarily inhibiting one. Deeply conservative on such issues, in practice the CBM has imposed an implicit 10 per cent interest ceiling on foreign MFIs' borrowings from offshore.[23] This is too low to attract the funds required given the risks, and especially given the cost of foreign exchange hedging required. CBM decision-making has also been notoriously slow in granting such approvals, with months usually passing before consideration is given. This not only negates the quick responses MFIs sometimes need when confronted by contingencies, it also makes long-term planning difficult.

A final restriction applied by the CBM that greatly inhibits foreign MFIs is that the thirteen foreign banks currently licensed to operate in Myanmar are forbidden from lending to them. No reason is given for this, which denies one of the few channels the foreign banks have of genuinely providing transformational capital to Myanmar.[24]

---

[22] Directive 3/2014 of the Microfinance Supervisory Committee (now the Financial Regulatory Department, Ministry of Finance), 13 October 2014. This Directive pertains to each of the subsequent two paragraphs too.

[23] Information sourced from interviews by the author with staff of foreign MFIs and of the CBM, February 2016.

[24] Author interviews with foreign MFIs and banks, February 2016.

What should be done about all of this? The recommendations of the MMFA (the microfinance industry body noted earlier), truncated in the following list, are, in the view of this author, compelling:

- The current limitations on access to funds [should be] liberalised to allow local and foreign-owned MFIs alike to source funds from both domestic and overseas organizations ...
- Eligible MFIs [should] be allowed to borrow at a higher debt-to-equity level than 5:1, the US$3 million limit is removed, and the prior approval for borrowing overseas should not be required ...
- The interest rate at which MFIs can borrow funds from overseas [should] not be capped, but should be determined by market rates and private due diligence ...[25]

Interest Rate Restrictions: Time for Incremental Liberalisation

Interest rates are regulated across the spectrum of formal financial services in Myanmar, and microfinance is no exception. For MFIs a maximum of 2.5 per cent per month (30 per cent per annum on a [mandatory] flat-rate basis) can be charged on loans, and a rate of 1.5 per cent per month (15 per cent per annum) must be paid on deposits. These rates compare to equivalent rates charged and paid by licensed commercial banks of 13 per cent per annum and 8 per cent per annum, respectively. Meanwhile, interest rates charged by informal moneylenders in Myanmar typically range from around 5 per cent per month on pledged collateral to 10–20 per cent per month unsecured.[26]

The interest rate caps and floors imposed on MFIs (especially when combined with the other constraints examined in these pages) make for considerable difficulties in such institutions achieving profitability and financial sustainability. The set margin of 15 per cent in other contexts would seem sufficient perhaps, but (and notwithstanding the low default rates claimed) lending micro sums to microenterprises is costly (according to CGAP, MFIs' operational costs typically range between 17 and 27 per cent of the value of a loan).[27] This, coupled with Myanmar's high current rate of inflation (estimated by the IMF at more than 10 per cent per

---

[25] These recommendations are drawn from an MMFA advocacy paper, 'Policy Reform Recommendations to Accelerate Micro-Finance in Myanmar', 17 February 2016, mimeo.

[26] For more on the range of interest rates applicable across different institutions in Myanmar, see Turnell (2016).

[27] CGAP operational expense estimates cited in Myint Zaw (2016: 98).

annum for 2015), makes microlending in the country a decidedly marginal proposition (IMF 2015: 5).

Nevertheless, the 30 per cent lending rate is similar to industry averages around the world, and assuredly to lift this ceiling would be to invite much unwanted publicity and criticism to microfinance in Myanmar.[28] Thankfully, there is a way out – keep the upper limit on the interest rates MFIs can charge, but liberalise the interest rates they must pay on deposits. In other words, allow an expansion of the interest rate *margin*, without raising the top line cost of credit to borrowers. Such a move should not deter potential depositors in MFIs. Their current deposit rate floor of 15 per cent is 7 per cent above the rate typically paid by banks on deposits, giving MFIs considerable downside flexibility, while continuing to position them as the deposit platform with the highest returns. Similarly suggesting that one need not fear them becoming an unattractive place to make deposits is the motivation for such savings. MFI customers are not, on the whole, searching for high interest rate returns. Rather, and overwhelmingly so, what they seek is a safe place to store their precautionary savings, and one that allows ready access to these in times of need.[29]

Product Restrictions: Riding the Wave of Mobile Payments

Under section 29c of the MFL, microfinance institutions are licensed to provide remittance services. No particular technologies for facilitating these services are specified. This has led to a not-unreasonable presumption amongst MFIs that they can engage in mobile phone–based payments and account services. Unfortunately, however, this presumption has not been realised in practice. Not through ad hoc proscription in this case – but simply because enabling regulations to allow MFIs to engage in this part of their lawful business have yet to be implemented.

Enabling regulations or not, Myanmar's MFIs themselves are much interested in the possibilities offered them by mobile financial services. In late 2015 a forum held exclusively for them by Wave Money, a mobile financial services outfit that is a subsidiary of Myanmar's Yoma Bank,

---

[28] The average yield on MFI loans in Cambodia is 31.6 per cent, 36.5 per cent in Indonesia, 46.5 per cent in Laos, 41.2 per cent in the Philippines and 19.9 per cent in Vietnam. Information was personally supplied to the author by researchers at the Livelihoods and Food Security Trust Fund, March 2016.

[29] A conclusion based on interviews with MFI staff conducted by the author in January–February 2016.

in partnership with the country's most successful foreign-owned telco, Norway's Telenor, was attended by more than thirty MFI representatives (including representatives from all of the largest MFIs). Notwithstanding the role of Yoma, Wave Money is an interoperable mobile financial services platform which (from their side) is open to any institution or their agents. Wave Money is as yet authorised to conduct only limited 'trials', and non-bank-based mobile financial services are yet to be authorised by the CBM.[30]

The denial thus far of allowing MFIs to take advantage of mobile phone–based technologies to provide better remittance and other products is an opportunity lost. As is widely celebrated, mobile phone–based financial services are dramatically expanding financial inclusion in many places around the world, but especially those hitherto furthest from the reach of formal banks. This outreach is especially prominent in Africa, where the Kenya-founded M-Pesa mobile money service has linked up with a number of MFIs to greatly reduce costs in loan disbursement, repayments and back-office processes, and even allowing for more efficient collection of deposits. A report commissioned by USAID on the possibilities of digital financial services was convinced that something similar could be achieved in Myanmar. Using the aforementioned PACT Global Finance Fund as an example, it noted that the MFI had '40,000 applicants waiting for loans ... Digitizing operations would help to significantly decrease time spent on loan processing and disbursement, allowing staff to focus attention on identification of new clients' (Evans, Akkram and Cuna 2015: 21).

Meanwhile, a report from one of the most active foreign legal/investment advisory firms in Myanmar was even more bullish, declaring that the 'liberalisation of the telecommunications market in under-banked Myanmar ... and the rise of microfinance investment set the stage for a stellar rise in electronic money'. More soberly (and accurately) comes the caveat that 'none of this is going to happen without proper regulation' (Vanderbruggen and Dharamsi 2014: 1).

Micro-Insurance

Poor households in Myanmar (indeed, everywhere) are more vulnerable to risk than are those with resources. They have less assets to fall back on when external shocks hit, and they are dramatically less likely to have

---

[30] The seeming authorisation of MFIs under the MFL are, clearly, yet to be tested.

anything in the way of formal insurance instruments. In Myanmar only around 3 per cent of the population have recognisable insurance of any form (Almekinders et al. 2015).

The provision of insurance by MFIs is allowed under the MFL (s 29d). Nevertheless, on this front once again practice is at variance to the legal formalities, and no enabling regulations have been written to allow for micro-insurance. Micro-insurance (which covers a range of risks, from life insurance, fire and accident, to snake-bite) is a more complex offering than loans and deposits, and could not (should not) be offered by any but the most professional of MFIs. Nevertheless, it seems a pity that an offering of such clear utility remains stymied.

Regulatory Problems

The FRD was created to mimic the institutions that elsewhere around the world regulate microfinance entities. Yet, in truth, the FRD struggles to properly implement the laws and regulations it is supposed to oversee, and has very little capacity to understand and incorporate the many new methodologies and technologies being applied elsewhere in the world. This has many implications for the sector, but not least the lack of confidence inspired by its supervision of what (as noted earlier) is now around 250 MFIs of varying qualities and capacities.

Meanwhile, exacerbating the problems for MFIs from dysfunctions within the FRD are rising concerns of regulatory arbitrage via growing incursions (justifiable and otherwise) by the Central Bank of Myanmar (CBM) in the MFI supervisory space. As we have seen, this has been clearly evident with respect to the external funding of foreign MFIs, but it has also caused confusion on the mobile payments front where, as noted, the CBM has thus far frustrated efforts by non-bank financial institutions.

Getting the supervisory structures right is a necessary condition for the health of the sector more broadly. International experience on this front, however, suggests the need for dedicated and singular microfinance supervision. MFIs are not banks, and their potential contributions arise from the extent to which they can surmount the cost and other barriers that have traditionally deterred more formal institutions from engaging the financially marginalised. Reinvigorating the FRD, and asserting its role as the regulatory 'one-stop shop' for MFIs, would seem useful policy for the Myanmar government, and for the international agencies supporting it in the quest for greater financial inclusion.

The Need to Move Beyond Peer-Group Lending

Beyond the regulatory restrictions on Myanmar's MFIs noted earlier are various industry practices that undermine the contribution that microfinance can make. One of these practices is the near-universal employment in Myanmar of the group-lending model, a methodology that has increasingly come under question elsewhere. In a nutshell the problem here is that the very virtue of such lending, that it *can* involve peer support to borrowers who fall behind, can also mutate into peer *pressure* to extract payment – at whatever the cost to the individuals afflicted.[31] Harper (2007: 36) writes that it would be hard to imagine that poor people enjoy pressure from their peers in such matters, and the resultant loss of privacy, any more than richer people with more options do. Putting the matter colourfully, Harper goes on to say:

> Group-based microfinance delivery systems are temporary low-quality expedients, like shared toilets, primary school classes of 60 children, or clinics without doctors. These are the best that can be provided at the present time for some people in some places, but they are recognised as fundamentally unsatisfactory.

Of course, and as Harper implicitly acknowledges in the previous quote, the reason for the all-pervasive persistence of group lending in microfinance comes down to cost – individual small loan assessment is expensive, while getting peer members to monitor each other is much less so. Is there any way out of the peer-group lending model?

A number of alternatives are available. One is potentially presented by the rise of mobile financial services outlined earlier in the chapter. Amongst the numerous possible virtues yielded through mobile financial services is the trove of data they allow that, in turn, tells potential creditors much about the individual they may want to lend to. Formal, regular payments in the otherwise informal economy, which, for many in Myanmar, is the real space in which they derive their living, are rare.

---

[31] The Smart Campaign is an international effort designed to make for better practices from MFIs, but especially in the context of lending. A joint effort of CGAP and Accion International's Center for Financial Inclusion, the Smart Campaign sets out six principles of MFI lending: 1. Avoid creating over-indebtedness; 2. Apply responsible and transparent pricing; 3. Always employ non-coercive repayment methods and practices; 4. Ensure the proper behaviour of staff; 5. Have procedures for redressing grievances; and 6. Ensure the privacy of customer data. For more on the Smart Campaign, see the organisation's website, http://www.smartcampaign.org/ (accessed 9 March 2016).

A growing exception to these, however, are the transactions undertaken to sustain mobile phone connectivity, and the use of this for commercial and financial purposes. In short, the information asymmetry that exists between borrower and lender, which prompted the creation of devices such as peer-group lending, might be coming to an end.

Another technology that would greatly aid Myanmar's MFIs in providing *individual* lending would come about via the creation of (one or more) 'credit bureaus'. Predating modern microfinance by many decades, credit bureaus are essentially information-sharing institutions that record the debt history of borrowers, and in this way also partially close the information asymmetry between debtors and creditors.[32] In so doing they aid financial institutions in making prudent lending decisions (and making them more financially sustainable in the process), while assisting 'good' borrowers to receive the funds they need by providing evidence of their creditworthiness. The lender is better off, the borrower is better off, the economy as a whole is better off, while the individual is free from group scrutiny.

Credit bureaus are fast making an impact throughout the international microfinance sector, within which they are also seen as a solution to the 'credit bubble' phenomenon of too much, too eager, money flowing into the system. In the words of one international industry network:

> In many markets, over-indebtedness and non-payment of loans has reduced portfolio quality and muted the benefits of microlending. Without systems to safeguard against negative outcomes, the ability of microfinance to significantly advance financial inclusion is at risk. Credit bureaus have proven to be crucial to the healthy development of the microfinance industry and are a critical link to bridging the informal and formal sector. (Montgomery and Montgomery 2010: 3)

Section 75 of the Central Bank of Myanmar Law (as well as ss 142 and 143 of the Financial Institutions Law of Myanmar) grants the central bank the authority to establish a credit bureau (or to license private credit bureaus) to 'collect, in a manner and to such extent, as it thinks fit, credit information or any other information relevant in the assessment of the creditworthiness of the customers and to inform of these information to financial institutions [sic]'.

---

[32] Under Myanmar's new (January 2016) Financial Institutions Law a credit bureau is defined as 'an entity specialized in the collection and sale of credit information for individuals and companies' (s 2w).

Alternatives to Microfinance: The Co-Operatives Cul de Sac

Often listed as microfinance providers in Myanmar are the various financial co-operatives that exist in the country. Separately organised under the Ministry of Cooperatives (itself posing something of a problem in terms of regulatory clarity) there is, and always has been, a very large gap between the presentation and rhetoric of what co-operatives do in Myanmar and the practical realities on the ground.[33] The co-operative movement has made enormous strides in many countries around the world, especially in terms of their contributions to financial inclusion. In Myanmar, the bald truth is that they have mostly been a failure, not least since they are based on levels of trust and social capital that have never been present – in the colonial era, the early independence years or the present. Yet, and notwithstanding this unpromising track record, it is claimed that there are around 1,700 financial co-operatives in Myanmar. Nearly 80 of these hold MFI licences. More than half a million borrowers are collectively claimed for the co-operatives, more than MMK20 billion (US$17 million) in loans and around MMK30 billion (US$26 million) in deposits (OECD 2015: 210). These numbers are not reliable, and many of the co-operatives are moribund in reality. Nevertheless, the claims themselves are illustrative of the regard in which the co-operative system has been held for many in authority in Myanmar.

The China Loan

Policy-making with respect to banking and financial affairs under the Thein Sein administration was, for the most part, mercifully absent of the sometimes eccentric initiatives that were hitherto a feature in Myanmar. In August 2013, however, echoes of the past could be heard when news broke of a large – up to US$900 million – loan negotiated between Myanmar's Ministry of Cooperatives and the Export-Import (Exim) Bank of China. This loan, to be drawn down in tranches, was to be on-lent to Myanmar's co-operatives which, in turn, would provide loans to individual borrowers. The Exim Bank loan was to be repaid in ten years, and came with an interest charge of 4.5 per cent per annum and a 'management fee' of

---

[33] In the wake of the coming to office of the NLD government in March 2016 the Ministry of Cooperatives has been abolished, and its activities transferred to an expanded Ministry of Border Affairs. The latter is a ministerial post reserved for a military appointee. Accordingly, it is likely the co-operative sector will remain outside of financial sector policy more broadly.

a further 1 per cent. Meanwhile, for the individual borrowers of the co-operatives the loan terms were very attractive – initially publicised at 1.5 per cent per month (it will be recalled that MFI loans are charged at 2.5 per cent), they were subsequently reduced to 1.1 per cent (Supetran 2015).

Under the 'new' system loans were meant to be used for a number of *business* purposes, but the expectation has been that farmers will use bor-rowings to go towards buying 'tractors, tractor trailers, trucks, engines, generators, water pumps and motorbikes'. Urban borrowers are expected to purchase 'taxis, sewing machines, trishaws and motorbikes'.[34]

The actual borrower of the US dollar loan from China was the Myanmar Foreign Trade Bank (MFTB), which then advanced the Ministry of Cooperatives an equivalent sum of *kyat*, for on-lending to co-operatives (Khin Oo Tha 2013). The reason the loan has been taken in US dollars appears to be because Chinese imported goods are the items borrowed against. As such, the whole arrangement is not unlike a vast hire purchase scheme.[35] The benefits to the Chinese suppliers from this are clear and apparent. Whether the arrangement locks Burmese borrowers into the purchase of items they might not otherwise choose is an open (and wor-rying) question.[36]

In reaction to the Ministry of Cooperative's announcements, Phyo Win, an MP with the opposition National League for Democracy (NLD), noted that co-operative enterprises had, in the past, 'always been a fail-ure'.[37] Other MPs at the time took a similar line, with representative Tin Nwe Oo rhetorically asking 'how many times has the co-operative system succeeded in our country?' while also noting in passing the high interest rate China was charging for its initiating credit.[38] The (now former) min-ister of Cooperatives himself acknowledged that 'the cooperative system has not succeeded in the past', before adding, 'but we will try to learn from our mistakes'.[39]

Upon this issue of the system's ability to cope with expansion, and of the Ministry and regulators' ability in directing it all, even outside

[34] Statement made at the aforementioned international conference on microfinance in Myanmar, held in Naypyidaw on 9–10 May 2013, op. cit.

[35] The 20 August report in the *New Light of Myanmar* supports the idea that this is the arrangement.

[36] Alas, it also cannot be assumed away that some of the foreign exchange proceeds of the loan may end up in places and pockets not properly intended.

[37] U Phyo Win is cited in Win Ko Ko Latt (2013).

[38] Tin Nwe Oo is cited in Khin Oo Tha (2013).

[39] Kyaw Hsan is cited in Win Ko Ko Latt (2013).

observers have been sceptical. Capturing the mood on this front was LIFT (2013: 17):

> A key issue facing the rapid growth of the cooperatives is the limited use of prudential standards and professional management systems, and, for example, clients are not required to undergo needs and risk assessments prior to disbursals. The supervisor (Ministry of Cooperatives) has limited tools to manage the funds, and the mandatory annual audits may be insufficient as the loan book grows. This is particularly important since, although Myanmar has had experience with cooperatives for a long time, sustainability at this scale is not yet proven and will require a few years of operation.

The MPs and others cited were (and are) surely right to be concerned. Put simply, co-operatives *have* always been a failure in Myanmar.[40] Established initially by the British colonial authorities to dilute the dominance of the *Chettiar* moneylenders, as well as to curry favour with the local populace, the first iteration collapsed in the 1920s amidst both economic depression and a widespread lack of faith in the system. The revival of the co-operatives post-independence (when they were seen as an acceptable device existing somewhere between capitalism and socialism) more or less went the same way, especially with respect to an all-pervasive belief that co-operative loans did not have to be paid back. Following the military coup in 1962, co-operatives were once again a chosen vehicle for credit provision. In reality, however, they were little more than elements of the security apparatus and distribution devices for petty (and not so petty) corruption, before disintegrating into irrelevancy. Up until the recent pronouncements it is perhaps fair to say that the consensus amongst financial sector stakeholders in Myanmar was that the co-operative credit system as it existed was essentially moribund, an artefact of history unsuited to modern financial practices.

Lessons for Microfinance

The lesson for microfinance in Myanmar from the long and sorry history (and recent past) of its financial co-operatives is a simple one. The provision of financial services, even in their micro form, is best left unburdened by aims and objectives that have little to do with such services, but much more to do with utopian visions of societal transformation. Such visions warped and distorted the co-operative movement in Myanmar,

---

[40] For details on the long history of financial co-operatives in Myanmar, see Turnell (2009).

and the phenomenon has been clearly apparent during the most hubristic moments of the global microfinance industry too. For Myanmar there is surely much value in simply providing reliable financial services to people otherwise denied them. Similarly, there is much to be said for microfinance in terms of creating in itself a viable industry of delivering financial intermediation, new products and new services to more and more people. There is, as Roodman (2012: 270) notes, 'few realms' where 'foreign aid and philanthropy point to such success in fostering Schumpterian development'.

Myanmar's difficult, constrained and broadly dysfunctional financial sector creates an environment in which microfinance institutions could play an unusually key role. At present they are not fulfilling this role, largely as a consequence of myopic policy-making by past governments of Myanmar. This is unfortunate, but, interpreting matters optimistically, it is a situation that allows present and future industry regulators and entrepreneurs to make rapid and relatively simple improvements. Microfinance is no panacea for the establishment of a fully functioning financial sector that properly aggregates and allocates capital, and allows ordinary people to better cope with risk. Nevertheless, microfinance represents an institutional complement and an important first step to such an end.

References

Almekinders, G., S. Fukuda, A. Mourmouras and J. Zhou. 2015. *ASEAN Financial Integration*. IMF Working Paper WP/15/34. Washington DC: International Monetary Fund.

Angelucci, M., D. Karlan and J. Zinman. 2013. *Win Some Lose Some? Evidence from a Randomized Microcredit Program Placement by Compartamos Banco*. May. Abdul LaJ-Pal Working Paper.

Armendariz de Aghion, B. and J. Morduch. 2005. *The Economics of Microfinance*. Cambridge, MA: MIT Press.

Attanasio, O., B. Augsberg, R. De Haas, E. Fitzsimons, and H. Harmgart. 2013. *Group Lending or Individual Lending? Evidence from a Randomized Field Experiment in Rural Mongolia*. CentER, Discussion Paper 2013–074. Tilberg: Tilberg University.

Augsburg, B., R. D. Haas, H. Harmgart and C. Meghir. 2012. *Microfinance, Poverty and Education*. Working Paper No. 1215. London: Institute for Fiscal Studies.

Banerjee, A., E. Duflo, R. Glennerster and C. Kinnan. 2014. *The Miracle of Microfinance? Evidence from a Randomized Evaluation*. Cambridge, MA: Massachusetts Institute of Technology, Department of Economics.

Collins, D., J. Morduch, S. Rutherford and O. Ruthven. 2009. *Portfolios of the Poor: How the World's Poor Live on $2 a Day*. Princeton: Princeton University Press.

Consultative Group to Assist the Poorest (CGAP). 2012. *A Guide to Regulation and Supervision of Microfinance: Consensus Guidelines*. Available at www .cgap.org/sites/default/files/Consensus-Guideline-A-Guide-to-Regulation-and-Supervision-of-Microfinance-Oct-2012_0.pdf (accessed 3 March 2016).

Crepon, B., E. Duflo, F. Devoto and W. Pariente. 2014. *Estimating the Impact of Microcredit on Those Who Take it Up: Evidence from a Randomized Evaluation*. Abdul Latif Jameel Poverty Action Lab (J-Pal). Available at http://economics .mit.edu/files/6659 (accessed 6 March 2016).

Evans, N., A. Akkram and T. Cuna. 2015. *Supporting Digital Financial Services in Myanmar: Assessment of the Potential for Digital Financial Services in Agriculture Value Chains*. Report prepared for the Mobile Solutions Technical Assistance and Research (mSTAR) programme. US Agency for International Development (USAID). Available at www.microlinks.org/sites/default/files/ resource/files/MyanmarDFSAssessment_Report_Long.pdf (accessed 14 March 2016).

Foerch, T., Om Ki, San Thein and S. Waldschmidt. 2015. *Myanmar's Financial Sector: A Challenging Environment for Banks*. Yangon: Deutsche Gesellshaft fur Internationale Zusammenarbeit GmbH (GIZ).

Harper, M. 2007. 'What's Wrong with Groups' in T. Dichter and M. Harper (eds), *What's Wrong with Microfinance*. London: Practical Action Publishing.

International Monetary Fund (IMF). 2015. *Myanmar: Staff Report for the 2015 Article IV Consultations*. Washington DC: IMF.

Khin Oo Tha. 2013. 'Chinese Bank to Loan $100 million'. 20 August. *Mizzima News*. Available at http://www.mizzima.com/business/economy/9883-chinese-bank-to-loan-100-million.

Livelihoods and Security Trust Fund (LIFT). 2013. *Myanmar: Financial Inclusion Roadmap, 2014–2020*. Yangon: LIFT.

Montgomery, K. and M. Montgomery. 2010. *Promoting Credit Bureaus: The Role of Microfinance Associations*. Washington DC: SEEP Network and Citi Foundation.

Myint Zaw. 2016. 'Paradign Shift of Microfinance in Myanmar' in Om Ki and San Thein (eds), *Collection of Papers on Myanmar's Financial Sector*. Yangon: GIZ-Myanmar and Thura Swiss.

Organisation for Economic Cooperation and Development (OECD). 2015. *Multi-Dimensional Review of Myanmar, Volume 2: In-Depth Analyses and Recommendations*. Paris: OECD.

Roodman, D. 2012. *Due Diligence: An Impertinent Inquiry into Microfinance*. Washington DC: Center for Global Development.

Sinclair, H. 2012. *Confessions of a Microfinance Heretic: How Microlending Lost its Way and Betrayed the Poor*. San Francisco: Berrett-Koehler.

Supetran, Jay. 2015. 'The China Loan: Managing and Sustaining Development'. August. *Myanmar Insider*. Available at http://www.myanmarinsider.com/the-china-loan-managing-and-sustaining-devel/.

Tarozzi, A., J. Desai and K. Johnson. 2013. *On the Impact of Microcredit: Evidence from a Randomized Intervention in Rural Ethiopia*. Working Paper No. 382. Bureau for Research and Economic Analysis of Development (BREAD). Available at ibread.org/bread/system/files/bread_wpapers/382.pdf (accessed 4 March 2016).

Turnell, S. R. 2009. *Fiery Dragons: Banks, Moneylenders and Microfinance in Burma*. Copenhagen: NIAS Press.

2014. 'Banking and Financial Regulation and Reform in Myanmar'. August, 31(2) *Journal of Southeast Asian Economies* 225–240.

2016. *Banking and Finance in Myanmar: Present Realities, Future Possibilities*. Yangon: United States Agency for International Development (USAID).

Vanderbruggen, E. and A. Dharamsi. 2014. 'Easy Money? Mobile Banking, Mobile Money and Myanmar's Financial Regulations'. 8 May. *VDB Loi Client Briefing Note*. Yangon: VDB Loi.

Win Ko Ko Latt. 2013. 'MPs Approve Loan Despite Concerns Over Interest'. 20 August. *The Myanmar Times*. Available at http://www.mmtimes.com/index.php/national-news/7947-mps-approve-loan-despite-concerns-over-interest.html.

World Bank. 2014. *Myanmar Agricultural Development Bank: Initial Assessment and Restructuring Options*. Bangkok: World Bank Group.

Laws

Central Bank of Myanmar Law No. 16/2013 (Pyidaungsu Hluttaw Law).
Financial Institutions Law of Myanmar No. 20/2016 (Pyidaungsu Hluttaw Law).
Microfinance Law No. 13/2011 (Pyidaungsu Hluttaw Law).

Regulations and Official Notifications

Central Bank of Myanmar. 2013. Directive 4–2013 (Mobile Banking Directive). 3 December.

Financial Regulatory Department, Ministry of Finance and Revenue. 2011. *Microfinance Procedures, Instructions and Accounting and Reporting Formats for the Microfinance Organization*. Notification 277/2011. 23 December.

Financial Regulatory Department, Ministry of Finance and Revenue. 2014. *Directive 3/2014 of the Microfinance Supervisory Committee*. 13 October.

Financial Regulatory Department, Ministry of Finance and Revenue. 2015. *Procedures in Borrowing Loans from Formal Financial Institutions Outside the Country, to be Followed by Foreign MFIs Doing Microfinance.* Regulation 13/2015. 5 January.

Financial Regulatory Department, Ministry of Finance and Revenue. 2015. *Receiving Voluntary Saving and Compulsory Saving by MFIs.* Regulation 39/2015. 13 January.

6

The Governance of Local Businesses in Myanmar

Confronting the Legacies of Military Rule

MATTHEW ARNOLD

Debates on law and development have more recently emphasised the importance of local governance in developing contexts (Bardhan and Mookherjee 2006). A range of countries – from Indonesia to Pakistan and China – have engaged in efforts at decentralisation and strengthening of local administration and governance institutions. But how is local economic governance important to development? This chapter demonstrates the connection between local economic governance and development in the context of Myanmar. Yet, given that Myanmar has been closed off from the outside world for so long, the preliminary step required is to map the current local governance administration system that exists and the ways in which it is already involved in local economic governance. This chapter offers an empirical overview of local governance in Myanmar, with an emphasis on the connection to economic development and reform.

For the purposes of this chapter, local economic governance entails the rules that govern businesses at the sub-national level and the actors and institutions that implement these rules, particularly at the township level and for small and medium-sized enterprises (Bissinger and Maung Maung 2014: 10).[1] Key processes and rules of local economic governance include granting permissions and licences, collecting revenue, providing services, and regulating and monitoring businesses. Improved local economic governance plays an important role for development, with the strengthening and expansion of small and medium-sized enterprises critical to job creation and local consumption and production.

---

[1] For a fuller review of local economic governance, see Bissinger (2016). As noted in that report, the businesses covered include both incorporated companies as well as individual entrepreneurs.

Local economic governance in Myanmar has evolved significantly since 2011 as the country decentralises power to fourteen new state and region governments mandated by the 2008 Constitution. Myanmar's efforts to open its economy after decades of military authoritarianism and towards a market economy are shaded by the residual bureaucratic structures of both socialist economic planning and a security state focused on surveillance and coercion. Two government departments are central to Myanmar's local economic governance: the General Administration Department (GAD) of the Ministry of Home Affairs and Development Affairs Organisations (DAOs), which are now under the new state and region governments following their transfer in 2011 from the Ministry of Border Affairs. The GAD is responsible for basic public administration across the breadth of Myanmar's sub-national governance, while DAOs are township-level agencies focused on municipal governance.

The GAD is primarily focused on administering Myanmar's 330 townships. However, within its very expansive remit, it has a wide range of local economic governance responsibilities. These include issuing licences for important economic activities, particularly the sale of alcohol and real estate. The GAD also provides the recommendations necessary for a variety of business licences and permits, including land transfers, construction permits and operating licences, and collects a significant amount of excise taxes as well as taxes on numerous types of land transactions. DAOs are important because they are the only civil service institution under the full control of state and region governments and are self-funded through the collection of local taxes and social service fees. The role of DAOs in local economic governance is paramount through the provision of most business operating licences, the issuance of construction permits, the management of local markets and the collection of building taxes. DAOs are also important to local businesses as primary service providers, and ensure the maintenance of basic functions such as water and sewage services, trash collection and road maintenance.

This chapter will first detail the roles, structures and functions of the GAD and DAOs for local economic governance. It will then assess how these two actors – which can be considered the principal providers of local economic governance – are shifting to account for national reform priorities, namely decentralisation and a liberalised economy, but also how the legacies of military rule continue to shape their basic functioning. Both of these organisations are significant in that they were long central to the military's control of the population and its management of the economy. However, with ongoing reforms, the respective roles of the

GAD and DAOs are slowly evolving to allow for more transparency and engagement with the public, including the business community. Growing Myanmar's economy through expanding and empowering local businesses is critical to alleviating poverty and boosting national economic growth. If the GAD and DAOs can be reformed further, they both have important roles to play in the country's economic development.

Economic Governance in Myanmar

Before proceeding, it is necessary to first articulate the basic parameters of local economic governance in Myanmar. The country has long maintained a 'graded territorial' system of sub-national governance, namely progressively smaller administrative units that are overseen by central administrators. Myanmar comprises seven states and seven regions, six self-administered zones and a self-administered division, and one Union territory – the capital Naypyidaw.[2] The smallest formal administrative units are the village tract, which consists of a cluster of villages, and wards, which are sister units to village tracts, but are in semi-urban and urban areas. Wards and village tracts are in turn grouped into 330 townships, where many Union ministry offices are located. Collections of townships are organised as seventy-four districts, which in turn form the fourteen states and regions.[3] Townships are the key building blocks of public administration in the country, and their administrations are headed by a GAD officer, who, as mentioned, is a civil servant from the Ministry of Home Affairs (Chit Saw and Arnold 2014). It is at the township level that many key functions of government take place, such as population registration, land management and most forms of tax collection.[4]

The 2008 Constitution made significant changes to the sub-national administration of Myanmar. The most significant of these reforms was the creation of fourteen new state and region governments, each with

[2] States and regions, despite the terminology distinguishing historically 'ethnic' states from majority *Bamar* regions, are constitutionally equivalent. The six self-administered territories are the zones of Naga in Sagaing Region, Danu, Pa-O, Palaung, Kokang and the Self-Administered Division of Wa (all in Shan State).

[3] 2008 Constitution of Myanmar, ss 49–51.

[4] The seventy-four districts form a middle tier of administration, linking the Union government and the fourteen state and region governments with all 330 townships, and they are headed by a senior official from the GAD. Self-administered zones, and the one self-administered division, have a constitutional status in many ways equivalent to a state or region, and can form their own indirectly elected and appointed 'leading bodies' led by a chairperson (2008 Constitution of Myanmar, ss 275 and 276).

executive, legislative and judicial functions (see Nixon, Joelene and Chit Saw 2013). However, Myanmar remains a highly centralised state. Although the new state and region governments have designated responsibilities and revenue sources, as stipulated by the 2008 Constitution, they do not have their own bureaucracy that functions independently of the Union government. Sub-national governance in Myanmar is still based upon the functioning of Union ministries that maintain offices at the state/region, district and township levels. The Ministry of Home Affairs' GAD is paramount within this system of sub-national governance. This means also that while Myanmar has two tiers of government – for example, the Union and state/region levels – there is effectively no third tier of government, namely 'local government' that has distinct responsibilities and revenue sources, and discretion over managing those.

Economic governance in Myanmar is dominated by the Union government. This stems from the historical legacies of socialist economic policies and centralisation under an authoritarian military regime. Providing permits and licences to do business in the most lucrative sectors, especially natural resources, is the exclusive domain of the Union government, as is issuing licences to import and export goods (Bissinger and Maung Maung 2014: 10). Although much of this interaction is channelled directly to Naypyidaw, especially in the case of large corporations, Union ministries maintain offices down through the administrative hierarchy to the sub-national administrations in states/regions and districts, and finally down to townships. It is at these lower levels, particularly in townships, that almost all of Myanmar's businesses, which are largely micro- and small and medium-sized enterprises (MSMEs), interact with government.[5]

The range of government actors involved in local economic governance is expansive (Bissinger 2016: 7–8). As mentioned, nearly all of these except for DAOs are local offices of Union ministries in the townships. Local economic governance actors include the ministries of Home Affairs; Cooperatives; Agriculture and Irrigation; Livestock, Fisheries and Rural Development; Environmental Conservation and Forestry; Finance; National Planning and Economic Development; Construction; and Labour, Employment and Social Security. At the township level of ministry offices, the focus is on issuing licences and collecting taxes, as well as basic implementation of national policies. At this level there has been little deconcentration of decision-making power, that is, local

---

[5] The Organisation for Economic Co-Operation and Development (2013: 104) notes that MSMEs comprise 99.4 per cent of all businesses in Myanmar.

officials implement policy rather than formulate it. Importantly, these local offices of Union ministries tend to be sector specific, such as agriculture or road construction for instance. Some of these local ministry offices will both report to superiors within their ministry as well as consult and co-ordinate with the state and region governments (Nixon et al. 2013: 26).

From 2011 to 2015, Myanmar had thirty Union ministries, which were subsequently reduced to twenty-three in 2016. Given this large number, they tend to be very sector focused. However, within Myanmar there is also an administrative tradition at local levels of governance for 'general administration', whereby some local officials will have a wide remit to engage in many sectors and form a primary interface with much of the population in terms of basic social service provision and revenue collection. The GAD is the most prominent example of this tradition whereby GAD officials are involved to one degree or another in the vast multitude of government functions at the local level. The GAD township administrator, an assistant director–level bureaucrat, acts as the senior-most civil servant locally. The DAOs are another example of a government agency with a diverse remit outside of one sector. DAOs are involved in everything from road construction and drainage, to licensing restaurants and hotels, to collecting building taxes and issuing construction permits. It is their more diverse mandates and extensive interfaces with the local communities that make the GAD and DAOs so important for basic public administration and local economic governance in particular. Lastly, in terms of interaction between the two, it should be noted that co-operation and routine interaction exist, but their mandates also allow for fairly distinct and largely complementary focuses. However, as Myanmar's paramount local administration agency, the GAD plays a leadership role for other local government agencies, including DAOs, such as by chairing local management committees. Rather than executive decision-making, this role mostly convenes meetings and enables communication between government agencies.

The GAD as Managers of Local Economic Governance

The GAD of the Ministry of Home Affairs is critically important to subnational governance in Myanmar, acting as a manager for a wide variety of government functions and processes, particularly for local economic governance. No other government organisation has such a wide presence in the country. Even the Tatmadaw (army) is not spread amongst the general population to the same degree anymore. The GAD's primary responsibility is the management of the country's public administrative structures, which, as detailed earlier, are hierarchical and geographically defined. The fourteen state and region governments rely upon the GAD to serve as their civil service, and the state/region executive secretary, a GAD deputy director-general, is the senior civil servant for each state and region. Below the states and regions, the district administrator is a GAD officer, and heads up the District General Administrative Office. In turn, the district level supervises the country's respective 330 townships, which are the critical building blocks of administration in Myanmar. A township administrator, who is always the GAD officer heading the township office, manages each township and provides direction to village tract and ward administrators. Nationally, the GAD supports co-ordination and communication amongst the Union government's twenty-three ministries. Given that role, the GAD plays a central role in connecting the capital, Naypyidaw, all the way down to approximately 16,700 wards and village tracts.[6] Considering this expansive presence, the GAD is the bureaucratic backbone of the Myanmar state.

The importance of the GAD depends not so much on what it explicitly controls, which is in fact a great deal, but rather on the GAD's ubiquitous presence, and its authority to co-ordinate, communicate amongst and convene other government actors. While governance reforms to reconstruct and reorient much of Myanmar's public sector have proliferated since the 2008 Constitution, with the exception of accruing new responsibilities at the state and region level, the GAD has experienced relatively limited reform of its own structures and processes. The GAD's parent ministry, Home Affairs, is one of three ministries which, according to the 2008 Constitution, must be led by a high-ranking military official on active duty and appointed by the commander-in-chief of the Armed Forces.[7] It is noteworthy that the other agencies of the Ministry of Home Affairs – the police, the Bureau of Special Investigation, and the prison and fire services – are all primarily focused on the security matters of the state. Within this group, the GAD officially places a very heavy

---

[6] Note that wards and village tracts are equivalent in terms of administration, but wards simply exist in urban areas rather than rural ones. For simplicity, this report uses 'village tracts' to represent the level of village tracts and wards. Moreover, note that village tracts do not simply correlate with 'a village', but rather a grouping of them. For perspective, there are 63, 938 villages in the country according to GAD statistics, which fall under 3,133 wards and 13,620 village tracts.

[7] 2008 Constitution of Myanmar, s 232. The other ministries in the military's 'gift' are Defence and Border Affairs.

ideational value on protecting peace and stability, albeit through public administration.

Overall, the relative power and institutional significance of the GAD has assuredly increased since the 2008 Constitution was enacted. The military-led Peace and Development Committees (PDCs) had been the paramount public administration body at sub-national levels under the military junta. These have been removed, and along with them, Tatmadaw officers are no longer routinely involved in general administration. At these sub-national levels, where before the GAD had played a secondary supporting role, the GAD has now become the paramount government presence. Moreover, while there are now state and region governments, with both legislative and executive powers, they depend on the GAD for basic and routine functioning as they have no dedicated civil service.[8]

The current legal basis for the GAD is the 2008 Constitution and the State and Region Governments Law and the Self-Administered Zone and Division Law. Under the 2008 Constitution, the GAD's pre-existing role as a primary link between the Union government and sub-national levels of governance continues, as well as the GAD's direct control of the country's core administrative institutions: the districts and townships. Moreover, the GAD also assumed responsibility for providing administrative support to the fourteen new state and region governments as well as the new Union territory that hosts the capital, Naypyidaw. The State and Region Government Law 16/2010 echoes constitutional provisions defining the GAD's central role, and also provides greater definition for the GAD's roles and responsibilities, functions and structures in the new level of sub-national governance created by the 2008 Constitution – state and region governments. Primarily, this entails the GAD acting as the civil service for the new state and region governments by setting up three attendant offices to support their functioning.[9]

Given these legal foundations, the GAD can be understood as currently playing two institutional roles.[10] The first is the continuation of its 'historic

---

[8] However, between 2013 and 2014, budget preparation for the state/region Hluttaw offices was separated from the GAD state/region office budget, possibly increasing the Hluttaws' autonomy, though all support staff are still GAD.

[9] The offices respectively support the state/region cabinet (led by the chief minister), the state/region parliament (Hluttaw) and a general administration office for the whole state/region.

[10] This dualism was highlighted in repeated interviews with senior GAD staff in October and November 2014, though there is no specific mention of it in the GAD's policy guidance. The Mon State executive secretary was most articulate in describing these roles.

role', which has been relatively untouched by the provisions of the 2008 Constitution or related laws. This historic role includes an eclectic variety of core mandates stretching from excise management to collecting assorted taxes, collecting demographic data, land management and local dispute resolution. Moreover, as mentioned, this historic role sees the continuation of the GAD's core function of providing administration for the country's basic units of administration, districts and townships, and the supervision of wards and village tracts. Its second main role is defined around the decentralisation occurring since April 2011 and the concomitant opening of the country to greater international development assistance.

The second role responds specifically to the creation of the fourteen state and region governments, as well as the Union territory of Naypyidaw and the burgeoning demands arising from President Thein Sein's efforts to promote 'people-centred development'. This has shifted the GAD from being a centralised actor working only for the Union government, albeit at local levels, to an increasingly decentralised department with a mandate to respond to the demands and dictates of new sub-national governments. As such, the GAD functions as the administrative core of Myanmar's vertical sub-national state structure, which revolves around its hierarchy of administrators. Beyond that, the expansion of local development funds and related co-ordination committees at the township and village levels, as well as processes to include communities' greater participation in development planning and budgeting processes, has resulted in the expansion of the responsibilities of GAD township administrators.

This wider context is important for understanding the current state of local economic governance. Long a socialist-leaning state defined by central planning and state-owned enterprises as well as an authoritarian security apparatus, Myanmar's current local economic governance must be framed against its recent origins stemming from this context. Although many changes are sweeping Myanmar's public sector, one of the great constants during this transition, as with previous ones, is the ongoing centrality of the GAD to the functioning of the Myanmar state, particularly at the sub-national levels, including for local economic governance.

As is the norm for all types of local governance, the GAD plays a particularly strong role in local economic governance, most notably through its township offices.[11] Economic governance functions provided by the

---

[11] At the state/region and district levels, the GAD has little direct engagement with businesses. In districts, GAD administrators approve licences for shops selling alcohol and can approve land grants.

GAD include excise management and fee and tax collection, as well as provision of the recommendations necessary for a range of licences and permits, including land transfers, construction permits and operating licences.[12] Much of the economic governance functions of the GAD fall under its 'historic' remit, and emphasise land administration, excise administration and tax collection.[13]

In terms of land management, the GAD is responsible for 'town lands', that is, urban areas, and it issues leases and licences for residential, industrial and commercial purposes.[14] The GAD also issues grants, free of land revenue, for the erection of a religious edifice or for an unremunerated public purpose. Lastly, when required, the GAD secures the acquisition of lands for public interest, such as for building schools, roads and special economic zones (SEZs) (see Nishimura; Wood this volume). GAD administrators are also widely involved in settling land disputes, primarily by functioning as the 'process manager' for disputes working through the assorted government committees that arbitrate disputes. Where possible, smaller land disputes are solved by the GAD administrators in districts and townships.[15]

Excise management is also the responsibility of the GAD. In the past, the GAD issued forty-one types of excise licences for four basic commodities (liquor, beer, yeast and wine). The GAD is now consolidating excise management for these four commodities in the states and regions. Presently, the GAD routinely issues twenty-eight types of excise licences, as some of the original forty-one categories date back to the British colonial era

---

[12] Town lands are primarily those in wards, which are deemed to be 'urban' areas. The specific criteria for this zoning appears to be a somewhat subjective judgement by local GAD officials but is primarily where there is a sufficient concentration of people to support local markets all the way up to major cities such as Yangon and Mandalay.

[13] As defined by GAD policy, the eight principal functions of the department are land administration; excise administration; collection of four kinds of tax; structural settlement of villages and towns; rural development; formation and registration of organisations and associations; conferring honourable titles and medals; and functions that restrict the transferring of the immovable properties (GAD brochure 2014).

[14] The Ministry of Agriculture keeps records for all 'farm lands' in the country, though the GAD manages 'grazing grants' for pasture land.

[15] According to Union government order number 59/2013, the Land Use Management Central Committee is chaired by the vice president and vice chaired by the minister of Home Affairs and the minister of Agriculture and Irrigation. Parallel committees exist from the central to the village level. These committees are responsible for trying to resolve land disputes, complaints and land-grabbing cases at their respective level. At the village tract level, these committees are often subsumed within the Farmland Management Committee.

and are no longer in use. Moreover, some of the state and region Hluttaws are passing new laws to amend excise licences and taxes. Excise management is based on the *Burma Excise Manual* of 1917. GAD headquarters in Naypyidaw only issues final approval for the licences that are issued by the district GAD and managed locally by the township GAD, including taxation.

Tax collection constitutes a major role for the GAD.[16] While the Land, Excise and Revenue Division bears overall responsibility for tax collection, collection is undertaken by township and district administrative offices. Four basic types of taxes are collected by the GAD:[17]

- *Excise tax*: for the excise licences issued for liquor, beer, yeast and wine.[18]
- *Land tax*: for usage of some urban residential areas and some lands where crops are planted.
- *Irrigation tax*: for usage of embankments, primarily along paddy fields and along rivers and irrigation canals. Primarily collected in Myanmar's coastal regions.
- *Mineral tax*: for collection of set minerals from state-owned public properties. These include laterite or 'stone metal' for municipal or local public roads; laterite for other purposes; limestone; stone for irrigation works, railway ballast or public works; clay; marble, gypsum and 'other minerals for which special rules do not exist'.

Interestingly, the GAD's land taxes are based upon six colonial-era laws:

1. Land and Revenue Act (1876)
2. The District Cesses Act (1880)
3. Upper Burma Land and Revenue Regulation (1889)
4. Lower Burma Towns and Village Lands Act (1898)
5. Revenue Recovery Act (1890)
6. Burma Excise Act (1917)[19]

Tax collection is generally undertaken annually. Excise taxes have historically been by far the most significant in terms of revenue. Land and

---

[16] Within the GAD, a district administrator is officially designated as the 'tax collector' while a township administrator is an 'assistant tax collector'. There is not a consolidated tax agency in Myanmar, such as the United States' Internal Revenue Service. Rather, tax collection is spread between a range of government agencies.

[17] *GAD 2012 Annual Record*, p. 70.

[18] These licences can vary between states and regions as they fall under the purview of state and region governments.

[19] Ministry of Home Affairs (MoHA), 2012, *GAD 2012 Annual Record*, p. 71.

mineral taxes have been moderately increasing in terms of total revenue, though they are still minimal. The GAD's tax collection for state and region governments is typically conducted at the township level (land and excise are two examples) and goes directly into state and region budgets.[20] As described previously, land tax rates were long held at very low levels (7 *kyat* per acre), but in the 2013–2014 fiscal year, land taxes were increased one hundred times by most states and regions (for example, by the Mon State Land Tax Law).[21] Regardless, levels of taxation for land remain minimal by international standards. These tax increases were legislated by the state and region Hluttaws because land tax, and indeed all of the GAD's tax mandates, fall under the jurisdiction of states and regions.

Myanmar's 330 townships are the building blocks for public administration in the country. Township General Administration Offices (township offices) are the primary focal point for the average Myanmar citizen's engagements with the state. The township office, under the leadership of a township administrator, is where key functions of government take place, including population registration, land registration and most forms of tax collection. While states and regions have seen significant changes to their governance structures since 2011, townships continue to function around the executive authority of GAD township administrators and do not yet have elected representative bodies.[22] The township office has a number of functions to fulfil in terms of local economic governance (Bissinger and Maung Maung 2014: 11–12). Indeed, one of the most important levels of GAD interaction with businesses is at the township level, which regularly engages with micro and small businesses. Licences for particular activities, including the sale of alcohol and real estate, are issued by the GAD. The GAD also provides the recommendations necessary for a range of licences and permits, including land transfers, construction permits and operating licences, and collects certain taxes on alcohol and land. In this way, the GAD acts as a broker and gatekeeper for many sectors. As noted by Bissinger and Linn Maung, while not a steadfast rule, township GADs are often involved in supporting economic activities that could be

---

[20] In rural areas, taxes are collected by the village tract administration, which receives 10 per cent as payment for collecting fees once the tax is remitted to the GAD. Interviews with township officers over late 2014.

[21] This rate of increase has varied as some state and region Hluttaws have yet to raise the land tax rates. For instance, Ayeyarwaddy Region has yet to change land tax rates.

[22] It is telling that while there have been additional laws since the 2008 Constitution that cover governance at both state/region (2010) and ward/village tract levels (2012), there has been no similar legislation for districts and townships.

perceived as having 'social' implications (Bissinger and Maung Maung 2014: 12).

DAOs as Implementers of Local Economic Governance

DAOs are the key actors responsible for the implementation of Myanmar's municipal governance outside of Yangon City, Mandalay City and Naypyidaw Union Territory.[23] In contrast to the GAD's role as a convener and facilitator for many government agencies, DAOs are focused more narrowly on their own remit in the country's towns and cities. Spread across the country, hundreds of DAOs manage local municipal affairs at the township level. The municipal governance of Yangon City and Mandalay City has unique provisions for the Yangon City Development Committee (YCDC) and the Mandalay City Development Committee (MCDC), which allow them their own distinct city administrations.[24] As one DAO officer noted regarding Myanmar's municipal governance, 'The rest of the country is not like YCDC or MCDC.'[25] For its part, Naypyidaw, the Union Territory, also has unique provisions for the Naypyidaw Council, which are based on the 2008 Constitution.[26]

For each state and region government, there is a DAO Office in the capital city, which is led by a director who supervises the township DAOs. The state/region government's minister of Development Affairs, with approval from the chief minister, sets development policies and oversees DAO work on the whole. Stemming from their historical origins, the core operational focus of DAOs is at the township level.[27] Township DAOs are composed of twin parts: a Township Development Affairs Committee (TDAC) that oversees and supports a Township DAO Office.[28] State/Region DAO Offices are led by a director who is the senior DAO civil servant for every state and region's DAO system. The State/Region DAO Office reports directly to the state/region government's minister of Development Affairs. A primary purpose of State/Region DAO Offices

[23] For a fuller review of DAOs, see Arnold et al. (2015).
[24] See MCDC Election Bylaw 2015.
[25] Interview with DAO director in Shan State, 12 March 2015.
[26] 2008 Constitution, s 284.
[27] The State/Region DAO Office in the state/region capital is, in turn, mainly responsible for co-ordination and staff management for the whole state/region. In contrast, at the township level, the TDAC and Township DAO Office work together to prioritise public works and municipal management.
[28] Interviews with state/region DAO directors in January and February 2015.

is to link their DAO systems – spread as they are around numerous townships – with the political leadership of the respective state/region government to ensure that DAO activities mesh with government priorities. State/Region DAO Offices play an important role in managing the DAO systems of their respective states and regions. This is a major shift for them in terms of purpose. Under the MoBA up until 2011, the Department of Development Affairs offices in the state and region capitals were largely intermediaries within the normal hierarchy of a Union ministry. After the placement of DAOs under the state and region governments, they became totally unique government actors in Myanmar as they now oversee a state/region system of government offices that provide a wide range of social services, manage local economic governance and collect significant amounts of revenue. For most states and regions, there is a State/Region DAO Office, but no parallel state-/region-level committee. There is no DAO presence at the district level. The key function of State/Region DAO Offices is to co-ordinate and supervise Township DAO Offices rather than any direct implementation.

The jurisdiction of these DAO offices has narrowed since the 2011 formation of state and region governments to focus on just the 'urban' areas of townships, for example, wards. This change stems from the abolition of MoBA's Department of Development Affairs in 2011, when its component parts were then split: DAO offices were to focus on urban wards while responsibilities for rural development were placed with the Department of Rural Development of the Ministry of Livestock, Fisheries, and Rural Development.[29]

The mandate of DAOs covers two general foci for urban areas: social service provision and economic governance. DAOs are one of the largest, though least understood, social service providers in Myanmar.[30] They deliver a significant range of services, which are directly funded through local taxes and fees, amongst the other revenues that DAOs collect. In

---

[29] The rationale for this change is unclear. Historically governance for urban and rural areas had been undertaken by municipal offices and district councils. Returning to this historical system may have felt like a comfortable transition. Moreover, the military generals drafting the 2008 Constitution may have felt a need to give at least one agency to the state and region governments as a sign of compromise, and allowing them control of the DAOs was perhaps the most comfortable option for them.

[30] According to the 2014 national census, 29.6 per cent of Myanmar's population of approximately 50.2 million is resident in urban areas. This varies extensively, from as high as 70.1 per cent in Yangon Region to as low as 14.1 per cent in Ayeyarwaddy Region. The criteria for 'urban' and 'rural' are not clear in the census's reporting, but are believed to be based on ward and village tract zoning.

contrast to other major social service providers in the country, such as the Ministry of Education and the Ministry of Health, DAOs have a diverse mandate to provide services ranging from water, sewage and trash collection to street lighting, roads, bridges and drainage.

Within the context of Myanmar's local economic governance, focused as it is on the township level, DAOs play a critically important role in providing the licences, permits and other approvals required for the basic functioning of local businesses, and especially MSMEs. These interactions with businesses are undertaken by dedicated DAO officers who work throughout urban areas collecting taxes and fees, licencing businesses and undertaking inspections. Some of the key economic functions provided by DAOs include licensing, construction permits and inspections.

A core legal mandate of DAOs is licences or the 'stipulation of conditions' for a wide range of businesses, which allows Township DAO Offices to issue certain business licences. These businesses vary widely, but include market vendors and roadside stalls, butchers, hotels and restaurants.[31] They also issue licences for businesses that are involved in a 'dangerous trade', including factories, health clinics, laboratories and blacksmiths. In this way, most MSMEs in urban Myanmar have an operating licence of some sort granted by a Township DAO Office; the most common of these are restaurants and small shops.[32]

Township DAO Offices also issue construction permits for both commercial and residential projects in urban areas. To erect buildings, businesses must obtain a construction permit from their Township DAO Office. This first entails collecting recommendations from the township fire and health departments, police and ward administrator. Along with proof of land ownership, these recommendations are then taken to the GAD township administrator who then checks land records and, if everything is in order, passes the recommendations to the Township DAO Office for final approval (Bissinger and Maung Maung 2014: 21).

---

[31] To obtain a DAO licence, businesses provide a completed application form, a fee, an ID card copy, a household list and a ward administrator's recommendation to the DAO. It is not always necessary to visit the Township DAO Office to obtain a licence, as the required paperwork and fee collection can be done by DAO field staff. Licences are renewed annually, again often by DAO field staff making visits to businesses.

[32] Township GADs are also a common place from which businesses must obtain licences and permissions. Licences for particular activities, including the sale of alcohol and real estate, are issued by the GAD. In rural Myanmar, where DAOs do not function, many types of operating licences are issued by the Department of Rural Development (DRD).

Conducting routine inspections of businesses is another core task of Township DAO Offices. DAO staff conduct some inspections on their own, such as those for market vendors. They also participate in larger inspection teams, such as for pharmacies, which receive annual inspections from a diverse team of civil servants that also includes officials from the Food and Drug Administration, township GAD, township medical office, police and fire department (Bissinger and Maung Maung 2014: 22).

In addition to these routine roles for a wide range of businesses, DAOs play unique roles for some key local businesses:

- *Slaughterhouses*: Township DAO Offices regulate slaughterhouses by conducting public auctions for operating licences and supervising the sale of meat. In this way, Township DAO Office approval is crucial in deciding where a slaughterhouse can be located and how many should be allowed. DAOs also establish and supervise livestock markets in urban areas.[33]
- *Ferries*: Township DAO Offices are responsible for the administration of small ferries across rivers and lakes in urban areas. This entails holding public auctions for ferry operating licences, as well as supervising the functioning of ferries, which are particularly prominent in the sprawling Irrawaddy River delta.
- *Markets*: Township DAO Offices manage local markets. Some of these markets are owned by DAOs, where they provide full supervision and maintenance. DAOs also grant permission for the establishment of privately owned markets and provide some supervision as well.

In addition to the technical requirements for economic governance, DAOs provide more general services to businesses. Businesses have wide-ranging infrastructure needs and can petition DAOs to construct roads and bridges and improve drainage. As with local communities, cost sharing for this local infrastructure is common between DAOs and business owners. For example, if a business or a group of businesses wants to improve the road in front of their business, the Township DAO Office may provide labour and machinery, but the business would be asked to provide the construction materials.[34] Other services to business duplicate those provided to the wider urban population – trash collection, street

---

[33] This also includes 'Supervising the keeping and breeding of animals within the development area and disposal of carcasses.'

[34] Multiple interviews with TDAC members and DAO staff in Ayeyarwaddy Region and Shan State, February and March 2015.

lighting and water, for instance (Bissinger and Maung Maung 2014: 27).[35] Lastly, it is important to note that for both social service provision and local economic governance, township DAOs are permitted to impose fines and penalties for violation of or non-compliance with DAO rules and regulations. In terms of penalties and punishment rates, there are significant variations between the states and regions.[36] Rates are set by each state and region government per township, and tend to be objective judgements about the relative capacity of communities and businesses to pay.

To fund their social service provision, DAOs must collect revenues locally. DAOs receive no funding from the Union government or state/ region governments.[37] Overall, revenues for DAOs come from three main sources: 1) user fees charged to households and businesses for services, 2) regular licence fees for businesses and 3) tender licence fees for certain businesses, primarily in relation to public auctions.

For local social services, individual households generally pay 'four property fees' – a 'building and land fee', and small charges for street lighting, garbage collection and water provision.[38] All of these user fees are collected directly by DAO staff.[39] While households are important consumers of social services, it is local businesses that are the mainstay for DAO revenue generation to pay for such social services. Of much more significance to overall DAO revenues than collection from households, businesses also pay common user fees, e.g. for street lighting, garbage and water, plus vehicle registration. DAOs also charge a service fee for inspecting new building construction, as well as building renovation projects,

---

[35] For assorted reasons, the quality of these services is sometimes rather poor, but does not seem to be a significant obstacle to business performance – instead it is more of a nuisance.

[36] For instance, in Sagaing Region, fines for prohibiting DAO staff from carrying out public works projects range from MMK5,000 to MMK20,000, while fines in Ayeyarwady Region range from MMK50,000 to MMK500,000. Overall, township DAOs have been raising fines and penalty rates for the past few years. Penalties can also include imprisonment such as one year in prison for the illegal slaughter of cows and buffalos, and six months in prison for the illegal slaughter of goats, sheep and pigs.

[37] Although DAOs are involved in allocating local development funds in collaboration with other township-level agencies, these are not in the form of direct transfers to them. For further information, see Robertson, Joelene and Dunn (2015).

[38] The calculation for the building and land fee is based on rent paid over a year, not the 'actual rent' but rather a valuation of possible rent, which is charged at 10 per cent. In this way, properties that are not actually rented are still paying the fee.

[39] However, there is some public criticism, particularly from businesses, that fees are collected, but services are not always delivered.

to assess if they comply with zoning and engineering requirements.[40] Additionally, DAOs collect revenue by annually charging businesses to use billboards and signs. However, it is from licensing fees that DAOs generate the vast majority of their revenues.

As described previously, almost all local businesses require a licence from DAOs to function. These include roadside stalls, bakeries and restaurants, small loan businesses, lodging houses and a vast array of 'dangerous trade' businesses (see Table 6.1).[41] Many of these licence fees are collected directly by DAO field staff who visit the businesses for this purpose. At times, however, DAOs hold an auction to select a contractor to collect fees from large numbers of local businesses and individuals, such as the licence fees paid by market vendors and roadside stalls. Market vendors and roadside stalls may also have to pay a small fee to DAOs to use public space if, for instance, they put chairs and tables out on a sidewalk or along a street. Fees for vehicles, namely the 'wheel tax', are also generally collected by a local firm that wins the bid for the right to collect such fees.

As mentioned previously, DAOs play a unique role issuing tender licences for a set of businesses that are acquired through public auctions, notably slaughterhouses and ferries.[42] Public auctions are also used for pawnshops and managing jetties, i.e. piers for large ships to dock. The by-laws for these auctions can vary significantly. For instance, slaughterhouse auctions in some states/regions focus on licences to run a slaughterhouse, regardless of the amount of livestock slaughtered, while in other states and regions, the auction is for the right to slaughter livestock, but the actual fee collected depends on the number of animals slaughtered, for example, the head count. Also as already explained, DAOs hold public auctions to allow businesses to collect certain DAO user fees, such as motor vehicle wheel taxes, and to implement some social services, such as garbage collection. However, the types of services that private businesses bid on to undertake for DAOs vary from one state/region to another.[43]

---

[40] The rate for this is set at 1 per cent of the total construction cost if the building is in an urban area where a DAO office has long demarcated the area as a development affairs area. The rate is only 0.5 per cent for a building outside an urban area where a development affairs area has only recently been demarcated.

[41] The criteria for 'dangerous' is unclear, but in general these tend to be businesses involved with food, local factories or general goods.

[42] Ferries under the DAO jurisdiction can be motorised or non-motorised, but tend to be 'taxi boats', i.e. those with oars, not motors, and used only locally.

[43] For instance, garbage is collected by a private business in Taunggyi, Shan State, but directly by the DAO in Pathein, Ayeyarwaddy Region.

Table 6.1. *Types of 'dangerous trade' businesses*

Food-related	Other
Tea shop; noodle shop; beetle nut shop; Myanmar traditional food shop; confectionary; cold storage for fish; soft drinks; *halawa* shop; soft drink factory; sausage shop; coffee shop; beverage shop for alcohol.	Small rice mill; cooking oil factory; salt factory; vermicelli factory; leather factory; furniture factory; health clinic and laboratory; printing house; boat maintenance facility; ship yard; lime powder factory; saw mill; beans factory; wholesale market; beauty salon; watch repair; photo shop; goldsmith; tailor; bicycle and motorcycle repair shop; lumber yard; car accessories shop; fish paste shop; fan without motor shop; blacksmith; firewood; CD/VCD shop; electronics shop; battery shop; stove and ceramics shop; gold shop; nail and hardware shop.

In most states and regions, tender licence fees, and particularly slaughterhouse tender licence fees, are the biggest sources of DAO revenue. For example, in Myangmya Township of Ayeyarwaddy Region, a fairly typical township, slaughterhouse revenue is 60 per cent of total revenue, while in Myeik Township of Tanintharyi Region, it is 50 per cent of total revenue.[44] It is also noteworthy that in Mandalay and Yangon Regions, outside of Yangon City and Mandalay City, the wheel tax is a major source of revenue given the rapid rise in vehicle ownership in recent years. Land taxes also play an increasingly important role for Mandalay and Yangon Regions, given booming real estate prices in those greater metropolitan areas.

The Legacies of Military Rule for Local Economic Governance

Full military rule in Myanmar ended in April 2011. However, overcoming the legacies of decades of such authoritarianism will take a long time. This is primarily because the military penetrated deeply into the bureaucracy starting in the early 1960s (Nakanashi 2013: 167).[45] Moreover, as

---

[44] DAO budget reporting. DAOs in various townships provided the author with examples of their annual budgets.

[45] As Nakanashi noted, 'The wholesale reorganization of administrative structures and accompanying distribution of government positions to Tatmadaw officers had an

Mary Callahan noted, 'In twentieth century Burma, warfare created state institutions that in many situations cannot distinguish between citizens and enemies of the state' (2005: 5). The influence of military authoritarianism on the bureaucracy had significant effects on economic governance as well. Namely, economic governance was not focused benignly on the full empowerment of the private sector, but rather part of a wider bureaucratic intent of surveillance and control of the population. Current economic realities in Myanmar are also compounded by the socialist tendencies of the junta. Starting during the early 1960s, during the Ne Win era, large swathes of the economy – including agricultural and industrial production, banking, transportation and communications – were nationalised (Tin Maung Maung Than 2006: 113).

While the 2008 Constitution changed some aspects of Myanmar's governance arrangements, other structures and practices have generally been left untouched.[46] In terms of sub-national governance, and by extension local economic governance, there are a couple fundamental realities. The first is that when the military removed itself from routine public administration in 2011, the GAD was for its part greatly empowered by the simple reality that it in turn became the paramount state agency for public administration at local levels; no longer were local army commanders supervising its work. It is also important to note that while Myanmar was indeed long an authoritarian state, the size of its bureaucracy was never particularly large, instead being fairly minimal and focused on surveillance and coercion rather than social services. For instance, the GAD has approximately 37,000 staff, with approximately half of those being clerks for the country's wards and village tracts. For a country of nearly 52 million, relatively there are not many local public servants.[47] Moreover, while the 2008 Constitution created fourteen state and region governments, it did little to shift the basic administration of the state at sub-national levels to them. State and region governments are led by a chief minister supported by a cabinet of nine ministers focused on assorted sectors. However, these ministers have no dedicated ministries to support their work and instead must rely on the local offices of Union ministries. Effectively, they are 'ministers without ministries' (Nixon et al. 2013: 28).

---

enormous impact on the Ne Win regime and on Burma's political system. It allowed the Tatmadaw to penetrate into the government administrative bureaucracy.' (2013: 167)

[46] For a review of the role of the military in the 2008 Constitution, see Pederson (2011).

[47] For further information about the size of Myanmar's public sector, see *Conceptualizing Public SectorReform in Myanmar* (Hook et al. 2015).

Given that, sub-national governance in the country is still dominated by Union ministries, such as those for health and education, and the omnipresence of the Ministry of Home Affairs' GAD.

Conversely, the one exception to this situation was the 2008 Constitution's placement of DAOs under the full control of the fourteen state and region governments, rather than a Union ministry. Each state and region government has a minister of development affairs whose mandate focuses on managing their DAOs, which no longer have a connection to any Union ministry. In this sense, DAOs are unique as they are answerable only to their respective state/region government. As such, DAOs stand out as a decentralised government agency that contrasts with the ongoing dominance of Union ministries functioning at sub-national levels. There are now fourteen 'DAO systems' across the country, each with its own legal mandate, policies, staffing and training programmes – with all reporting only to their respective state and region government. In this manner, DAOs are the nascent bureaucracies of the states and regions, albeit focused on only municipal governance.

The legal mandate of DAOs also represents an important precedent for Myanmar's current transition. Municipal governance in Myanmar can be traced to the 1898 Municipal Law, which in its general form lasted for ninety-five years, being fully repealed only in 1993. It was replaced by the Development Committees Law 1993, which was amended in 1997, transferring responsibility for municipal affairs from the GAD under the Ministry of Home Affairs to the newly created Ministry of Border Affairs and its Department of Development Affairs, which then became responsible for both urban and rural development. In 2011, in accordance with Schedule II of the 2008 Constitution, the only government agency to come under the full control of the new state and region governments were DAOs. Subsequently, each state and region parliament enacted Development Affairs Laws to define municipal governance for their respective areas.[48] The fourteen state and region Development Affairs Laws which have been

---

[48] Specifically, the legal basis for DAOs is the State Law and Order Restoration Council's (SLORC) Law No. 5/93, namely the 1993 Development Committees Law. According to the 2008 Constitution's section 188, state and region Hluttaws have the right to enact laws for the entire or any part of a state or region, related to matters listed in the constitution's Schedule II. 'Development Matters' is listed under the Management Sector of Schedule II. Within the 2008 Constitution there is no explicit mention of DAOs, or municipal governance more generally. Within Schedule II, 'Development Matters' is listed as *si-bin-tha-ya-ye* in the Myanmar copy of the constitution, which directly translates as 'development affairs'.

passed since late 2012 are all based on the Development Committees Law 1993, and are therefore largely similar.

In this way, DAOs currently have a distinctly awkward present reality: they are uniquely empowered to be decentralised through new state/ region laws, yet their renewed legal mandates stem from the previous SLORC/SPDC junta era, namely of centralised authoritarian rule by the military. Rather than a malicious conspiracy by the military, this situation arguably stems from the exigency to move quickly with new laws following the movement of DAOs to the newly created state and region governments and the expediency of needing to write new municipal laws by the inherently weak nascent state and region parliaments. In a similar vein, many DAO officers are former military officers given the long tradition during junta rule for retiring military officers to be transferred into the bureaucracy, especially the Ministries of Home Affairs and Border Affairs (Taylor 2009: 451).

While the state and region Development Affairs Laws share great commonality based around older structures of centralised authoritarianism, it is also important to caveat this. First, future state and region parliaments can amend the laws as they see fit. This represents one of the more significant areas of social service provision and economic governance under the sole discretion of the states and regions. Moreover, while state and region parliaments generally have demonstrated limited ambitions since 2011, one area where they have shown great interest is in the township by-laws that set the rates of fees and taxes collected locally, both by the GAD and DAOs.[49] This is significant for future reforms in that state and region parliaments can adjust the rates for revenue collection by the GAD; and the DAOs, states and regions can do likewise and also amend their basic legal mandates. This has had, and will continue to have, great significance for local economic governance.

---

[49] It is important to note how the assorted rates are set for DAO revenue collection. Somewhat uniquely, DAOs have by-laws for every township that define all rates and how to issue licences and tenders. The by-laws also set the prices that can be charged by private businesses that win public auctions. For example, slaughterhouses that win an auction must sell meat at the rates set in their township's respective by-law. To set licence rates, DAOs periodically announce prospective rates to the public and ask for feedback. If businesses have problems with rates, they can complain at a Township DAO Office. Moreover, business owners can also check the rates at Township DAO Offices. TDACs review the feedback and make suggestions, which are then posted again for public feedback. When there are no complaints received after a certain period, these rates are then sent to the state/ region government and parliament for final approval. The rates set vary greatly between townships. There is an implicit emphasis on establishing lower rates in poorer townships.

Decentralisation is fundamental to Myanmar's political and economic development. However, given decades of ethnic secessionism and centralised military rule, it remains a politically sensitive topic. From 2011 to 2016, Myanmar's Union government, under the leadership of President Thein Sein, publicly emphasised improving sub-national service delivery and inclusive economic growth. It can be expected that the current National League for Democracy government will continue to do the same. While the 2008 Constitution enshrines structures that maintain much of the centralised nature of the Myanmar state, there are also genuine possibilities for greater decentralisation to occur, most significantly through the structures of the state and region governments. It is within this context that local economic governance may move quickest towards greater decentralisation as compared to further political and democratic reforms.

It is interesting that DAOs – paramount to local economic governance and essential to basic administration in urban areas – were the one government agency fully given to the states and regions. It is also telling that the sister half of the DAOs under the old Ministry of Border Affairs, the Department of Rural Development, was simply transferred to another Union ministry.[50] In this sense, there seems to be a preference within Myanmar's military-driven elite that some of the most extensive decentralisation reforms occur in its cities and towns rather than the countryside. Tellingly, the other precedents for greater administrative autonomy in Myanmar concern its two largest cities of Yangon and Mandalay, which have unique legal mandates for city administrations but share most of the same responsibilities as DAOs. The YCDC and the MCDC both existed before the 2011 transition began and allow for those cities to be governed more directly than anywhere else in the country. However, they are still under the authority of the respective region governments and do not have fully elected city councils,[51] but are nonetheless significant markers for the types of decentralisation that could potentially occur in other parts of the country.

However, in contrast to this bureaucratic context and political dynamics for the DAOs sits the GAD, which is the archetype of a centralised

---

[50] The Department of Development Affairs had responsibility for both rural and urban governance issues. While the DRD did not exist as a distinct entity before 2011, the basic functions for rural governance were under the Department of Development Affairs until they had a dedicated home in the DRD.

[51] As with many government committees, community representatives serve alongside bureaucrats. Moreover, these community representatives are not chosen through universal suffrage but rather by each household head casting a vote.

bureaucracy and the ongoing involvement of the military in the country's public administration. Removing DAOs from the Ministry of Border Affairs was a significant step for the demilitarisation of the bureaucracy (though perhaps not an intentional step), but removing the GAD from the Ministry of Home Affairs is much more difficult in terms of challenging the military's ongoing dominance of key parts of the state bureaucracy.[52] Regardless, there is significant potential for further decentralisation to occur even in terms of the GAD's economic governance remit. For instance, the state and region parliaments have been passing new by-laws to raise the excise and land taxes that the GAD collects. Overall, however, it is still DAOs that represent the most viable opportunities for decentralising economic governance given their unique characteristics: a dedicated committee with majority community representation, full detachment from the Union government, self-funded from local communities and an expansive mandate covering many essential services. Considering this, one future possibility is that the DAOs may evolve into a more distinctive third tier of government, and a truer form of a 'municipal government'.[53] This could be achieved through national legislation.

Against these wider bureaucratic and political questions rest more tangible needs to transition local economic governance away from its historical legacies of socialist planning and military rule. The rules governing local business still tend to emphasise surveillance and control rather than empowerment and flexibility. It is telling that much of the interaction with and revenue collection by government officials focuses on the granting of permission to do something rather than collection against wealth actually created. There exist many deeply flawed structural issues for local economic governance (Bissinger 2016). These include service fees charged to businesses being arbitrary and not based on the actual costs of provision, and inconsistent and ad hoc collection of major taxes, such as that for land and buildings. In some areas, such as the issuance of tendered licences for slaughterhouses, state agencies such as DAOs continue to set

---

[52] How deliberate moving DAOs was is open to speculation regarding the 2008 Constitution's design and intent. On the one hand, it could be seen as a form of compromise by the military to hand over at least one significant local governance actor. On the other, it may be that the functions of DAOs were simply not attractive for keeping within the purview of the military in a manner similar to the GAD's functions as a key part of the Ministry of Home Affairs.

[53] 'Municipal' is defined, according to the *Oxford Advanced Learner's Dictionary*, as pertaining to a town or city or its governing body. 'Municipality' is defined as a town, city or district with its own local government.

prices for basic commodities such as beef and pork. Moreover, the structuring of public auctions for key services, such as ferries, tends to create local monopolies, but the short time for such licences (one year) leaves little incentive for infrastructure investments or service improvements.

Following decades of limited economic growth and military authoritarianism, the governance reforms needed in Myanmar are many. Local businesses are still confronted with a system of economic governance that is archaic and unsuited for a national transition towards a free market and democratisation. Such challenges faced by local businesses highlight that the wider social contract in Myanmar remains fraught, even traumatised, by decades of military rule. Local businesses widely perceive the payment of taxes and fees to be a necessary burden to ensure permission to operate but which does little to actually support their growth in terms of better government services or improved infrastructure.[54] For example, as actors who bear much of the burden of paying fees and taxes to DAOs, local businesses often feel that there is not enough transparency and accountability in terms of how DAOs function (Bissinger and Maung Maung 2014: 24). For instance, while other government agencies are creating online portals to share information, DAOs remain without systematic means of sharing basic information. Generally speaking, neither businesses nor the public know how much DAOs collect nor how and where revenue is spent. Inherently, businesses want to know how the processes of municipal affairs work, for example, why the DAO chose a particular road or building for renovation, how it did so and when the work will finish.

Overall, this dynamic of mistrust between the state and both the private sector and general public is a significant challenge for Myanmar's local development as much of its local revenue collection, used for many social services, comes from businesses.[55] Non-compliance with tax and fee collection remains rampant. In this regard, improving local economic governance to raise revenues is critically important to strengthening and expanding local social services. It is somewhat of a vicious cycle as without

---

[54] As Bissinger notes, 'Businesses often [do] not perceive that taxes translate into goods and services that helped the private sector; instead taxes [are] used to keep the oppressive state apparatus functioning.' Bissinger, J. 2016. *The Local Governance of Business in Myanmar.* Yangon: The Asia Foundation.

[55] There is also a need to reduce opportunities for corruption – for instance by scrutinising the system of 'recommendation letters' necessary to secure permits and licences, and considering the adoption of a self-declaration system for businesses, with concomitant risk-based auditing.

revenues, it is hard to improve local services.[56] But without improved local services, businesses and communities will remain hesitant to pay taxes and fees. This dynamic creates immense challenges for local governance actors: few resources to fulfil their mandate and a citizen-government relationship that is perpetually fraught and distrusting. Identifying ways to increase revenues is a priority, but there is also concern about avoiding overburdening local businesses and the public.[57]

Conclusion

While a lot of international attention and media focus has centred on the national governance reforms that have taken place since 2011, this chapter has demonstrated that there have been significant shifts in the structures of sub-national governance as well. Though Myanmar remains a highly centralised country, it is slowly but surely decentralising, including in terms of how it governs businesses. As such, any effort to understand the regulatory framework in Myanmar must include consideration of the GAD and DAOs functioning at local levels.

The GAD is the paramount actor for local governance in Myanmar, playing a critical role as a 'process manager' able to convene and co-ordinate many important government processes, including for businesses. As such, the GAD effectively acts as a gatekeeper for various business sectors to secure government permission to operate. However, its role is somewhat structurally confusing for state and region governments. On one hand, it remains steeped in the ideology of past regimes with its focus on protecting peace and stability, albeit through basic public administration. On the other, it is clearly a key point of interaction between individuals and the state, particularly in contentious areas such as land disputes and SEZs, which will remain an issue of ongoing concern. Considering this, the GAD's structures and roles have wider impacts on prospects for governance reforms. For instance, given its critical role in land management, reforming the GAD will be essential for improving Myanmar's system of land management.

---

[56] A priority must be placed on improved public relations. This can provide better incentives for improved revenue collection, i.e. it must be made clear to businesses and the public how revenues are utilised, and in what ways increased revenues will improve municipal services in line with public priorities.

[57] Interview with minister of Development Affairs, Shan State, 13 March 2015.

In contrast to the GAD's acting as the general manager of local governance the DAOs are more narrowly focused on the routine implementation of just municipal governance. As such, they are the key interface that Myanmar's micro- and small and medium-sized businesses have with government for everything from business licences to construction permits to assorted local taxes. The DAOs' traits of self-funding and an expansive mandate define them as a significant experiment in Myanmar's move towards greater decentralisation. DAOs also represent one of the most prominent examples of the demilitarisation of the bureaucracy, which contrasts starkly with the GAD's continuing placement within the military-led Ministry of Home Affairs.

Overall, both the GAD and DAOs have significant roles to play in Myanmar's decentralisation reforms. As the country continues to experiment with democratisation, and presuming the peace process advances further, there will be greater calls for a truer form of local government, namely a third tier of government. Given that the GAD acts as local administrators across Myanmar and that the DAOs are the most decentralised actors in the country, both will be central to this national discourse. Moreover, both have a significant role to play in improving Myanmar's fractured social contract, particularly between the state and businesses.

Improving their operational effectiveness can enable them to play a particularly strong role in improving local social services and economic growth. Both the GAD and DAOs serve as primary interfaces between the general public and the government for a wide range of issues. In terms of the governance of businesses, the relationships still remain fraught. Overall, this interaction tends to emphasise surveillance and control, rather than empowerment and flexibility. Improving the relationships between DAOs and the GAD with local businesses is thus of critical importance to boosting 'inclusive growth' across Myanmar. Given their importance, future efforts at law and business reform must pay close attention to the sub-national level, and particularly to the GAD and DAOs. Critical to such reforms will be further moving both organisations away from their historic origins as key functionaries of the military dictatorships of decades past.

References

Arnold, M., Ye Thu Aung, S. Kempel and Kyi Pyar Chit Saw. 2015. *Municipal Governance in Myanmar: An Overview of Development Affairs Organizations.* Paper No. 7. Yangon: The Asia Foundation, www.theasiafoundation.org.

Bardhan, Pranab and Dilip Mookherjee (eds). 2006. *Decentralization and Local Governance in Developing Countries: A Comparative Perspective*. Cambridge, MA: MIT Press.

Bissinger, J. 2016. *The Local Governance of Business in Myanmar*. Yangon: The Asia Foundation, www.theasiafoundation.org.

Bissinger, J. and L. Maung Maung. 2014. *Subnational Governments and Business in Myanmar*. Paper No. 2. Yangon: The Asia Foundation, www.theasiafoundation.org.

Bonoan, M. et al. 2011. *Innovations in Strengthening Local Economic Governance in Asia*. Yangon: The Asia Foundation, www.theasiafoundation.org.

Callahan, Mary. 2005. *Making Enemies: War and State-Building in Burma*. Ithaca, NY: Cornell University Press.

Cheesman, Nick. 2015. *Opposing the Rule of Law: How Myanmar's Courts Make Law and Order*. Cambridge: Cambridge University Press.

Chit Saw, Kyi Pyar and Matthew Arnold. 2014. *Administering the State*. Paper No. 6. Yangon: The Asia Foundation, www.theasiafoundation.org.

GAD brochure. 2014. Given to visitors at the GAD Headquarters in Naypyidaw, on file with author.

Hook, D. et al. 2015. *Conceptualizing Public Sector Reform in Myanmar*. Yangon: The Asia Foundation, www.theasiafoundation.org.

Ministry of Home Affairs. 2012. *GAD 2012 Annual Record*. Myanmar.

Nakanashi, Yoshihiro. 2013. *Strong Soldiers, Failed Revolution: The State and Military in Burma, 1962–88*. Singapore: National University Press.

Nixon, Hamish and Cindy Joelene. 2014. *Fiscal Decentralisation in Myanmar*. Paper No. 5. Yangon: The Asia Foundation, www.theasiafoundation.org.

Nixon, Hamish, Cindy Joelene, Kyi Pyar Chit Saw, Thet Aung Lynn and Matthew Arnold. 2013. *State and Region Governments in Myanmar*. Yangon: The Asia Foundation, www.theasiafoundation.org.

Organisation for Economic Co-Operation and Development (OECD). 2013. *Multidimensional Review of Myanmar: Volume 1 Initial Assessment*. Paris: OECD.

Pederson, Morden. 2011. 'The Politics of Burma's Democratic Transition: Prospects for Change and Options for Democrats'. 43(1) *Critical Asian Studies* 49–68.

Robertson, Bart, Cindy Joelene and Lauren Dunn. 2015. *Local Development Funds in Myanmar*. Yangon: The Asia Foundation, www.asiafoundation.org.

Taylor, Robert. 2009. *The State in Myanmar*. London: Hurst Press.

Tin Maung Maung Than. 2006. *State Dominance in Myanmar: The Political Economy of Industrialization*. Singapore: Institute of Southeast Asian Studies.

Union Government Order No. 59/2013. The Land Use Management Central Committee. Myanmar.

Laws

Constitution of Myanmar – 2008.
Development Committees Law No. 5/1993.
Mandalay City Development Affairs Law No. 11/2014.
MCDC Election Bylaw – 20 February 2015.
Mon State Land Tax Law No. 9/2012.
Yangon City Development Affairs Law No. 6/2013.
YCDC Election Bylaw Notification No. 1/2014.
YCDC Election Bylaw, Amendment – 30 September 2014.

7

Special Economic Zones

Gateway or Roadblock to Reform?

JOSH WOOD

Economic reform is a key component of any political transition, as both a direct goal of political actors and an unintended consequence of new institutional arrangements. Myanmar's transition, which began in 2011, has been characterised by the former. After decades of insularity, command-style planning and low economic growth, the government has implemented numerous economy-wide reforms. These have included substantive changes to banking, exchange rate, trade and natural resource policies, to name just several examples, as well as the beginning of a long overdue transition towards a market economy (Turnell 2015). The lifting of international sanctions by Western powers which has accompanied related reforms in the political system has been equally important, allowing new capital goods, firms and financial products to enter Myanmar for the first time. Although the economy remains backward by regional standards, the country's steady progress suggests a new, outward-looking approach to economic management which may finally unlock Myanmar's long-recognised potential.

One of the most commonly cited examples of Myanmar's new-found reformist zeal are the three special economic zones (SEZs) which passed into law in January 2011 and were significantly revised in early 2014. The three sites selected by the parliament in Dawei, Kyaukphyu and Thilawa were granted unique regulatory status aimed at supporting export-orientated industries. The policy, however, is not a product of new thinking in Naypyidaw. Rather, the three sites chosen have been unofficial government policy for almost twenty years and have inherited many undesirable traits from the pre-reform era.

As has been seen in many instances of transition, an underperforming economy constrains government action and can accentuate civic unrest in a time of political vulnerability (Hughes 2003). Not only do the chances of violence and military intervention increase in times of economic flux, but the entire transition itself, and related notions of opening up democracy and transparency, can be tarnished if the benefits are not seen to be fair or far-reaching. The success or otherwise of Myanmar's SEZs can therefore be expected to have far-reaching consequences for the country's transition overall.

The focus of this chapter is to explore whether SEZs can contribute to economic reform in a period of political transition. First, it will explore the origins of Myanmar's SEZs and show decisively that they are anything but the spearhead of economic reforms they have often been touted to be. Second, it will assess the likely economic benefits to be derived from each of the zones and provide commentary on the likelihood of positive economic return to government investment in each location. Finally, it will explore some of the key economic forces in Myanmar today which are not only more important indicators of Myanmar's economic openness, but in many instances undermine the necessity for SEZs altogether. As this chapter will demonstrate, Myanmar's poorly conceived economic plans are not likely to increase national welfare and could put at risk the country's broader reform agenda.

The Importance of SEZs for Economic Reform in the Asia-Pacific

Depending on the definition employed, there are approximately 3,000 SEZs currently operational in more than 135 countries (World Bank 2015). All of the Association of Southeast Asian Nations (ASEAN) economies, with the exception of Brunei, have attempted some form of SEZ or export processing zone in the last three decades.

Of the many schemes implemented across the globe, the impacts upon both the economy and the polity have varied enormously. While increased employment and economic activity is the most common benefit, highly successful zones have achieved other development goals as well. New technologies, management techniques, taxation revenue and the acceleration of domestic industrialisation have been effectively promoted when zones are optimally designed and well-implemented. Generally, however, rigorous studies of SEZs have employed a cost-benefit analysis methodology. This approach tabulates all of the additional benefits to the host country such as wages, taxes, local purchases and even electricity tariffs and compares them with the costs of construction, operation and all other subsidies and incentives offered to foreign firms. The aim is to capture the overall welfare gain resulting from the investment from government into the scheme. To properly determine the overall success of an SEZ several years of operation are required, and therefore benchmarking of Myanmar's zones is not yet possible. However, qualitative evidence from within Myanmar alongside comparable case studies gives a strong indication of the zone's likely performance in a future cost-benefit analysis.

Despite the large number of regional equivalents, the vast majority of zones in the Asia-Pacific cannot be fairly compared with Myanmar's three proposed locations. Within India alone there are 392 SEZs (Anwar 2014) which often bear little resemblance to one another. For example, around 38 per cent are focused entirely on an individual industry such as textiles or biotechnology. Around 19 per cent are government-run, but the vast majority are privately owned. Some are coastal, others urban; others still are planned cities altogether.

Similarly diverse are the size, structure and objectives of SEZs throughout the Asia-Pacific region. While all hope to promote investment and domestic employment, some have aimed to attract particular industries, others to decentralise industry from the major cities; a small number had the primary objective of promoting a particularly undeveloped region.

A very small number of zones in the Asia-Pacific such as Bataan in the Philippines, Shenzhen in China and Penang in Malaysia are directly comparable to the large-scale projects currently under way in Myanmar. Wei (1999) and Warr (1987a, 1987b) provide an in-depth analysis of the three respective sites, and these studies are required reading for those wishing to understand where the costs and benefits of SEZs actually accrue. To briefly summarise these outstanding pieces of scholarship, both Shenzhen and Penang were an unambiguous success, encouraging millions of dollars in foreign investment, providing thousands of well-paid jobs and supporting the wider implementation of economic reforms. The key to their success was the ability to leverage pre-existing physical and business infrastructure. Situated in close proximity to pre-existing shipping routes, endowed with excellent natural harbours and able to access the services, entrepreneurialism and labour available in nearby urban areas, the zones were well-positioned to attract foreign investment which had proven elusive elsewhere in the country. The second key to their success was management and adaptability. Both Penang and Shenzhen were capably governed and given relative autonomy from the political process, which allowed fast and responsive decision-making. Bataan, in contrast, was built from scratch in a remote part of the Philippines and proved a disastrous investment of taxpayer money. Each requirement of industry, including port facilities, roads and electricity, was provided by the government. Labour, spare parts, food and other essential services were sourced from elsewhere, inflating costs and causing debilitating shortages. Although several firms took advantage of the site, the benefits were too small to justify the enormous outlays that were borne by the central government.

These instructive case studies do not, of course, dictate the destiny of Myanmar's SEZs. However, they clearly demonstrate that winning over foreign investors is only half the battle, as the economic gains which result must exceed the tax breaks, construction costs, administrative burden and other subsidies if the scheme is to be cost-positive. Leveraging of existing infrastructure, physical and otherwise, alongside good management is therefore crucial for Myanmar's three proposed zones if they are to avoid becoming a fiscal burden.

The Origins and Regulation of Myanmar's Special Economic Zones

The origins of Myanmar's SEZs provide a crucial insight into the likelihood of their success and subsequent influence on the reform process. As Farole and Moberg (2014) explain, because of the many design variables which can be employed, SEZs are most effective when focused on the achievement of specific and tangible goals. Once established, they posit, a successful reconfiguration is almost impossible to achieve. Not only are the capital costs of alteration enormous, the branding of the zone is also affected, as the original design and purpose of the zone have already been established in the mindset of international investors.

The origin of the SEZ policy, like much in Myanmar throughout the pre-reform period, is shrouded in mystery. Little is known about how the idea first gained traction, why the three locations of Dawei, Kyaukphyu and Thilawa were chosen and at what point external actors began to have an influence on the process. Undoubtedly, the success of China's Shenzhen and similar schemes throughout Asia was influential, presenting a means through which exports could be boosted without significantly reducing government control of the economy (Walsh 2013). But exactly who championed the idea, their reasoning and their motivations remained opaque until the first feasibility study on Dawei was undertaken in 1996 followed by another in Kyaukphyu the following year. What is clear is that these SEZs were planned long in advance of the introduction of legal regulation.

Dawei, it soon became clear, was to be a joint venture with Thailand, spearheaded by the well-connected conglomerate Italian-Thai Development (ITD). Road and rail connections with Bangkok were a key characteristic of the scheme which sought to provide an alternative, overland trade route to the Malacca Straits. The Kyaukphyu SEZ, in Rakhine State, was tailored towards Chinese interests and was expected to receive substantial financing to support its development. An oil and gas pipeline to Yunnan Province, road and rail connections with the Chinese border and manufacturing investment from Chinese companies were all key tenets of the proposed zone. The Thilawa Port and Industrial Zone, which was eventually elevated to SEZ status in 2011, was opened in 1998 with the assistance of the Hong Kong-based Hutchinsons.[1] Located in close proximity to Yangon, the site hoped to attract new investors and improve the logistics of the country's most important maritime asset.

While the specifics of each location will be explored in depth later in the chapter, it is worth emphasising that from the very beginning each zone had specific international investors in mind. Formulated during a period of severe economic sanctions, co-operation from two of the very few countries which maintained full economic relations with Myanmar was seen as necessary if the zones were to be successful.

However, it was only after fifteen years of planning and indecision that the Myanmar Special Economic Zone Law No. 8/2011 and the Dawei Special Economic Zone Law No. 17/2011 were introduced to provide the legislative framework required for the policies to progress beyond the preliminary stages. The basic principle of the legislation was to enforce a duty-free area for industry in which investors, both foreign and domestic, would be permitted only to export their produce (Turnell 2014). Tax incentives were also prescribed, on both the income paid to employees and the profits made by corporations.

While the underlying principles of the laws were generally accepted, the new government decided to revise the legislation only ten months after its passing. An independent consulting firm was hired to explore the weaknesses in the existing laws, and a rigorous discussion took place inclusive of the relevant stakeholders. Finally, after months of debate, the Myanmar Special Economic Zone Law No. 1/2014 was passed, abolishing

---

[1] Although the port has remained active since its construction, the industrial zone was a failure with only a small number of local enterprises becoming established in the area under a particularly opaque process.

the existing laws and covering the three existing zones as well as any others which may follow.

Interestingly, government oversight was rearranged to connect the management of all zones to a central body which was in turn overseen by the president. Contrary to the government's push for decentralisation of decision-making in other policy areas, Myanmar's SEZs have become increasingly centralised due to their perceived importance and their notable failure to progress without executive assistance. Such changes contradict both SEZ best practice and the broader transition away from top-down economic planning (an issue explored by Arnold in Chapter 6, this volume).

Other key features include an up to seven year income tax holiday, followed by a 50 per cent exemption for a further five years which can be extended by another five years if profits are reinvested. Custom duties and related taxes were also exempted for imported raw materials and machinery, and access to land, a big concern for potential investors, was made possible through the establishment of fifty-year leases.

However, the most pressing question surrounding Myanmar's SEZ laws is whether they are needed at all. In the many years which have followed initial planning for the zones, Myanmar has changed dramatically. Most critically, the degree of economic control commanded by the state has been significantly reduced in a range of areas. Equally important is the removal of most economic sanctions, which prevented the vast majority of international firms from investing. The main purpose of the zones, to provide employment opportunities and boost exports, is still highly desirable. But given the political and economic reforms which have been successfully implemented since 2011, these goals are already being met as a result of large-scale foreign direct investment.

The reform that has most undermined the need for SEZs is the Foreign Investment Law No. 21/2012. This important piece of legislation provided greater certainty for foreign firms on a wide range of issues and was warmly welcomed by the international business community (Allens 2012). One of the most welcomed features was the removal of many industry-specific restrictions, allowing foreign firms to invest in all but the most sensitive sectors of the Myanmar economy. Greater certainty over land use, local employment regulations, administrative procedures and dispute resolution was also included, along with a particularly attractive five-year income tax holiday from the moment of commenced production.

In tandem with the well-received foreign investment law was the gradual removal of international sanctions. Beginning with the European

Union in 2012, the vast majority of non-military sanctions have now been removed, clearing a major obstacle for foreign direct investment. Equally important, however, is the removal of sanctions on international financial flows. Once an enormous barrier to investment, access to credit and other essential banking services has greatly improved the ease of doing business (Findlay, Park and Verbiest 2015). Incredibly, as a result of these developments, foreign direct investment into Myanmar has more than tripled in the last three years and now stands at more than US$8 billion (DICA 2015). China's once dominant position has dwindled, but remains the fourth largest source of investment in the 2014–2015 financial year. Rather, investment has flowed from a variety of countries which had no presence in the pre-reform era such as Korea, India, the United Kingdom and Norway.

A further component of the foreign investment law which threatens the viability of Myanmar's SEZs is its overly generous tax concessions. According to article 27, foreign investors in any part of Myanmar are granted a five-year tax holiday, exemptions from custom duties and tax-relief incentives for export industries. As Farole and Akinci (2011) explain, these are the key provisions of an SEZ based on the assumption that such policies are unfeasible throughout the rest of the economy. While the concessions are fractionally smaller than those offered to investors within SEZs, they are very generous nonetheless and largely nullify one of the zones' chief selling points.

One final point of consideration is the industrial mix of investment which has arrived in Myanmar over the last three years. While the SEZs are explicitly focused upon attracting investment into manufacturing and industry (rather than natural resources, agriculture and services) the current arrangements have already had considerable success in those areas. Despite what has often been assumed about the nature of foreign direct investment into Myanmar, a diversity of sectors have benefited since 2012. For instance, in 2014–2015, manufacturing received around 20 per cent of foreign investment with an almost equal share being attracted into transport and communication projects (DICA 2015).

Because of the high-quality legal protections, reasonably efficient administrative procedures, generous taxation policies and other prerequisites for industrial activity already in place, there is little evidence to suggest that SEZs are required in Myanmar. While schemes of this kind may have been very useful in the pre-reform era when less liberal economic conditions were present, recent reforms and the arrival of foreign firms have undermined their reason of being. Recognising the monumental shifts which have occurred in the Myanmar economy should prompt a rethink of SEZ policy and refocus of priorities towards more meaningful reforms of the entire economy.

To conclude, it is misleading to associate Myanmar's SEZs with the recent push towards economic openness and international engagement. Rather, the zones were designed and refined under vastly differing conditions to today, when Myanmar's trade and investment relationships were greatly curtailed by international sanctions, but have remained as government policy into the present era. Ironically, as the economic policies of the central government have shifted, SEZ policy remains much to its detriment, wedded to the government mindset of the 1990s. As such, the government's current goals are misaligned with the already established characteristics of the zones and will prove enormously difficult to change. As the next section highlights, the destiny of the zones is by no means pre-determined by past mistakes but greatly reduces the probability for a positive economic outcome and puts at risk Myanmar's broader goals for economic reform.

The Potential Contribution of SEZs to Economic Reform

Myanmar's SEZs are evidently long-standing policy initiatives which have been fast-tracked in the pursuit of economic liberalisation and development (Harding and Carter 2010). Not only are the zones premised on outdated geopolitical considerations, they must also compete with hundreds of similar and well-resourced schemes throughout the Asia-Pacific if they are to be successful. The big question surrounding Myanmar's SEZs is therefore whether they will help or hinder the country's transition to a market economy. The creation of distinct legal entities can be advantageous in some situations, but can distort other regions and sectors and could potentially retard momentum for more far-reaching reforms. The considerable financial and reputational risks attached with a failed SEZ must also be considered. The collapse of the SEZs in Madagascar, for instance, contributed to a substantial downgrading of the broader investment climate and had long-lived negative repercussions (Farole 2011). A setback in one of Myanmar's zones would be a fiscal catastrophe, could spook foreign investors and could potentially reduce the appetite for economic reform for both policy-makers and the public. Considering these risks, Myanmar's three prospective zones could greatly impede the country's progress and should, in two of the three locations, be abandoned forthwith.

Dawei: A Costly Indulgence

In the remote city of Dawei, Tanintharyi Division, the establishment of Myanmar's first SEZ was proposed by the central government. Following a feasibility study by the Myanmar Port Authority and Thai conglomerate ITD in 1996, the site was chosen over several alternatives along the Andaman Sea and has been mired in controversy ever since. Shortly after Dawei had been selected for development, the Thai economy was hit by the Asian financial crisis. Its largest construction company, ITD, was unable to avoid the downturn and suffered significant losses for several years after the shock had subsided. Enthusiasm for the development of Dawei quickly evaporated in the company's headquarters, sinking the ambitious plan in its formative stages.

Nevertheless, as the region's growth rates began to improve the zone's development was once again on the agenda. The ousting of Thai Prime Minister Shinawatra in 2006, with whom ITD was closely aligned, reinvigorated the company's international ambitions, and a preliminary deal was finally struck in 2008. Under a sixty-year Build, Operate, Transfer agreement, ITD would construct and maintain the zone with work to begin on the 250 km^2 estate right away. A local conglomerate, Max Myanmar, was also granted a 25 per cent stake.

Unlike the case with similar schemes of this nature, however, ITD was granted the additional responsibility to manage the zone and spearhead the search for international investors. As land was cleared and service roads began to be built, the absence of committed companies became a serious concern. This anxiety prompted Max Myanmar to unceremoniously withdraw their support in 2012, and construction stalled to a standstill. With no power source, no investors and few signs of progress, ITD was relieved of its position in 2013, and the zone fell under the direct control of the increasingly frustrated Thai and Myanmar governments. Considering the acute absence of private sector interest, this was a bold and potentially costly move.

Following the departure of ITD, the zone's future looked bleak, but hopes have been buoyed in recent months. In July 2015, Thailand, Myanmar and Japan signed a memorandum of intent to hold equal shares in the Dawei SEZ Development Company which will manage the zone and lead efforts to attract investors. Despite being previously dismissed for incompetence, ITD have once again been contracted to build the 'first phase' of the SEZ with additional details to be determined over the next three years.

While the zone's master plan will most likely be refined with Japanese input, most of the key features have already been decided upon. For instance, the exact parcel of land to be used is settled, stretching over 250 km² and serviced by basic roads, wells and maintenance facilities constructed by ITD. A small service dock has already been finished, and a great deal of land has been cleared for future construction. The key to the zone's progress, however, is the necessity of a deep-sea port. The coastal inlets at the site are far too shallow for international shipping and will require substantial deepening. Breakwaters, berths and docking facilities will all need to be built from scratch.

The construction of other essential facilities has also been proposed by the Myanmar government (METI 2014). An electricity plant, the damming of a nearby river, the establishment of local quarries and the paving of what are at present completely inadequate roads are all required if the zone is to function properly. Alongside essential infrastructure, facilities for the manufacture of petrochemicals, steel and other heavy industries have been proposed. Factories for light industries, such as food processing, will also be given a large share of the zone's area. Finally, as well as housing, hospitality and temporary accommodation, a five-star resort and golf course have been allocated for the coastal sections. Whether anyone would want to holiday next to a petrochemical plant has clearly not been considered carefully enough.

Evidently, this is economic planning of the most wasteful variety. Even for firms with a desire to invest in Myanmar, there are simply no bankable characteristics which make Dawei any more desirable than Pathein, Yangon or Mawlamyine where the necessary facilities for production and export already exist. Indeed, the problems of the Dawei SEZ are so insurmountable that it threatens to drain government resources away from other, more meaningful economic reforms.

To begin with, Tanintharyi Division is a sparsely populated region from which foreign firms will have great difficulty sourcing both skilled and unskilled labour. The region's educational focus and tiny industrial sector mean that only a very small number of local people will be adequately prepared for work in the SEZ. Training or importing workers would be prohibitively expensive and time-consuming, a cost that alone is sure to deter more-sophisticated industries. Unlike in much of Myanmar, finding sufficient quantities of unskilled labour in Dawei is also a concern. The relative prosperity of the region and the close proximity of better-paid opportunities in Thailand suggest that labour costs will be significantly above the national average.

The absence of high population densities will also be problematic for foreign investors seeking auxiliary services. The Dawei region's legal, financial and accounting firms are basic and domestically orientated. The tiny industrial sector, which is almost entirely situated in Dawei, will struggle to supply the capital goods, spare parts and repair services that an advanced industrial zone would require. Until the region develops organically, which could take many years, investors will need to be prepared for all contingencies and rely upon internal resources to address problems as they occur.

The other major concern for Dawei is the absence of infrastructure which will be essential to the zone's success. In addition to the electricity, water and port facilities which have been incorporated into the master plan, the surrounding area will also require extensive upgrades to meet the demands of industry. The region's roads are narrow, mostly dirt and in poor condition. There are no rail services connecting Dawei to the rest of Myanmar, and the proposed line to Bangkok will need to overcome dozens of geographic, legal and financial hurdles if it is ever to eventuate. The major airport in Dawei is adequate but small, and will undoubtedly require expansion for the zone to maintain connection with key cities in the region. Indeed, for almost every requirement of industry more work needs to be done.

Finally, being hundreds of kilometres from Yangon, Mandalay and the vast majority of the country's largest population centres, Dawei will hold limited appeal to firms seeking an entry into Myanmar. The prospect of access to more than fifty million new customers has generated excitement, and some tentative steps, from some of the world's largest companies. Enticing more investment of this kind is a key goal of the central government which will be in no way advanced by the development of Dawei.

The final concerns of the Dawei SEZ are ongoing social and environmental issues. Although debate, and legal disputes, continue to be unresolved, there can be no doubt that public opinion has unambiguously turned against the project. Not only have the local residents of Dawei frequently voiced their opposition, but throughout much of Myanmar the damage to communities and ecosystems which may occur as a result of the zone's development is considered too severe to warrant the project.

Despite these reservations, Dawei does have several advantages which are worthy of note. To begin with, the region is politically stable and does not suffer from ethnic, religious or separatist conflicts which threaten many areas of Myanmar today. Second, Dawei is welcoming to expats, boasting clean air and wonderful beaches surrounded by stunningly green mountains. Finally, influential overseas partners are evidently interested. With the assistance of Tokyo and Bangkok, a handful of companies may be directly induced to invest, which could help to build momentum for the site's success. Encouraging additional investors will undoubtedly remain an enormous challenge, but having several respected international firms on board will bring prestige to an otherwise unattractive investment option.

Despite these positives, Dawei looks set to remain a costly and embarrassing project. Due to the absence of natural advantages, the enormous cost of construction and the low likelihood of attracting international investors, the state's investment into the Dawei SEZ will never be recouped. Such profligate behaviour has not been driven by rent-seeking behaviour as has been the case in other projects throughout Myanmar. Rather, it reflects an economic ideology in which the state attempts to control and redirect resources rather than allowing market forces to dictate where industry can most profitably flourish. Aside from the financial cost, and the considerable burden upon economic ministries, ongoing speculation around the zone has highlighted some uncomfortable truths about doing business in Myanmar. The glacial pace of progress, constant renegotiations and ongoing claims of environmental and social damage give the impression that little has changed since the pre-reform era.

Kyaukphyu and the Chinese Dream

The Kyaukphyu SEZ, like Dawei, is unlikely to attract a sufficient quantity of foreign investment or additional employment opportunities to justify its multi-million-dollar cost of construction. After almost twenty years of planning the zone and negotiating over who will pay for what, a concrete design and operating structure are still yet to be determined. As previously mentioned, Kyaukphyu was conceived with Chinese interests (and finance) in mind. Since the late 1990s, however, both China and Myanmar have undergone significant changes which leave the much publicised SEZ almost entirely redundant.

In fact, the perceived strategic value of the tiny Kyaukphyu Township has been the most influential factor in its elevation to SEZ status. Situated on the coast of Rakhine State, facing west towards the Persian Gulf, the natural harbour was identified by Chinese strategists concerned about energy security. By transporting oil and gas overland, they reasoned, China would be less vulnerable to uncertainty in the Malacca Straits through which the vast majority of hydrocarbon imports currently pass. A pipeline through central Myanmar to Yunnan Province, originating at Kyaukphyu, was thus conceived and appeared to Myanmar policy-makers as a sensible location for an SEZ.

Despite the successful completion of a feasibility study in 1997 and the ongoing support of China, progress on the zone has been remarkably slow. Although the delays can largely be attributed to reluctance within the Myanmar government about the plausibility of such a large-scale project, the ambiguous role of China has also been influential. A succession of five-year plans has outlined support for an SEZ alongside several other infrastructure investments in western Myanmar. Translating these promises into concrete financial support, however, has been an ongoing frustration for ministries in Myanmar. While the passing of legislation in 2011 and 2014 should have removed any lingering concerns about the project internally, even the most basic construction has yet to begin. In fact, so far behind schedule is the Kyaukphyu SEZ that in July 2015 the land set aside for use was deemed unsuitable due to the eruption of a mud volcano. It is still yet to be determined exactly where the SEZ will be situated.

However, it is important to separate the progress of the Sino-Burmese pipeline from the inaction which has plagued the Kyaukphyu SEZ. Stretching 771 km to Kunming in Southern China, this project has connected the gas fields surrounding Kyaukphyu Township with China since 2013. The construction of a shipping terminal and treatment plant has enabled oil to be imported from the Middle East by ship and transported along the same pipeline to China since 2014. Indeed, due to the rapid success in achieving its primary aim of diversifying its energy sources, China would seemingly have much less interest in supporting the SEZ. Nevertheless, the Myanmar government is at present committed to the project and continues to woo Chinese money, firms and expertise.

The plan for the Kyaukphyu SEZ, which remains in flux, differs in several respects from the plan for Dawei. Most notably, heavy industries are not the major focus of the zone which is much more attuned to its natural advantages than its southern sibling. For instance, fish processing and related products are expected to take almost 50 per cent of the available land within the zone, recognising the rich coastal resources of the region, high labour intensity and the relatively unsophisticated techniques required to compete with neighbouring countries. The remainder of the zone is to consist of textiles, light industries and others related to gas and oil processing and transportation. Overall, the focus is rational, and the scale more realistic.

Several other advantages of the Kyaukphyu SEZ are worthy of mention. In particular, the natural harbour is one of the finest in Myanmar, reaching depths of up to 30 metres and offering multiple approaches for ships of almost any size. Equally notable is the presence of several international firms, such as Daewoo, already involved in oil and gas exploitation. Although only tangentially related to industry, their success in the region is a glowing endorsement for the business environment and will assist in stimulating the arrival of supplementary services to the town. Finally, the abundance of unfarmed lands surrounding the township will provide a pleasant setting for visiting business people and provide considerable flexibility in construction.

Yet despite these attributes, the glaring weaknesses of the site are almost certain to render the Kyaukphyu SEZ an unprofitable investment for the Myanmar government. In particular, the area lacks the necessary transportation infrastructure to support industrial activity. Given the township's remoteness, this is in no way surprising, but the costs of construction will dwarf the gains that additional foreign investment could possibly deliver. Due to a historical reliance upon maritime transport, the roads surrounding Kyaukphyu are of the most basic variety. Electricity supplies are limited, and a new plant will be required to be built. A new reservoir will be necessary to provide fresh water for both industrial and residential use as the township's population increases. The local airport, which has limited services to Sittwe and Yangon, will undoubtedly require expansion.

The great hope of the project, of course, is Chinese finance, which could potentially reduce the costs incurred by the central government. However, despite many (non-binding) assurances of support over the years, there is growing evidence that Beijing's enthusiasm for the project is cooling. The successful completion of the oil and gas pipeline aside, there is no doubt that China's waning influence in Myanmar has also played a major part. The thawing of diplomatic relations with the West, the entry of international agencies and the return of many multinational corporations further eroded the special treatment China had been able to attain in the pre-reform era. Although some form of Chinese support may still be forthcoming, expecting China to shoulder the bulk of the financial burden would be to ignore rapid geopolitical shifts which have occurred in the last five years.

Attracting foreign investors, from China and elsewhere, will also be enormously challenging. Putting aside the enormous uncertainty surrounding so much of the SEZ, there is little to entice foreign firms beyond favourable tax treatment and other sweeteners. The township is surrounded by the nearly impenetrable Arakan mountain range and hundreds of kilometres from Myanmar's primary population centres. With only 20,000 inhabitants, Kyaukphyu has few of the necessary services that foreign firms will require. Hotels, banks, conference facilities and telecommunications are all in short supply. Like Dawei, Kyaukphyu is also lacking in skilled tradespeople and technicians. Unskilled labour, though able to be sourced from the surrounding countryside, will need to be housed and their assimilation into the local community carefully managed.

Perhaps the biggest concern for Kyaukphyu, however, is its location in Rakhine State. Having been ravaged by communal violence in 2012, the state's Buddhist and Islamic communities remain in a high state of tension. The Kyaukphyu Islamic quarter was burnt to the ground at the height of the violence, prompting the thousands of Muslim residents to move into military-protected camps on the outskirts of town. The distinct, though related issues surrounding the Rohingya minority are a further risk for foreign firms. Although not residing in the township itself, the displacement and ongoing persecution of the Rohingya are a significant barrier to the zone's success. The recurrence of hostilities against either group could bring about damage to property, delays to transport and harm to employees, the types of eventualities that foreign firms aim to avoid at all costs. A secondary risk, by association with violence and human rights abuses, is also to be considered. Even if Kyaukphyu itself remains safe, the reputational damage that could occur from operating within such a volatile environment remains a significant barrier to investment.

Considering all of these concerns, and the huge number of uncertainties which remain unresolved, the Kyaukphyu SEZ will remain a burden upon the Myanmar economy as long as it remains official government policy. The absence of investor interest, the high cost of construction and the unreliability of Chinese co-operation suggest that the scheme should be scrapped immediately or at least modified to support only the most relevant industries. The region's plentiful oil and gas reserves, Kyaukphyu's natural harbour and the pipeline to China are clear advantages that could encourage new sources of foreign investment. However, a large-scale SEZ underwritten by the Myanmar taxpayer is the wrong approach which risks enormous losses for the government and a diversion of resources away from more pressing structural issues in urgent need of attention.

Thilawa and the Benefits of Proximity

In contrast to the remote townships of Dawei and Kyaukphyu, the Thilawa SEZ is just 25 km away from Myanmar's largest city and has a promising future. Dozens of firms have already committed to the project, construction of the first phase is nearing completion and, if carefully managed, the zone could bring considerable economic benefits.

Although its future looks relatively bright, the Thilawa SEZ like the other zones is not a product of recent economic reforms. In 1998 the area was demarcated as a free trade zone in which operating firms were exempted from import and export duties. This was part of the previous military regime's efforts to attract foreign investment. A new, five-berth port was constructed by Hong Kong conglomerate Hutchison Port Holdings, and several factories were erected in the late 1990s. However, following the Asian financial crisis and the withdrawal of key investors, the improvement and expansion of port facilities in Yangon itself became a much higher priority. While the Thilawa port continued to operate (well below capacity), a plan to reboot the scheme with SEZ status was finally realised in 2011. Thus, the Thilawa SEZ Management Committee was established and granted the difficult task of overseeing construction and attracting new investors.

The zone's first major victory, after several years of negotiations, was the formal entry of Japan as a development partner in late 2013. A new consortium consisting of three Japanese firms (Mitsubishi, Marubeni and Sumitomo), nine Myanmar companies, the Japan International Cooperation Agency and the already-formed Thilawa SEZ Management Committee was duly established to develop, market and operate the 2,400-hectare zone. Since the establishment of the consortium progress has been swift. The first phase of the zone is nearing completion, more than forty foreign firms have already agreed to invest and low-interest loans from Japan have been secured to finance the project.

Although the design of the zone is relatively simple, it skilfully incorporates natural advantages which will minimise capital outlays. Most critically for the zone's future is the underutilised Thilawa Port. Operating twenty-four hours per day but at less than 15 per cent capacity, the fractionally deeper Thilawa is able to avoid the sandbars that restrict Yangon's major port during low tides and that can delay incoming ships for up to two days (Gomez-Ibanez, Bok and Nguyen 2012).

In regards to road connections Thilawa is also well-positioned. Sitting fractionally to the southeast of Yangon's downtown, freight trucks will have easy access to the city's arterial roads without the necessity of passing through the increasingly gridlocked downtown. A pre-existing (though basic) railway line which connects the area with the Yangon Circular Railway will need to be extended and upgraded, but once complete will give the zone excellent access to the entire city. Yangon international airport, which connects with most major cities in Asia, is only forty-five minutes away.

Industrially, the zone is welcoming to firms from a variety of fields, but is most favourable to labour-intensive export industries. The zone's administrative structure is particularly focused upon providing the conditions in which the production and export of shoes, toys, electrical products, automobile parts and other light industrial products can flourish. Such an approach, which recognises Myanmar's comparative advantages and will not require industrial planning or subsidies, is sensible.

The second likeable aspect of the design is its eventual integration with Yangon itself. As the city continues to grow, increasing pressure will be placed on the city's transport, office space and electricity supply. However, by preparing the nearby Thilawa for a large working and residential population, future population growth can be absorbed with minimal disruption. Of course, the city is already suffering from congestion and the inconvenience caused by long-neglected but necessary improvements. But if carefully managed, the Thilawa SEZ can help to improve the city's functionality overall, which could have potentially enormous economic benefits.

Unfortunately for many of the local inhabitants, the land upon which the Thilawa SEZ is quickly taking shape is hotly disputed. The 1997 purchase of the area under the military government has been questioned for the low price paid (around US$20 per acre) and the subsequent years of inaction which allowed farming to continue until very recently. Additional compensation has been provided by the current government, but claims of its inadequacy, given the land's enormous value, and government coercion to sign have been well-publicised. So far, at least, the issue has not significantly dampened the zone's chances of success. In fact, an independent report presented to and subsequently published by JICA (2014) examined whether the project contravened the organisation's environmental and social guidelines. It concluded that the purchase, notice given and additional compensation were both fair and reasonable, and should in no way impede Japanese support. The subsequent involvement of more than forty firms, including several from Europe, Australia and the United

States, clearly shows that the controversy may hinder but is unlikely to extinguish investor interest in the zone.

Despite the many strengths of the Thilawa SEZ, absolute success in an economic sense may still prove elusive. To begin with, the politics of the zone are highly sensitive to change. A new government in Naypyidaw could very easily lose interest in an expensive, controversial plan so overtly associated with their predecessors. Several politicians from the National League for Democracy (NLD) have publicly criticised the project, but so far, no policy position has been taken by the party leadership. Equally plausible is a change of heart in Tokyo – a pivot in strategy could doom the zone entirely.

Second, management of the zone will remain hotly contested and may not always make the most prudent decisions. The competing visions of Japan, the private sector partners and aspiring Myanmar politicians could foreseeably constrain effective decision-making. Unlike the independent and autonomous management committees of successful zones such as Shenzhen, Thilawa may lack the necessary flexibility to alter zone policies where necessary.

Finally, even if the zone is carefully managed, the competition for foreign investment will remain unrelentingly fierce. The vast majority of Myanmar's neighbours have already developed SEZs and other incentives for foreign firms to operate within their borders. Indeed, low corporate tax rates and high-quality infrastructure can be acquired in dozens of locations in Southeast Asia alone. As such, the Thilawa SEZ may not provide Myanmar with an edge on its foreign competitors but may simply elevate it to a level playing field for the first time in decades.

The Future of the Zones

Incongruously, Myanmar's SEZs look set to be complete after the foreign investment boom currently underway has subsided. Rather than providing a toehold for foreign capital with more liberal regulations, the zones look set to provide a comparable legal environment to prospective investors which could be acquired and profitably operated throughout the country. In this respect, the zones proposed in the late 1990s have failed to achieve their stated goal, wasting considerable government resources in the process.

Yet a complete abandonment of the policy is not necessarily the best option. As already mentioned, Thilawa provides many of the most desirable characteristics needed in SEZs and should be developed as the industrial hub of Yangon. Whether its status as a zone remains is not important, but providing good infrastructure, reliable electricity and additional industrial space for the city's expansion is a critical development goal. The key objective of Thilawa, it must be remembered, is to attract investment and create employment opportunities. The means employed to achieve that goal should therefore remain flexible.

Dawei, on the other hand, will not play a major role in Myanmar's economic future. Because it possesses so few natural advantages and private sector interest remains minimal, the site can at best be a productive port for the city of Dawei. The creation of an industrial hub in this location was always a stretch, built on geopolitical considerations rather than the needs of potential investors. Nevertheless, the willingness of Thailand and Japan to assist in the zone should continue to be explored, and a more modest facility with road connections to Thailand could in fact be cost positive.

The most difficult SEZ to diagnose is Kyaukphyu, which has shown the least progress of the three. Because the site has not yet been chosen, and work has yet to begin, abandoning the zone concept may be the most sensible option. However, as the township possesses one of the finest natural harbours in the country and sits in close proximity to considerable natural gas deposits, it may still attract investment from a small number of both foreign and domestic firms. The most important point to recognise in Kyaukphyu is that there simply is no rush. Gas exploration licences have been successfully sold, the oil and gas pipeline is operational and the state's ethnic and religious tensions are an ongoing threat to future investment. The central government should therefore wait and see how the needs of the region's investors evolve and when approached by a private firm or foreign government to develop Kyaukphyu (or any alternative port on the Arakan coastline) consider the proposal on its likely economic benefits. If no private developer is forthcoming, public investment in what is a high-risk, low-return venture should be redirected to more economically viable infrastructure projects.

Conclusion

Myanmar's three SEZs, despite much commentary to the contrary, loom as serious impediments to economic liberalisation and development. Although implemented to encourage foreign investment and boost export industries, policy baggage from the pre-reform era has handicapped the zones' design and incorporated outdated and unhelpful characteristics which will drastically reduce their chances of success. As similar schemes in China, Malaysia and the Philippines attest, attracting an adequate number of investors is only half the challenge. To provide substantial economic benefits, these case studies highlight, construction and service costs need to be minimised. Utilising existing infrastructure, something that both Dawei and Kyaukphyu have failed to do, should be a central characteristic of Myanmar's SEZs.

While the prospects for success of the zones are not encouraging, the rapidly changing business environment in Myanmar suggests that they will not significantly hinder the benefits of foreign investment. Since the Foreign Investment Law was passed in 2012 the inward flow of capital has been remarkably swift. Not only has investment been sourced from a larger variety of countries, it has also flown into previously neglected sectors such as manufacturing and communication infrastructure (DICA 2015). Such positive developments suggest that the current policy settings are working effectively and SEZs are in and of themselves unnecessary. However, the likely failure of the zones to make a positive contribution to national welfare carries additional risks for the country's development. The financial cost, administrative burden, loss of political capital and broader reputational damage that can accompany failed SEZs should be a major concern for policy-makers. While abandonment remains the most sensible option in many respects, a more modest, demand-driven policy could still be cost positive if foreign firms and governments remain willing to support the zones financially. However, considering the high bureaucratic costs of implementation and the political viability of liberalising measures which can cover the entire economy, lasting structural reform should undoubtedly remain the priority of policy-makers from this point forward.

As the case of Myanmar demonstrates, SEZs can be a slow, expensive and ineffective way to undertake economic reform in transitional regimes. Although a focus on small geographic areas would seemingly attract less resistance than economy-wide reforms, it is essential that the sites are well-chosen and offer significantly more attractive investment conditions than the rest of the country can afford. As a broader lesson for transitional economies, Myanmar's failings are instructive. In isolation, SEZs can be effective reform instruments, particularly if resistance is strong within sections of the government or broader population. Quarantining the risks can allow for more expansive changes which can then pave the way for broader reforms, a method effectively employed in China throughout the 1980s. However, if forming part of a suite of economic reforms, the potency of an SEZ is greatly diminished. By offering a similar package of legal and taxation incentives, the perceived value of the site itself and its accompanying infrastructure will determine the quantity of foreign investment and related economic opportunities. Considering the low potential of the chosen sites, it is clearly time for the SEZs to play a smaller role in future reform efforts and enable more-important, welfare-enhancing policies to take their place.

References

Allens. 2012. 'Myanmar's new Foreign investment Law'. Available at www.allens .com.au/pubs/res/fores7.

Anwar, M. 2014. 'New Modes of Industrial Manufacturing: India's Experience with Special Economic Zones'. 24 *Bulletin of Geography* 7–25.

Directorate of Investment and Company Administration (DICA). 2015. *Yearly Approved Amount of Foreign Investment*. Available at dica.gov.mm.x-aas.net/.

Farole, T. 2011. *Special Economic Zones in Africa: Comparing Performance and Learning from Global Experiences*. Washington DC: World Bank Publications.

Farole, T. and G. Akinci. 2011. *Special Economic Zones: Progress, Emerging Challenges, and Future Directions*. Washington DC: World Bank Publications.

Farole, T. and L. Moberg. 2014. 'It Worked in China so Why Not Africa? The Political Economy Challenge of Special Economic Zones'. WIDER Working Paper No. 2014/152. United Nations University.

Findlay, R., C. Park and J. Verbiest. 2015. 'Myanmar: Unlocking the Potential. A Strategy for High, Sustained, and Inclusive Growth'. Economics Working Paper Series No. 437. Asian Development Bank.

Gomez-Ibanez, J., D. Bok and X. T. Nguyen. 2012. *Yangon's Development Challenges*. Cambridge: Ash Center for Democratic Governance.

Harding, A. and C. Carter (eds). 2010. *Special Economic Zones in Asian Market Economies*. London: Routledge.

Hughes, C. 2003. *The Political Economy of the Cambodian Transition*. London: Routledge.

Japan International Cooperation Agency (JICA). 2014. *Thilawa Special Economic Zone Development Project in the Republic of the Union of Myanmar: The Examiner for the JICA Guidelines for Environmental and Social Considerations*. Tokyo: JICA. Available at www.jica.go.jp/english/our_work/social_ environmental/objection/c8h0vm00008zvp4f-att/report.pdf.

Ministry of Economic, Trade and Industry (METI). 2014. *Research on Technical Evaluation for Promoting Dawei SEZ Development in FY2014*. Tokyo: METI.

Tantri, M. 2011. 'Trajectories of China's Integration with the World Economy through SEZs: a Study on Shenzhen SEZ'. Working Paper 261. Bangalore: The Institute for Social and Economic Change.

Turnell, S. 2014. 'Legislative Foundations of Myanmar's Economic Reforms' in M. Crouch and T. Lindsey (eds), *Law, Society and Transition in Myanmar*. Oxford: Hart Publishing, pp. 183–201.

2015. 'Burma's Economic Transition: Hopes and Hurdles'. 82(2) *Social Quarterly Research* 479–506.

Walsh, J. 2013. 'Social Policy and Special Economic Zones in the Greater Mekong Subregion'. 3(1) *International Journal of Social Quality* 44–56.

Warr, P. 1987a. 'Malaysia's Industrial Enclaves: Benefits and Costs'. 25 *The Developing Economies* 30–55.

1987b. 'Export Promotion via Industrial Enclaves: The Philippines Bataan Export Processing Zone'. 23(2) *The Journal of Development Studies* 220–241.

Wei, G. 1999. *Special Economic Zones and the Economic Transition in China*. Singapore: World Scientific.

World Bank. 2015. *Special Economic Zones, Poverty Reduction and Economic Management Network*. Washington DC: International Trade Department.

Laws

Dawei Special Economic Zone Law No. 17/2011 (State Peace and Development Law).

Foreign Investment Law No. 21/2012 (Pyidaungsu Hluttaw Law).

Myanmar Special Economic Zone Law No. 1/2014 (Pyidaungsu Hluttaw Law).

Myanmar Special Economic Zone Law No. 8/2011 (State Peace and Development Law).

8

Facing the Concentrated Burden of Development

Local Reponses to Myanmar's Special Economic Zones

LAUREN NISHIMURA

With the easing or elimination of economic sanctions and shift away from authoritarian military rule, Myanmar is now attracting large-scale foreign investment. One strategy of the Myanmar government to attract foreign investment is the creation of special economic zones (SEZs).[1] An SEZ is a designated geographical area or zone with differing applicable domestic laws or mechanisms meant to attract and enable development and investment. Investor incentives can include tax holidays or benefits, streamlined permitting, favourable regulations and rules, and the promise of improved infrastructure.

Three SEZs are underway in Myanmar: in Dawei in Tanintharyi Region, Thilawa near Yangon and Kyaukphyu, located on the Bay of Bengal in Rahkine State. These SEZs are governed by a legal regime that began with two SEZ laws adopted in 2011, which were then superseded by a third general SEZ law in 2014. While these SEZs have not all been able to attract steady flows of foreign capital they are nonetheless proceeding. Even in the early stages of development, the SEZs have had a negative effect on local communities living in and nearby project areas. Affected communities, Myanmar civil society and international rights groups have responded vigorously, seeking to participate in decision-making and have their concerns addressed, and in some instances opposing the projects entirely.

In this context, it is important to consider the degree to which the applicable laws provide tools for communities and civil society in their efforts to influence project development, convey their needs and seek

---

[1] Sean Turnell characterises the legislation establishing SEZs as one of Myanmar's 'foundational legal reforms of an economic nature', although the implementation of SEZs internationally has had mixed results (Turnell 2014: 184).

redress for the negative effects of SEZs. This chapter does not presume that well-written inclusive laws alone will create desirable outcomes. Yet laws that do not contemplate community participation or redress create further barriers.[2] This chapter argues that the SEZ law creates such barriers. It shows this using two perspectives: by assessing the law as it compares to international standards and through an analysis of how affected communities and civil society are – and are not – using domestic law in their attempts to make demands and have them met.

This chapter is situated as part of an ongoing discussion in literature on the operation – and existence – of laws and rights in Myanmar. It takes as a premise that the importance of formal legal protections and remedies is dependent on context and how one conceives of social change. In Myanmar, the lived experience of legal processes often differs from outside conceptions of the law and how it should operate. In the past, this translated into uses of the law to maintain order and suppress dissent. This resulted in the use of non-legal strategies to address grievances. Despite recent legal reforms, local actors see non-legal strategies as necessary due to perceived and real obstacles. This includes difficulties accessing formal legal processes and the belief that other strategies are more reliable for local communities to resist large-scale development. However, this chapter does not argue that strategies that avoid domestic law are more effective, but rather that they remain necessary in the absence of a trusted, consistent legal process.

Myanmar's SEZ development has placed the burden of development on local communities without the opportunity to benefit or influence the decision-making process. Local responses to these projects can be viewed as examples of transnational strategies of social movements and advocacy networks familiar to scholars studying Myanmar. Yet the inclusion of domestic strategies by affected communities shows that work towards solutions – legal or otherwise – is not located exclusively abroad. Accordingly, this chapter begins with a discussion of domestic and transnational social movements literature and positions the chapter within debate about the utility and conception of law in Myanmar. It next assesses the SEZ law from the perspective of international law and analyses its use by affected communities, and then turns to the local effect of the projects

---

[2] This brings to mind Andrew Harding's statement at the end of his chapter on law and development in Myanmar that 'the law may not be Myanmar's biggest problem but it does lie consistently somewhere at the root of many other problems, and in this sense is extremely important' (Harding 2014: 399).

and responses by communities and allied civil society groups. This chapter concludes by arguing that these responses provide an example of local actors drawing from strategies used by social movements, while incorporating new tactics and concerns due to the nature of SEZ projects and status of law in contemporary Myanmar.

Law, Rights and Social Movements in Myanmar

The legal processes affecting daily life in Myanmar and ideas about how law should function are not always aligned. Indeed, there is analytical push-back about whether legal 'rights' exist in Myanmar or whether they are instead 'a political concept, always contingent and contested rather than durable and guaranteed' (Prasse-Freeman 2014). During military rule, law came to mean the maintenance of order – or the perception of order – through exercise of what Nick Cheesman calls the principle of 'sovereign *cetana*'. The use of this principle meant that legal rights could be employed, but only in a manner consistent with the goals of those in power and not as a challenge to authority (Cheesman 2015). This legacy still affects the way that law is perceived and operates in Myanmar. New domestic laws, including the SEZ law, can be criticised for their failure to provide communities with access to information and opportunities to participate in decision-making on development projects. But these shortcomings in the law may not be the only obstacle to legal action. Non-legal responses may appear more viable or present an alternative to avoid a legal system that is still used to suppress community dissent and protest. Legal challenges brought by local communities can have high costs, require a significant amount of resources and time difficult for local communities to garner, and necessitate a revision to how courts have operated in the past.

Yet, in the context of Myanmar's SEZs, reliance on non-legal strategies has not meant that the law is ignored. As outlined later in the chapter, international law is being used where domestic law seems to be lacking and as a strategy with its own merits. The government's accession to two international human rights conventions in the 1990s opened up space for certain human rights discourse and projects (Cheesman and Kyaw Min San 2014).[3] Historical use of this space might contribute to current legal strategies relying on human rights arguments. Recourse to international

---

[3] Myanmar acceded to the Conventions on the Rights of the Child and Conventions on the Elimination of All Forms of Discrimination Against Women in 1991 and 1997, respectively.

law could be motivated by a confluence of this and other factors: transnational input and actors' support may shape communities' claims, or affected communities could view human rights and their utility in a different way than rights conceived under domestic law.

The use of international legal arguments also places these SEZ responses within work on, and analyses of, social movements. Community mobilisation and formation of social movements to address identified injustices have a long history in Myanmar (Dale 2011). Domestic and transnational Burma pro-democracy movements are examples of new models of social movements that draw on conventional tactics, coalescing around common goals and strategies to push for social and political change or resolution of shared grievances. Community and civil society responses to Myanmar's SEZs, however, are not necessarily motivated by a common goal or coherent interest. This lack of shared purpose between groups does not align responses to SEZs with concepts of social movements, where collective action targets shared grievances to seek state action, legal recourse or policy changes to address these grievances. Instead, the goals of communities and civil society vary across SEZs, resulting in mobilising efforts to achieve different ends: some groups seek to halt development of the project, while others do not oppose the creation of the SEZ but want compensation for losses and replacement land.

Despite these differences, those responding to Myanmar's SEZ development share the common goal of achieving a concrete outcome, and most are not pursuing changes to law and policy for the sake of the change in itself. Thus, a push for legal reform may be viewed as instrumental, a means to achieve the varying goals of those facing SEZ development. This does not diminish the potential benefits such reform could provide. Legal processes that provide for community participation offer the possibility of inclusion, although issues of implementation and efficacy may also arise. Indeed, participation that forecloses the opportunity to voice opposition or that merely seeks to affirm consent risks shifting the burden of development projects onto the communities they are intended to benefit (see Carothers and Gramont 2013: 80–81). Advocating for inclusive legal processes is a part of a transformative justice project in Myanmar – an effort to restore law to a place where formal application of rules is consistent rather than contingent (Cheesman and Kyaw Min San 2014). However, where trusted domestic legal tools remain largely absent, as the responses to SEZs in Myanmar illustrate, communities and civil society employ a variety and combination of other strategies to achieve desired outcomes.

The strategies used against SEZ development can be understood with reference to the literature on transnational social movements. Margaret E. Keck and Kathryn Sikkink, for example, argue that social change can be accomplished through transnational advocacy networks. These networks work on an issue across state boundaries, to articulate a clear harm and bring pressure on the state from outside through a 'boomerang effect'. The boomerang effect is needed where domestic actors are unable to engage with the state and therefore use the pressure of an outside state to accomplish their goals (Keck and Sikkink 1998). Aspects of community and civil society campaigns, media and targeting of foreign government involvement to respond to Myanmar's SEZs fit the kinds of strategies used by the transnational advocacy networks Keck and Sikkink describe. Yet community and civil society groups continue to engage local government as well. The involvement of private investors further complicates the analysis. The transnational advocacy networks envisioned by Keck and Sikkink seek to apply pressure upon the state, whereas SEZ-affected communities and networks target state actors *and* the businesses developing and investing in SEZs (see Dale 2011).

Social change does not have a clear roadmap. As responses to Myanmar's SEZ show, no single conceptual category will capture the strategies used by local communities and civil society. Law is not entirely irrelevant in Myanmar, and transnational strategies are not the only way to accomplish advocacy goals. There is value in domestic, transnational, legal and non-legal approaches. The variety of responses discussed later in the chapter shows this to be the case, and further establishes that understanding the ways people try to solve problems is essential to the application of theoretical approaches.

Assessment of Myanmar's SEZ Law

On 23 January 2014, the Myanmar Parliament approved a new general SEZ law, superseding two 2011 SEZ laws – one general and one governing the Dawei SEZ. Aside from their geographical focus, these laws were nearly identical. They also preceded the revision or promulgation of other domestic land use or investment laws and regulations. This section analyses the current SEZ law from the perspective of affected communities, exploring whether provisions provide for local participation in decision-making, consideration in land confiscation issues or an opportunity to object to SEZ development. Along the way, it also applies principles of international law, including Myanmar's obligations with respect to resettlement and its duties to protect and respect human rights and provide access to a remedy. These principles provide an important framework of analysis, as Myanmar undertakes a process of legal reform and seeks to provide the perception of a stable legal environment to other states and foreign investors.[4]

Participation and Access to Information for Affected Communities

The objectives of the SEZ law focus on facilitating economic growth and investment, with incentives offered to developers and investors in the form of tax relief and exemptions. The priority placed on investment by the law is in itself not problematic. Yet failure to account for those affected by such investment coupled with a lack of other domestic legal protections results in a legal framework that is apt to shift the burden of development to local communities without appropriate consideration or compensation. The SEZ law creates duties for investors and developers in labour and logistical matters, but does not mention consultations or the provision of information to stakeholders. The law does not discuss whether or how information can be accessed, and if affected persons can participate in decision-making or object to a project. This is inconsistent with the government's international obligations. Under international law, including instruments that Myanmar has ratified, every person is entitled to participate in the decisions of his or her government.[5] This includes approval of development projects with large-scale environmental and social consequences such as an SEZ.

Effective participation means that those who are affected by a decision should at a minimum be involved in and able to influence the decision-making process. For those affected by an SEZ, this translates into inclusion in impact assessments and approval for SEZ development.[6] The SEZ law, however, does not contemplate impact assessments. The effect of an SEZ is mentioned only in the context of investors' duties to avoid negative social and health implications. Environmental effects

---

[4] Melissa Crouch's chapter in this volume puts this reform in historical context, describing past moments of legal reform and how they contribute to or influence current efforts.

[5] See UDHR, art 21 (right to participate in government); CEDAW, art 7 (right to participate in formulation of government policy); CRC, art 13 (right to information). See also UDHR, arts 19, 20 (rights to information, association, assembly, and freedom of expression, which includes the right to receive and impart information); ICESCR, art 13 (component of right to education is the right to participate effectively in a free society).

[6] See supra footnote 4; Rio Declaration, principle 10.

are not specifically addressed, although investors have a duty to abide by Myanmar's Environmental Conservation Law (ECL) (SEZ law, s 35). The ECL assigns the establishment of a system of environmental and social impact assessments (EIAs and SIAs) to the Ministry of Environmental Conservation and Forestry (MOECAF), and subsequent Environmental Conservation Rules provide some general guidelines on EIAs (ECL, s 7m). This might be sufficient if it had resulted in such a system. However, nothing has formally materialised for the SEZs currently underway. Myanmar's EIA Procedure, which remained in draft form for several years, was released in January 2016. How it will be implemented and the effect it will have on community engagement in the process are not yet clear. Curiously, the SEZ law does not impose a parallel duty on developers to follow the ECL, which is a shift from the 2011 SEZ laws that created the same environmental obligations for investors and developers (2011 SEZ law, s 34; Dawei SEZ law, s 31).

The creation of a 'one-stop service' to facilitate permits, licences and registration also risks sacrificing impact analyses and consideration of affected communities to ensure speedy approvals and construction. This is highlighted by the SEZ rules, which name various administrative departments involved in the 'one-stop service department' such as immigration, customs, internal revenue, and the ministries of industry, construction and energy (SEZ rules, ch 4(20)). MOECAF is not mentioned, nor are impact assessments.

The SEZ management structure creates further obstacles to accessing information; its lack of independence and transparency about how decisions are made makes it difficult for affected persons and communities to understand whom to direct communications to or how to monitor development decisions. Under the current SEZ law, a Central Body formed by the Myanmar government holds overall authority for SEZ decision-making, management committees oversee individual SEZ sites and a Central Working Body serves as an intermediary between the two. The composition of these bodies is not clear, although information released about the Thilawa SEZ indicates that Myanmar's president and vice president chair the Central Body and Central Working Body, respectively. The only mention in the law of the inclusion of non-government personnel is with respect to management committees (SEZ law, s 9(a)). This is also inferred by the SEZ rules, which give the Central Working Body authority to appoint members of the management committees and permit non-civil servants on these committees to receive a salary (SEZ rules, ch 2 (4)–(5)). The potential for non-government personnel on management committees, however, does not provide a sufficient means to include affected persons' concerns or interests in the development process. The ability of the Central Body to increase the tax exemptions and relief periods in the law with government approval is also problematic (SEZ law, s 5(j)). It is difficult to imagine such a decision would not be endorsed with the president as chair. This authority allows the Central Body to offer incentives beyond what the law provides, granting a great deal of discretion to unknown decision-makers to undo constraints imposed by the law.

Land, Livelihood and Resettlement Issues

Affected communities are also not guaranteed protection from arbitrary displacement or adequate compensation. Arbitrary displacement in cases of large-scale development occurs when projects are not justified by compelling and overriding public interests that are necessary and proportional (Kälin 2008: 32). To avoid this, states must protect against forced evictions by ensuring that safeguards are in place through legal protections, legislation and other measures (CESCR, General Comment 7 para 9). The UN Basic Principles and Guidelines on Development-Based Evictions and Displacement (Guidelines) provide further instruction. The Guidelines permit evictions in exceptional circumstances only, mandate that they comply with international human rights and humanitarian law, and require those evicted to receive full and fair compensation (Guidelines, paras 6, 21). If people are evicted, then resettlement must be offered along with alternative land of equal or better quality; accessible, affordable housing; and essential services (Guidelines, para 16).

The SEZ law does not prohibit forced evictions or provide safeguards for those who face relocation. It does not explicitly guarantee or protect the substantive rights or interests of affected communities or residents in or around an SEZ site. Nor does the law discuss compensation for confiscated land. While the SEZ law need not account for every aspect of land confiscation and use that should be covered by other domestic laws, the lack of a coherent body of law that would cover these issues combined with the failure to ensure their inclusion make addressing land rights issues difficult. The few mentions relevant to those affected by the SEZs place an obligation on developers or investors to handle the costs of resettlement. Under the SEZ law, the developer or investor is required to pay the agreed expenditures for transfer, resettlement and compensation if houses, buildings, gardens, paddy fields, fruit-bearing plants and plantations on the land must be cleared or transferred. They must also negotiate with the management committee to ensure that those forced to leave the land do not fall below their previous standard of living and have their fundamental needs fulfilled (SEZ law, s 80(a)–(b)). There is no further guidance on how negotiations should proceed and if or how these obligations should be shared amongst developers and investors, despite the requirement that the government maintain transparent procedures in establishment and management of SEZs (SEZ law, s 39(b)).

Land confiscation and tenure issues are also problematic. The Ministry of Home Affairs is tasked with confiscating land, in accordance with existing laws (SEZ law, s 82). The government has relied on Myanmar's 1894 Land Acquisition Act and 2012 Farmland Act to acquire land at current SEZ sites. While these laws require that compensation for land be given at market value or above, and for farmland, in accordance with specified rules,[7] in practice this has not occurred. Land remains a key issue for communities living in and around SEZ sites. The law, however, does not fill the void in legal uncertainty for land compensation or tenure and does not acknowledge entitlement to alternative land if displaced. Moreover, without land, people will be unlikely to maintain their standard of living or fulfil their basic needs, as developers and investors are obliged to ensure under the SEZ law. This puts developers and investors at greater risk of legal non-compliance and shifts responsibility from the government to those with business interests. This does not accord with the government's duty to protect the property rights of citizens or ensure an adequate standard of living.[8]

The SEZ law also requires investors to follow international standards and norms and prevent social and health effects in accordance with existing law (SEZ law, s 35). The inclusion of a reference to international standards is positive but does not, alone, entail clear obligations or responsibilities for investors. The SEZ rules do not clarify which international standards apply or how investors can meet this obligation. This ambiguity makes it difficult for affected persons to challenge implementation issues, but provides decision-makers with the ability to add requirements that might fall under the broad ambit of 'international standards and norms'. As with

---

[7] See Land Acquisition Act, s 23 (compensation at fair market value plus a 15 per cent payment for the compulsory nature of the acquisition); 2012 Farmland Law, s 26; Farmland Rules, s 67.

[8] See Myanmar Constitution, art 356; UDHR, art 25; ICESCR, art 11; CRC, art 27; CEDAW, art 14.

environmental obligations, there is no parallel provision for developers to comply with international standards.

In addition, the labour provisions make it impossible for non-citizens to benefit from the operation of the SEZ. Investors are consistently required to hire only Myanmar citizens for work that requires no expertise and use a set percentage of citizens for skilled workers, which increases over time after the commencement of commercial operations (SEZ law, s 74). This could create discrimination and international rights issues given the government's refusal to recognise some ethnic groups and minorities as citizens. Under the law, these groups could not apply for the employment opportunities promised to citizens.

Ability to Object or Access a Remedy

The Myanmar government must provide access to an effective, adequate and enforceable remedy.[9] As the Committee on the Rights of the Child explained for 'rights to have meaning, there must be effective remedies to redress violations' (2003, General Comment 5). The Committee provides guidance and monitors the Convention on the Rights of the Child (CRC), which Myanmar has ratified. The Guidelines also require the government to provide an effective remedy for any person claiming a violation of his or her right not to be forcibly evicted (para 17).

The government does not accomplish this in the SEZ law. Any disputes arising from the SEZ are shifted to businesses to settle: the law allows disputes to be resolved in accordance with the agreed-upon mechanism in the relevant contract or existing law if no such mechanism exists (SEZ law, s 54). Furthermore, the SEZ rules make clear that the law contemplates business disputes, referring to disputes that involve investors, developers or the management committee and not affected persons (see SEZ rules, ch 13). Contractual dispute resolution mechanisms are not a substitute for an effective remedy, and risk varying remedial outcomes depending on the contract, most of which would likely ignore communities' needs entirely. There is no guarantee that dispute resolution mechanisms will be fair or produce enforceable outcomes. Yet Myanmar's existing law does not offer any clear recourse for violations stemming from an SEZ: a consistent and independent judiciary is not available, and the legal system has

---

[9] See UDHR, art 8; CEDAW, art 2; ICCPR, art 2(3); ASEAN Human Rights Declaration (AHRD), principle 5 (right to effective and enforceable remedy); see also UNDRIP, art 8(2) (states should provide for effective mechanisms to prevent and redress various abuses).

proven unreliable historically for community- and land-based claims.[10] The law must also be perceived as fair and equitable, and applied in such a manner to bolster confidence in the legal system.[11]

Domestic law that accounts for affected communities in the development process and provides access to remedies is in itself not a guarantee that decision-making and outcomes will reflect the guarantees of such laws. However, when the law fails to offer even this baseline, as is the case with Myanmar's SEZ law, then seeking recourse under the law is an option unavailable to affected communities. The SEZ law has a number of shortcomings and gaps, and makes little mention of affected people or communities and their role and rights related to SEZs. While the law's focus on developers and investor activities and incentives is expected given its purpose, the absence of other domestic laws that clarify the rights of other stakeholders makes it difficult for affected communities to use domestic law to address grievances or push for inclusion in the development process.

The Effects of Myanmar's SEZs on Local Communities

There are three SEZs currently being developed in Myanmar – Dawei, Thilawa and Kyaukphyu. This section details the scope of negative effects in the SEZ project areas, and identifies three central problems that affected communities have been seeking to respond to: 1) lack of information and prior notice; 2) lack of meaningful consultation and participation in the decision-making process; and 3) loss of land and inadequate compensation. The discussion focuses on these problems at the two most developed SEZs – Dawei and Thilawa – that have been in the planning or construction phases for several years. While each SEZ poses unique challenges, similar consequences are expected at Kyaukphyu, the most recently announced SEZ. This section does not discuss the economic prospects of the SEZs, or how they fit into Myanmar's broader economic goals.[12]

Initiated in 2008, the Dawei SEZ was the first to begin in Myanmar, but stalled due to financing issues and changes to the project plan. Project

---

[10] Connie Carter argues that Myanmar law directly and indirectly contributes to land tenure insecurity and facilitates land grabs (Carter 2015: 100–116). See also ICJ 2014.

[11] For more on this in the context of resource extraction, see Adam Simpson, Chapter 3 of this volume.

[12] For more on the development and economic prospects of these SEZs see Wood, Chapter 7 of this volume.

developers envision the SEZ as a regional transport hub that will connect shipping lines from South Asia to Southeast Asia and China. The
Myanmar and Thai governments currently share responsibility for project development and management. The Dawei SEZ has faced significant opposition since its conception. The preparatory and initial phases
of development have already negatively affected local communities, and
reports from civil society and residents highlight concerns surrounding
loss of land, lack of information about development progress and plans,
issues with compensation and other human rights concerns. According
to a report by Burmese non-governmental organisation (NGO) Paung Ku
and international research organisation Transnational Institute (TNI), a
fully realised SEZ project could result in the displacement of 33,000 people, with infrastructure supporting the SEZ displacing thousands more.
This report also estimates that as many as 500,000 people could be indirectly or directly affected by 'massive land grabs, economic speculation,
and the decimation of the current rural economy' stemming from the SEZ
(Paung Ku and TNI 2012).

Affected communities consistently highlight concerns about land
loss: a survey by community-based organisation Dawei Development
Association (DDA) of nearly 1,600 households in twenty villages that
will be directly affected by the project found that nearly three-quarters
of those surveyed rely on agriculture as their primary occupation. Nearly
three-quarters of those surveyed also anticipate losing land as a result of
the SEZ (DDA 2014: 5, 26–27). This fear is already a reality for villages in
and around an access road: land from at least thirteen villages has reportedly been confiscated for its construction (DDA 2014: 15). Despite this
land seizure, only 15 per cent of those surveyed by DDA received any
form of compensation, and most of these households were still awaiting
full payment at the time of the survey (DDA 2014: 40, 44). Moreover, due
to gaps in domestic law, there is no guarantee that those displaced will
receive proper compensation or replacement land, and there is no clarity
about who is responsible for ensuring this occurs.

Most households affected by the SEZ report receiving little to no information about the project. Two-thirds of those surveyed by DDA had not
received any information from the government or companies, and 80
per cent learned about the SEZ through word of mouth or local media
(DDA 2014: 6, 33). As a result, affected persons are not provided prior
notice about activities, are unaware of the status of the project and do not
know if and when they will be relocated (DDA and SSDN 2012: 11, 16).
Most people who received information were told about the benefits of

the project and not any potential risks or negative consequences (DDA 2014: 6). Consultations, much less adequate or meaningful consultations, also appear lacking for the Dawei SEZ: villagers have claimed that they were not consulted or provided information about the project (DDA 2013). Likewise, the EIA and its process have failed to include local community or their opinions. Public meetings were not held prior to the commencement of the project, which occurred before any EIA process began. Meaningful consultations are meant to convey information on the project and provide space for public participation and comment. Without information the local community cannot participate in decision-making, question the project plans or share concerns about project effects. Thus, affected communities are effectively silenced in the formal decision-making process, forced to find other means to express opposition to the project and seek redress.

Similar challenges have arisen in the context of the Thilawa SEZ. Located approximately 25 km from Yangon, the Thilawa SEZ is being developed in two phases. The Thilawa SEZ project began as a joint venture between the Myanmar and Japanese governments in 2012, with the memorandum of co-operation (MoC) between the two countries including recognition that the SEZ should develop in line with international environmental standards. It is currently being developed and will be managed by a company that includes a consortium of Japanese and Myanmar corporations, the Japan International Cooperation Agency (JICA) and the Thilawa SEZ Management Committee.

At the end of January 2013, residents in both phases of the SEZ received eviction notices, instructing them to vacate their homes within fourteen days or face imprisonment. This deadline passed without event, however, after the Japanese government urged the Myanmar government to consult with community and follow international environmental standards as agreed upon in the MoC. Yet meaningful consultation did not occur, and by September 2013, all affected households in the Phase I area had signed resettlement and compensation agreements. Some reported facing threats of destruction of property, removal of offers for compensation and arrest if they did not sign (ERI 2014a). The NGO Physicians for Human Rights (PHR) reports that nearly all households it surveyed at the relocation site – 93 per cent – felt threatened or afraid of the repercussions if they did not move (PHR 2014). According to residents, there was no advance notice that an eviction was being contemplated or opportunity to object to the proposed plan. This process, along with the failure to provide full consultations or an opportunity to challenge the proposed plan and eviction, and the lack of legal or technical advice offered to the affected community, runs afoul of the Guidelines and other international standards (Guidelines, para 37).

The relocation site has been criticised for its conditions and cramped living situation: each household was provided a housing space of 25 by 50 feet and the choice between an already constructed home or money to build one (ERI 2014a). PHR found that the resettlement process failed to meet international guidelines in a number of significant ways, which resulted from threats by the government, inadequate compensation, contaminated water supplies and loss of livelihoods (PHR 2014). According to the Guidelines, the Myanmar government must also provide access to basic resources and services for those evicted, including food, potable water, shelter, sanitation, medical care, education and livelihood sources (Guidelines, para 52). The relocated community, however, reports difficulty accessing or loss of these resources, which are necessary to their continued survival (PHR 2014: 6, 16).

Phase II of development is expected to displace much more of the local community and will require relocation of 846 households, or 3,869 people (PHR 2014). As with Dawei, land tenure and access are primary concerns of affected persons. Attempts to confiscate the land through the Myanmar domestic legal process have resulted in confusion and criticism. According to affected communities, the process prescribed by the law was not followed.[13] Many residents of the Phase I area did not receive notice of the confiscation until July 2014, sent to the relocation site well after land was taken. There was no publicly posted notice, no opportunity to object and no chance to dispute or alter compensation agreements.

The project has also been marked by a lack of information offered to local communities. An EIA for Phase I was completed *after* villagers were told to sign their resettlement and compensation agreements. There were two meetings held as part of this EIA process. No known public notice or information was offered in advance of these meetings. Nor did these meetings reportedly include individuals who represented affected communities' interests (ERI 2014a). An EIA and a strategic environmental assessment (SEA) are underway for Phase II, but have stalled due to uncertainty over development plans (Ko Ko Gyi 2014).

---

[13] Under the 1894 Land Acquisition Act, the Myanmar government must provide public notice of the intended confiscation and its location at a convenient public location, an opportunity to object and, if any objections are lodged, a chance for such objections to be heard (Land Acquisition Act s 4(1)–(2), 5A(1)–(3)).

Finally, as with Myanmar's other SEZs, information about the Kyaukphyu SEZ is difficult to access – especially for local communities – and the project development process and approvals lack transparency. The SEZ Management Committee holds meetings with little notice, and there is currently little known about how land issues will be handled. Informal or customary land ownership practices will exacerbate problems with compensation and land confiscation that are borne out in other SEZ areas. There are already claims that compensation for lost land is inadequate, inconsistent and below market rate in contravention of international standards and domestic law (*Asian Correspondent* 2015). Unlike Dawei and Thilawa, where foreign government actors are involved, Kyaukphyu is being privately developed with a Singapore-based consortium leading efforts. This may affect community engagement and responses that target foreign investment and states' human rights obligations. In Thilawa, for example, affected community members were able to object to development because JICA has its own objection procedure. In Dawei, Myanmar organisations used strong advocacy ties with Thai organisations, which do not yet exist with Singapore groups.

Community and Civil Society Responses to SEZ Development

Affected communities have not been sufficiently included in the decision-making process or given important information about SEZ projects. They have also lost land and report difficult relocation conditions and inadequate or no compensation for their losses. Yet the SEZ law does not provide a tool to request information or inclusion in the decision-making process, and does not provide a remedy for community grievances. This has led communities and civil society to use a variety and combination of other strategies to achieve desired outcomes. Civil society and community responses to SEZ development include formation of civil society groups and coalitions; protest and opposition campaigns; the use of international law and standards, including human rights legal arguments; reports and media highlighting risks to communities generally and women and vulnerable populations specifically; and the pursuit of non-legal remedies.

The nature of SEZ development, with foreign investment and foreign state involvement, strengthens transnational responses and provides opportunities to make arguments and use mechanisms that are not available to opponents of domestic development or land confiscation. For the Thilawa and Dawei SEZs, this translated into legal strategies that utilise international human rights bodies and objection mechanisms. Foreign investment also draws media attention and bolsters transnational campaigns and networks. These strategies have been used successfully in the past to oppose large-scale development projects (Khagram 2004). They are also familiar to civil society in Myanmar, which has previously countered foreign investment and the government's support for projects with human rights arguments (Dale 2011).

Below is an analysis of some of the strategies used by civil society and affected communities to confront injustices and negative effects caused by SEZ development. The breadth and variety of strategies, and the near absence of domestic legal strategies, show that affected communities and those representing their interests will go to great lengths and use non-judicial mechanisms that might intuitively seem less appropriate than recourse to a functioning legal system.

Organising, Campaigns and Direct Actions

Local communities have formed groups to represent the interests of those affected by the SEZ in both Dawei and Thilawa areas. DDA, Dawei Watch and Tavoyan Women's Union are examples of groups focused on the Dawei SEZ. Community members from Thilawa have also organised to represent local interests, with villages on or near the SEZ site forming the Thilawa Social Development Group (TSDG). Other groups focused on one or more SEZs include Thailand-based Towards Ecological Recovery and Regional Alliance (TERRA), Yangon-based Paung Ku, EarthRights International, TNI, Human Rights Watch, Oxfam and the International Commission of Jurists. These groups work both independently as well as in coalitions, and through their efforts have raised awareness and interest in Myanmar's SEZ beyond its borders. The organisation and networking of groups across geography – from the local level to the national, regional and international levels – is an aspect of the 'boomerang model' advanced by Keck and Sikkink. These organisations also establish networks characteristic of transnational advocacy groups, bringing pressure to bear from outside Myanmar (Keck and Sikkink 1998).

These organisations have succeeded in some of their objectives. Community-organised campaigns and protests have slowed or stalled construction of infrastructure. In Dawei, the community-based organisation DDA has long voiced concerns over the project, displacement and the lack of local input or proper impact assessment. The organisation was involved in a campaign against project developer Italian-Thai Development PLC's proposed 4,000 MW coal-fired power plant intended to provide power to the SEZ. Efforts directed against this plant succeeded, and in January 2012 the minister of Electric Power for Myanmar halted plans for its construction citing expected harmful environmental effects. DDA has organised or supported campaigns to raise visibility – both domestically and abroad – about the negative effects of SEZs that have included tactics such as a ten-day bicycle ride, press conferences, information-sharing events, community surveys and reports, and monitoring. DDA now has a monitoring team to track development at the SEZ site, which collects information about what developers are communicating to local communities about the project's progress and assessment processes. This team reported that villagers continue to get differing or unclear information about resettlement plans and learn about the EIA plans only from contractors, as this information is not available to the broader public (DDA 2015).

Since learning about the SEZ's development in Thilawa, TSDG has repeatedly requested more information from project developers about the SEZ. However, unlike some groups in Dawei, TSDG does not oppose the SEZ development. Instead, they seek adequate compensation, replacement land and inclusion in the decision-making process. Using both letter writing and press conferences, TSDG pursued responses from the Myanmar government and JICA. During and after the resettlement process, TSDG sent close to twenty letters to the local authorities at the Yangon regional government and JICA requesting meetings to discuss issues with compensation. They also sent more than a dozen letters to the Thilawa SEZ Management Committee without response. These letters detailed issues with the relocation and at the site, including poor living conditions and lack of jobs and access to education (Snaing 2014; Requesters 2014a: 8). TSDG accompanied these letter-writing campaigns with press conferences, highlighting the lack of response from JICA, questioning JICA's financial support given the social and environmental effects of the SEZ, and expressing concern that the problems created by Phase I's development could be repeated for Phase II (TSDG 2014). Although these strategies prompted little response from the regional government or JICA, it raised the visibility of communities' concerns through press coverage and articles.

Community-based groups or organisations such as DDA and TSDG have used both public campaigns and direct appeals to decision-makers to influence the development of SEZs. Others affected by the SEZs who oppose the project have used physical forms of protest. In respective actions, protesters blocked road construction and access at the Dawei

SEZ site. In 2011, the Karen National Union (KNU), an ethnic armed organisation representing the Karen people, stopped construction of a road being built to access the Dawei SEZ after communities claimed that land was taken without compensation. These allegations have persisted, and in September and November 2013, villagers – acting independently of the KNU – again blocked roads citing Italian-Thai Development's failure to compensate for losses stemming from the SEZ (TERRA 2014). Similarly, those affected by a proposed reservoir and dam, which could displace approximately one thousand residents of Kalonthar Village, oppose development (DDA 2014: 15–16). Communities have repeatedly and visibly protested the dam and the relocation that will result. They have criticised the reservoir project and asked then President Thein Sein to ensure that foreign investment is environmentally friendly and protects the country's people (TERRA 2014). These events are not impulsive, but are planned for a strategic purpose and push back against the regime in place.

International Standards, Obligations and Human Rights-Based Claims

In addition to campaign tactics and protests, community members and groups have argued that international standards, laws or rights have been violated and looked to human rights mechanisms to seek redress or hold project developers accountable. Both Thilawa and Dawei SEZs have prompted accusations of human rights violations. Both communities have also filed complaints outside of Myanmar, despite the existence of a Myanmar National Human Rights Commission. This is likely due to the perceived lack of independence of the Myanmar Commission, which has been criticised for its reliance on the executive and support for government decisions (Crouch 2013). The submission of human rights complaints outside of Myanmar further underscores the difficulty communities face accessing an effective remedy or a legitimate rights-based grievance mechanism in the country.

In March 2013 in Dawei, DDA and communities affected by the SEZ submitted a complaint to the National Human Rights Commission of Thailand (NHRCT), claiming that the human rights of local ethnic and indigenous people had been violated (DDA 2013). The complaint outlined examples of involuntary resettlement and inadequate compensation, and alleged a lack of information and proper consultation during the environmental assessment process. It also called on Thailand to uphold human rights, and for the NHRCT to investigate the behaviour of the Thai government and Thai company Italian-Thai Development.

Community members followed this letter with testimony to the NHRCT that provided further detail about the violations claimed in their complaint letter, and submitted DDA's second report documenting the negative effects and human rights issues (DDA 2014). In November 2014, the NHRCT validated the communities' claims and sent a letter, from the Community Rights Subcommittee of the Commission to the Thai prime minister, which outlined the human rights violations and urged compliance with human rights principles. The Commission recognised violations that included forcible land confiscation without warning or consent, no public hearings, no EIA or social or health impact assessment prior to construction, involuntary relocation, and inadequate or no compensation for damaged crops and lost land (NHRC 2014).

The negative consequences of foreign investment are also an issue at the Thilawa SEZ. In June 2014, three residents from the SEZ area filed a complaint under JICA's objection procedures, bringing their objection directly to JICA's examiner in Tokyo, as the office responsible for receiving objections under the JICA Guidelines. The objection was the first to be lodged under JICA's objection procedures, and it detailed the substantial damages villagers incurred or would likely incur as a result of JICA's violation of its Guidelines for Environmental and Social Considerations at Thilawa. The applicants sought the provision of clean water, improvement of housing conditions and solutions for flooding issues, adequate compensation, access to education for relocated children, development of a new Livelihoods Restoration and Support Plan that acknowledges and accounts for villagers' desire to maintain their land-based livelihoods, and a mechanism to ensure meaningful participation between communities and other stakeholders and developers. Although the examiner did not find any serious violations of JICA's Guidelines for Environmental and Social Considerations, a set of recommendations was included with its findings. These recommendations focused on providing participatory opportunities to affected communities and improving conditions at the relocation site (Examiner for the JICA guidelines and for environmental and social considerations 2014). The requesters, TSDG and other civil society groups rejected these findings, criticising the investigation and issuing comments questioning the process and its outcome (Requesters 2014b; Mekong Watch 2015).

The Japanese government's involvement in Myanmar's SEZs has also been the target of other civil society scrutiny. In May 2013, DDA sent a letter to the Japanese prime minister, JICA and other Japanese minsters expressing concerns that if Japan became involved with the Dawei SEZ, then it would be contributing to human rights abuses and social and environmental effects (TERRA 2014). Human Rights Watch also sent a letter to the Japanese prime minister, in December 2013, focusing on the human rights concerns at the Thilawa SEZ. The letter encouraged Japan to prioritise human rights in an upcoming Japan-ASEAN summit and presented Thilawa as a 'cautionary tale'. Human Rights Watch urged Japan to press the Myanmar government to protect the rights of communities such as those in Thilawa 'facing widespread displacement and forced eviction for infrastructure, development, agriculture and natural resource extraction projects by Burmese and foreign investors' (Human Rights Watch 2013).

Community and civil society groups also advocated for better impact assessments by foreign developers and inclusion in the decision-making process. For both Dawei and Thilawa, villagers consistently allege that they have not been provided with information, are not included in meaningful consultations and are not aware of the status of EIA processes. According to principles accepted by Myanmar in ratified international instruments and in other international declarations, local community members are entitled to participate in decisions that will affect them, and to be included in the analysis of consequences for development projects with significant environmental and social effects (Rio Declaration, principle 10; CEDAW, art 7; CRC, art 13). Stakeholders have invoked these rights to push for inclusion in decision-making and highlight instances where the government and developers have fallen short of their obligations. In Dawei, for example, community members and civil society have complained that impact assessments occurred after the commencement of construction and that communities were not properly included (DDA 2013; TERRA 2014). Civil society groups have also pushed the Thai government to stop its participation in the Dawei SEZ development, conduct impact studies and consider all viable alternatives, and ensure engagement of all stakeholders at every stage of the process (Statement 2012). Similarly, Japanese NGO Mekong Watch has supported communities and TSDG at Thilawa, calling for improvement at the relocation site and pushing for more transparent EIA processes for the SEZ (Mekong Watch 2014a; 2014b). They requested clarification from JICA on the current EIA process, its methodology, compliance with laws and international standards, and inclusion of communities. JICA responded that it would comply with its Guidelines and Myanmar's Environmental Conservation Law and Rules, the SEZ law and the Draft EIA procedures, but deferred to the Myanmar government for questions of methodology (Mekong Watch 2014b).

The focus on transnational human rights abuses and decision-making reflects an inability or reticence to bring human rights claims against the Myanmar government. Even with the creation of the Myanmar Commission, human rights are still in the process of institutionalisation. The government only recently signed the International Covenant on Economic, Social, and Cultural Rights (ICESCR), one of the two covenants that comprise the International Bill of Human Rights.[14] Unlike the vast majority of UN member states, it has yet to sign the second – the International Covenant on Civil and Political Rights. Sikkink and Thomas Risse have tried to capture the varying stages of domestic incorporation of human rights through their 'spiral model'. This builds upon the boomerang model and includes a progression of five phases that ultimately ends with human rights norms that are consistently applied (Risse, Ropp and Sikkink 1999; Risse, Ropp and Sikkink 2013). Moreover, while human rights are conceptually global, in practice they are driven by context and localised understandings (Goodale and Merry 2007: 11). Responses to SEZs indicate that human rights are not yet fully integrated into Myanmar, and thus norms will not be consistently applied or enforced. This leads to human rights claims that seek recourse elsewhere, in foreign states that might have progressed further in their implementation.

Raising Awareness through Reports and Media Coverage

Civil society and community groups have undertaken studies, produced analyses and reports, and used the media to raise communities' concerns; document environmental, human rights and social effects; and make demands and recommendations. Some of these studies have provided evidence for complaints alleging human rights violations, such as DDA's comprehensive reports. These reports have used focus groups, surveys and interviews. In 2012, DDA and the Southern Society Development Network (SSDN) conducted six focus group discussions and twenty-four interviews. They then issued a report detailing the results of this research, which explored local peoples' understandings of the Dawei SEZ and the losses already incurred (DDA and SSDN 2012: 9–12). In 2014, DDA conducted a survey of almost 1,600 households in twenty villages that will be directly affected by the SEZ project. DDA's report detailed the effects and

---

[14] Myanmar signed ICESCR in July 2015, but it has yet to be ratified.

risks from the SEZ, and the domestic and international legal responsibilities not being met by its development. DDA found communities lacked information and were not consulted, land was taken with inadequate or no proper compensation, and livelihoods and access to basic needs were already being compromised.

Transnational advocacy networks are most effective when they focus on issues involving harm with a short, clear causal chain and identifiable responsible parties (Keck and Sikkink 1998). SEZ development is such an issue. Along with DDA, local, foreign and international civil society groups have highlighted land grabbing and forced resettlement as troubling consequences of SEZ development. Paung Ku and TNI published a report highlighting land grabbing and forced resettlement as risks and consequences stemming from the Dawei SEZ. This report also highlights a loss of rural livelihoods resulting from the SEZ (Paung Ku and TNI 2012). At the Thilawa relocation site, PHR conducted interviews with 78 per cent of households at the site and twenty-two key informants. Their resulting report outlined the shortcomings of the resettlement process and relocation site, which it found fell well short of international guidelines (PHR 2014). EarthRights International subsequently released two analyses of Thilawa, one detailing the rights of affected communities, questioning the legality and illustrating the effects of the SEZ, and the other outlining concerns with the process and substance of the EIA for Phase I (ERI 2014a; 2014b). Three Thai groups – TERRA, a project under Thai non-profit organisation Foundation for Ecological Recovery (FER); Ecological Alert and Recovery; and Healthy Public Policy – have also criticised assessment of environmental effects at Dawei, calling into question the project and highlighting the risks of proceeding without a strategic environmental assessment that considers cumulative effects (TERRA 2012). In each of these reports, risks and harm are directly linked to SEZ development and the behaviour of project proponents.

The negative consequences of an SEZ on specific groups are the focus of some community organisations. In Dawei, the Tavoyan Women's Union documented the detrimental effects of the SEZ to rural women, who reported suffering loss of income and having land confiscated. Women received little to no compensation, in part because title for land between a husband and wife may be held in a man's name. They were given less information than men and were not included in decision-making (Tavoyan Women's Union 2014).

The media has also been used as a tool to prompt greater coverage of and interest in Myanmar's SEZs. Many of the reports or analyses produced by civil society are accompanied by press conferences. Protests and campaigns have generated media coverage of the SEZ projects. Some groups have used the media to share their concerns about stakeholder behaviour. TSDG regularly called press conferences to highlight JICA and the Myanmar government's lack of responses to their letters and requests for meetings. Other groups, such as Dawei Watch, provided content to the media directly through feature stories, news analysis, photos and video.

Domestic Law and Non-Legal Remedies

As part of its human rights obligations, the Myanmar government has a duty to provide access to an effective remedy. The right to such a remedy is enshrined in international law and the regional ASEAN human rights declaration.[15] Yet those affected by SEZs have little recourse to address grievances as they have few legal options in Myanmar. Communities also face heavy barriers to seek an injunction or other legal means to halt construction. Domestic laws have yet to be used in lawsuits related to the SEZs, although several reports have highlighted the violation of various domestic laws stemming from project development (DDA 2014: 70–72; ERI 2014a: 9–11). The first tort case to include evidence of environmental degradation and damages was filed in May 2014, for the damage caused by the Heinda mining project, located in the Dawei District outside the SEZ area.[16] Otherwise, cases challenging large-scale development projects remain virtually untested. This does not mean that there are no domestic cases challenging government decision-making: legal claims have been brought opposing government land confiscation. Such cases are also viewed as an effort to advocate for more consistent application of the law (Cheesman and Kyaw Min San 2014). But the prospects of success are limited, and reprisals are often expected when law is used to punish dissent. In Thilawa, for example, the first notice of SEZ development for villagers was an eviction notice accompanied by the threat of imprisonment for failure to comply.

---

[15] See UDHR, art 8; ICCPR, art 2(3); CEDAW, art 2; ASEAN Human Rights Declaration, principle 5.

[16] This case is still ongoing. For more on this lawsuit, see Business & Human Rights Resource Centre, 'Myanmar Pongpipat lawsuit (re environmental & health effects of Heinda tin mine)', http://business-humanrights.org/en/myanmar-pongpipat-lawsuit-re-environmental-health-impact-of-heinda-tin-mine-0.

In one attempt to fill this gap, discussions are underway at Thilawa between civil society, project developers and their consultants to develop an operational grievance mechanism (OGM). It is hoped that the OGM will provide a space for affected communities to address past or ongoing issues related to the SEZ, and that the community will be involved in the process of its creation and implementation. Even if an OGM is launched, and succeeds in its purpose, it will not replace the government's legal obligations and the need to provide an effective remedy. The push for a community-driven OGM, however, again highlights the need for non-traditional strategies when legal solutions are unavailable or ineffective.

Civil society and community groups responding to SEZs share some of the non-legal strategies used by social movements, including collective action, community organisation and protest. Unlike many social movements, however, the various groups taking on SEZs are not united by a single objective or cause. Some oppose SEZs, while others support development but want compensation for lost land and income. SEZ development also presents a broader set of advocacy options than exclusively domestic projects or development. Foreign involvement creates opportunities to bring transnational legal actions and attract international attention and networks. These kinds of advocacy strategies are indicative of transnational advocacy networks or social movement models that target government and project developers.

Yet those affected by SEZ development should not have to file human rights complaints in neighbouring countries, write dozens of letters, stage multiple protests or seek international intervention to access information or have their voices considered. The absence of strong, clear domestic laws or access to such laws creates another barrier in a struggle to promote sustainable growth in Myanmar and address past and future issues arising from continued large-scale development. The reform of Myanmar's domestic laws is not an end in and of itself. Other obstacles exist that prevent the law from becoming a reliable tool for those facing the risks and negative consequences of development, and communities will continue to use a variety of strategies with mixed results until these are addressed.

Conclusion

Myanmar's three SEZ projects risk concentrating the burden of development on local communities, who do not have formal access to the decision-making process or a remedy for negative effects suffered. While encouraging foreign investment, these SEZs have created insurmountable social barriers by displacing communities and disrupting livelihoods. They also risk harming health and local environments in both their immediate areas and, potentially, wider regions. Myanmar's SEZ law does little to reduce these risks. The SEZ law does not ensure affected communities are consulted, can access information or can participate in decision-making and impact assessments. The focus on incentives for investors and developers provides limited to no options for communities' grievances, leaving those affected by SEZs to look elsewhere for information and solutions. Meaningful solutions, however, are not readily accessible through Myanmar's other relevant domestic laws, which at best create vague protections that are not often enforced.

Concerns over the negative effects of SEZ development and the shortcomings of Myanmar's legal regime have led to the variety of responses and strategies described in this chapter. Some of these strategies have included reference to international standards, domestic law and other rights-based claims. But most have not; the bulk of response to the SEZ projects has been in the form of organising, campaigns and direct action akin to strategies of other social movements, along with evidence-gathering and uses of media. However, because SEZs involve foreign actors, transnational advocacy and action are possible. Consequently, strategies have also included complaints to foreign human rights bodies or objection procedures and other joint actions used by transnational advocacy networks.

The strategies used also speak to how international and domestic law is perceived in Myanmar. Community groups brought human rights claims against foreign developers but not Myanmar government actors. Domestic legal action has not yet been pursued. This is due in part to a lack of clear, justiciable legal rights for affected communities. It also reflects the nascent role formal law plays in opposing government decisions, and the government's failure to provide a consistent and effective remedy for grievances that threaten the status quo. While non-legal strategies seek to achieve desired outcomes for people affected by the SEZs, these will remain unpredictable and ad hoc without accompanying legal protections. More inclusive legal processes are a first step towards providing the opportunity for just outcomes. Consistent and adequate compensation and replacement land should be part of the SEZ process. A formal process of engagement with local communities could also reduce the need to send dozens of letters or hold press conferences to simply get a meeting with decision-makers. Changes to the law, however, do not guarantee better outcomes. There is also a need to address other structural barriers, and strategies like those used by those facing SEZs will continue to be necessary to give affected communities a voice and shift some of the burden of development back on project developers.

References

Asian Correspondent. 2015. 'Kyaukphyu: History to Repeat Itself in Burma's Newest Special Economic Zone?' 20 April. Available at asiancorrespondent.com/132248/kyaukphyu-history-to-repeat-itself-in-burmas-newest-special-economic-zone.

Business & Human Rights Resource Centre. 'Myanmar Pongpipat lawsuit (re environmental & health impact of Heinda tin mine)'. Available at http://business-humanrights.org/en/myanmar-pongpipat-lawsuit-re-environmental-health-impact-of-heinda-tin-mine-0 (accessed 3 April 2016).

Carothers, Thomas and Diane de Gramont. 2013. *Development Aid Confronts Politics: The Almost Revolution.* Washington DC: Carnegie Endowment for Int'l Peace.

Carter, Connie. 2015. 'Winners and Losers: Land Grabbing in the New Myanmar' in Andrew Harding and Connie Carter (eds), *Land Grabs in Asia: What Role for the Law?* New York: Routledge, pp. 100–116.

Cheesman, Nick. 2015. *Opposing the Rule of Law: How Myanmar's Courts Make Law and Order.* Cambridge: Cambridge University Press.

Cheesman, Nick and Kyaw Min San. 2014. 'Not Just Defending; Advocating for Law in Myanmar'. 31(3) *Wisconsin International Law Journal* 702–733.

Crouch, Melissa. 2013. 'Asian Legal Transplants and Rule of Law Reform: National Human Rights Commission in Myanmar and Indonesia'. 5(2) *Hague Journal on the Rule of Law* 146–177.

Dale, John G. 2011. *Free Burma: Transnational Legal Action and Corporate Accountability.* Minneapolis: University of Minnesota Press.

Dawei Development Association (DDA) and Southern Society Development Network (SSDN). 2012. 'Local Peoples' Understandings of the Dawei Economic Zone. Available at http://www.terraper.org/web/sites/default/files/key-issues-content/1348571885_en.pdf.

Dawei Development Association (DDA). 2013. Letter to National Human Rights Commission of Thailand, 'Re: Concerns on Violation of Human Rights and Community Rights Related to Dawei Deep Sea Port and Special Economic Zone Project'. 5 March. Available at http://www.inebnetwork.org/attachments/files/DDA_Letter_NHRC_05March2013.pdf.

Dawei Development Association (DDA). 2014. 'Voices from the Ground: Concerns Over the Dawei Special Economic Zone and Related Projects'. Available at http://www.ddamyanmar.com/wp-content/uploads/2014/10/Voice-from-the-Ground-Engonline-1.pdf.

Dawei Development Association (DDA). 2015. 'Dawei SEZ Monitoring Team Report' (on file with author).

EarthRights International (ERI). 2014a. 'A Briefer on the Thilawa Special Economic Zone: Analysis of the Affected Communities' Rights and Remedies Under Myanmar Law and JICA's Guidelines'. Available at https://www.earthrights .org/sites/default/files/thilawa_briefer_-_earthrights_international_0.pdf.

(ERI). 2014b. 'Analysis of the Environmental Impact Assessment for Phase I of the Thilawa Special Economic Zone Project'. Available at http://www .burmalibrary.org/docs21/ERI-2014-11-analysis_of_Thilawa_EIA-Phase_1- en-red.pdf.

Examiner for the JICA guidelines and for environmental and social considerations. 2014. 'Investigative Report: Thilawa Special Economic Zone Development Project in The Republic of the Union of Myanmar'. Available at http://www.jica.go.jp/english/our_work/social_environmental/objection/ c8h0vm00008zvp4f-att/report.pdf.

Goodale, Mark and Sally Engle Merry (eds). 2007. *The Practice of Human Rights: Tracking Law between the Global and the Local*. Cambridge: Cambridge University Press.

Harding, Andrew. 2014. 'Law and Development in Its Burmese Moment: Legal Reform in an Emerging Democracy' in Melissa Crouch and Tim Lindsey (eds), *Law, Society and Transition in Myanmar*. Oxford: Hart Publishing, pp. 377–400.

Human Rights Watch. 2013. 'Re: Making Human Rights a Cornerstone of the Japan-ASEAN Summit'. 11 December. Available at www.hrw.org/print/news/ 2013/12/11/letter-prime-minister-abe-making-human-rights-cornerstone- japan-asean-summit.

International Commission of Jurists (ICJ). 2014. 'MYANMAR: Country Profile Prepared by the ICJ Centre for the Independence of Judges and Lawyers'. Available at http://icj.wpengine.netdna-cdn.com/wp-content/uploads/2014/ 06/CIJL-Country-Profile-Myanmar-June-2014.pdf.

Kälin, Walter. 2008. 'Guiding Principles on Internal Displacement – Annotations'. 38 *Studies in Transnational Legal Policy*. The American Society of International Law.

Keck, Margaret E. and Kathryn Sikkink. 1998. *Activists beyond Borders: Advocacy Networks in International Politics*. Ithaca, NY: Cornell University Press.

Khagram, Sanjeev. 2004. *Dams and Development: Transnational Struggles for Water and Power*. Ithaca, NY: Cornell University Press.

Ko Ko Gyi. 2014. 'EIA on Thilawa SEZ Second Phase Faces Delay, Company Says'. 25 September. *Mizzima*. Available at http://archive-3.mizzima.com/ mizzima-news/myanmar/item/13108-eia-on-thilawa-sez-second- phase-faces-delay-company-says/13108-eia-on-thilawa-sez-second-phase- faces-delay-company-says.

Mekong Watch. 2014a. 'JICA Continues to Ignore People Affected by Thilawa Special Economic Zone (SEZ) in Burma (Myanmar); Mekong Watch Appalled by JICA Decision to Provide Investment Financing for SEZ and Calls for Improved Relocation and Compensation Measures to Prevent Deterioration of Villagers' Living Conditions'. Available at https://mekongwatch.files .wordpress.com/2014/04/20140425_statement_thilawa_mw_final-2.pdf.

2014b, 'Recommendation Letter Regarding the Process Related to Environment Impact Assessment for "the Thilawa SEZ Development Project" in Burma (Myanmar)'. Available at https://mekongwatch.files.wordpress.com/2014/08/ 20140722_jica-response-to-mw-0701-sea-letter_english.pdf.

2015. 'Mekong Watch Comments on JICA Examiner's Report on Thilawa SEZ'. Available at https://mekongwatch.wordpress.com/2015/03/13/mekong-watch-comments-on-jica-examiners-report-on-thilawa-sez/.

Memorandum on the Cooperation for the Development of the Thilawa SEZ, between JICA and Myanmar SEZ Management Committee. 21 December 2012. Available at http://www.meti.go.jp/press/2012/12/20121227003/ 20121227003-2.pdf.

National Human Rights Commission of Thailand (NHRC), Community Rights Subcommittee. 2014. 'Re: Urging to Comply with Human Rights Principles' (on file with author). November.

Paung Ku and Transnational Institute (TNI). 2012. 'Land Grabbing in Dawei (Myanmar/Burma): A (Inter)National Human Rights Concern'. Available at https://www.tni.org/files/download/dawei_land_grab.pdf.

Physicians for Human Rights (PHR). 2014. 'A Foreseeable Disaster in Burma: Forced Displacement in the Thilawa Special Economic Zone'. Available at https:// s3.amazonaws.com/PHR_Reports/Burma-Thilawa-English-Report-Nov2014 .pdf.

Prasse-Freeman, Elliott. 2014. 'Conceptions of Justice vs. the Rule of Law' in David Steinberg (ed.), Myanmar: The Dynamics of an Evolving Polity. Boulder, CO: Lynne Rienner Publishers, Inc., pp. 89–114.

Requesters. 2014a. 'Objection Regarding the Thilawa Special Economic Zone Development Project in Myanmar'. 2 June. Available at http://www.jica.go.jp/ english/our_work/social_environmental/objection/c8h0vm00008zvp4f-att/ objection_status_01.pdf.

Requesters. 2014b. 'Opinions on the Examiners' Report Regarding the Thilawa Special Economic Zone Development Project in Myanmar'. 3 December. Available at https://mekongwatch.files.wordpress.com/2015/03/20141203_ requesters-opinions-on-jica-examiners-thilawa_webe68eb2e8bc89e794a8 .pdf.

Risse, Thomas, Stephen C. Ropp and Kathryn Sikkink (eds). 1999. The Power of Human Rights: International Norms and Domestic Change. Cambridge: Cambridge University Press.

2013. *The Persistent Power of Human Rights: From Commitment to Compliance.* Cambridge: Cambridge University Press.

Snaing, Yen. 2014. 'Relocated Thilawa SEZ Villagers Persist in Calls for JICA Meeting'. 9 April. *The Irrawaddy.* Available at www.irrawaddy.org/burma/relocated-thilawa-sez-villagers-persist-calls-jica-meeting.html.

Statement by thirty civil society networks and organisations. 2012. 'Government Must Review Its Plan to Engage with Dawei Project: Stop Patronizing Dawei Project, Stop Public Debt Hikes'. Available at http://www.terraper.org/web/sites/default/files/key-issues-content/1348570623_en.pdf.

Tavoyan Women's Union. 2014. 'Our Lives Not for Sale: Tavoyan Women Speak out against the Dawei Special Economic Zone Project'. Available at http://womenofburma.org/wp-content/uploads/2015/02/Our-Lives-Not-for-Sale_English.pdf.

Thilawa Social Development Group (TSDG). 2014. 'Japanese Agency Fails to Meet Villagers over Serious Problems with Thilawa Special Economic Zone'. Available at https://mekongwatch.wordpress.com/2014/04/29/thilawa-villagers-hold-press-conference-dismayed-by-jicas-failure-to-respond/.

Towards Ecological Recovery and Regional Alliance (TERRA). 2012. 'Dawei: Points of Concerns'. Ecological Alert and Recovery, Health Public Policy. Available at http://www.terraper.org/web/sites/default/files/key-issues-content/1348571066_en.pdf.

Towards Ecological Recovery and Regional Alliance (TERRA). 2014. 'Dawei Deep Seaport and Special Economic Zone – Chronology of Key Events (from 2008–2013)'. Available at www.burmapartnership.org/wp-content/uploads/2014/10/Dawei_Chronology_KeyEvents2008-2013_Jan2014.pdf.

Turnell, Sean. 2014. 'Legislative Foundations of Myanmar's Economic Reforms' in Melissa Crouch and Tim Lindsey (eds), *Law, Society and Transition in Myanmar.* Oxford: Hart Publishing, pp. 183–200.

Regional and International Documents

Association of Southeast Asian Nations (ASEAN). 2012. ASEAN Human Rights Declaration (AHRD). 18 November.

Committee on the Rights of the Child. 2003. 'General Comment No 5, General Measures of Implementation of the Convention on the Rights of the Child (arts 4, 42 and 44, para 6)'. UN Doc CRC/GC/2003/5.

Convention on the Elimination of All Forms of Discrimination Against Women (CEDAW). 1979. 1249 UNTS 13. 18 December.

Convention on the Rights of the Child (CRC). 1989. 1577 U.N.T.S. 3. 20 November.

International Covenant on Civil and Political Rights (ICCPR). 1966. S. Treaty Doc No. 95-20, 6 ILM 368 (1967), 999 UNTS 171. 16 December.

FACING THE CONCENTRATED BURDEN OF DEVELOPMENT   227

Social and Cultural Rights (ICESCR). 1966.

International Covenant on Economic, Social and Cultural Rights (ICESCR). 1966. S Treaty Doc No. 95-19, 6 ILM 360 (1967), 993 UNTS 3. 16 December.
Office of the United Nations High Commissioner for Human Rights. 2007. 'Basic Principles and Guidelines on Development-Based Evictions and Displacement, Annex 1 of the Report of the Special Rapporteur on Adequate Housing as a Component of the Right to an Adequate Standard of Living'. A/HRC/4/18. Available at http://www.ohchr.org/Documents/Issues/Housing/Guidelines_en.pdf.
Rio Declaration on Environment and Development. 1992. UN Doc. A/CONF.151/26 (vol I); 31 ILM 874.
UN Committee on Economic, Social and Cultural Rights (CESCR). 1997. 'General Comment No 7: The right to adequate housing (Art 11.1): forced evictions'. E/1998/22. 20 May.
Universal Declaration of Human Rights (UDHR). 1948. GA res 217A (III), UN Doc A/810 at 71.

Laws and Regulations

Constitution of Myanmar – 2008.
Dawei Special Economic Zone Law No. 17/2011 (State Peace and Development Law).
Environmental Conservation Law No. 9/2012 (Pyidaungsu Hluttaw Law).
Environmental Conservation Rules, Notification No. 50/2014.
Environmental Impact Assessment Procedure – 2015.
Farmland Law No. 11/2012 (Pyidaungsu Hluttaw Law).
Farmland Rules, Notification No. 62/2012.
Land Acquisition Act – 1894.
Myanmar Special Economic Zone Law No. 1/2014 (Pyidaungsu Hluttaw Law).
Myanmar Special Economic Zone Law No. 8/2011 (State Peace and Development Law).
Myanmar Special Economic Zone Rules, Notification No. 1/2015.

9

Top-Down Transitions and the Politics of US Sanctions

CATHERINE RENSHAW

Introduction

US sanctions had negligible effects on Myanmar's transition to democracy. By the end of 2015, it was clear that those sanctions which remained in place, such as the US Treasury Department prohibition on dealings with Specially Designated Nationals (SDNs), were in fact counter-productive to Myanmar's economic development. This was highlighted in dramatic fashion in November 2015, when the US Treasury's Office of Foreign Assets Control (OFAC) advised US banks to refrain from financing shipments to Yangon's main terminal. The terminal is controlled by Asia World Co Ltd, and the company's managing director, Steven Law, was subject to sanctions because of his involvement with the former military regime. Asia World is one of Myanmar's largest and most successful companies. It is a sprawling conglomerate with stakes in shipping, trade, construction and mining. Asia World helped in the construction of Naypyidaw and in 2013 was awarded the contract for the upgrade of Yangon's international airport. In 2015, Steven Law was amongst those honoured in Myanmar's 2015 Annual Presidential Awards for service to Myanmar's development.

In December 2015, the US announced a six-month suspension of sanctions, permitting shipments through all ports and airports controlled by Steven Law and other SDNs. In October 2016, following a visit to Washington DC by Special Counsellor of State Aung San Suu Kyi, US President Barack Obama issued an Executive Order that effectively eliminated all remaining sanctions against Myanmar. The lifting of sanctions signalled belated acceptance by the United States that the price of peaceful transition in Myanmar is the ongoing and considerable influence of Myanmar's crony capitalists over the trajectory of reform. It was inevitable that the United States would overcome its moral opprobrium and permit US companies to engage in trade with business persons such as Steven

Law. What is far from clear is whether there are economic strategies the United States can now implement which could divert Myanmar from the path of uneven development and demi-democratisation taken by so many of its Southeast Asia neighbours, where the systematic privileging of oligarchs and capitalist elites undercuts the benefits of democratisation for the majority of people. This chapter examines the US sanctions regime in the context of Myanmar's democratic transition, assesses its objectives and shortcomings, and considers the prospects for effective influence through economic engagement in the future.

Sanctions and the Business of Transition

There is near-uniform consensus amongst scholars and analysts that the US policy of sanctions against Myanmar in the period 1990–2010 was manifestly ineffective in encouraging political change (Mintier 1997; Hadar 1998; Pedersen 2000; Steinberg 1999; Sachs 2004b; Badgley 2004; McGillivray and Stam 2004; Holliday 2005a; Taylor and Pedersen 2005; James 2006; Rarick 2006; Pedersen 2007; Abramowitz and Kolieb 2008; Howse and Genser 2008; Kudo 2008; Selth 2010; Pedersen 2013; Wilson 2014a; Jones 2014). Indeed, in the view of many scholars, US sanctions were in fact counter-productive. The primary consequence of sanctions was to prolong the political stalemate that existed between the military government and the opposition, while at the same time exacerbating the suffering and impoverishment of the Burmese people (Taylor 2004; Pedersen 2014; Jones 2014). That this was the consequence of sanctions comes as no surprise to those who are familiar with Myanmar and the nature of its military regime (Taylor and Pedersen 2005). Myanmar is surrounded by neighbours such as China, India and Thailand which did not join the West and its allies in implementing sanctions (Ott 1998). Myanmar is also rich in extractive resources. These factors mitigated the loss of US foreign direct investment as a source of funding for development projects and reduced the regime's dependency on the West, greatly diminishing any economic leverage the United States might have had. Furthermore, the military regime did not fear isolation. Burma's colonial history and its leaders' fears of external interference fostered a culture of xenophobia, which sanctions merely exacerbated (Holliday 2005b).

This chapter is concerned with the legacy of US sanctions and the way this legacy continues to shape the business of transition in Myanmar. In part, this is a historical inquiry into the untidy history of sanctions and their deleterious effect on the economic and political landscape of

Myanmar (Haacke 2015; Holliday 2005a; Pedersen 2014). As late as 2016, the US Treasury maintained a list of SDNs (SDN list) whose assets were blocked and with whom US persons were generally prohibited from dealing. This list contained the names of some of Myanmar's most prominent business people, their families and the companies they manage. The industries with which these entities are associated include mining, construction, tourism, shipping, manufacturing, oil and gas, farming, banking, transport, real estate development, forestry, electrical and power, and foreign trading. So extensive are the interests of these people and so labyrinthine are their networks of business relationships that it was almost impossible to engage in any commercial activity in Myanmar without coming into contact with a prohibited person. This chapter considers the effects, tangible and intangible, these ongoing sanctions had on the fragile process of transition.

In this chapter, I focus specifically on US sanctions because US policy in relation to Myanmar was largely replicated by its major allies (the European Union, Canada, Switzerland and Australia). The European Union's Myanmar sanctions package, for example, was atypically broad compared to other EU sanctions regimes, primarily because the European Union and others followed the United States in expressing disapprobation of the junta through a broad range of sanctions (Portela 2014). It is notable, however, that other countries moved far more swiftly than the United States in removing all sanctions (excluding those related to arms trading) after 2012. As I show in this chapter, although US sanctions policy was scaled down significantly post-2012, some elements remained in place until October 2016. The reason for this, and the ongoing problems posed by sanctions for Myanmar's development, is one of the central themes of this chapter. Studying US sanctions in the early period of Myanmar's democratisation highlights several important aspects of the business of transition. First, sanctions throw into sharp relief the centrality of *timing* as an independent variable in the success of economic policies underpinning transition. In the wake of Thein Sein's accession to power, the European Union, Canada and Australia moved with alacrity to embrace Myanmar's transition. Most sanctions, with the exception of embargoes on arms dealing, were swiftly removed. The United States reacted far more slowly, the pace of its sanctions reform well out of kilter with the pace of change on the ground in Myanmar. The consequences of this were felt not just by US companies that suffered a competitive disadvantage because of delay in access to Myanmar's markets, but also by third-party countries that were unnerved by the uncertainty created by the US position and were therefore slower than they would otherwise have been to engage in Myanmar.

Second, the issue of sanctions highlights the fact that the business of transition is not merely about economic costs and benefits. It also raises questions about prevailing conceptions of political morality, both inside Myanmar and outside, and the correct point at which judgements about past collusion and profiteering with an oppressive regime should be made by the citizens and politicians of the country in question, instead of by outsiders. Aung San Suu Kyi hinted at an answer to this question in 2012, when she asked US Congress to lift sanctions. Suu Kyi said 'we must learn to stand on our own two feet and not depend on sanctions to push us towards democracy' (NBC 2012). The evolution of Suu Kyi's thinking on sanctions, and the effect her early views on sanctions had on US policy, form part of the discussion in this chapter.

US Sanctions Regime (1990–2010)

In 1989, in response to the military junta's brutal suppression of the 1988 pro-democracy movement, President Bush suspended Burma's eligibility for benefits under the Generalised System of Preferences (Ewing-Chow 2006). In 1990, the US Senate and Congress passed the Customs and Trade Act, which requires the US president to impose economic sanctions on Burma if specific conditions were not met, such as progress on human rights and suppression of the flow of narcotics. In 1991, invoking the Customs and Trade Act, President Bush refused to renew its bilateral tex-tile agreement with Myanmar. In 1994, US Congress placed Burma on the list of international 'outlaw states' (together with Libya, North Korea and Iraq), which meant that US funds available under the Foreign Assistance Act could not be used towards financing the US share of international assistance programmes in Myanmar. In 1996, President Clinton signed the 1997 Foreign Operations Act, which prohibits the United States from giving any new assistance to Myanmar and gives the president discretion to prohibit US individuals from initiating new investments in Myanmar. In 1997, citing a constant and continuing pattern of severe repression, President Clinton exercised this discretion.

The administration of President George W. Bush (2001–2009) contin-ued the policy of sanctions against Myanmar. In 2003, President Bush signed the Burmese Freedom and Democracy Act 2003 (BDFA). As well as freezing the assets of senior members of the Burmese government, indi-viduals and corporations, the BFDA banned the importation of any goods produced, manufactured, grown or assembled in Burma; prohibited US firms from providing financial services to any Burmese entity including credit card services provided by American Express, MasterCard and Visa; expanded the visa ban; codified the policy of opposition to international loans and technical assistance to Burma; and required US financial institutions to freeze assets of senior individuals of the State Peace and Development Council (SPDC). The BFDA stated that the United States would block any application by Myanmar for soft loans from the International Monetary Fund and the World Bank. The ban would remain in effect until the US president certified to Congress that Myanmar's government had made substantial progress towards ending human rights violations and implementing a democratic government. All political prisoners must be released, and freedom of speech and press, as well as freedom of association and religion, must be reinstated. In addition, the SPDC would have to reach an agreement with the National League for Democracy (NLD) and other democratic forces in that country, including Burma's ethnic nationalities, on the transfer of power to a civilian government. On 1 August 2006, President George W. Bush extended the BDFA for another three years.

In 2007, following the regime's violent crackdown on protestors in the Saffron revolution, President Bush announced a new Executive Order aimed at tightening economic sanctions and blocking property and travel to the United States by senior leaders of the SPDC, as well as individuals who provide financial backing for the SPDC, and individuals responsible for human rights violations and impeding democracy in Burma. In 2008 the Tom Lantos Block Burmese Junta's Anti-Democratic Efforts (JADE) Act of 2008 was passed by the Senate and Congress, which amongst other things prohibits the importation from Myanmar of jadeite and rubies and articles of jewellery containing jadeite or rubies.

It was not only the US federal government that levelled sanctions against Myanmar. In a move of dubious constitutionality, state legislatures such as Massachusetts and city governments such as New York City, Washington DC and Seattle also imposed bans on companies dealing in products from Myanmar or investing in Myanmar (Brandon 1998; Schmahmann, Finch and Chapman 1997). These bans were highly effective in encouraging US companies to abandon engagement in Myanmar. In 1996, for example, citing the Massachusetts law, Apple Computers pulled out of Myanmar, shortly followed by Eastman Kodak and Hewlett-Packard (Mintier 1997). In other cases, informal sanctions, including lobbying campaigns, consumer boycotts, shareholder protests, street marches and letter-writing initiatives, led to foreign firms divesting their interests in Myanmar. Levi Strauss, Pepsico, Heineken, Carlsberg, Eddie Bauer and Liz Claiborne all withdrew from Myanmar in the period between 1995 and 2005 (Holliday 2011:118). In 2003, the American Apparel and Footwear Association announced that due to the repressive nature of the regime in Myanmar, including its use of child labour and forced labour, restrictive worker rights and the banning of unions, it was implementing an immediate and total ban on US textiles, apparel and footwear imports from Myanmar (Falco 2003). In 2003, Saks Fifth Avenue and the May Company banned the sale of Burmese products in their stores.

The threat of litigation provided a further disincentive to US firms considering engaging in Myanmar. Prior to the implementation of sanctions, Unocal Oil Corporation contracted with the Burmese government to build the Yadana Natural Gas Pipeline, close to the Andaman Islands. In 1996, a group of ethnic minority farmers sued Unocal under the Alien Torts Claims Act for complicity in human rights abuses carried out during the construction of the pipeline. Unocal's argument, that its presence in Myanmar was a positive force, providing jobs for Burmese citizens and increasing economic growth which would ultimately lead to democratisation, played poorly in the US media.[1] In December 2004, Unocal reached a multi-million-dollar settlement with the plaintiffs (Dale 2011).

Throughout this period, the people of Myanmar slipped further into poverty. Myanmar's profound economic problems did not result solely from the withdrawal of US companies or the prohibition on economic trade between Myanmar and the United States. As McCarthy (2000) points out, the Asian financial crisis was responsible for decimating trade with Myanmar's neighbours in the Association of Southeast Asian Neighbours, and this, coupled with the SPDC's own economic ineptitude, probably caused more harm than US sanctions. By mid-1998, all investment from Thailand and Indonesia had ceased, and investment from Malaysia and Singapore had slowed considerably (Brandon 1998). Nonetheless, it is possible to point to some examples – the depletion of the Burmese garment industry is one infamous case – where US sanctions had a direct and profoundly negative effect on the livelihood of ordinary Burmese citizens. At its peak, Myanmar's Garments Manufacturing Association had four hundred factories employing 400,000 workers. By 2007, as a direct result

---

[1] However, the National Foreign Trade Council, an association of more than 680 transnational corporations, intervened in the lawsuit, arguing amongst other things, that isolating Burma actually hindered efforts towards reform.

of trade sanctions, it had contracted to one hundred factories employing 60,000 workers (Jones 2014). In addition, the severe reduction in multilateral and bilateral financial aid that resulted from the US opposition to Burma's membership in various multilateral financial organisations made the lives of Burmese citizens much harder than those of their neighbours in Cambodia, Vietnam and Laos.

More broadly, one of the enduring effects of the sanctions regime was to cause Myanmar's economy to be channelled down a particular development pathway, largely shaped by demands for energy and commodities from neighbouring states such as China (Jones 2014). Growth occurred in areas of state control, primarily the extractive industries, where there were few constraints on exploitation of the workforce or protection against environmental damage. Conglomerates supported by the military were assigned major infrastructure projects, often involving land grabs and forced displacement. The benefits of these projects flowed to army commanders, cronyist businessmen, investors and local ethnic minority elites. Meanwhile, sanctions curtailed the potential development of labour-intensive manufacturing and agricultural enterprises. In the wake of sanctions, small enterprises and private factories collapsed. Jones (2014) argues that one effect of this was to stymie the emergence of an organised working class, which might have protested for higher wages and greater political and civil liberties.

In sum, despite the existence of broad agreement amongst most analysts that deploying sanctions against Burma was futile and destructive, the United States persisted with sanctions for a little more than two decades. The US policy was followed, with various degrees of enthusiasm, by its allies in Canada, the European Union and Australia. The sanctions policy was justified, publicly, on three principle grounds. First, sanctions would deny Burma's rulers the hard currency they use to fund the tools of repression (weapons and military equipment). Second, economic hardship caused by sanctions would cause the people to rise against the government, forcing it from power, or pressure it for changes, which the regime would have to comply with. Finally, engagement with the Burmese military regime would entail collaborating with (and enriching) dictators and human rights abusers and was thus morally indefensible.

History has shown that the first and second of these arguments were deeply flawed. First, Burma's leaders did not need the West to supply them with military equipment: China stood ready to oblige. Second, after the 1988 uprising, there was no indication whatsoever that a widespread destabilising popular protest was imminent. It is the final reason therefore – the moral reason – that explains why the US policy of sanctions endured, even though it palpably failed to influence political developments in Myanmar and in likelihood harmed ordinary Burmese people. The US sanctions policy was in the end a reflection of prevailing domestic political considerations in the United States, including public sentiments regarding pro-democracy leader Aung San Suu Kyi.

Suu Kyi played a central role in maintaining the policy of US sanctions. In the mid-1990s, while Burma was still firmly under the control of the State Law and Order Restoration Council (SLORC), it seemed for a brief moment that a new age of economic openness might be dawning in Myanmar. The SLORC abandoned the 'Burmese Way to Socialism' and began to privatise government-controlled enterprises, liberalise external trade, legalise cross-border trade with neighbours such as Thailand and accept foreign direct investment (Cingranelli and Richards 1999). By 1995, the Myanmar Investment Commission had approved 95 per cent of foreign investment proposals (McCarthy 2000). The SLORC established joint ventures with foreign companies Total (France) and Unocal (US), and granted mining exploration licences to companies such as Gold (Canada). Foreign-backed investment projects in manufacturing were established, taking advantage of Burma's low labour costs. The SLORC named 1996 'Visit Myanmar Year' and embarked on a programme of hotel construction, backed by foreign investment (Hadar 1998). In 1997 Myanmar was accepted as a full member of the Association of Southeast Asian Nations (ASEAN), which brought with it the prospect of integrating Burma's markets with those of its Southeast Asian neighbours, some of whom were the 'tiger economies' of the developing world. Japan and ASEAN's wealthier members, such as Singapore, increased levels of aid to Myanmar.

The hope of many was that political glasnost would follow these promising economic developments, perhaps through the creation of a middle class that would agitate for democratic change from within. The United States, together with Japan and the European Union, initially sought to encourage economic development in Burma with precisely this aim. As Holliday points out, throughout the 1960s, constructive engagement and positive sanctions (incentives) were central to mainstream thinking about how to encourage political change (Holliday 2005b). Optimistic observers pointed to the economic liberalisation and democratisation of South Korea and Taiwan in the 1980s as examples of a potential pathway for Myanmar (Holliday 2005b). In a detailed report on sanctions prepared for the National Bureau of Asian Research, John Badgley (2004) brought together an impressive group of Myanmar scholars and analysts who all concurred in the view that 'involving states and societies in the web of international trade and finance is the best way to link them to norms of transparency and the rule of law' (Badgley 2004: 9).

But in July 1996, in a videotape smuggled from Myanmar, Aung San Suu Kyi called for economic sanctions to 'make it quite clear that economic change in Burma is not possible without political change' (Reuters 1996). On 3 February 1997, in a press conference with foreign media, Suu Kyi firmly rejected the argument that foreign investment in Burma would raise living standards and increase the prospects for freedom. She urged the international community to implement sanctions, arguing that 'what the international community is doing now is putting more and more money into the pockets of a small privileged group, who become more keen on preserving the status quo' (Associated Press 1997). Two months later, in the wake of Suu Kyi's call, the United States imposed sanctions on all new foreign investment in Burma.

Suu Kyi was still calling for caution in engaging with Burmese industries as late as 2012. In June 2012, Suu Kyi advised foreign companies not to invest in the state-run Myanmar Oil and Gas Enterprise until it became more accountable and open.

Aung San Suu Kyi, and the vocal and well-funded Burmese diaspora, believed that sanctions strengthened the ability of the democratic opposition to gain concessions from the regime (Haacke 2015). The view that sanctions are an effective tool for influencing policy was given credence by occasional suggestive sequences of events which were read by some as indicating a level of responsiveness on the part of the military to external pressure. For example, in1990, he regime made the somewhat surprising decision to proceed with elections. The decision followed Suu Kyi's call on foreign countries to impose a complete economic boycott, including a trade embargo, until the regime held elections Five years later, the regime's announcement that Suu Kyi was to be released from house arrest in July 1995 came one day before US Congress was to debate the banning of all economic contact with Myanmar (Hadar 1998). Again, some read this as evidence that political action by the United States was capable of shaping decision-making in Myanmar. Suu Kyi and her supporters were successful in convincing US politicians and interest groups that sanctions must remain in place for the military government to understand that it could not achieve its economic goals without first striking a deal with the opposition (Falco 2003). Coupled with this was the strong public sentiment in the United States that something must be done in response to the repression of Suu Kyi and the people of Burma. US politicians were eager to be seen as responsive to this sentiment, and few politicians were willing to risk being labelled as apologists for the military dictators by calling for a rethink of the sanctions policy (Lintner 2008).

The South African experience also loomed large in US thinking, and perhaps in Suu Kyi's as well. Nobel laureate and anti-apartheid activist Desmond Tutu named Suu Kyi 'the Mandela of Burma' and urged the world to 'do for Burma what was done for South Africa' (Tutu 1995). Sanctions and the isolation of the apartheid regime in South Africa were seen as contributing to its undoing. The South African experience seemed to overturn the liberal theory that Western states should engage dictatorships in trade and commerce, rather than isolate them, because engagement would lead to greater wealth and the creation of a middle class no longer satisfied with having no economic or political power (Corker 1986). Senator Mitch McConnell, a leading figure in the history of US political engagement with Myanmar, stated: 'Sanctions worked in South Africa and they will in Burma too' (Schuman 2006). Yet in South Africa, there was broad agreement from neighbouring countries to support the sanctions policy (Badgley 2004). Burnell (2004) argues that South Africa is in fact perhaps the *only* example where international economic sanctions were a major success, and that even there the relative importance of their contribution to South Africa's break with apartheid is a matter of dispute.

For US legislators, 'sanctions had a moral, public policy value for the special interest groups in their own constituencies', and the United States chose to 'privilege these groups and their perspectives over the welfare of the majority of Myanmar's people' (James 2006: 134). The cost to US interests in pursuing this course of action was minimal. Seattle, for example, which imposed bans on companies trading with Burma, did not consider a similar move against China, which was a major buyer of aircraft produced by local company Boeing Corporation (*Seattle Post Intelligencer* 1997). As McCarthy writes, 'evidently, the Burmese political activists have been more successful than their Chinese counterparts in swaying the support of the United States congress' and 'Chinese business interests and the US-China business lobby groups are also far more powerful, and far more organised, than their Burmese counterparts' (McCarthy 2000: 260). US policy towards China from the mid-1990s followed a path of what Madeleine Albright called 'purposeful engagement' with trade as the modus operandi of relations between the two countries. Trade with China was too profitable to forgo, while trade with Myanmar was dispensable. However, opinion about the appropriateness of sanctions in the United States was not uniform. Jerry Jasinowski, president of the US National Association of Manufacturers, said that, 'Unilateral economic sanctions are no substitute for a serious foreign policy. The measures will harm the interests of the very people the law was designed to help – the impoverished Burmese people – while doing nothing to advance human rights' (Mintier 1997).

There is some evidence that opinion in Myanmar ran along similar lines. A 2004 editorial in the *Myanmar Times* said that,

> It is so obvious that America will definitely benefit from a democratic Myanmar, yet Washington ignores our invitations to work constructively towards this goal, whilst decisions taken in Washington are hampering efforts in Myanmar to develop the economy, fight the drug trade and play a bigger role in the international community. (quoted in James 2006: 136)

On another occasion, the *Myanmar Times* opined that, 'the US should be more responsible and realistic in helping the people of the developing countries reach their common objective in becoming peaceful, stable and sustainable democracies' (quoted in James 2006: 137). It is difficult to gauge the extent to which these sentiments were widespread. Former political prisoners such as Khin Zaw Win argued that demands for sanctions were unpatriotic: 'there can be no greater sacrilege or transgression than to actively advocate for punitive measures against one's own land and people' (Jones 2014: 124). In contrast, the National League for Democracy's 2011 study of the impact of sanctions denied that sanctions had affected Myanmar's economic performance. The NLD study attributed economic underperformance to cronyism and the junta's economic mismanagement (NLD 2011). For its part, Myanmar's military government used the opposition's support for sanctions to denounce them as the tools of foreign powers.

In the case of Myanmar, aiming for the 'art of the possible' and accepting a military-led transition and the gradual empowerment of the people through development assistance and economic investment were not a policy option that could be countenanced while Suu Kyi stood in public opposition to it (Taylor 2004). In the end, sanctions were an expensive reassurance to Suu Kyi and the Burmese diaspora that their cause was just and that the Western world agreed with them. In his book *Societies Under*

Siege (2014) Lee Jones provides an insightful quote from NLD Central Executive Committee member Han Tha Myint:

> Sanctions are meant to offer moral support, to convince our people that the world has not abandoned us ... we have been working only on our moral principles ... it might not be very useful for us politically, but it is very useful for us spiritually. (Jones 2014: 104)

An editorial in the *Irrawaddy* magazine in August 2005 provides one response to this view of the utility of sanctions:

> Treating Burmese Generals as pariahs may draw newspaper headlines and applause from dissidents, but it just makes the regime become more introverted, xenophobic, oppressive and isolationist. You are dealing with a medieval dictatorship, not sophisticated politicians. It is no secret that the US has no strategy on Burma apart from sanctions ... there should be more down-to-earth considerations for the hardships of ordinary Burmese, and not just more lofty ideals of freedom and democracy. (quoted in James 2006: 146)

The aim of US sanctions policy in the period 1990–2008 was regime change. But as the events of 2007 and the Saffron revolution made very clear, if it was not clear enough already, regime change resulting from a successful popular uprising was a fantasy. The number of protestors who took to the streets in 2007 was very small, and the government's disposal of the protest was ruthless and efficient. The difficulty was that despite its ineffectiveness, and the hardship it brought to ordinary Burmese people, once the policy was in place it was very difficult for US legislators to abandon it without infuriating domestic constituencies in the United States and the vocal Burmese diaspora (James 2006).

New Directions in US Sanctions Policy

In 2009, the incoming Obama administration conducted a review of the sanctions policy. The ultimate result of this review was a new era of 'pragmatic engagement' – later to be relabelled 'principled' engagement (Haacke 2015). The policy was close to what Holliday (2005a) had earlier called for in terms of a *robust* form of constructive engagement, involving positive sanctions as well as investment. Principled engagement involved an 'action for action' policy, aimed at sending a clear signal of support to reformers, whereby positive indicators of reform would be rewarded with financial benefits. It also involved increasing the focus on targeting selected individuals who had colluded with the military regime (US State Department 2012).

The shift to pragmatic engagement under the Obama administration meant that the actions of Congress were sometimes out of step with White House policy. In 2011, for example, US Congress extended the general imports restriction in the 2003 BDFA for another year. It also reaffirmed existing sanctions, which meant that as well as barring the use of funds for military purposes, the State Department's Economic Support Fund could be used only for humanitarian assistance, while the United States continued to block loans, agreements or other developmental assistance from international organisations to Myanmar. In 2012, Congress renewed the General Import Ban, allowing the Obama administration to decide when to selectively ease or waive existing sanctions. Insofar as sanctions fulfil a 'signalling' function, indicating the disapprobation of the sanctioning state, conflicting messages from the administration and Capitol Hill clearly have the potential to undercut their utility.

Following the election of Aung San Suu Kyi to parliament in 2012, US investment activity in Myanmar was permitted, with the exception of investment agreements with the Ministry of Defence, state or non-state armed groups, and individuals and entities blocked under the sanctions programme. To encourage responsible investment by US companies, particularly in the oil and gas sector, reporting requirements were introduced in cases where new investment by US companies exceeds US$500,000. In May 2013, as part of President Thein Sein's visit to Washington DC, the two governments signed a Trade and Investment Framework Agreement. The import ban of jadeite and rubies as well as articles of jewellery containing them, prohibited by the 2008 JADE Act, continued.

In May 2013, the Obama administration also lifted the 1996 ban on granting US entry visas to the former military rulers of Myanmar, their business partners and immediate families. At the same time, however, President Obama extended the National Emergencies Act, which prohibits US individuals and businesses from dealing with Burmese people or companies involved in repression of the democracy movement since the 1990s. Some of Myanmar's major conglomerates, including the Asia World Group, the Htoo Group of Companies, the Max Group of Companies and the military-run Myanmar Economic Corporation and Union of Myanmar Economic Holdings Ltd, remained on the US Department of the Treasury's list, as did the individuals who owned and directed these groups, such as U Tun Myint Naing (Steven Law), the managing director of Asia World; Zaw Zaw, founder of the Max Myanmar group of companies; and U Tay Za, founder and chairman of the Htoo Group of Companies. The families of those on the SDN list were also subject to sanctions.

As Sean Turnell notes, wealth and economic activity in Myanmar are concentrated in very few hands, and these hands are inevitably linked to the military regime (Hodge 2015). Asia World, for example, was one of two major contractors that built the capital Naypyidaw, and which developed, constructed and currently operate the Naypyidaw international airport. As the major partner of China Power Investment Corporation, Asia World was engaged in building the controversial Myitsone Dam, along the Irrawaddy River in Kachin State. Since 2000, Asia World has operated a port and three wharfs in Yangon's Ahlone Township. The company has been granted licences and permissions to import and sell fuel, and distribute and supply electricity, in townships in Eastern Bago Region and other states and regions (Min and Kudo 2014), and has interests in industrial development, construction, transportation, import and export, garment manufacturing, paper mills, palm oil, road infrastructure and supermarket chains. In September 2012, a subsidiary of Asia World, Asia Mega Link Ltd, was granted a joint venture with the Myanmar Post and Telecommunications Department to sell cellular phone SIM cards. Asia World is involved in the development of the Thilawa special economic zone near Yangon (see Nishimura; Wood, this volume). A 2007 Wikileaks cable to the US State Department, titled 'Dropping the Hammer on Crony Steven Law', details Law's relationship with General Than Shwe and shows how this relationship resulted in lucrative construction and trading contracts for Asia World (Wikileaks 2007a).

Until October 2016, the two military-owned and -operated corporations, the Myanmar Economic Corporation and the Union of Myanmar Economic Holdings Ltd (UMEHL), and the managing directors of these corporations, remained on the SDN list. UMEHL was the first business venture formed by Myanmar's military after its takeover in 1988. It is jointly owned by two military departments, with 40 per cent of shares owned by the director of defence procurement and 60 per cent owned by active and veteran defence personnel, including high-ranking military officers of the former junta, the State Peace and Development Council. UMEHL, which is exempt from commercial and profit taxes, has joint ventures or partners with affiliates in mining, banking, manufacturing, livestock and fisheries, trading, logistics and transportation, food and beverages, steel and pharmaceuticals; a monopoly on sectors such as gems, jade and cigarettes; and exclusive access to preferential contracts with foreign firms (Holliday

2005b). The Myanmar Economic Corporation, which has thirty-four sub-sidiaries, is operated by the Ministry of Defence Quartermasters General Office, and its private shares are owned exclusively by active-duty military personnel. The managing director of the company is retired Brig. Gen. Thant Swe. The military's two sanctioned conglomerates still own or control much of Myanmar's land, factories and import licences and almost all of the country's jade mines (Mahtani and Paddock 2015). In 2014, UMEHL took control of the country's largest brewery, Myanmar Brewery.

Under President Thein Sein, foreign direct investment was permitted and policies of economic liberalisation were expanded. Myanmar Government Notification No. 11/2013, relating to foreign direct investment, provides that joint ventures cannot give foreign partners more than 80 per cent equity. It is therefore necessary for overseas investors to partner with local companies, in the same way that Chinese businesses and partners in countries that did not have sanctions against Burma have partnered with Asia World, UMEHL and other conglomerates. The larger, more established local companies, and the complicated web of subsidiaries related to these companies, are central to the business life of Myanmar. US companies such as General Electric Co., Coca-Cola Co. and the Gap Inc, which began operating in Myanmar soon after Thein Sein's election and the political thaw began, experienced the complexity of avoiding actors on the SDN list, and actively lobbied the US administration to review the SDN sanctions policy (Hookaway and Rubenfeld 2015). Even where US companies and individuals avoided entering into formal partnerships with prohibited Burmese conglomerates and subsidiaries, they found it difficult if not impossible to avoid entanglement with them.

The political impetus towards engagement with Myanmar, coupled with the continuing disapprobation of certain Burmese nationals and their presence on the SDN list, led to some farcical situations. When Hillary Clinton visited Myanmar as US secretary of state in December 2011, she stayed at the Thinagaha hotel, owned by blacklisted crony U Chit Khaing (Szep and Marshall 2012; Wikileaks 2007b). When John Kerry visited Naypyidaw as US secretary of state in August 2014, he stayed at a hotel built and owned by sanctioned Myanmar businessman Zaw Zaw and his Max Myanmar Group. In 2015, newly elected NLD parliamentarians attended a training programme sponsored by regime crony Tay Za, who made his fortune in logging and arms sales, and who remains on the SDN list (Mahtani 2016). Kentucky Fried Chicken, which is owned by Kentucky-based Yum Brands, established an outlet in Yangon's new airport terminal under its local franchisee, Yoma Strategic Holdings. The new terminal was built and financed by Asia World subsidiary Yangon Aerodrome.

A serious problem arose in September 2015, when US companies discovered that a significant amount of trade from the United States to Myanmar was moving through Asia World Port Terminal in Yangon. The port, a critical artery for foreign trade for Myanmar, is owned and operated by a subsidiary of Asia World, which until October 2016 was subject to US sanctions as a SDN. When alerted to the fact that US companies and financiers were using the port, the US Treasury's OFAC confirmed the requirement to block all payments referencing Asia World Port Terminal. The result of this was a sharp decline in US shipments to Myanmar and a decision by US banks such as Citigroup, Bank of America and PNC Financials to halt backing any further trade with Myanmar. The uncertainty also discouraged third-country exporters and third-country financial institutions from engaging in trade with Myanmar (Schectman and Torbati 2015). In December 2015, OFAC issued a special six-month licence to authorise transactions that would otherwise have been prohibited (Hookaway and Rubenfeld 2015). Announcing the licence, the White House said that its purpose was to permit US trade with Myanmar to continue by removing uncertainty: constraints on American companies were a 'completely unintended and unfortunate consequence of our sanctions and something that we want to rectify immediately' (Hookaway and Rubenfeld 2015). The announcement specifically stated that the licence was not a response to the 2015 election results in Myanmar, and that it was still too soon to determine whether to drop sanctions entirely.

The danger was that given the other hurdles facing US companies wishing to invest in Myanmar – such as poor infrastructure, an unskilled workforce and an uncertain regulatory environment – investors found the potential for running afoul of US sanctions policy sufficient reason to delay engaging with Myanmar at all (Schectman, Henry and McLaughlin 2015). Penalties for US sanctions violations amount to US$250,000 per violation or twice the value of the transaction, while criminal penalties are US$1 million per violation and/or twenty years' imprisonment (Culvahouse 2009). The net result of the uncertainty and constraints caused by targeted sanctions was that despite foreign direct investment approvals in Myanmar amounting to more than US$8 billion in the fiscal year to 31 March 2014, few significant investments came from the United States (Lewis 2015).

The first to be removed from the SDN Myanmar list, on 23 April 2015, was U Win Aung and his two companies, Dagon International Ltd and

Dagon Timber Ltd. A 2007 US diplomatic cable published by Wikileaks described Win Aung as 'a regime crony' who had given financial support to the military regime (Wikileaks 2007c). But in the new Myanmar, as president of the Myanmar Federation of Chambers of Commerce and Industry (UMFCCI), Aung was in constant contact with potential US foreign investors, who found themselves unable to sign memorandums of understanding with the Federation because its president was on a US blacklist. OFAC's announcement that U Win Aung and his companies had been delisted simply stated that U Win Aung had submitted verifiable information demonstrating that changed circumstances warranted delisting, including taking positive steps and changing behaviour (Dinmore and Phyo Win 2015).

OFAC did not provide public guidance on the nature and strength of the evidence required by those seeking delisting, other than to say they must have taken positive steps and changed their behaviour. In a visit to Myanmar in June 2014, the US assistant secretary of state for democracy, human rights and labor, Tom Malinowski, advised those on the sanctions list 'to demonstrate to [the United States] that they are engaging in responsible business practices' (Mahtani 2014a). It seems that wholehearted engagement with bodies such as the Myanmar Centre for Responsible Business, a body established in Myanmar by the Institute for Human Rights and Business and the Danish Centre for Human Rights, provided one possible path to redemption. The director of the Centre said that U Win Aung's company was amongst the top nine companies in the Centre's 2014 report on transparency: 'As with the other leading companies on that list, they have engaged actively with the process and participated in ongoing discussions' with the Centre (Dinmore and Phyo Win 2015). The director said that U Win Aung had been very supportive of the objectives and work of the Centre, both as president of the Chamber of Commerce and Industry and in the development of the Thilawa special economic zone. Reportedly, Win Aung's removal followed years of lobbying (Lewis 2015).

The official statement announcing that U Win Aung had been removed from the SDN list also noted that individuals or entities would continue to be added 'as appropriate, for example, where there is evidence that they have undermined the reform or peace process, committed human rights abuses in Burma, or participated in military trade with North Korea' (Lewis 2015; Dinmore and Phyo Win 2015). In 2014, the US Treasury announced that Aung Thaung, a parliamentarian in the lower house and former minister of industry, had been added to the SDN list. The stated reason for the addition was that Thaung had been 'intentionally under-mining the positive economic and political development of Myanmar'. Human Rights Watch, amongst others, claimed that Aung Thaung backed the radical Buddhist 969 Group, a movement that has been accused of inspiring sectarian attacks by majority Buddhists against Muslims (Mahtani 2014b). The movement's leader denied any relationship with Aung Thaung (Preston 2015). The listing threatened to cause a run on the United Amara Bank, in which Thaung's son has an interest. The bank was forced to make a public statement declaring that Thaung was not involved in the bank.

At the time it was introduced, principled engagement, particularly targeted sanctions in the form of the SDN list maintained by OFAC, seemed to offer US policy-makers a *via media* between the problematic options of isolation or engagement. Targeted sanctions were intended to affect only regime leaders, their business associates, those responsible for human rights abuses, those who undermined political reforms or the peace process, and those who engaged in military trade with North Korea. They were viewed as less harmful to ordinary Burmese people than wholesale embargoes, as they maximised personal cost to the regime leaders while minimising the suffering of the general population (Cortright and Lopez 2002; Howlett 2004).

The difficulty was that the criteria for deciding who should be placed on the list and removed from the list are extremely unclear. For example, under the former regime, Zaw Zaw, of the Max Group of Companies, took control of several companies that were being privatised in the 2010 rush of privatisations that occurred before the junta handed over power to the civilian government in 2010. Max Myanmar, a company belonging to the Max Group of Companies, acquired twelve gas stations, part of the land for Yangon's new Novotel Hotel and a banking licence for the Ayeyarwaddy Bank, and was awarded almost all the construction projects for the stadia and gymnasium for the 2013 Southeast Asia Games (Min and Kudo 2014). More troublingly, Zaw Zaw's companies bought land off the military that had been confiscated from farmers (Karen Human Rights Group 2009). Yet under the new regime, Zaw Zaw made large donations to the NLD (Thibaut 2015), and Aung San Suu Kyi does not seem to regard him as a persona non grata. Zaw Zaw is head of the Myanmar Football Association, and in 2012 Suu Kyi accepted Zaw Zaw's invitation to attend a soccer game with him (Szep and Marshall 2012). The Myanmar Centre for Responsible Business has lauded Zaw Zaw because his companies engage actively and participate in ongoing discussions with the Centre, and demonstrate transparency and understanding of what responsible business means (Dinmore and Phyo Win 2015). Yet Zaw Zaw remained on the SDN list until October 2016.

The failures of due process inherent in the process of SDN listing and delisting were well-documented in Fitzgerald's 1999 article 'If Property Rights Were Treated Like Human Rights, They Could Never Get Away with This: Blacklisting and Due Process in US Economic Sanctions Programs'. Although OFAC improved transparency and increased efficiencies since 1999, the process of listing and delisting remained opaque. Appealing OFAC's decision in relation to listing was expensive and often unsuccessful (Fitzgerald1999). Culvahouse (2009) points out that the US government's interpretation of sanctions did not generally establish binding precedents and was subject to political considerations, and that courts tended to defer to the executive branch's interpretation of its economic sanctions regulations and foreign policy purposes.

The larger consideration is what purpose these sanctions had. To survive under Myanmar's military regime, businesses had to engage with the military. Successful businesses were the ones that learned to engage deeply. These businesses were rewarded with licences, concessions and contracts. Zaw Zaw, of the Max Group of Companies, openly acknowledges that he was friendly with the old military regime, pointing out that there was simply no other way to succeed. 'Only the government has projects. If I don't do projects with them, who will I do projects with?' (Kinetz 2013). The claim of many cronies is that 'they never did anything that was illegal' (Zaw Zaw, quoted in Szep and Marshall 2012). But the law in Myanmar was the servant of the military regime (Cheesman 2015). A claim that one did nothing illegal is merely saying that one stood on the right side of the military government. The difficult question is at what point during a transition from military rule does sanctioning by an external power such as the United States become counter-productive.

Setting aside the obvious and justifiable imposition of sanctions against Burmese nationals who traded in weapons with North Korea, there seems to be a fundamental confusion about the policy purposes of targeted sanctions. Derek Tonkin, longtime Myanmar analyst, believes that the United States continued to 'fine-tune sanctions in the misguided belief that they represent some kind of calibrated pressure on the outgoing or incoming Myanmar administration' (Tonkin 2015). Others suggest that the purpose of the SDN list was punitive: in the words of an unnamed US State Department official, 'The sanctions list does not allow for redemption.

It is designed to hold people accountable for past wrongs, regardless of whatever good work they may be doing now' (Kinetz 2013). On still other accounts, the purpose of sanctions was to act as an incentive for good corporate behaviour. Derek Mitchell, the US ambassador to Myanmar, said that it was the responsibility of sanctioned tycoons to show that they were committed to helping the country after making money during the military regime (Wong and Barta 2012).

Conclusion

If US sanctions against Myanmar were remnants of the belief that US economic pressure could influence the course of political change in Myanmar, then they were misguided. The entire history of US sanctions against Myanmar demonstrates this. The shift to 'smart' or 'targeted' sanctions did not change the logic that the level of political responsiveness in Myanmar was unrelated to any economic leverage obtained by the United States through the implementation of sanctions (see Chesterman and Pouligny 2003). If targeted sanctions were intended as punishment for individuals who aided the former military regime, then they were deficient in almost every respect. The United States had no remit to apply punishment to Myanmar's citizens, and under the sanctions regime there were few of the requirements of procedural fairness and due process that we would expect to find in a criminal justice system. In short, as a form of punishment, the targeted sanctions regime was unjust. Finally, if targeted sanctions were intended to provide a moral signal of disapproval about the way in which certain individuals prospered under the military regime, then they lacked legitimacy, because there was insufficient clarity and certainty about the reasons why names were added to and removed from the list, which led to a perception of arbitrariness and undercut the moral function of the sanctions regime.

It is most likely that the purpose of targeted sanctions during the period of transition was to spur Myanmar's business people and former political leaders to act with integrity. But if this was the aim of US sanctions, then there should have been more diligent consideration of their actual effect. There appears to have been little attention given by US policymakers to questions about how Myanmar's business elite, new political leaders and the general population experienced the sanctions regime, or how the sanctions regime affected the decision-making of those who remained on the SDN list. For example, if the main effect of sanctions was to restrict economic options for local actors, then what circumvention strategies did these actors develop to minimise the intended effect? Were these strategies positive? What was the local perception of the legitimacy of sanctions, given that they were previously applied to so little effect, and then implemented and removed arbitrarily against individuals and their companies? What of the emerging body of scholarship that seeks to show how material incentives and disincentives applied by third parties have the potential to 'crowd out' intrinsic motivation for engaging in pre-scribed behaviour, and are thus detrimental to the development of long-term principled compliance with international standards by target actors (Goodman and Jinks 2013; Renshaw 2016)?

As several chapters in this book show, the business of transition is complex and often traumatic. On balance, the US sanctions regime exacer-bated this complexity and trauma. The chaos, absurdity, ineffectiveness and injustice of most of the regime lead us back to the question with which this chapter began. At what point in time should the new regime be responsible for implementing its own sanctions?

References

Abramowitz, Morton and Jonathon Kolieb. 2008. 'A New Strategy on Myanmar'. 107(712) *Current History* 393.

Associated Press. (1997). 'Unocal Chief Meets Daw Aung San Suu' (17 May 1997).

Badgley, John (ed.). 2004. *Reconciling Burma / Myanmar: Essays on US Relations with Burma*. Seattle: National Bureau of Asian Research.

Biron, Carey. 2012. 'Suu Kyi Backs end of US sanctions'. 20 September. *Asia Times*. Available at http://www.atimes.com/atimes/Southeast_Asia/NI20Ae03.html.

Brandon, J. 1998. 'Burma: 17 Months after the United States Sanctions'. October. Paper delivered at the Burma Studies Conference, Northern Illinois University.

Burnell, Peter. 2004. 'Democracy Promotion: The Elusive Quest for Grand Strategies'. 4 *International Politics and Society* 100.

Cheesman, Nick. 2015. *Opposing the Rule of Law: How Myanmar's Courts Make Law and Order*. Cambridge: Cambridge University Press.

Cheesman, Nick, Nicholas Farrelly and Trevor Wilson (eds). 2014. *Debating Democratization in Myanmar*. Singapore: Institute of Southeast Asian Studies.

Chesterman, S. and B. Pouligny. 2003. 'Are Sanctions Meant to Work? The Politics of Creating and Implementing Sanctions through the United Nations'. 9 *Global Governance* 503.

Cingranelli, David L. and Richards, David L. (1999). 'Respect for Human Rights after the End of the Cold War'. 36(5) *Journal of Peace Research* 511.

Clymer, Kenton. 2015. *A Delicate Relationship: the United States and Burma/ Myanmar since 1945*. Ithaca, NY: Cornell University Press.

Corker, Christopher. 1986. *The United States and South Africa, 1968–1985: Constructive Engagement and its Critics.* Durham, NC: Duke University Press.

Cortright, David and George A. Lopez (eds). 2002. *Smart Sanctions: Targeting Economic Statecraft.* Lanham, MD: Rowman and Littlefield.

Crispin, S. 1998. 'Burma's Economy Edges towards Collapse'. 161 *Far Eastern Economic Review* 56.

Culvahouse, A. B. Jr. 2009. 'Practical Guide to International Sanctions Law and Lore: Mamas, Don't Let Your Children Grow up to Be Sanctions Lawyers'. 32 *Houston Journal of International Law* 587.

Dale, John G. 2011. *Free Burma: Transnational Legal Action and Corporate Accountability.* Minneapolis, MN: University of Minnesota Press.

Dapice, D. 1998. 'Development Prospects' in Robert Rotberg (ed.), *Burma, Prospects for a Democratic Future.* Washington DC and Cambridge, MA.: Brookings Institution Press and World Peace Foundation.

Dinmore, Guy and Su Phyo Win. 2015. 'US Offers Path to Redemption for "Cronies"'. 29 April. *Myanmar Times.* Available at http://www.mmtimes .com/index.php/business/14179-us-offers-path-to-redemption-for-cronies .html.

Ewing-Chow, Michael. 2006. 'First Do No Harm: Myanmar Trade Sanctions and Human Rights'. 5 *Northwestern University Journal of International Human Rights* 153.

Falco, Martha. 2003. *Burma: Time for Change.* Report of an Independent Task Force Sponsored by the Council on Foreign Relations.

Fitzgerald, Peter L. 1999. 'If Property Rights Were Treated Like Human Rights, They Could Never Get Away with This: Blacklisting and Due Process in US Economic Sanctions Programs'. 51(1) *Hastings Law Journal* 93.

Goodman, Ryan and Derek Jinks. 2013. 'Social Mechanisms to Promote Human Rights' in Thomas Risse, Stephen C. Ropp and Kathryn Sikkink (eds), *The Persistent Power of Human Rights: from Commitment to Compliance.* Cambridge: Cambridge University Press.

Haacke, Jürgen. 2015. 'The United States and Myanmar: From Antagonists to Security Partners?' 34(2) *Journal of Current Southeast Asian Affairs* 55.

Hadar, Leon T. 1998. 'US Sanctions Against Burma: a Failure on All Fronts'. 26 March. Trade Policy Analysis No. 1. Available at http://www.cato.org/pubs/ trade/tpa-001.html.

Hodge, Amanda. 2015. 'Myanmar Election: The Australian Set to Shape the Economic Future'. 6 November. *The Australian.* Available at http://www.theaustralian .com.au/news/world/myanmar-election-the-australian-set-to-shape-the- economic-future/news-story/8d8013f3911532adbbee0c4fd0777994.

Holliday, Ian. 2005a. 'Rethinking the United States Myanmar Policy'. 45(4) *Asian Survey* 603.

2005b. 'Doing Business with Rights Violating Regimes: Corporate Social Responsi- bility and Myanmar's Military Junta'. 61(4) *Journal of Business Ethics* 329.

2011. *Burma Redux: Global Justice and the Quest for Political Reform in Myanmar.* New York: Columbia University Press.

Hookaway, James and Samuel Rubenfeld. 2015. 'US Temporarily Lifts trade Restrictions on Myanmar'. 7 December. *Wall Street Journal.* Available at http://www.wsj.com/articles/u-s-temporarily-lifts-trade-restrictions-on-myanmar-1449539262.

Howlett, Amy. 2004. 'Getting "Smart": Crafting Economic Sanctions That Respect All Human Rights'. 73 *Fordham Law Review* 1,199.

Howse, Robert L. and Genser, Jared M. (2008) 'Are EU Trade Sanctions on Burma Compatible with WTO Law?', 29 *Michigan Journal of International Law* 165.

James, Helen. 2006. *Security and Sustainable Development in Myanmar.* Oxon: Routledge.

Jones, Lee. 2014. 'Explaining Myanmar's Regime Transition: The Periphery Is Central', 21(5) *Democratization* 780.

Karen Human Rights Group. 2009. 'Land confiscation and the business of human rights abuse in Thaton District'. 2 April. Report from the Field/KHRG #2009-F6. http://khrg.org/2009/04/khrg09f6/land-confiscation-and-business-human-rights-abuse-thaton-district.

Kinetz, Erika. 2013. 'How a Myanmar Tycoon is Profiting from Change'. 3 June. *Associated Press.* Available at https://www.yahoo.com/news/myanmar-tycoon-profiting-change-041812031.html.

Kudo, Toshihiro. 2008. 'The Impact of US Sanctions on the Myanmar Garment Industry', 48(6) *Asian Survey* 997.

Lewis, Simon. 2015. 'US Move Could Signal Softening on Myanmar Blacklist'. 4 May. *Nikkei Asian Review.* Available at http://asia.nikkei.com/Politics-Economy/Economy/US-move-could-signal-softening-on-Myanmar-blacklist.

Lintner, B. 2008. 'Regrettable Apology for Myanmar: Review, Promoting Human Rights in Burma by Morten B Pedersen'. 9 February. *Asia Times.* Available at http://www.atimes.com/atimes/Southeast_Asia/JB09Ae01.html.

Mahtani, Shibani. 2014a. 'U.S. Urges Myanmar Nationals to Work Harder to Get Off Sanctions List'. 29 June. *Wall Street Journal.* Available at http://www.wsj.com/articles/u-s-urges-myanmar-nationals-to-work-harder-to-get-off-sanctions-list-1404059697.

2014b. 'Myanmar's Government Not Targeted by Blacklist, U.S. Says'. 4 November. *Wall Street Journal.* Available at http://www.wsj.com/articles/myanmars-government-not-targeted-by-blacklist-u-s-says-1415088559.

2016. 'US Business in Myanmar Stuck in Sanctions Limbo'. 29 March. *Wall Street Journal Asia.* Available at http://www.pressreader.com/china/the-wall-street-journal-asia/20160329/282454233124272.

Mahtani, Shibani and Richard Paddock. 2015. '"Cronies" of Former Regime Thrive Despite US Blacklist'. 12 August. *Wall Street Journal.* Available at http://www.wsj.com/articles/cronies-of-former-myanmar-regime-thrive-despite-u-s-blacklist-1439433052.

McCartan, Brian. 2010. 'A Crony Rises in Myanmar'. 22 December. *Asia Times Online*. Available at http://www.atimes.com/atimes/Southeast_Asia/LL22 Ae02.html.

McCarthy, Stephen. 2000. 'Ten Years of Chaos in Burma: Foreign Investment and Economic Liberalization under the SLORC-SPDC, 1988 to 1998'. 73(2) *Pacific Affairs* 233.

McGillivray, F. and A. C. Stam. 2004. 'Political Institutions, Coercive Diplomacy, and the Duration of Economic Sanctions'. 48(2) *Journal of Conflict Resolution* 154.

Min, Aung and Kudo Toshihiro. 2014. 'Business Conglomerates in the Context of Myanmar's Economic Reform' in Hank Lim and Yamada Yasahiro, *Myanmar's Integration in the Global Economy: Outlook and Opportunities*. Bangkok: Bangkok Research Centre.

Mintier, Tom. 1997. 'U.S. Businesses Criticize Burma Sanctions'. 24 April. *CNN World News*. Available at http://edition.cnn.com/WORLD/9704/24/burma/.

National Broadcasting Corporation (NBC). 2012. 'Myanmar's Suu Kyi delivers freedom message'. 21 September. Available at http://www.nbcnews.com/video/nightly-news/49126187#49126187.

National League for Democracy (NLD). 2011. 'Sanctions on Burma'. 8 February. Available at www.burmacampaign.org.uk/index.php/news-and-reports/news-stories/nationalleague-for-democracy-statement-on-sanctions/8.

Nyein, Susanne Prager. 2009. 'Expanding Military, Shrinking Citizenry and the New Constitution in Burma'. 39(4) *Journal of Contemporary Asia* 638.

Ott, C. 1998. 'From Isolation to Relevance: Policy Considerations' in Robert Rotberg (ed.), *Burma, Prospects for a Democratic Future*. Washington DC and Cambridge, MA: Brookings Institution Press and World Peace Foundation, pp. 69–83.

Pedersen, Morten. 2000. 'International Policy on Burma: Coercion, Persuasion, or Cooperation? Assessing the Claims' in Morten Pedersen, Emily Rudland and Ronald James May (eds), *Burma Myanmar: Strong Regime, Weak State?* Canberra: Crawford House Publishing, p. 240.

    2007. *Promoting Human Rights in Burma: A Critique of Western Sanctions Policy*. Lanham, MD: Rowman and Littlefield.

    2013. 'How to Promote Human Rights in the World's Most Repressive States'. 67(2) *Australian Journal of International Affairs* 190.

    2014. 'Myanmar's Democratic Opening: The Process and Prospect of Reform' in Nick Cheesman, Nicholas Farrelly and Trevor Wilson, *Debating Democratisation in Myanmar*. Singapore: Institute of Southeast Asian Studies, pp. 19–42.

Pedersen, Morten, Emily Rudland and Ronald James May (eds). 2000. *Burma Myanmar: Strong Regime, Weak State?* Canberra: Crawford House Publishing.

Portela, Clara. (2014) 'The EU's use of "Targeted Sanctions": evaluating effectiveness'. Centre for European Policy Studies Working Paper 391/2014.

Preston, Alex. 2015. 'Saffron Terror: An Audience with Burma's "Buddhist Bin Laden" Ashin Wirathu'. 12 February. *GQ*. Available at http://www.gq-magazine .co.uk/article/ashin-wirathu-audience-with-the-buddhist-bin-laden-burma.

Rarick, Charles A. 2006. 'Destroying a Country in Order to Save It: The Folly of Economic Sanctions against Myanmar'. 26 *Economic Affairs*. Available at http://papers.ssrn.com/sol3/papers.cfm?abstract_id=904854.

Renshaw, Catherine. 2016. 'Human Trafficking in Southeast Asia: Uncovering the Dynamics of State Commitment and Compliance'. 37(4) *Michigan Journal of International Law* 611.

Reuters. 1996. 'Burmese Dissident Urges Western Sanctions to Oust Military'. 19 July. Available at http://www.nytimes.com/1996/07/19/world/burmese-dissident-urges-western-sanctions-to-oust-military.html.

Ruland, Jurgen. 2001. 'Burma Ten Years after the Uprising: The Regional Dimension' in Robert H. Taylor (ed.), *Burma: Political Economy under Military Rule*. New York: Palgrave Publishers.

Sachs, Jeffrey. 2004a. Interview. 25 August. Radio Free Asia Burmese Service.

2004b. 'Myanmar: Sanctions Won't Work'. 27 July. *The Financial Times*. Available at http://yaleglobal.yale.edu/content/myanmar-sanctions-wont-work.

Schectman, Joel, David Henry and Timothy Mclaughlin. 2015. 'Sanctions fears choke nascent US Trade with Myanmar'. 7 November. Reuters. Available at http://www.reuters.com/article/usa-myanmar-sanctions-idUSL1N12T1J T20151107.

Schectman, Joel and Yeganeh Torbati. 2015. 'US temporarily lifts trade restrictions on Myanmar shipping hubs'. 7 December. Reuters. Available at http://www.reuters.com/article/us-usa-myanmar-sanctions-trade-idUSKBN0TQ 2IM20151207.

Schmahmann, D. R., J. Finch and T. Chapman. 1997. 'Off the Precipice: Massachusetts Expands its Foreign Policy Expedition From Burma to Indonesia'. 30 *Vanderbilt Journal of Transnational Law* 1,021.

Schuman, Michael. 2006. 'Going Nowhere'. 30 January. *Time*. Available at http://www .burmanet.org/news/2006/01/23/time-asia-going-nowhere-michael-schuman/.

Seattle Post Intelligencer. 1997. 'City's Burma Policy an Endless, Bad Idea'. 18 August. Available at http://archives.usaengage.org/archives/news/970818spi.html.

Selth, Andrew. 2010. 'Civil-Military Relations in Burma: Portents, Predictions and Possibilities'. Griffith Asia Institute. Available at https://www.griffith.edu.au/__ data/assets/pdf_file/0016/215341/Selth-Regional-Outlook-25.pdf.

Steinberg, David I. 1999. 'Burma/Myanmar and the Dilemmas of U.S. Foreign Policy'. 21 *Contemporary Southeast Asia* 283.

2003. in Martha Falco (ed.), *Burma: Time for Change*. Report of an Independent Task Force Sponsored by the Council on Foreign Relations.

2015. 'Aung San Suu Kyi and US Policy toward Burma/Myanmar'. 29(3) *Journal of Current Southeast Asian Affairs* 35.

Szep, Jason and Marshall, Andrew A.C. 2012. 'Special Report: An Image Makeover for Myanmar Inc'. 12 April. Reuters. Available at http://www.reuters.com/article/us-myanmar-cronies-image-idUSBRE83B0YU20120412.

Taylor, Robert. 2004. 'Myanmar's Political Future: Is Waiting for the Perfect the Enemy of Doing the Possible?' in John Badgley (ed.), *Reconciling Burma / Myanmar: Essays on US Relations with Burma*. Seattle: National Bureau of Asia Research, pp. 29–40.

Taylor, Robert and Morten Pedersen. 2005. 'Supporting Burma/ Myanmar's National Reconciliation Process: Challenges and Opportunities'. January. An independent report for the European Commission. Available at http://www.ibiblio.org/obl/docs3/Independant_Report-Burma_Day.htm.

Thibaut, Marion. 2015. 'Myanmar Cronies Still Pull the Strings as the Economy Creaks Open'. 1 November. *AFP*. Available at https://www.yahoo.com/news/myanmar-cronies-still-pull-strings-economy-creaks-open-025901148.html.

Tonkin, Derek. 2015. 'The US Sanctions Fiasco over Myanmar Persists'. 11 December. NetworkMyanmar.org

Tutu, Desmond. 1995. *The Daily Yomiuri* (Editorial). 30 March. Available at http://www.burmalibrary.org/reg.burma/archives/199503/msg00138.html.

US State Department. 2002. *Burma: Country Reports on Human Rights Practises 2002*. Washington DC: Bureau of Democracy, Human Rights and Labor. Available at http://www.ibiblio.org/obl/docs3/Independant_Report-Burma_Day.htm.

2012. 'Background Briefing on Burma'. Press Release. Available at http://www.state.gov/r/pa/prs/ps/2012/04/187446.htm.

Wikileaks. 2007a. 'Dropping the Hammer on Crony Steven Law'. 28 December. Available at https://wikileaks.org/plusd/cables/07RANGOON1211_a.html.

2007b. 'Eden Group Prospering Due to Regime Connections'. 16 November. Available at https://wikileaks.org/plusd/cables/07RANGOON1113_a.html.

2007c. 'Win Aung – a Rising Crony with Connections'. 26 December. Available at https://wikileaks.org/plusd/cables/07RANGOON1203_a.html.

Wilson, Trevor. 2013a. 'The Politics of Investing in Myanmar'. Australia Myanmar Chamber of Commerce Report. Available at http://www.a-mcc.com/wp-content/uploads/2013/06/130623-Investing-in-Myanmar-Trevor-Wilson.pdf.

2013b. 'Myanmar: International Perspectives on Reform – Responses from the US, UK, EU, China, Japan, and Australia'. 1 *Foreign Policy Research Centre Journal* 56–78.

2014a. 'Debating Democratization in Myanmar' in Nick Cheesman, Nicholas Farrelly and Trevor Wilson (eds), *Debating Democratization in Myanmar*. Singapore: Institute of Southeast Asian Studies, pp. 11–17.

2014b. 'Why Corporate Behaviour is under Scrutiny in Myanmar'. 15 *East Asia Forum* 3.

Wong, Chun Han and Patrick Barta. 2012. 'In Myanmar, a Mogul Tries to Skirt Sanctions'. 23 August. *Wall Street Journal*. Available at http://www.wsj.com/articles/SB10000872396390444082904577606952614200254.

Zaw, Htet Naing. 2013. 'A "Crony" with a Conscience'. 24 April. *The Irrawaddy*. Available at http://burmanationalnews.org/burma/index.php?option=com_content&view=article&id=3732.

Laws (US)

Burmese Freedom and Democracy Act of 2003 (Public Law 108–161; 50 U.S.C. 1701 note).

Customs and Trade Act of 1990.

Foreign Operations, Export Financing, and Related Programs Appropriations Act of 1997 (Public Law 104–208).

International Emergency Economic Powers Act of 1997 (IEEPA) (Public Law 95–223; 50 U.S.C. 1701 et seq.).

National Emergencies Act (NEA) (Public Law 94–412; 50 U.S.C. 1601 et seq.).

Tom Lantos Block Burmese Junta's Anti-Democratic Efforts (JADE) Act of 2008 (JADE Act) (Public Law 110–286; 50 U.S.C. 1701 note).

10

The Politics of Aid in Myanmar

TIM FREWER

Myanmar is an aid frontier, a new site for the aid work of a large number of international organisations. After historic elections in 2015, Myanmar could go from being an 'aid orphan' due to neglect as a recipient of technical programming and Western aid over the last sixty years (Duffield 2008) to the new poster-child of international development. This chapter seeks to consider the changing contours of aid, development, non-governmental organisations (NGOs) and transformation in Myanmar. This chapter will attempt to avoid the prescriptive literature that holds that the expansion of good governance, technical assistance, civil society organisations (CSOs) and NGOs is an inherently positive phenomenon that marks the maturing of a democratic society. Nor will it follow the path of the critical literature that sees development assistance in merely instrumental terms.

This chapter will assess the changes in the aid landscape and NGOs in Myanmar to demonstrate that the expansion of CSOs and the international aid sector in Myanmar has not been the driving force behind the democratic transition. Rather, NGOs and donor-supported programmes in Myanmar have generally expanded as Myanmar's transition has increasingly afforded these actors new institutional, geopolitical and economic opportunities.

This chapter begins by outlining the contemporary debate in the literature on aid, and against this context it explains the more recent expansion of aid networks in Myanmar specifically. It then identifies how Myanmar has shifted from being a relative aid orphan to a new hub for international aid. In the final section, this chapter focuses on some of the unintended effects of aid: the importance of interactions between elites and the aid industry in authoritarian regimes, the potential impact of aid on state provision of public services, and the effect of donors using aid to pursue aims that have greater salience for their own geopolitical and economic interests. Overall, this chapter argues that for Myanmar to avoid the pitfalls of aid-dependent countries such as Cambodia, the political effects of aid, rather than abstract notions of good governance and civil society, need to be at the forefront of discussions over development.

Situating Aid in Myanmar's Transition

Most academic literature on aid, NGOs and 'civil society expansion' in Myanmar has been optimistic, if not overly prescriptive. Many academics, well-known for their nuanced work on the politics and history of Myanmar, have tended to offer less than nuanced accounts of aid and NGOs. Renowned historian Thant Myint U (Thant Myint U 2012) has identified that increases in aid are not only inevitable but much needed for regime transformation. He singles out technical assistance from international donors as crucial for the success of Myanmar's transition (a general theme of the volume within which his article is published). While there is no doubt that there are major technical limitations especially at lower administrative levels, the question is really what form such technical assistance will take. Avowing the political aspects of technical programming tends to by default legitimise dominant neoliberal approaches to 'good governance' which are currently in vogue (Godfrey et al. 2002; Walker et al. 2008). David Steinberg, another renowned scholar on Myanmar, similarly has pushed for 'the build-up of indigenous civil society through the international NGO community' (US Senate Subcommittee on East Asian and Pacific Affairs 2010). Once again this avows the contested politics surrounding Western NGOs and the role they may play in promoting neoliberal approaches to development (Mercer 2002; Roberts, Jones III and Fröhling 2005; Srinivas 2009). Since the mid-2000s there has been a steady stream of academic literature pursuing similar themes and promoting the expansion of 'civil society', NGOs and aid through international assistance in Myanmar (Dorning 2006; Kramer 2011; Lorch 2007; Morgan 2014; South 2008; Tegenfeldt 2006; Ware 2012). NGOs have a lot to offer Myanmar, and each of these publications contributes detailed and useful empirical data and insights into the topic. Yet none of them aims to engage with the critical literature on NGOs, nor do they situate the expansion of aid and NGOs within recent experiences of nearby aid-dependent countries such as Cambodia.

Much of the critical literature on the other hand has explored the relationship between NGOs, aid expansion, business interests (Baur and Schmitz 2012), capital accumulation (Bumpus and Liverman 2008; Roberts 2014; Roy 2010), security (Duffield 2007; Grove 2010; Reid

2013) and the neoliberal[1] rationalities within which aid chains tend to be embedded (Bebbington 2004; Chandler 2013; Craig and Porter 2006; Wallace, Bornstein and Chapman 2007). In places such as Cambodia that have undergone similar transitions, aid and NGO expansion have gone hand in hand with authoritarianism and state-backed pilfering of natural resources (Biddulph 2011; Milne, Pak and Sullivan 2015). Aid programmes and NGOs there have expanded exponentially, yet been extremely limited in countering the effects of liberalisation and state kleptocracy (Ear 2013; Hughes 2009; Un 2005) – and in some cases even intensified these problems (Frewer 2013; Frewer and Chan 2014). More generally, an increasing body of literature has shown that for the most part development bureaucracies tend to focus on donor interests, technical programming, buzz words and institutional survival over long-term political engagement with the forces that create poverty in particular locales (Cooke and Kothari 2001; De Sardan 2005; Escobar 2011 [1995]; Ferguson 1990; Lewis and Mosse 2006; Li 2007; Mosse 2005).

To understand the current situation in Myanmar, it is important to consider why the push for NGOs and increased aid to Myanmar has taken place. Apart from the broader context of neoliberal aid networks[2] that seek out localities to establish new governance experiments (for instance the World Bank and Asian Development Bank; see Craig and Porter 2006; Goldman 2006; Rich 2013; Simpson 2013), there are also a number of Myanmar-specific factors that are salient. The broad, multi-faceted transition to 'discipline-flourishing democracy'[3] is particularly important. Yet rather than assuming that Myanmar will follow an imagined gradual

---

[1] The term 'neoliberal' in relation to development in this chapter refers to two things. First, the *project* of attempting to transform and organise structures, mechanisms and discourses put in place to govern over the poor, towards market-based principles, or, as Foucault put it, constantly asking 'how the overall exercise of political power can be modelled on the principles of a market economy' (Foucault 2004: 150). Second, 'neoliberalism' refers to the actual process and material transformations that come out of this project. This includes the increasing pressure on states to provide (or outsource to NGOs and private entities) social services in line with the principle of competition, the increasing pressure to replace aid disbursements with private finance, an emphasis on 'bottom-up' solutions to problems which posit the poor as primarily economic agents whose capabilities are to be worked upon, and the rise of social enterprises and social entrepreneurialism within development (see Chandler 2013; Craig and Porter 2006).

[2] See for instance Wallace et al. (2007) who provide a general overview of how networks of donors/NGOs/experts ('aid chains') facilitate the expansion of international development, and the spread of neoliberalism.

[3] In 2003 Prime Minister General Khin Nyunt publicly announced the 'Seven Steps Roadmap to Democracy'.

linear transition towards democracy where increasing amounts of aid and NGOs will result in the opening of 'civil society' and increased 'good governance', it is important to keep in mind the 'messy' and multidimensional nature of change. Myanmar's transition is a complex, non-linear process that retains much of the former military-based disciplinary modes of governing (Jones 2014), and is as such vulnerable to falling back on the use of violent oppression – or having violent oppression work alongside liberal democratic institutions.

More importantly, the significance of Myanmar's nominal democratic transition in terms of changed bilateral relationships cannot be merely explained in terms of the actual 'on the ground' results of such reforms. Rather, it is often at the broad level of democratic reform, transition and 'good enough governance' (Harrison 2004) where elections, new laws and policies resonate with bilateral donor governments, NGOs and multilateral institutions. In this way these changes become accepted as legitimate democratic reform, regardless of the complex and contradictory nature of actual regime change.

From Aid Orphan to Aid Hub?

Throughout much of the former General Ne Win's Burma Socialist Programme Party (BSPP) regime (1962–1988), aid flows from OECD countries were modest – mainly as a result of Ne Win's insular policies, although as with other Southeast Asian nations, aid flows fluctuated with the serendipity of the Cold War. Australia, Germany and Japan were the exceptions here where Myanmar was a major recipient of Australia's Colombo Plan (Australia was Burma's fourth biggest donor between 1950 and 1980) (McGregor 2005) and Japan provided almost half of all Myanmar's aid from 1962 to 1988 (Seekins 1992). Compared to the aid to other least-developed recipient counties, aid to Myanmar was however much lower. As can be observed in Figure 10.1 the events of 1988 had a major influence on UK, US, German and Japanese aid – where all four countries slashed their already humble aid disbursements by more than 50 per cent. However, Australia and Japan continued to provide money to the military regime (in 1989 Japan provided US$71 million, and Australia US$4 million – and Australia was the first country to officially recognise the new name 'Myanmar').

It was not until Daw Aung Suu Kyi formally requested the Australian government to divert money to the border regions in 1990 that money to the military stopped flowing (McGregor 2005). Two years after the

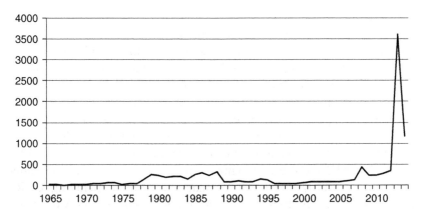

Figure 10.1. ODA disbursements to Myanmar (US$ millions).
Data Source: OECD Statistics (http://stats.oecd.org/Index.aspx?DatasetCode=
TABLE2A#).

events of 1988 the European Union imposed an arms embargo against
Myanmar – showing that the relationship between violent events and aid
flows may sometimes be delayed. In the wake of these events and the 1990
elections, a consensus emerged on the part of the US, EU and Australia
governments that the State Law and Order Restoration Council (SLORC)
was unbearably authoritarian due to its unwillingness to relinquish power
to the opposition National League for Democracy (NLD) party which had
technically won the elections, and so aid flows were dramatically reduced.
Instead, aid flows began to concentrate on border areas, and only Japan
and Association of Southeast Asian Nations (ASEAN) neighbours continued to support the SLORC regime (Steinberg 2007).

Throughout the 1990s and early 2000s, NGOs set up on the Thai borders
were increasingly becoming the targets of bilateral aid flows. During this
period, the Border Consortium, which consists of various organisations
that have been involved in refugee issues on the Thai/Myanmar border
since 1984 (and has had a variety of related names), received a significant
share of bilateral aid from the traditional donors. By 2005, US$30 million
per year was going to border-based NGOs (South 2007). During this time
the US Senate passed legislation that blocked US funds from supporting the government through multilateral institutions such as the World
Bank and Asian Development Bank, preventing them from conducting
any major activities in Myanmar. So too the United States successfully
pushed the United Nations Development Programme (UNDP) to enact a

policy of only conducting activities that had Aung San Suu Kyi's specific approval (Steinberg 2007). Donor country policy towards Myanmar was dictated not only by ideological consensus, but fluctuated with domestic donor politics, and the rise and fall of particular leaders, for example, Prime Ministers Paul Keating and John Howard in Australia who pushed for increasing bilateral aid (McGregor 2005), and President Bush who vehemently opposed bilateral aid (Steinberg 2007), not to mention the actions of Burmese expatriates on foreign constituencies (Oo 2006).

During the 1990s a handful of large, predominantly US-based international NGOs (INGOs) began to initiate programmes from Yangon under the military's fairly restrictive bureaucratic system, including CARE (1995), Save the Children (1995), PACT (1997) and Action Aid (1999). The military regime used bureaucratic means, including visa restrictions, organisational registration and approval/disapproval from line ministries, as well as restriction of access to particular areas, to curtail both the number of NGOs and the scope of their activities (Currie 2012). In the early 1990s such restrictions were eased under Prime Minister Khin Nyunt, but once again enforced with his sacking after 2004. Throughout this whole period it was also excessively difficult for local NGOs to become established. A range of United Nations agencies however continued and expanded their work in the 2000s – including the United Nations International Children's Emergency Fund (UNICEF), UNDP, United Nations High Commissioner for Refugees (UNHCR), United Nations Office on Drugs and Crime (UNODC) and World Health Organization (WHO). One major setback however was the 2005 termination of US$37.5 million of grants from the Global Fund to the UNDP and Myanmar government, which was cited as being due to excessive travel restrictions placed upon implementing agencies.[4] The programme was however quickly re-established in 2006 under the Three Diseases Fund (3D) through funds from the European Commission, Sweden, Netherlands, United Kingdom, Norway and Australia.

The 2008 Cyclone Nargis turned out to be a catalysing factor for the expansion of aid activities. Coming only a year after the Saffron revolution which involved extra-judicial killings and widespread state repression, the largely paranoid and inept response of the state (Seekins 2009; Selth 2008) had the unexpected effect of opening Myanmar up to greater numbers of INGOs and increasing amounts of aid (Ware 2012). As the

[4] There were also claims that the United States – the largest donor of the Global Fund – had put excessive pressure on the fund to pull out.

military government began to realise that it had severely mismanaged the crisis, it granted greater freedom to INGOs and foreign donors. The Triparite Core Group, formed three weeks after Cyclone Nargis hit, and composed of Myanmar officials, ASEAN representatives and UN agencies, saw involvement of not only local and international NGOs but also the World Bank and Asian Development Bank. This was in contrast to the first two weeks of the disaster where NGOs were blocked from accessing the Irrawaddy delta, and where aid was diverted to the military (Seekins 2009).

Due to these events, Organisation for Economic Co-Operation and Development (OECD) aid to Myanmar in 2008 more than doubled (with Australia's and the European Union's aid more than tripling). According to Morgan (2014) there were only forty NGOs operating in Myanmar prior to Cyclone Nargis, yet one year after there were more than one hundred. Once again, and although aid remained limited in the years after Cyclone Nargis, the entire event opened up space for humanitarian-based aid operations, and shows that fluctuations and shifts in aid flows are not necessarily determined by the degree to which recipient states demonstrate an ability to work in the interests of local populations. If anything, Cyclone Nargis demonstrated a long-held tendency of the state to prioritise security over wellbeing (Callahan 2004; Seekins 2009). Like other disasters in the global south (Schuller 2012), such events and the responses they evoke cannot be merely understood in moralistic terms, but also in terms of facilitating the expansion of NGOs and donors.

In the same year, only days after Cyclone Nargis hit,[5] a constitutional referendum was held which formed a larger part of the military's '7 steps roadmap to democracy' (step 4 – 'enact a new democratic constitution'). Along with the 2010 elections (step 5), both formed important events in the transition to a nominally civilian government, and saw General Thein Sein abandon his position within the military to take up the position of president. Although both events were widely rejected as fraudulent by donor countries, they nonetheless resulted in the gradual interest and re-engagement with the Myanmar state on the part of the United States, European Union and Australia. In fact Australia, Norway, Sweden and the United Kingdom had gradually been increasing their bilateral aid to Myanmar since the early 2000s. Although Myanmar formed only a

[5] Cyclone Nargis made landfall on 2 May, while the referendum was held on 10 May, but postponed in the 'most heavily effected townships' (totalling forty-seven townships in Irrawaddy division and Yangon).

relatively small part of their aid portfolios, such assistance was not without controversy – for example, the Australian programme of training Myanmar state officials on human rights from 2000 to 2003.[6] But much more importantly these donors and the large INGOs they supported had by 2010 signalled what would come to be a major shift in patterns of aid distribution, namely away from border-based NGOs that were highly critical of the Myanmar government and which operated outside the state, to a gradual focus on Yangon-based operations that worked under the control of the state.

By 2011, when a suite of reforms were publicly revealed by the Thein Sein government, donors began to display unprecedented enthusiasm for Myanmar's state-led reform process. This largely coincided with a major shift in US policy where both President Obama and Secretary of State Clinton sought to more closely engage with Myanmar's democratisation process and position Myanmar, at least discursively, closer within the orbit of US geopolitical interests. A 2009 US State Department review of Burmese relations which led to a new focus on 'pragmatic engagement' and Thein Sein's 2013 visit to Washington DC to sign a Trade and Investment Framework Agreement were both significant events which marked a shift in relations between Myanmar and the United States (Steinberg 2015). Sanctions were gradually lifted or suspended starting in 2011, and by 2015, the only sanctions that remained were targeted against key individuals.[7]

In 2013, the World Bank, which up until that time had formally refused to provide any significant loans or grants to Myanmar due to it being in arrears of US$420 million, provided a bridging loan which opened Myanmar up to significant inflows of credit – more than US$500 million over the following year. Following suit, the European Union also suspended all sanctions in 2012 and established an office providing US$100 million for democratic reform and various other development activities. The Asian Development Bank opened an office in 2013 and immediately began a number of major projects. Australia doubled its aid between 2010 and 2012 and also dramatically reduced the number of individuals on its sanctions list. By 2013 Myanmar had become the second highest recipient of OECD aid (after Afghanistan).[8] By 2015 bilateral donors had more enthusiastically begun to support the reform

---

[6] The programme was terminated in 2003 due to human rights abuses that occurred due to an attack on the NLD: see Wilson and Kinley (2007).

[7] With the exception of sanctions on jade produced from Myanmar.

[8] Although 40 per cent of this was debt relief.

process. A range of donors such as the European Union, UK Department for International Development (DFID), Norway and Australia began to directly support initiatives surrounding both the ceasefire process and the November 2015 general elections.

President Then Sein's inaugural speech in 2011 was also a landmark event, as for the first time in recent Myanmar history, the state publicly acknowledged the problem of poverty (Than 2015). This opened up Myanmar to a wide ambit of technical, social and welfare interventions –that is programmes that more systematically sought to understand and improve the living standards and resilience of the Myanmar population. Conservation programmes also expanded.[9] There was a significant expansion of multi-donor Yangon-based consortiums such as the Three Millennium Development Goal Fund (3MDG) and Livelihoods and Food Security Trust Fund (LIFT), and a number of agencies became involved in the formulation of new policies and state programmes in the fields of health, education and agriculture. In 2011 the Global Fund returned to Myanmar and has since disbursed US$115 million of grants on more than sixty-eight different projects. There has also been an expansion of smaller local, but foreign-funded, NGOs working in the field of 'social enterprises', women's empowerment and microfinance. Indeed there has been a flurry of donors (Burke 2013). In addition, new state regulations that apply to NGOs under the Association Registration Law have eased former restrictions. It is no longer a legal requirement for NGOs to get formal permission from the government to operate.[10] Myanmar is thus on the verge of a major influx of aid, NGOs and expertise. As a mark of this, parts of Yangon, much like Phnom Penh and Vientiane, are increasingly inhabited by conspicuous 'aidlanders' (Apthorpe 2011; Fechter 2011), those working directly in the aid industry, who inhabit premium coffee shops, boutique restaurants and bars.

In Myanmar's shift from aid orphan to one of the largest recipients of international aid, the last five years have seen major increases in the numbers of NGOs operating in Myanmar, OECD inflows and donor-led governmental initiatives. These changes have largely occurred due to a changed domestic political environment that is open to aid and expertise

---

[9] For instance the UN Reduction of Emissions from Deforestation and Degradation programme (REDD+) made moves throughout 2014–2015 to establish Myanmar as a country under the programme.

[10] To the criticism of many NGOs, by-laws passed in July 2015 still required NGOs to go though a formal registration process before being able to be operate.

inflows, with a simultaneous eagerness on the part of influential donors such as the United States and World Bank to gain a foothold in Myanmar by actively engaging and supporting Myanmar's transition. The next section will consider some of the political–economic effects of the expansion of aid in Myanmar.

The New Cambodia? Authoritarianism, Elites and Aid

From aid orphan to aid frontier, Myanmar could take the place of Cambodia as Asia's 'donor playground' (Fforde and Seidel 2010) for post-conflict, development interventions. Foreign donors have provided advice and technical assistance on a range of major issues such as democratisation, ceasefire arrangements, electoral reform and policing. The European Union has controversially been training the Myanmar police force and has opened a National Crisis Management Centre in Naypyidaw. Norway is a major sponsor and supporter of the government's ceasefire process, via the Myanmar Peace Centre. The United States has started to provide 'non-combative' technical assistance to the Tatmadaw, and the Australian government has been providing substantial assistance on 'strengthening borders'.[11] Many of these reforms are targeted at Myanmar as a democratic pivot away from China.

Much like the case in Cambodia, where authoritarian power structures have sat comfortably with a bewildering array of development structures and initiatives (Ear 2013; Hughes 2009), the penetration of donor–NGO–aid chains into Myanmar appears to be primarily dictated by opportunity – namely the opportunities that have arisen from the United States easing sanctions and its new policy of 'pragmatic engagement', and the Myanmar government opening up to aid and NGOs. There is often ambiguity between the opportunity to provide assistance to increase the well being of the desperately poor, and the opportunity to expand programming, activities and funding. At the same time, the broader project of liberalisation that large numbers of OECD donors and NGOs are now pursuing brings about a range of political and economic effects – often unintended as much as intended. This section will briefly consider three such broad effects of aid expansion in Myanmar: the creation of economic opportunities it provides to elites, the creation of a division of labour

---

[11] In 2014 it was reported by Australia's then Immigration Minister Scott Morrison that Australia was dedicating A$5 million to strengthening Myanmar's borders. Australia has also funded the creation of Border Liaison Offices across the country.

between donor-driven politics and state-led resource extraction, and the effects of the pursuit of national political and economic interests by donors.

First, the increase in aid in Myanmar is taking place within a regime that at its core remains authoritarian, and so this raises concerns about the interaction between the aid assemblage and elite interests. As with Cambodia, the Myanmar elite seem to have crossed a threshold where technical neoliberal programmes are not only seen as posing no major threats to their interests, but offer the possibility of broadening them. As Burke (2013: 12) puts it, 'There is a risk that foreign aid provision will end up backing a central government agenda' that will 'enable development as a tool of pacification, also serving as a conduit for private sector investments that benefit well-connected individuals and bypass local people'. As Turnell (2015), Jones (2014) and Meehan (2011) have pointed out, for those who have amassed wealth from the illicit cross-border trade in the Khin Nyunt ceasefire era, or from state-backed monopolies of key industries thought the 1990s and 2000s, liberalisation is set to facilitate new investment opportunities for them. From the border, militia-based elite who accumulated wealth by facilitating cross-border flows of opium, teak, jade and ruby trading – such as Kokang drug lord Lo Hsing Han, Mong Tai militia leader Kun Sa or Myanmar National Democratic Alliance Army (MNDAA) leader Yao Ming Liang,[12] a new generation of 'cronies', based in Yangon – have now become the state's 'favoured entrepreneurs' and control the majority of wealth in the formal economy. As Jones states, the emerging 'state mediated capitalism' has 'fostered a re-emergent business class and created a layer of crony capitalists in an increasingly symbiotic relationship with the state' (Jones 2014: 146). These include the late Lo Hsing Han's son Stephen Law, who runs the Asia World Company (which has a large array of investments in Naypyidaw and downtown Yangon, and hydropower projects such as Myitsone and Salween); Zaw Zaw, who owns the powerful Max Myanmar conglomerate; owner of Ayeyarwady bank Tay Za, who owns Htoo company and amongst other things the extravagant Kandawgyi Palace hotel; and Kyaw Win, who owns SkyNet.

Important here is that the accumulated capital of the Myanmar elite is looking for new outlets, and liberalisation and its associated opportunities will likely bring them – whether this be from Western *or* regional

---

[12] In 1993 head of rebel group MNDAA and drug lord Yang Mao Liang established the Peace Myanmar Group company – a major water and alcoholic beverage manufacturer (including producer of the ubiquitous Myanmar Rum and Myanmar Whisky).

investment. This not only includes export industries such as the garment industry which is based on cheap labour, or construction and service industries, in places such as Yangon, Mandalay, Naypyidaw and other cities, but also agro-industrial enterprises such as rubber plantations which are rapidly taking large swathes of land in the northeast (Woods 2011). The reform process and partial democratisation of the state will no doubt help to facilitate this process by reducing risks to investment through new fiscal policies and mechanisms[13] – and Western governments have recently been flaunting this process and the investment opportunities it will likely bring.[14] At a broad level then, the interests of NGOs and donors – who form a part of recent liberalisation efforts – and elites – who are interested in investing surplus capital in the rapidly expanding formal economy – overlap to some extent. As in nearby Cambodia, new laws, government policies, democratic reform and increasing foreign investment will no doubt accrue new opportunities to those elite who are well-positioned to take advantage of Myanmar's transition.

The second broad effect of aid to be considered here concerns the delivery of state services. It is not the case that NGO and donor programmes push Myanmar along a linear trajectory towards democratisation and rising standards of living. Nor is it the case that neoliberal development interventions merely abandon the vulnerable to the market. Rather the influx of aid and expertise has differentiated effects on the complex relations between the state and the population it claims to govern. One particular effect which is of interest here is the way in which donor-funded programmes tend to concentrate on highly visible social and governmental reforms, while state interests into military affairs and natural resource extraction remain enclosed within much more opaque channels. This often has the effect of producing a division of labour where donors and particular government departments (or even specific individuals) focus on expanding and improving health, education, judicial and agricultural

---

[13] Since 2011 there has been a flurry of wide-ranging reforms, from new banking and fiscal regulation – often led by former opponents of the regime, for instance renowned Yangon economist U Thant – to new laws such as the 2012 Vacant, Fallow and Virgin Lands Management Law, and the 2012 Foreign Investment Law, which open Myanmar up to formal state-sanctioned foreign investment.

[14] In 2015 the US State Department's Investment Climate Statement for Burma was optimistic about 'the unique opportunities the country presents – including a rich natural resource base, a large market potential, a young labor force ... '. A report from the UK Department of Trade and Investment in the same year was similarly optimistic about Myanmar's oil and gas reserves.

services, while on the other hand, others are left to pursue military agendas and natural resource exploitation.[15]

Where significant sums of aid begin to flow into health and education, it becomes tempting for the state to increasingly rely upon international donors to fund social welfare activities, while normalising the practice of diverting state revenues into military expenditure and into the hands of the elite. The case of Rakhine State epitomises this. Since major bouts of violence in 2012, close to a million people have been placed in displacement camps. Under a military-administered state of emergency, a large number of Muslims (especially those who identify as Rohingya) in the state have been unable to leave camps and villages, and have major restrictions on accessing basic health and education services. Many authors have pointed out that the pursuit of a xenophobic politics that blames Muslims, and especially the marginalised Rohingya, for the woes of Rakhine State effectively shifts grievances away from the state and towards the Rohingya who have already experienced a long history of state repression (Grundy-Warr and Wong 1997; Human Rights Watch Asia 1996; Medecins Sans Frontieres – Holland 2002). There is clearly both state and local elite interest in repressing the Rohingya (Irrawaddy 2012; Lewa 2005; Linter 1996; Zarni and Cowley 2014; Zin 2015). Responding to the crisis, international agencies have been highly restricted to providing only extremely basic welfare services on an ad hoc basis (which the state decided to exclude communities from in the first place) while being entirely unable to address the political aspects of the issue (i.e. not even being able to refer to the group as Rohingya) (see also Roughneen 2014). The common-sense perspectives frequently reiterated in popular and academic literature see Myanmar as one of the poorest countries in the world with minimal government expenditure on health, education and infrastructure, and therefore in urgent need of aid and investment.

---

[15] A salient example of this is the Myanmar Peace Centre (2012–2015) established under the Thein Sein regime, which was supported through aid disbursements of US$2.5 million from the European Union and Japan (with the European Union providing US$33.5 million for the subsequent peace process). During the period of funding, including the historic 2015 ceasefire agreement, conflict in border areas escalated where the Tatmadaw launched a number of fierce military campaigns in Shan and Kachin States that led to tens of thousands being displaced. At the same time the situation of the Rohingya in Rakhine State also dramatically declined. In 2016, after the government disbanded the Myanmar Peace Centre (where donor-provided assets were transferred to two NGOs established by senior government officials who had worked at the centre), donors pledged more than US$100 million for a Joint Peace Fund.

This narrative of the need for aid in Myanmar neglects the way in which aid subsidises the responsibility of the state to provide social or welfare services and allows it to normalise the practice of diverting large chunks of state revenue towards other agendas.

Since 1988, even in the face of sanctions, the military state generated windfall revenues from mining, timber and especially gas and oil. The Yadana and Yetagun natural gas fields that came on-line in 1988 and 2000 have provided billions of dollars for the state. With the Shwe gas block (currently being sold) and lucrative pipelines across northern Myanmar connecting China and India, the state is likely to continue to gain substantial foreign exchange from natural resources. For instance Turnell (2015) notes that for the 2011 financial year, the state-owned Myanmar Oil and Gas Enterprise brought in net revenues of around US$1.5 billion; mining and gems brought in around US$1.3 billion; and teak and other hardwood brought in around US$600 million. Yet up to 2011, the state displayed revenues in the public budget at the official rate of US$1:MMK6, which grossly underestimates earned revenue by trillions of *kyat*, giving the impression that the state is facing a budget deficit.

Revenues gained from these lucrative enterprises are placed in a State Fund Account which allows for discretionary spending for the military – which for most of the 2000s ate up around half of the formal budget. Since the Yadana gas field came on-line the state has pumped significant revenues from foreign exchange directly into the military. In 1988 the Tatmadaw was composed of 186,000 personnel. By 2007 that figure had jumped to 400,000. So desperate was the Tatmadaw for military hardware that in the early 1990s it mortgaged future oil revenues to buy US$1.2 billion of Chinese arms (Skidmore and Wilson 2012). While donors and NGOs were footing the multi-million-dollar bill for providing services to those fleeing the state's brutal war over the last two decades (South 2007), the state was spending unprecedented amounts on the military. Now with the transition from full military rule, state services will no doubt rapidly expand. The question remains however to what degree Myanmar will follow countries such as Cambodia and East Timor where even after the cessation of conflict, the provision of health and education services are still highly dependent upon a patchwork of donors and NGOs (Hughes 2009).

The final broad effect of aid examined here concerns the effects of donors as they pursue their geopolitical and economic institutional interests. As scholarly research produced over the last three decades has shown, donors who fund development programmes – whether they be small-scale NGO projects or large-scale infrastructure projects – cannot be considered as merely benevolent actors solely acting in the best interests of the poor. Rather, both bilateral and multilateral donors tend to be enmeshed in broader geopolitical and economic rationalities that go well beyond the particular host country within which they run projects (Duffield 2007; Essex 2013). For instance in the contemporary neoliberal aidscape most bilateral donors are fairly blunt about pursuing national interests – whether they be the 'aid for trade' policies of Canada, DFID or Australia which seek to open up new markets to nationally produced goods or access cheap land and natural resources, or geopolitical and security interests which both Australia and the United States pursue.

Many of the largest donor countries operating in Myanmar have aggressively pursued trade deals and the opening of the Myanmar market to their national goods and services, alongside their aid programmes. With the changing political–economic landscape afforded by Myanmar's liberalisation, new economic opportunities have begun to materialise. Since 2012 when the European Union signed a number of trade deals with Myanmar, EU investments into Myanmar were more than US$5 billion (in 2014) and included companies such as Carlsberg, Heineken, British American Tobacco, Nestlé and Mercedes Benz. Australia has seen a much more humble trade relationship with Myanmar (with A$189 million worth of exports to Myanmar in 2014), although major investments from the Australian company Woodside have been made into four gas and oil blocks off the coast of Rakhine State[16] – which the Department of Foreign Affairs and Trade (DFAT) helped to facilitate – and an international NGO with DFAT funding has helped to run a livelihoods programme (also in Rakhine State). One of Myanmar's biggest donors of recent times – Norway, which has also been a major proponent of the peace process – is also home to Telenor, one of the largest telecommunication operators in Myanmar, and Statoils, which also has made large investments into gas and oil blocks off the Rakhine coast. The intertwining of aid and trade on the part of donors has often produced unintended consequences on conflict and instability.

Investments into oil and gas for instance are only fuelling conflict in Rakhine State by contributing to the long-held belief of people in the state that the massive revenues generated from natural resources are not being fairly shared with the state. As another example, the Australian company Snowy Mountains Engineering Corporation has been

---

[16] Along with investments by British company BG, more than US$1 billion has been invested in four offshore blocks.

contracted to conduct an environmental impact assessment for the proposed Mong Ton dam on the Than Lwin (Salween) River in Shan State. This has directly exacerbated conflicts between the Shan State Army – North, which has refused to allow staff of the company to enter the site, and the Tatmadaw. So too the Asian Development Bank's support for the upgrade of a major highway through Karen State has resulted in unprecedented fighting between the Tatmadaw and Democratic Karen Benevolent Army (which has historically fought as a proxy of the state) due to conflicts over formal and informal taxation of goods crossing the border with Thailand (Simpson 2013). At the same time, as Woods (2011) and Kramer (2015) have pointed out, the state-dominated peace process which donors have strongly backed may potentially reproduce new patterns of inequality as land, forests and rivers come under government control, and are opened up to domestic and foreign investment. This 'ceasefire capitalism', just as in Laos and Cambodia, will no doubt lead to new tensions and vulnerabilities (see for example Dwyer 2014 on Laos and Cambodia; Le Billon 2002)

In summary, this section has briefly highlighted the importance of considering the unintended as well as intentional impacts of aid. As critical scholars of aid have pointed out, the challenge of conceptualising development in the twenty-first century lies not so much in evaluating to what degree aid organisations pursue stated aims and goals, but in coming to grips with the wide range of non-intentional effects that aid inevitably brings about (Duffield 2010; Grove and Pugh 2015; Sidaway 2007) – for example focusing on how lower-case 'd' development reorganises economic and political relations as it expands across space, rather than focusing on 'civil society', 'good governance' and other abstract buzz words associated with upper-case 'D' Development (Bebbington 2004). By merely focusing on the intentional aspects of international development there is the risk that Myanmar will go down the path of Cambodia – where kleptocracy, elite-based natural resource exploitation and aid all sit side-by-side.

Conclusion

Myanmar is on the verge of seeing a major influx of aid. This chapter has demonstrated how changing circumstances within Myanmar (namely the transition to 'discipline-flourishing democracy') and changing attitudes of major donors towards the country (namely enthusiastic support for the country's transition) have resulted in a major influx and increase of

NGOs, multi-actor development programmes, aid flows and expertise. Against the common understanding of NGOs as emerging in a bottom-up manner with the expansion of 'civil society', it was argued that a more careful reading of development in Myanmar reveals that NGOs and development programmes have also increased in a top-down, opportunistic manner which is more a function of the space available to pursue institutional agendas.

While there are many reasons to be optimistic about Myanmar's recent changes, this chapter has critically interrogated three aspects of aid in the Myanmar context. First, it looked at the relation between aid and elite interests and argued that in many ways the interests of the elite and of donors and NGOs overlap. Using the example of other donor-dependent countries such as Cambodia, it was shown how elite interests and authoritarian structures can potentially not only work in harmony with increasing quantities of aid and development programmes, but even be legitimised by aid and NGO activities. Second, this chapter identified how aid can potentially create a division of labour between donor money, which is invested into highly visible programming surrounding human rights, basic services, welfare and technical programming, while elites and certain military actors are left to pursue less-visible activities surrounding military campaigns, land confiscation, citizenship and natural resource exploitation. Finally, the chapter demonstrated how aid also legitimises the political and economic interests of donors, and in many cases pursuing such interests can exacerbate the already existent and multi-faceted tensions within Myanmar.

While this chapter can offer only a glimpse into the complex politics of aid in Myanmar, it has argued for the importance of placing politics at the centre of understandings of aid and development. In terms of aid and development, Myanmar is currently at a crucial juncture and could potentially go down a number of different paths. To avoid the deeply problematic trajectory of aid in places such as Cambodia, a careful and deep engagement with the politics of land, natural resource usage, patrimonialism, citizenship and ethnic grievance should be prioritised over framing aid and development in technical, non-political terms.

References

Apthorpe, R. 2011. 'CODA – With Alice in Aidland: A Seriously Satirical Allegory'. *Adventures in Aidland: The Anthropology of Professionals in International Development*. New York: Berghahn, pp. 199–220.

Baur, D. and H. P. Schmitz. 2012. 'Corporations and NGOs: When Accountability Leads to Co-optation'. 106(1) *Journal of Business Ethics* 9–21.

Bebbington, A. 2004. 'NGOs and Uneven Development: Geographies of Development Intervention'. 28(6) *Progress in Human Geography* 725–745.

Biddulph, R. 2011. 'Tenure Security Interventions in Cambodia: Testing Bebbington's Approach to Development Geography'. 93(3) *Geografiska Annaler: Series B, Human Geography* 223–236.

Bumpus, A. G. and D. M. Liverman. 2008. 'Accumulation by Decarbonization and the Governance of Carbon Offsets'. 84(2) *Economic Geography* 127–155.

Burke, A. 2013. *Myanmar and Foreign Aid – Recent Changes, Risk and Opportunity.* Sydney: The Policy Practise.

Callahan, M. P. 2004. *Making Enemies: War and State Building in Burma.* Singapore: NUS Press.

Chandler, D. 2013. 'Where is the Human in Human-Centred Approaches to Development? A Critique of Amartya Sen's "Development as Freedom"' in J. R. Sandro Mezzadra and Ranabir Samadar (eds), *The Biopolitics of Development.* London: Springer, pp. 67–86.

Cooke, B. and U. Kothari. 2001. *Participation: The New Tyranny?* New York: Zed Books.

Craig, D. and D. Porter. 2006. *Development beyond Neoliberalism?: Governance, Poverty Reduction and Political Economy.* Cambridge: Cambridge University Press.

Currie, K. 2012. *Burma in the Balance: The Role of Foreign Assistance in Supporting Burma's Democratic Transition.* Yangon: Project 2049 Institute.

De Sardan, J.-P. O. 2005. *Anthropology and Development: Understanding Comtemporary Social Change.* London: Zed Books.

Dorning, K. 2006. 'Creating an Environment for Participation: International NGOs and the Growth of Civil Society in Burma/Myanmar' in T. Wilson (ed.), *Myanmar's Long Road to National Reconciliation.* Canberra: Asia Pacific Press, pp. 188–217.

Duffield, M. 2007. *Development, Security and Unending War.* London: Polity.
    2010. 'Risk-Management and the Fortified Aid Compound: Everyday Life in Post-Interventionary Society'. 4(4) *Journal of Intervention and Statebuilding* 453–474.

Duffield, M. R. 2008. *On the Edge of 'No Man's Land': Chronic Emergency in Myanmar.* Bristol: School of Sociology, Politics, and International Studies, University of Bristol.

Dwyer, M. B. 2014. 'Micro-Geopolitics: Capitalising Security in Laos's Golden Quadrangle'. 19(2) *Geopolitics* 377–405.

Ear, S. 2013. *Aid Dependence in Cambodia: How Foreign Assistance Undermines Democracy.* New York: Columbia University Press.

Escobar, A. 2011 [1995]. *Encountering Development: The Making and Unmaking of the Third World (New in Paper).* Princeton: Princeton University Press.

Essex, J. 2013. *Development, Security, and Aid: Geopolitics and Geoeconomics at the US Agency for International Development* (Vol. 16). Georgia: University of Georgia Press.

Fechter, A.-M. 2011. 'Anybody at Home? The Inhabitants of Aidland' in A.-M. Fechter and H. Hindman (eds), *Inside the Everyday Lives of Development Workers: The Challenges and Futures of Aidland.* New York: Kumarian Press, pp. 131–149.

Ferguson, J. 1990. *The Anti-politics Machine: 'Development', Depoliticization and Bureaucratic Power in Lesotho.* Cambridge: Cambridge University Press.

Fforde, A. and K. Seidel. 2010. 'Donor Playground Cambodia?' *What a look at aid and development in Cambodia confirms and what it may imply.* Berlin: Heinrich-Böll-Stiftung.

Foucault, M. 2004. *The Birth of Biopolitics – Lectures at the College de France 1978–79.* New York: Palgrave Macmillan.

Frewer, T. 2013. 'Doing NGO Work: The Politics of Being "civil society"and Promoting "good governance" in Cambodia'. 44(1) *Australian Geographer* 97–114.

Frewer, T. and S. Chan. 2014. 'GIS and the "Usual Suspects" – [Mis]understanding Land Use Change in Cambodia'. 42(2) *Human Ecology* 267–281.

Godfrey, M., C. Sophal, T. Kato, L. Vou Piseth, P. Dorina, T. Saravy, ... S. Sovannarith. 2002. 'Technical Assistance and Capacity Development in an Aid-Dependent Economy: The Experience of Cambodia'. 30(3) *World Development* 355–373.

Goldman, M. 2006. *Imperial Nature: The World Bank and Struggles for Social Justice in the Age of Globalization.* New Haven, CT: Yale University Press.

Grove, K. and J. Pugh. 2015. 'Assemblage Thinking and Participatory Development: Potentiality, Ethics, Biopolitics'. 9(1) *Geography Compass* 1–13.

Grove, K. J. 2010. 'Insuring "our common future?" Dangerous Climate Change and the Biopolitics of Environmental Security'. 15(3) *Geopolitics* 536–563.

Grundy-Warr, C. and E. Wong. 1997. 'Sanctuary under a Plastic Sheet – The Unresolved Problem of Rohingya Refugees'. 8(23) *IBRU Boundary and Security Bulletin.*

Harrison, G. 2004. *The World Bank and Africa: The Construction of Governance States.* Oxon: Routledge.

Hughes, C. 2009. *Dependent Communities: Aid and Politics in Cambodia and East Timor.* Ithaca, NY: Cornell University.

Human Rights Watch Asia. 1996. *Burma – The Rohingya Muslims – Ending a Cycle of Exodus?* (Vol. 8). London: Human Rights Watch.

Irrawaddy, T. 2012. 'History behind Arakan State Conflict'. *The Irrawaddy.*

Jones, L. 2014. 'The Political Economy of Myanmar's Transition'. 44(1) *Journal of Contemporary Asia* 144–170.

Kramer, T. 2011. *Civil Society Gaining Ground. Opportunities for Change and Development in Burma.* Amsterdam: Transnational Institute, Burma Center Netherlands.

2015. 'Ethnic Conflict and Lands Rights in Myanmar'. 82(2) *Social Research: An International Quarterly* 355–374.

Le Billon, P. 2002. 'Logging in Muddy Waters: The Politics of Forest Exploitation in Cambodia'. 34(4) *Critical Asian Studies* 563–586.

Lewa, C. 2005. 'The Rohingya: Forced Migration and Statelessness' in O. Mishra (ed.), *Forced Migration in the South Asian Region: Displacement, Human Rights and Conflict Resolution*. Washington DC: Centre for Refugees Studies.

Lewis, D. and D. Mosse. 2006. *Development Brokers and Translators: The Ethnography of Aid and Agencies*. London: Kumarian Press.

Li, T. M. 2007. *The Will to Improve: Governmentality, Development, and the Practice of Politics*. New York: Duke University Press Books.

Linter, B. 1996. 'Diversionary Tactics: Anti-Muslim Campaign Seen as Effort to Rally Burmans'. 29 August. *Far Eastern Economic Review*.

Lorch, J. 2007. 'Myanmar's Civil Society–a Patch for the National Education System? The Emergence of Civil Society in Areas of State Weakness'. 26(3) *Journal of Current Southeast Asian Affairs* 55–88.

McGregor, A. 2005. 'Geopolitics and Human Rights: Unpacking Australia's Burma'. 26(2) *Singapore Journal of Tropical Geography* 191–211.

Medecins Sans Frontieres – Holland. 2002. '10 Years for the Rohingya Refugees in Bagladesh: Past, Present and Future'. Dhaka.

Meehan, P. 2011. 'Drugs, Insurgency and State-Building in Burma: Why the Drugs Trade is Central to Burma's Changing Political Order'. 42(03) *Journal of Southeast Asian Studies* 376–404.

Mercer, C. 2002. 'NGOs, Civil Society and Democratization: A Critical Review of the Literature'. 2(1) *Progress in Development Studies* 5–22.

Milne, S., K. Pak and M. Sullivan. 2015. 'Shackled to Nature? The Post-Conflict State and Its Symbiotic Relationship with Natural Resources' in S. Milne and S. Mahanty (eds), *Conservation and Development in Cambodia: Exploring Frontiers of Change in Nature, State and Society*. Oxon: Routledge, pp. 28–50.

Morgan, A. J. 2014. 'Remarkable Occurrence: Progress for Civil Society in an Open Myanmar'. 23 A. *Pacific Rim Law & Policy Journal* 495.

Mosse, D. 2005. *Cultivating Development: An Ethnography of Aid Policy and Practice (Anthropology, Culture and Society Series)*. New York: Pluto Press.

Oo, Z. 2006. 'Exit, Voice and Loyalty in Burma: The Role of Overseas Burmese in Democratising Their Homeland'. *Myanmar's Long Road to National Reconciliation*. Singapore: ISEAS Publications, pp. 231–262.

Reid, J. 2013. 'Interrogating the Neoliberal Biopolitics of the Sustainable Development-Resilience Nexus'. 7(4) *International Political Sociology* 353–367.

Rich, B. 2013. *Foreclosing the Future: The World Bank and the Politics of Environmental Destruction*. Washington DC: Island Press.

Roberts, S. M. 2014. 'Development Capital: USAID and the Rise of Development Contractors'. 104(5) *Annals of the Association of American Geographers*.

Roberts, S. M., J. P. Jones III and O. Fröhling. 2005. 'NGOs and the Globalization of Managerialism: A Research Framework'. 33(11) *World Development* 1,845–1,864.

Roughneen, S. 2014. 'MSF, Human Rights Commission at Odds Over Maungdaw Violence'. *The Irrawaddy*.

Roy, A. 2010. *Poverty Capital: Microfinance and the Making of Development*. Oxon: Routledge.

Schuller, M. 2012. *Killing with Kindness: Haiti, International Aid, and NGOs*. New Brunswick, NJ: Rutgers University Press.

Seekins, D. M. 1992. 'Japan's Aid Relations with Military Regimes in Burma, 1962–1991: The Kokunaika Process'. 32(3) *Asian Survey* 246–262.

2009. 'State, Society and Natural Disaster: Cyclone Nargis in Myanmar (Burma)'. 37(5) *Asian Journal of Social Science* 717–737.

Selth, A. 2008. 'Even Paranoids Have Enemies: Cyclone Nargis and Myanmar's Fears of Invasion'. 30(3) *Contemporary Southeast Asia: A Journal of International and Strategic Affairs* 379–402.

Sidaway, J. D. 2007. 'Spaces of Postdevelopment'. 31(3) *Progress in Human Geography* 345–361.

Simpson, A. 2013. 'Market Building and Risk under a Regime in Transition: The Asian Development Bank in Myanmar (Burma)' in T. Carroll and Darryl S. L. Jarvis (eds), *The Politics of Marketising Asia*. London: Palgrave Macmillan.

Skidmore, M. and T. Wilson. 2012. 'Interpreting the Transition in Myanmar' in N. Cheeseman, M. Skidmore and T. Wilson (eds), *Myanmar's Transition: Openings, Obstacles, and Opportunities*. Singapore: ISEAS.

South, A. 2007. *Burma: The Changing Nature of Displacement Crises*. Geneva: Refugee Studies Centre.

2008. *Civil Society in Burma: The Development of Democracy Amidst Conflict*. Institute of Southeast Asian Studies.

Srinivas, N. 2009. 'Against NGOs? A Critical Perspective on Nongovernmental Action'. 38(4) *Nonprofit and Voluntary Sector Quarterly* 614–626.

Steinberg, D. I. 2007. 'The United States and Its Allies: The Problem of Burma/ Myanmar Policy'. 29(2) *Contemporary Southeast Asia: A Journal of International and Strategic Affairs* 219–237.

2015. 'Myanmar and the United States, Closing and Opening Doors: An Idiosyncratic Analysis'. 82(2) *Social Research: An International Quarterly* 427–452.

Tegenfeldt, D. 2006. 'More than Saving Lives: The Role of International Development Agencies in Supporting Change Processes in Burma/Myanmar' in T. Wilson (ed.), *Myanmar's Long Road to National Reconciliation*. Canberra: Asia Pacific Press, pp. 218–230.

Than, T. M. M. 2015. 'Myanmar's Economic Reforms: Hard Choices Ahead'. 82(2) *Social Research: An International Quarterly* 453–480.

Thant Myint U. 2012. 'White Elephants and Black Swans: Thought on Myanmar's Recent History and Possible Futures' in N. Cheeseman, M. Skidmore and T. Wilson (eds). *Myanmar's Transition: Openings, Obstacles and Opportunities.* Canberra: ISEAS.

Turnell, S. 2015. 'Burma's Economic Transition: Hopes and Hurdles'. 82(2) *Social Research: An International Quarterly* 481–506.

Un, K. 2005. 'Patronage Politics and Hybrid Democracy: Political Change in Cambodia, 1993–2003'. 29(2) *Asian Perspective-Seoul* 203.

US Senate Subcommittee on East Asian and Pacific Affairs. 2010. Hearings on Burma: Testimony of David I. Steinberg, Professor, School of Foreign Service, Georgetown University. Washington DC: US State Department.

Walker, M., S. M. Roberts, J. P. Jones III and O. Fröhling. 2008. 'Neoliberal Development through Technical Assistance: Constructing Communities of Entrepreneurial Subjects in Oaxaca, Mexico'. 39(1) *Geoforum* 527–542.

Wallace, T., L. Bornstein and J. Chapman. 2007. *The Aid Chain: Coercion and Commitment in Development NGOs.* New York: Practical Action Pub.

Ware, A. 2012. *Context-Sensitive Development: How International NGOs Operate in Myanmar.* London: Stylus Publishing, LLC.

Wilson, T. and D. Kinley. 2007. 'Engaging a Pariah: Human Rights Training in Burma/Myanmar'. 29(2) *Human Rights Quarterly* 368–402.

Woods, K. 2011. 'Ceasefire Capitalism: Military–Private Partnerships, Resource Concessions and Military–State Building in the Burma–China Borderlands'. 38(4) *Journal of Peasant Studies* 747–770.

Zarni, M. and A. Cowley. 2014. 'Slow-Burning Genocide of Myanmar's Rohingya'. 23 *The Pacific Rim Law & Policy Journal* 683.

Zin, M. 2015. 'Anti-Muslim Violence in Burma: Why Now?' 82(2) *Social Research: An International Quarterly* 375–397.

INDEX

Accion International, 128
ACLEDA Myanmar, 127t5.1, 128
Action Aid, 260
Acumen, 104
aid, 21, 27, 255–56, 270–71. *See also*
    donors; *also specific countries*
    academic literature on, 256–58
    from aid orphan to aid hub,
        xvii, 258–64
    authoritarianism, 265–66
    current situation, 257–58
    and elite interests, 265
    and geopolitical and economic
        institutional interests, 268–70
    from OECD countries, 258
    political-economic effects, 264–70
    and state services delivery, 266–68
Alien Torts Claims Act (US), 233
American Apparel and Footwear
    Association, 233
anti-sweatshop campaigns, 34
Anti-trafficking in Persons Law
    (Philippines), 20
arbitrary displacement, 205
Ashoka, 103
Asia, 19, 59, 94, 96
    financial crisis 1997, 6, 184,
        191, 233
    social inequality, 89–92
Asia-Europe Foundation, 84
Asia Mega Link Ltd, 241
Asia World Co Ltd, 228, 241, 242
Asia World Port Terminal, 243
Asian Development Bank (ADB), 14,
    19, 38, 84, 88, 93, 94, 95, 96, 97,
    259, 261, 262, 270
    on knowledge-based economies, 93

regional strategies for economic
    growth, 92
on social inequality, 89
social innovations, 102
Association of Southeast Asian Nations
    (ASEAN), 20, 177, 220, 235,
    259, 261
Association of Southeast Asian
    Neighbours, 233
Association Registration Law, 108,
    110, 263
Associations Registration Law, 85
auditing requirements of global
    buyers, 46, 49
Aung San Suu Kyi, 22, 59, 74, 228,
    231, 235, 236–37, 238, 240, 245,
    258, 260
Aung Thaung, 244–45
Australia, 59, 234, 259, 261, 262, 263,
    264, 269
    aid from, 258
Australian AID, 64
Azerbaijan, 57

Bangladesh, 19
banking sector, 9
Bataan, Philippines, 178
British Council, 6, 90, 110
British Indian empire, 8
building and land fee, collected by
    DAO, 163
Building Markets, 115t4.1
Burma Code, 8
Burma Excise Act, 157
Burmese Freedom and Democracy Act
    (BDFA) (US), 231–32, 240
Bush, George W., 231, 232, 260